Dear Valued Customer,

We realize you're a busy professional with deadlines to hit. Whether your goal is to learn a new technology or solve a critical problem, we want to be there to lend you a hand. Our primary objective is to provide you with the insight and knowledge you need to stay atop the highly competitive and ever-changing technology industry.

Wiley Publishing, Inc. offers books on a wide variety of technical categories, including security, data warehousing, software development tools, and networking - everything you need to reach your peak. Regardless of your level of expertise, the Wiley family of books has you covered.

- For Dummies – The *fun* and *easy* way to learn
- The Weekend Crash Course –The *fastest* way to learn a new tool or technology
- Visual – For those who prefer to learn a new topic *visually*
- The Bible – The *100% comprehensive* tutorial and reference
- The Wiley Professional list – *Practical* and *reliable* resources for IT professionals

In the book that you now hold in your hands, Darren Broemmer shares best practices and lessons learned for J2EE development. As you design and build a banking application with J2EE and design patterns, you'll also utilize metadata-driven configurable foundation components to help automate much of the development for Web-based business applications. And of course, the tools and technologies used to construct the sample application are not from any one vendor, but best of breed—Jakarta Struts, Servlets, JSP, XML, EJB, UML, WebLogic, WebSphere, and many more.

Our commitment to you does not end at the last page of this book. We'd like to open a dialog with you to see what other solutions we can provide. Please be sure to visit us at www.wiley.com/compbooks to review our complete title list and explore the other resources we offer. If you have a comment, suggestion or any other inquiry, please locate the "contact us" link at www.wiley.com.

Thank you for your support and we look forward to hearing from you and serving your needs again in the future.

Sincerely,

Richard K. Swadley

Richard K. Swadley
Vice President & Executive Group Publisher
Wiley Publishing, Inc.

Bible

DUMMIES

Independent Thinkers

*more information
on related titles*

J2EE™ Best Practices Java™ Design Patterns, Automation, and Performance

Darren Broemmer

Wiley Publishing, Inc.

Publisher: Bob Ipsen
Editor: Theresa Hudson
Developmental Editor: Kenyon Brown
Editorial Manager: Kathryn A. Malm
Managing Editor: Pamela Hanley
New Media Editor: Brian Snapp
Text Design & Composition: Interactive Composition Corporation

This book is printed on acid-free paper. ∞

Published by Wiley Publishing, Inc., Indianapolis, Indiana
Published simultaneously in Canada

For general information on our other products and services please contact our Customer Care Department within the United States at (800) 762-2974, outside the United States at (317) 572-3993 or fax (317) 572-4002.

Wiley also publishes its books in a variety of electronic formats. Some content that appears in print may not be available in electronic books.

Library of Congress Cataloging-in-Publication Data:

ISBN 0-471-22885-0

Printed in the United States of America
10 9 8 7 6 5 4 3 2 1

*This book is dedicated to my mother, Joan,
and in loving memory of my father, Gary,
for all of their love, support,
and encouragement.*

Contents

Acknowledgments

I owe countless thanks to my parents, John and Joan, Shirley and my late father Gary, for always being there and giving so much of themselves to help me. Without question, this book would not have been possible without everything that they have done for me. Special thanks also goes to John Abbey, Jeff Nelms, and Ken Young for reviewing the chapters, providing their insight, and contributing to this effort. John and I have collaborated for years on J2EE development and had many a lively and entertaining discussion on the topic. Likewise, Jeff and I have debated the finer points of business objects many times and much of the performance slant in this book can be traced back to his influence. Ken's early feedback helped to shape the perspective that the book eventually took. I would also like to recognize Ron Carden for his influence in my work and the development of this material. Another person who made this book possible is my wife Caroline who enthusiastically supported me throughout the effort. I would also like to acknowledge Bill Hough who unquestionably supported this effort. Special thanks to Jack Greenfield, Terri Hudson, and all the folks at Wiley for their support and help in putting this book together. Finally, thanks to God through whom all things are made possible.

Darren Broemmer

September 2002

About the Author

Darren Broemmer is an application architect working on next-generation J2EE software solutions in the mortgage industry at Freddie Mac. His previous work includes architecture, development, and management experience in Internet and client-server systems implementations for consulting clients in North America, Europe, and the Middle East. Darren specializes in Java and J2EE technology and is the coinventor of a Java application development framework called jPylon, a set of reusable, extensible software components based on J2EE. JPylon was chosen to be a part of the Sun Microsystems ONE Studio Developer Resources program (formerly Forte for Java Extension Partners Program). Throughout his career, Darren has regularly consulted with projects on best practices for J2EE development and has spoken at corporate conferences about jPylon and J2EE technology. When he is not busy thinking of ways to abstract and automate software development, Darren tries to stay in shape by playing basketball and running, although he will never be able to keep up with his wife at Ultimate Frisbee.

Introduction

Java 2 Enterprise Edition (J2EE) technology is becoming a pervasive platform for the development of Internet-based, transactional business applications. It provides a robust development platform upon which to build flexible, reusable components and applications. It is a powerful standard that is well-suited for Internet-based applications because it provides many of the underlying services such as HTTP request processing (Java servlet API), transaction management (Enterprise JavaBeans), and messaging (Java Message Service), just to name a few. However, J2EE is also a complex and changing standard that leaves the technologist with many design decisions and performance considerations. Each component service adds a level of overhead to the application processing that must be considered. Additionally, there are a number of common business logic functions, such as error handling, that must be designed and developed for each component and application.

An application development effort using J2EE should give careful consideration to the services provided by the platform and how application components can best utilize them. There are a number of best practices one should consider in order to be highly effective in building J2EE components and integrating them into applications. These practices include evaluating and selecting the right set of software components and services to do the job. This is no different than in other professions; a carpenter or a steelworker both use an architecture plan to build things, although the tools they use to do so are quite different. A scalable, modular architecture built upon J2EE will likely comprise a selection of the appropriate set of J2EE services combined with a custom foundation of common business logic functions.

Overview of the Book and Technology

This book will supply a set of best practices for J2EE software development and then use them to construct an application architecture approach referred to as the reference architecture. The reference architecture will provide a basis for rapidly building transactional business applications using J2EE technology. The design and implementation of the reference architecture is based on a set of guiding principles that will be used to optimize and automate J2EE development.

Guiding Principles of the Reference Architecture

The goal of constructing the reference architecture is to create a development environment that can be used to build applications faster and with better performance, quality, and reusability. The following set of guiding principles are used to accomplish these goals:

- Applying proven design patterns to J2EE
- Automating common functions
- Using metadata-driven, configurable foundation components
- Considering performance and scalability

These principles are essential in driving the architecture and building the foundation for development. These concepts will be discussed throughout this book in detail and applied to each segment of the J2EE architecture. Much of software development in general and J2EE development in particular can be optimized and automated through these concepts and their realization in the form of common foundation logic. Solid analysis of design choices as input to the architecture and application components is essential in order to provide solutions that balance the needs of rapid development, faster performance, higher quality, and greater reusability.

Figure I.1 shows the inputs and outputs of the architecture. This diagram essentially represents the guiding principles and the benefits that can be derived from applying them to application development.

These principles provide the motivation and the basis for the approach to this study of developing applications using J2EE. Each aspect of the enterprise architecture within J2EE will be studied for its behavior and characteristics. By using this information and applying the development principles and best practices, you can create an approach to effectively use the technology to reach our application development goals.

The goals at the right side of Figure I.1, such as flexibility and reusability, should be considered and addressed from the beginning of any software development project. These types of goals are realized at two different levels: the software architecture level described earlier and the application component design. The reference architecture will guide much of the application design, so it is important to understand and distinguish these levels before undertaking enterprise software development. Each of the two levels will provide different types of benefits to both the end users and the development organization.

Applying Proven Design Patterns

A design pattern is a defined interaction of objects to solve a recurring problem in software development. There are a number of documented design patterns (E.

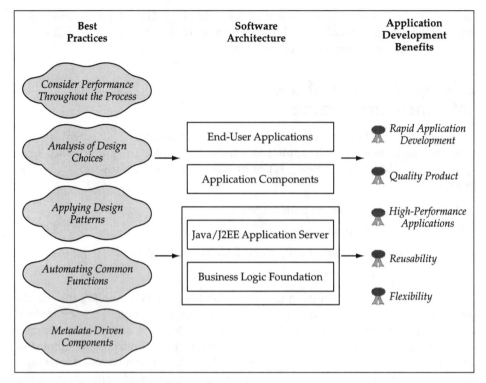

Figure I.1   Architecture Principles and Benefits.

Gamma, R. Helm, R. Johnson, J. Vlissides, 1995. *Design Patterns.* Boston, MA: Addison-Wesley) that represent proven solutions that you can use to solve common problems in object-oriented (OO) development. You can also apply many of these patterns to the J2EE architecture. One example is the concept of a service within the Service-Based Architecture. The service component layer of the reference architecture will resemble both the Façade and Mediator patterns (Gamma et al. 1995). The service component provides a simple interface to the client and decouples the presentation components (JavaServer Pages or servlets) from the back-end business logic components. This provides the benefit of increased reusability and a simplified view of the world from the client perspective. If you add a standard interface to the service components, you can now implement the Command pattern (Gamma et al. 1995) from a front-end component. This allows you to build a generic, configurable controller component in the front end that invokes these standardized back-end services.

If you apply these well-documented, proven design patterns to J2EE architecture, you will see that the stateless Session Bean is the perfect implementation for the Service-Based Architecture. This becomes the Session-Façade pattern (D. Alur, J. Crupi, D. Malks. 2001. *Core J2EE Patterns.* Mountain View, CA: Sun Java Center), an implementation of the Façade pattern applied to a Session Enterprise Java Bean. If you consider a Session Bean component merely to be a wrapper around your service object that adds the ability to distribute the service and manage transactions around it, you utilize the J2EE component-based services without changing the object-oriented view of the world very much at all. In the case of stateless Session Beans, you also gain these benefits without adding much overhead to the processing time. The session façade acting as an EJB component wrapper around a service implementation object is referred to as the Service Component pattern in the reference architecture.

Figure I.2 illustrates the UML representation of this service component pattern.

The business objects and presentation components also contain numerous examples of proven design patterns that can be applied. The Template Method pattern (Gamma et al. 1995) provides an excellent mechanism for providing extensible foundation components for both business objects and service objects. In the case of business objects, it provides a template for common operations such as a *save* operation to cause the object's data to persist in the database. The base class, or template, provides hooks for subclasses, the specific business objects, to implement validation rules and presave or postsave logic. Enterprise JavaBeans uses a number of design patterns applied to the Java language. Some of them are variations of existing patterns that use Java interfaces, such as with Entity Beans. Entity Beans must implement a common interface `javax.ejb.EntityBean` that provides hooks for insert, update, and delete logic. Each architecture layer discussed builds on these existing patterns and looks at some additional patterns that provide flexibility and reusability within the software architecture on top of J2EE.

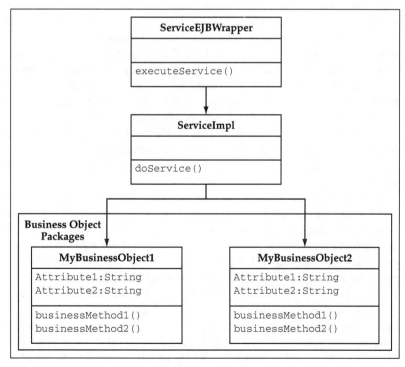

Figure I.2 UML Diagram of Service Component Pattern.

Automating Common Functions

The approach of automating common functions provides a number of benefits:

- Time is not wasted on monotonous, error-prone tasks.

- A higher-quality product through better-tested software; there is less total code to run through and it gets hit on every request; in essence, the foundation of much of the processing becomes a black box process with inputs.

- Automated functions and their common interfaces make it easier to develop and maintain consistent software across the application.

Even with easy-to-use APIs such as the Java servlet API, there are still many functions that must always be done in an application. For example, one of the common elements of business applications is the ability to process user form submissions. On each of these requests, the data from the form submission needs to be read out of the `HttpServletRequest` object, packaged in some data structures, and sent to the requested service or back-end function. One alternative is to write a custom servlet or JSP to handle every form on all pages. This usually isn't very efficient because the number of forms in a typical business application is relatively high. You might find that the logic to handle each form is repetitive and even has the same blocks of code in it. The other alternative is to abstract the basic flow of handling a form request and put it into a common servlet that can be used by all of the Web pages that have forms. Using a configuration service, you could define each form, its input data, and a service that should be used to process the request. Almost any function or process that is repeatable is a candidate for automation. This book looks at the nature of transactional Web applications in order to define a set of common elements that can be automated. As it turns out, due to the nature of Web applications and J2EE application architectures, many of these common elements need to be implemented for any given application. A set of configurable foundation components that implement these functions will increase both the quality and quantity of application functionality built on the reference architecture. As this book goes through the process of discussing the set of common elements and applying them to the Java platform, additional requirements for this foundation layer will be flushed out. Some basic work can be done at this level that provides immense value in meeting the overall goals of a scalable, modular architecture.

A set of configurable foundation components that automate basic elements of an application is often referred to as a framework. Building upon an earlier principle, many of these foundation components will be implemented using proven object-oriented design patterns. These framework components and patterns are what make up the reference architecture that will be used to rapidly develop quality J2EE applications. As many developers know, there is a gap between the total sum of services needed to develop just purely application-specific logic and those that are currently provided with the development platform. A software layer, referred to in this book as the Business Logic Foundation (BLF), will attempt to bridge this gap. The Java and J2EE platform continues to evolve and close the gap. However, it still remains even as a large number of people and organizations are working to add services to the platform. Due to the complexity of enterprise development, the widely varying set of requirements that different businesses and organizations have, and the many design considerations, it will take a significant amount of time for the standard to mature to the point where it addresses all of these needs. In fact, even as the underlying platforms and standards evolve, technology and problem domains also grow, thus making it likely that closing the gap will resemble a calculus equation represented by a curve which slowly approaches zero, but never actually gets there.

The automation capabilities within technical frameworks provide a high level of reusability across applications. Reusability is of course the "Holy Grail" of object-oriented software development. However, it has been very hard to achieve in many practical settings. Given a strategic application architecture and the set of guiding principles, you can position yourself to benefit from software reuse. The Enterprise JavaBean specification goes a long way toward having standard, reusable business components across applications. However, it is the role of the application architecture on top of J2EE to enable those components to be reused. It is important to have an application architecture that easily allows components to be plugged in to the rest of the system without adding significant overhead.

One way to plug in different components is through a messaging layer that buffers the different interfaces and systems. In complex architectures, this is the right solution, but for many applications, the overhead is too much of a price to pay. Two primary strategies to promote and enable the reuse of domain components are realized through the first two principles, design patterns and automated foundation components. One such example is that of the Service-Based Architecture layer that provides a standard interface for process-based components. By creating a standard interface that is used by the user presentation layer, a service such as Retrieve Account Data can be reused from different screens that require customer data. Services such as Account Deposit and Account Withdrawal can be reused as building blocks in an overall service, Transfer Funds. The fact that there is a service layer at all in the architecture allows the services themselves to be reused from different client devices. Finally, the standard interface of the service components allows you to automate their invocation through a configurable foundation layer within the reference architecture.

Use Metadata-Driven Components

Metadata is usually defined as data that describes other data. This book also uses the term "metadata" to refer to the many data elements that define the attributes and behaviors of various software components. Some examples of this could be the list of properties and their respective data types for a given business object, or it could be the form name and associated configuration information for a Web page. Much of the metadata that defines these components comes from design models described in UML.

The principle of using metadata to drive components again builds upon a previous principle, that of automating the tasks of software development. Metadata is used as an input to the "framework" services that automate and drive the behavior of J2EE components. This is applicable at all levels of the architecture. In the case of business objects, metadata can be used to define the business entities and their attributes. At the workflow or transaction level, metadata can be used to drive the process flow of complicated tasks. At the user interface level, it can define a particular Web page form and how it should be processed. All of these elements of applications can be abstracted and defined using metadata. The J2EE specifications themselves rely on different forms of metadata to configure and deploy components. A perfect example is the abstract approach taken by EJB 2.0 toward Container-Managed Persistence (CMP). The EJB deployment descriptors contain the metadata that maps the bean's properties to database tables, as well as defining any relationships that the bean may have with other components.

Not every process or function should be defined using metadata (everything in moderation, as they say). There are some drawbacks to this approach that should be considered and that may not make it the right approach for every task. A metadata-driven abstraction usually will add some overhead to the execution of the task when compared to explicit lines of code used to do the same job. This overhead is typically negligible when compared to something like a single database I/O request. However, it should be considered nonetheless in the overall approach to software development, especially where transaction throughput is essential to the success of an application.

Another potential drawback of this approach is the fact that it can make reading and debugging code a bit more difficult. A separate file or repository that contains the metadata determines portions of the flow through the code. There are a number of arguments to counteract this point, some of which have been mentioned here already. The primary argument is that these foundation components, which are configurable through metadata, become highly tested components that become almost like a black box to the rest of the application. Once you have these components working correctly, very little time is spent looking at the "framework" code. The behavior of an application can be determined simply by looking at the client code and the metadata inputs to the service. Consistent use of these foundation components rapidly makes this contention less of an issue. Another less structured argument is that well-written object-oriented code is difficult to sit down and read in the first place because the methods are typically very small and you often have to jump back and forth from object to object anyway in order to decipher what is going on. This issue was dealt with on a different level when software development moved in large part from procedural code to object-oriented development. It is usually easier to read and understand a contiguous block of procedural code than it is object-oriented code, but the many benefits found in OO development far outweigh this minor and perhaps even debatable disadvantage. Some of these same arguments apply to a metadata-driven approach as well.

As in many aspects of the J2EE architecture, both the pros and the cons must be weighed for a given design decision before making a choice. As is the case with so many architecture decisions you will see, the solution is often a middle-of-the-road choice in which metadata is used for key components that provide the maximum benefit. Elements of business applications that are data intensive and heavily used, such as forms processing and business object persistence, will use metadata to rapidly develop quality implementations.

The industry seems to be moving to storing many pieces of data in XML format, and metadata is no exception. Storing metadata as XML provides a number of benefits:

- XML data provides a standard format that can be stored either in a file or in a database table.

- Most design tools can generate XML data from their models; many tools now support XMI (XML Metadata Interchange), a standard XML format for object metadata.

- XML can be created or modified using a number of different tools including XML editors, custom-written tools, or in many cases, even a simple text editor.

An interesting effect of using metadata is that it separates pieces of the application design from the code. This is helpful for a number of reasons:

- A higher number of application functions driven by the design imply that fewer application changes will require actual code changes. This increases the speed of maintenance cycles and deployment.

- XML supports a model-driven development approach; the design models become accurate pieces of documentation for the system and are used to generate application components or the metadata input to foundation components.

- Much of the input to application code can originate from design models. The object models for the business entities contain the properties and the relationships between the entities. This metadata can be exported from design tools into XML. The XMI specification provides one such format to do so, and design tools are starting to support it. If a configurable business object base class can manage the properties and relationships for a business object, you have now automated this portion of the business object through metadata input almost completely through the design process. Of course, specific business methods and other application components will also modify the properties of the business object and create instances of relationships, but the logic to do so has been automated through the metadata-driven process.

Practicality: Performance and Scalability

The last principle, essentially performance engineering, is one that underlies all else. Avoiding this topic until the final phases of any project can have serious consequences. The quickest thing (no pun intended!) that will keep people from using your system is poor performance, especially in today's fast-paced Internet world. Business application users are accustomed to the performance of client-server applications over private networks and consumers or Internet users are very impatient when it comes to waiting for a Web-site page to load. Thus, although it is true that computers are getting faster and more hardware is always an option (if you built a scalable solution), you must keep a watchful eye and build performance into the development process from the very beginning. It must be a part of the design process because it often involves trade-offs with other aspects of a system, most often the flexibility that an application provides to the user.

Java, the language itself, can quickly approach the performance of C/C++ in many situations, a language widely regarded as a high-performance choice for even the most demanding applications. This is primarily due to the evolution of just-in-time (JIT) compilers that now aggressively translate Java byte code and perform code optimizations.

This is particularly true on the server side, where you typically have a large set of Java classes that will be executed many times. The initial overhead of performing the translation into native instructions is usually not worth mentioning, and thus in theory, the majority of the code should be comparable to compiled C++ code. One weakness that Java still has when compared to C++ is the garbage collection process, which adds some overhead. However, the programming benefits are well worth the minimal cost involved in terms of memory allocation and management, so this really does not even become an issue. In fact, as processor speeds continue to increase, the difference between the two languages themselves is likely to become almost insignificant. However, component services provided by J2EE add another layer on top of the language, and you must look very closely at the impact that component services have on the application's overall performance. While J2EE provides many valuable services, such as object persistence and naming and directory services, their benefits must be weighed against their costs.

Many solutions will involve using Enterprise Java services in cases in which they provide the most benefit, but not as a standard across the board. This is a common tendency of building J2EE architectures, to use the enterprise components across the board from front-to-back in the software architecture. A key example of this is the use of Entity Beans. Relatively speaking, Entity Beans are fairly heavyweight components, and thus should not be used to model every business object in an application, particularly if each business object maps to a row in the database. Doing this can quickly degrade the scalability, and thus the usability, of an application. A scalable architecture is a must for almost any system, and design guidelines discussed in this book for each layer of the architecture must be applied when deciding on the foundation for software components as well as in building the individual components themselves.

How This Book Is Organized

The structure of this book starts with a conceptual view of business applications and moves all the way to the realization of a corresponding application architecture and sample application. An introduction is first given to the reference architecture approach and how it is applied to J2EE technology. The three basic layers of the reference architecture (business objects, services/processes, and user interaction) are each built from the ground up, starting with design concepts, moving to relevant J2EE best practices, and ending with a J2EE implementation. Each layer is discussed as a general foundation for development in addition to its practical use in the form of a sample bank application that is constructed throughout the book. After having moved through the architecture vision, best practices, and implementation, the last set of chapters then take a step back and look deeper into topics such as application security, performance, and reuse.

Chapter 1, "Building Business Applications with J2EE," introduces and discusses the common elements of business applications. The common characteristics are abstracted out as a foundation for an application architecture approach. The layers of the reference architecture are introduced, and the components within each layer are defined. The J2EE platform is briefly covered, and the reference architecture is mapped to its implementation as J2EE components. The Model-View-Controller architecture pattern, also commonly known as the Model 2 approach in Web development, is presented as an overarching aspect of both J2EE technology and the reference architecture.

Chapter 2, "The Business Object Architecture: Design Considerations," covers design elements of the business object layer of the reference architecture. This chapter introduces the bank application's object model as an example to study. The elements of business object components are discussed and the implementation options in J2EE are considered. Design elements discussed include stateful versus stateless, Entity Beans versus regular Java objects, persistence mechanisms, and transaction concurrency.

Chapter 3, "Building Business Objects: Managing Properties and Handling Errors," walks through an implementation of the first half of business object responsibilities, which include property management, business validations, and handling error conditions. Due to the amount of functionality within business objects, their implementation is divided into chapters 3 and 4. An explicit implementation of the Account business object is discussed and then a generic property management approach is introduced. A metadata-driven base class implementation is described that can be used for all business objects. A standard interface for business objects is introduced so that all objects can be dealt with generically and consistently. Value objects and bulk accessor methods are also discussed. An error list mechanism is introduced and implemented that manages a set of configurable business errors for an object. General error and exception-handling techniques are discussed and applied to the business object implementation.

Chapter 4, "Building Business Objects: Persistence, Relationships, and the Template Method Pattern," walks through an implementation of the second half of business responsibilities, which include persistence of the object's data to a database, management of interactions with other objects, and the use of the Template Method pattern to build extensible, reusable business logic templates. Options for persistence that are discussed include the explicit use of JDBC, a metadata-driven JDBC framework, third-party and open-source persistence frameworks, and Entity Bean Container-Managed Persistence. Sample implementations are shown and discussed for each of the options. The business object lifecycle is abstracted through the construction of a business object factory, and implementations are shown for JDBC, Entity Beans, and Castor, a popular open-source persistence framework for Java. Object collection services are also discussed as a faster alternative to using business objects for read-only operations, and best practices are provided for using JDBC if that alternative is chosen. Data caching and a JMS-based refresh mechanism are also addressed as an option to prevent unnecessary database I/O. The responsibilities of aggregated business objects are discussed and corresponding methods are added to the standard business object interface. The Template Method pattern, which enables a key concept of the reference architecture, automation with extensibility, is discussed. Implementations of a save template, an object creation template, and an aggregated object template are constructed to automate basic business object functionality. The overall metadata DTD and implementation are then discussed. At the end of this chapter, readers will have a set of design concepts and code that can be used to quickly build robust business object components.

Chapter 5, "The Service-Based Architecture: Design Considerations," covers design elements and the rationale behind the service component layer of the reference architecture. The basic elements of these process-oriented objects are discussed, and implementation options are considered. Services are categorized as either update or data retrieval. The concept of the Session Bean as a component wrapper to regular

Java implementation classes is introduced. The majority of the chapter then covers the interface of the service components, the benefits of choosing a standard interface, and the considerations for different data structures such as XML, value objects, and argument lists.

Chapter 6, "Building Service-Based Components," walks you through the implementation of service components in the reference architecture. Examples are given for both explicit interfaces and a standard interface. A service data class is created that encapsulates value objects, argument lists, and error data in order to create a standard service interface. The implementation of an EJB wrapper around a regular Java class implementation is constructed. A service component base class is introduced for standard error handling, transaction management, and the invocation of the implementation classes. The general responsibilities of both data retrieval and update services are discussed. Some service implementations from the bank application are constructed such as TransferFunds, ChangeAddress, and GetAccountList. Strategies for building generic reusable services, invoking services within other services, and using the controller pattern are also discussed.

Chapter 7, "The User Interaction Architecture: Design Considerations and an Overview of Jakarta Struts," covers design elements and the common aspects of the user interaction layer of the reference architecture. The key aspects of web-based user interaction are abstracted as events, actions, services, and Web pages. These abstractions and the design considerations are used so that the core responsibilities of the controller architecture can be broken down into eight steps. These steps are automated to the extent possible and partitioned effectively between the controller and the action classes. Design considerations for state management are discussed with a brief overview of scope within the JSP/servlet architecture. Best practices for applying the Model-View-Controller architecture to J2EE are discussed including managing the session size, and JSP templates and encapsulating presentation logic in reusable custom tags. The last part of this chapter provides an overview of the Jakarta Struts project, an open-source implementation of the Model 2 architecture. The controller architecture of Struts is discussed, but the real power is shown to be within the JSP tag library that easily integrates request-handling functionality into dynamic Web pages.

Chapter 8, "Building the User Interaction Architecture," walks through the implementation of the user interaction layer using Struts. Implementation aspects are discussed and illustrated through practical examples of constructing the bank's Web site. The change address and view accounts pages are constructed as examples of simple update and data retrieval functions. The new customer wizard is constructed as an example of a multipage form. Strategies for the implementation of the user interaction components are discussed. Options are shown for implementing the event object and service data objects both independently and separately. Integrating error handling from front to back in the reference architecture is discussed and implemented. Some custom tags are created to illustrate the power of reusable presentation logic that integrates with the reference architecture, such as the drop-down tag, which automatically gets its data from a specified object cache. The implementation of the JSP template mechanism, as used by the bank's pages, is defined and discussed. The creation of extensible base action classes for standard logic is discussed and implemented. At the end of this chapter, readers have a complete set of tools and design concepts to rapidly build transactional Web sites using J2EE technology and a Business Logic Foundation.

Chapter 9, "Strengthening the Bank Application: Adding Security and Advanced Functionality," gives a brief overview of application security in J2EE and its use in the bank application. Some of the more interesting design aspects of Web-based applications are discussed through advanced pages within the bank application. A set of administrative pages that introduce implementation strategies for multiple submit buttons on a form and multiple objects being updated on the same form are developed.

Chapter 10, "Performance," presents an approach to performance engineering that balances the focus throughout the software development lifecycle. An emphasis is placed on scalable architectures and benchmark testing up front to determine the validity of proposed solutions. Strategies for measuring and optimizing performance are discussed including object instantiation, object caching, and the use of J2EE components such as Entity Beans.

Chapter 11, "Moving toward Reuse in the Reference Architecture," focuses on common roadblocks to reuse and best practices that can be used to offset these hurdles. Roadblocks range from the social aspects all the way to technical limitations. Both J2EE and the reference architecture are positioned as key aspects of a reuse architecture based on configuration and extensibility, the use of standard interfaces, and a layered modular architecture. Reuse and adaptability are considered in a strategic view of the reference architecture.

Who Should Read This Book

This book is intended for those who have already had some exposure to J2EE technologies such as EJB and JSP/servlets, although architects and software engineers of all skill levels will find the design considerations, implementation techniques, and reusable code useful. Technically astute managers and other information technology professionals will also find many sections of the book, such as the chapters on security, performance engineering, and reuse and strategic architecture, helpful.

This material will be of interest to any Java technologist building business applications using J2EE because it provides concepts and examples of how to build applications faster and with greater quality. Many J2EE books on the market provide basic API examples but do not go into detail about the design implications of different J2EE architectures or how to automate the development of J2EE components. This book does those things on both a theoretical and practical level.

Tools You Will Need

To run the sample application and use the business logic foundation software, you will need the following:

- Any J2EE 1.3–compliant application server such as BEA Weblogic 6.1
- Jakarta Struts v1.0 or greater, which is available at
  `http://jakarta.apache.org/struts`
- (Optional) The Castor Data Binding Framework, part of the ExoLab project, which is available at `http://castor.exolab.org/`

What's on the Web Site

The companion Web site contains all of the code from the Business Logic Foundation that is discussed as part of the reference architecture. It also contains the code for the sample bank application. You will also find links to relevant Web sites, open-source projects, and industry information on:

- J2EE and J2EE Blueprints
- The Jakarta Struts project
- The Jakarta Commons project
- The Castor project
- Performance testing

Summary

The concepts and principles that are discussed here provide a foundation for a set of best practices that will be used effectively to build Internet applications using J2EE technology. These design and development guidelines feed into the creation of a powerful architecture that is used to develop Internet applications faster and with greater performance, quality, and reusability. J2EE provides a powerful standard upon which you can build components and applications; with the right set of development practices and software assets, Web-based business application development moves closer to a process known as software fabrication, in which applications are built using prefabricated components and frameworks.

Building Business Applications with J2EE

The approach to developing Web applications with J2EE (Java 2 Enterprise Edition) is based on a number of factors, which include:

- The common elements of business applications
- The vision of the software architecture; that is, the definition of the components and their interaction
- The J2EE technology platform used to implement the software

Business applications share a number of common elements because they are all used to implement business processes and manage the information of a business. Consequently, business entities and processes can be modeled as software components. In today's world, users access many business applications and their underlying components through the Internet, usually by using a Web browser but increasingly through wireless and other Internet devices. The vision of the software architecture should integrate the common elements into a component structure that models the business today and positions it for the future. On the technical side, the architecture should position the development organization to meet the requirements of flexibility, performance, and time-to-market constraints. The execution of the software architecture vision is driven by the guiding principles discussed in the introduction and a number of J2EE best practices described in this book.

This chapter defines a set of fundamental elements that are common among Web-based business applications. This set of key elements drives the definition of a reference architecture that comprises three layers: business objects, process-oriented or service-based objects, and user interaction components. The basic theory behind the J2EE platform approach is briefly discussed and followed by an introduction to a central design pattern that is predominantly used to implement J2EE applications, the Model-View-Controller (MVC) architecture pattern.

Elements of Transactional, Web-Based Business Applications

Business applications, especially Web-based transactional applications, share many common characteristics. It is important to take a step back and look at these characteristics because they form the basis of many application architectures. In fact, these elements are the model on which the software architecture is based. From these characteristics, you derive the different types of application components and services that are required. The architectures discussed in the remainder of this book are based on these elements. These elements map to software layers and components, and a thorough analysis of how the mapping should be done is given in the following chapters. In short, these elements provide the foundation of the architecture, and they drive the software layers that enable flexibility and reusability.

Business Entities

Businesses deal with different entities all of the time. These range from higher-level entities such as a customer or a supplier down to lower levels such as purchase orders or even perhaps individual line items on a contract. These entities share a number of common characteristics:

- Behaviors
- Properties
- Relationships with other entities
- Rules or policies

An example used throughout the book is a bank. Two primary entities that banks deal with are customers and accounts. Accounts have properties, such as a current balance and minimum allowed balance, as well as rules that enforce policies of what happens when the current balance falls below the minimum. Accounts also have behaviors such as deposit and withdrawal, and they interact with customers, the other entity in the bank example.

Entities become participants in business processes. They often have different sets of business policies or rules that must be enforced. An application will likely be interested in the persistence of the state of the entities, for example, the status of a purchase order or the current balance of a bank account.

Business entities are of course the foundation of object-oriented design and development. While this book is not meant to be a discussion of object-oriented theory, it is important to take note of these primary characteristics to motivate further discussion on their place in the software architecture and on how a technical solution can address this element of business applications.

Business Processes

Businesses use many processes to carry out the work of their business. These processes often have some sort of specified workflow and often involve one or more business entities. They must be executed in a secure manner, and they involve units of work that cannot be broken apart. One example that illustrates both points is the process of transferring money from a checking account to a money market account. The bank providing the service does not want the deposit credited without also accounting for the withdrawal, or it loses money.

The accessibility of these business processes, or services, is becoming ever more of an issue. In the example, a bank's customer may want the ability to transfer the funds from a home PC through a browser or from a wireless device while on the road. Businesses exchange funds all of the time, and a Web service for a transfer of funds through a secure, B2B (business-to-business) Internet client provides another potential access point.

Based on the bank example, business processes share the following characteristics:

- Include some flow of activities
- Involve business entities as participants
- Need to be executed in a secure manner
- Comprise units of work essential to the business
- Need to be accessible from different clients:
    - Browser-based applications
    - Wireless devices
    - B2B Web services
    - Other Internet clients

User Interaction

Many business processes would not be very helpful or effective if end users could not access them. As described in the previous section, the types of access points are growing, and the requirements can vary widely based on how the information or service should be presented to each access device.

The user interaction portions of applications typically share the following characteristics:

- Application presentation, such as HTML or XML over HTTP
- Access to business functions and services

- Static and dynamic content
- Screen flow, or page navigation
- Forms processing
- Error handling

The sample bank Web site exhibits these characteristics. There are both static content (account holder policies) and dynamic content (list of customer accounts and detailed information about each). In order to transfer funds between accounts, the user must fill out a quick form to select the amount and the from and to accounts. Any data entry mistakes, such as entering an amount greater than the balance, must be handled accordingly and the user must be given the opportunity to retry the transaction.

A bank customer accessing this service from a handheld wireless device would encounter all of the same elements. The application itself would need to tailor the content to fit onto the smaller screen and communicate using WML instead of HTML, but the same issues exist.

NOTE A Web service that can be used by a B2B partner to transfer funds would share many of the same characteristics except for the content-generation and screen-navigation elements, but all of the forms-processing and error-handling logic would still be needed. A Web service is actually a simpler example than the first two, although it does introduce its own set of challenges. For the most part, the user interaction layer in the case of a Web service is an HTTP wrapper around the business process.

The Reference Architecture

The primary elements of business applications naturally fit into layers, starting with the business entities themselves. They are at the core of what the business deals with every day. Every business has processes or transactions that involve these entities. Finally, these processes and transactions need to be accessible to users or business partners. Figure 1.1 shows how these layers fit together in a reference architecture. Once you move toward technical solutions to implement these layers, you will see that your software architecture diagrams closely resemble this diagram.

The software architecture models the three primary elements of business applications and provides technical implementations for each of them. Each of these categories is a conceptual layer in the architecture: business entities, business processes, and user interaction. This book defines a set of terms to describe these software layers in relation to the reference architecture. Note that these are not standard J2EE terms, simply a shorthand notation used to communicate the vision of the application architecture and describe how the components fit together.

Business Object Architecture.   The business entities become the core of the "Business Object Architecture." This term is used to describe the layer of business object components that model these entities and interact with enterprise information systems. This typically involves some combination of

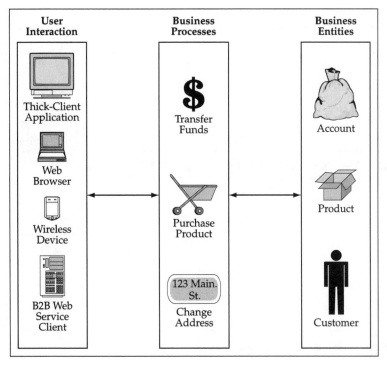

Figure 1.1   The Structure of a Business Application.

regular Java classes and Entity Beans in J2EE architectures. Business entities within the bank example include a *Customer* and an *Account*.

Service-Based Architecture.   The business processes become a part of the "Service-Based Architecture." This term is used to describe the layer of the business components that implement the processes and workflows of the business. The typical incarnation of a "service" in this reference architecture is a stateless Session Bean, although your definition is not limited to this. In this book, "service" describes a process-oriented object as opposed to an object that models a particular business entity. A Session Bean can act simply as a component wrapper to one of your process-oriented objects, although these objects could be invoked directly from another service or business component as well. Business processes within the bank example include *TransferFunds* and *ChangeAddress*.

User Interaction Architecture.   The user interface and client interaction aspects are simply called the "User Interaction Architecture." In a J2EE architecture, this is typically implemented under the Model 2 approach, which uses servlets and JavaServer Pages (JSP) to implement a Model-View-Controller (MVC) Web architecture. User interaction within the bank example includes Web pages with which the user can transfer funds and change their address.

As described in this book, these layers define interaction points in the software architecture. Note that at this point you should not consider network or hardware

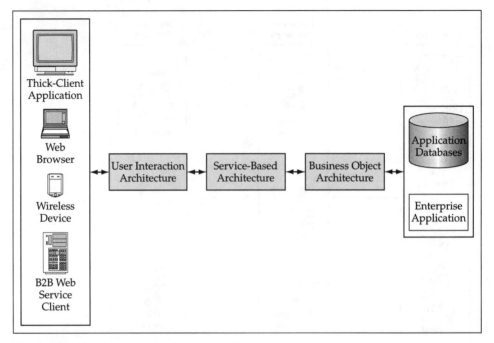

Figure 1.2   The Basic Architecture Layers Diagram.

architecture. These software layers could reside on the same physical tier or be distributed across a network. For now, this is somewhat irrelevant. The interaction of the software components and the partitioning of functionality is the key point to be drawn from this view of the architecture.

Figure 1.2 illustrates the software architecture diagram, which closely resembles the diagram that represents the flow of business application characteristics.

Business Object Architecture

The Business Object Architecture contains the components that implement the business entities in the system. Each of these components manages the data and business logic associated with a particular business entity. This includes the persistence of that object's data, typically to a relational database. This database access can be implemented by the container in the case of CMP (Container-Managed Persistence) Entity Beans or by the developer in the case of BMP (Bean-Managed Persistence) Entity Beans or regular Java classes. In the last two cases, in which the developer does the work, it is a best practice to isolate the database access into a separate data-access layer. If there is any data access outside of the business object model, this should also be included in this layer. This includes database queries that are run in order to retrieve read-only data for presentation to the user.

In the bank application, a business object could represent entities such as a customer, a bank account, or even an individual transaction on the bank account such as a withdrawal. These business objects can be implemented either as Java classes, Entity Beans, or some combination of the two. The persistence of each business object is abstracted out to the extent possible so that separate data objects, persistence frameworks, or Container-Managed Persistence services can be used to have the object data persist in the database.

Service-Based Architecture

The Service-Based Architecture contains the components that implement the business processes and transactions of an application. These typically are process-oriented objects that represent units of work or implement a business workflow. Many of the service components are relatively small in content because the business objects are used to do much of the work. Other services are quite complicated in nature. Not all software architectures include a service-based layer; however, it can add tremendous value in terms of flexibility, reusability, and component design. The concept of services allows the front end to be decoupled from the back-end business object components. Service objects are used to coordinate transactions that involve multiple business components and provide a simple interface to the user interaction layer. Services themselves become reusable across screens, applications, and different client access points. As you will see, a simple stateless Session Bean wrapper around a service object allows you to easily distribute the service and manage the transaction as well, one of the greatest benefits of the EJB (Enterprise JavaBeans) architecture.

One important aspect of the Service-Based Architecture is that services typically fall into one of two categories: read-only and update. Remember that in the architecture diagram, all the back-end functionality that is required to create the presentation layer needs to be provided by a service. Thus, many services within the application architecture will be data retrieval services.

> **NOTE** Depending on the technical architecture, the presentation layer may or may not be able to contact the data-access layer directly. Some configurations will separate the user interaction layer (Web container) and the Business Object Architecture (EJB container) onto different physical tiers with no direct path from the user interaction layer to the database. Other architectures combine the two layers on one physical tier. Thus, for maximum efficiency, you would not need a service to retrieve a result set. This issue is hotly contested in the industry, and will be covered later in the chapters on User Interaction and Service-Based Architecture.

In the bank application, the business processes include allowing customers access to their account information, transferring funds between accounts, and changing the customer address. These services are implemented as process-oriented objects and then wrapped with stateless Session Beans to implement the service component pattern discussed in the introduction. They are initially deployed as remote EJB components so that the services can be potentially accessed from a number of different clients. However, a deployment with local interfaces would work equally well in cases where the Web tier and EJB tiers are colocated on the same physical machine. The J2EE platform section later in this chapter discusses the different tiers and the nature of the respective J2EE components in more detail.

User Interaction Architecture

The User Interaction Architecture contains components that process user requests, invoke application services, and generate responses sent back to the user. In a Web-based application, this layer would process HTML form submissions, manage state within a user session, generate Web-page content, and control navigation between pages. It is easy to see that the user interaction layer has a large number of responsibilities. Thus, it is not surprising that the User Interaction Architecture has more types of components than the other two layers combined. Whereas there are only service components in the Service-Based Architecture and only data and business objects in the Business Object Architecture, the User Interaction Architecture contains page components, request-processing components, state management, tag libraries, and user action components just to name a few. And that doesn't count content generation, personalization, portals, and other complexities that factor into many business applications.

The point is that this layer encompasses a lot of functions. The good news is, however, that many of the functions within this layer can be automated through configurable foundation components. Web design will always require people skilled in graphics design and human factors, but integrating business functionality into Web pages can be done in a flexible, robust manner through the Model 2 paradigm, the MVC (*Journal of Object-Oriented Programming* 1988) architecture pattern applied to the J2EE Web tier architecture. Both Java Swing and the J2EE Blueprints (Kassem and the Enterprise Team 2000) sample applications are based on this architecture pattern. A major portion of the reference architecture discussed in this book is a generic, configurable implementation of the Model 2 architecture. This allows you to automate the processing of user requests and page navigation, a major portion of the responsibilities within the User Interaction Architecture. Reusable libraries can be used for many of the other functions, such as tag libraries and style sheets for the purpose of content generation.

For each layer of the architecture and each element of the business application within these layers, design choices will be considered that impact the overall goals of the system, such as performance and flexibility. The four guiding principles discussed in the introduction will be applied to each element in order to use proven design patterns and automate as much of the processing as possible. The Business Logic Foundation will cut across these different elements to provide configurable, metadata-driven components to automate the work.

The User Interaction Architecture encompasses any application components resident on the client device as well. In the case of client-server applications, this would include the entire thick-client, Java Swing GUI (graphical user interface) application. However, in the case of thin-client Web applications, this is typically limited to some amount of JavaScript that runs within the browser. The JavaScript code comes from the Web server, although it is actually run on the client side. Java applets are an additional possibility, although they are not often used in enterprise Web development. Thus, the majority of the user interaction processing for Web applications is handled on the server.

In the bank application, user interaction is primarily through a set of pages for the bank's Web site, which provides customers with access to accounts and Internet banking functions. There is also a set of Web pages for bank administrators to facilitate management of some aspects of the application as well as provide the ability to make adjustments to account transactions. Almost every page pulls in dynamic content from the application database and provides secure access to the appropriate set of service components.

The J2EE Platform Approach

As defined in the J2EE Blueprints, the Java 2 Enterprise Edition platform provides a component-based approach to implementing a multitiered software architecture. This architecture can be used to model the elements that typically characterize business applications. The components that make up the architecture are executed in run-time environments called containers. Containers are used to provide infrastructure-type services such as lifecycle management, distribution, and security. In a Web-based, thin-client application, the majority of the software resides on two containers running inside of an application server. J2EE application servers provide both a Web container and an Enterprise JavaBean container. These two environments provide the basis of an excellent foundation on which to build transactional business applications.

Containers and components in the J2EE architecture are divided into three tiers. The tiers are defined as:

Client Tier.   The Web browser or Java application client.

Middle Tier.   Comprising the Web container and the EJB container, the middle tier contains the business logic of the application and provides any services available to the client tier.

Enterprise Information Systems Tier.   The rest of the enterprise information architecture including databases and existing applications.

Figure 1.3 shows how the tiers and containers fit together in the J2EE platform.

Note that multiple containers and software layers in the architecture are housed on the middle tier of the J2EE architecture. This is where the bulk of the work resides; thus the focus of this book is on this tier. The client tier for a Web application is typically a Web browser. Other types of clients include a thick-client Java GUI application, Java applet, and B2B Web service clients. The enterprise information tier consists primarily of data sources and other existing applications. J2EE provides a number of interfaces and APIs (application programming interfaces) to access resources in this tier.

The two primary containers of the J2EE architecture, both found on the middle tier, are the Web container and the EJB container. The function of the Web container is to process client requests and generate a response, while the function of the EJB container is to implement the business logic of the application.

Table 1.1 provides a summary of the primary software components that are found on the middle tier of the J2EE architecture. Note that this list excludes J2EE interfaces to enterprise tier resources, which are discussed in detail later in this chapter.

It is important to note, and your study of the entire architecture will demonstrate, that not all of these components are required for every application. In fact, you will find that many applications are better off using only those components that provide substantial value for the type of solution being addressed.

Table 1.1   J2EE Containers and Components

CONTAINER	COMPONENT	DESCRIPTION
Web	Servlet	Component that processes HTTP requests and generates HTML or XML responses
	JSP	Text-based document used to generate dynamic content that can contain both HTML content, scriptlets of Java code, and JSP custom tags
EJB	Session Bean	Provides a service to a single client
	Entity Bean	Persistent object that represents an instance of data across all clients
	Message-Driven Bean	A consumer of asynchronous messages

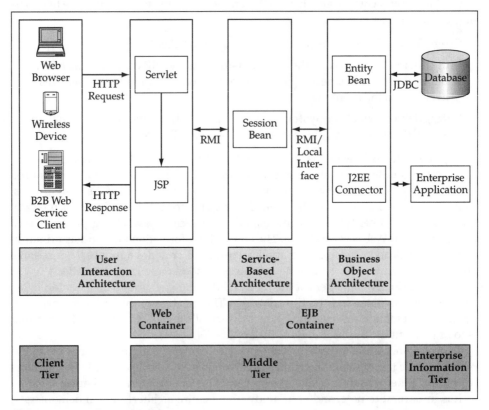

Figure 1.3   Basic J2EE Architecture.

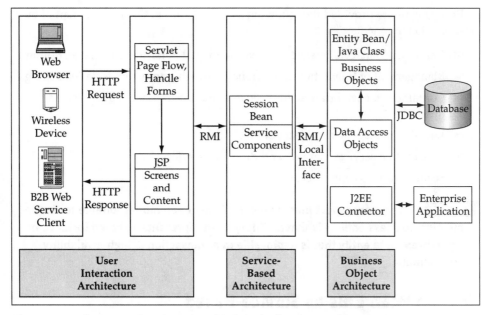

Figure 1.4   Elements of Business Applications in the J2EE Architecture.

Figure 1.4 shows the elements of business applications that were discussed previously. These elements are overlaid on top of the J2EE architecture and components.

The following gives you a look at how the primary J2EE components provide implementations for the different layers of the business application architecture.

Entity Bean EJBs as Business Object Components

Entity Beans are meant to represent persistent data entities within an application. An instance of an Entity Bean typically represents a "row" in a database, but is not necessarily limited to this definition. You can also implement much more coarse-grained Entity Beans that use either dependent objects (regular Java classes) or other local Entity Beans to encapsulate logic for a number of related business entities. One of the major component services that are provided to Entity Beans is that of Container-Managed Persistence, where the container causes the component's data to persist in a relational database. In the EJB 2.0 specification, however, CMP persistence is limited to one table. Any object-relational mapping scheme more complicated than a one-to-one table-object mapping is not explicitly supported by the EJB specification except through Bean-Managed Persistence (BMP), in which you write the persistence code yourself. It turns out that there are few compelling reasons to take the BMP Entity Bean approach, but this is only one of a number of persistence options that will be discussed thoroughly in the upcoming chapters on the Business Object Architecture.

Entity Beans are provided the following services to aid in the development of business object components:

- Container-Managed Persistence (Bean-Managed Persistence is also an option.)
- Management of transaction concurrency through transaction isolation settings
- Container-managed transactions (Bean-managed transactions are also an option.)
- Lifecycle management; object pooling
- Distribution services; naming and directory services
- Security (access control lists)

NOTE The primary aspect that makes the Entity Bean model suitable for implementing business entities is that an Entity Bean represents a shared instance of a persistent data entity that is deployable in a transactional, high-availability environment.

Session Bean EJBs as Service-Based Components

A Session Bean represents a service provided to a client, which makes it a natural fit for a service-based model. Unlike Entity Beans, Session Beans do not share data across multiple clients. Each user requesting a service or executing a transaction invokes a Session Bean to process the request.

Session Beans can be either stateful or stateless. Stateless Session Beans do not maintain any state between method calls for a given client, and a given instance is typically multithreaded, servicing multiple clients. After a stateless Session Bean processes a given request, it goes on to the next client and next request without maintaining or sharing any data. Stateful Session Beans are often constructed for a particular client and can maintain state across method invocations for a single client until the component is removed.

Session Beans are provided the following services to aid in the development of business processes or service-based components:

- Container-managed transactions (Bean-managed transactions are also an option.)
- Lifecycle management; object pooling
- Distribution services; naming and directory services
- Security (access control lists)

JavaServer Pages and Java Servlets as the User Interface

JavaServer Pages (JSP) and Java servlets are the two primary components of the Web tier in the J2EE architecture. The primary job of the Web tier and these two components is to process and respond to Web user requests. Thus, aspects of the User Interaction

Architecture such as forms processing and content generation are handled by these components. The servlet API provides an easy-to-use set of objects that process HTTP requests and generate HTML/XML responses. The concept of a servlet is to provide a Java-centric approach to programming Web tier functionality.

JavaServer Pages provide an HTML-centric version of servlets. JSP components are document-based rather than object-based, but they provide the ability to integrate anything that can be done in Java as well as some other nice conveniences. JSP documents have built-in access to servlet API objects such as the request and response objects, as well as the user session object. JSP also provides a very powerful custom tag mechanism that enables you to encapsulate a reusable piece of Java presentation code in an HTML tag that can be placed directly into the JSP document.

JSP and servlets provide the following user presentation services:

- HTTP request processing
- HTTP response generation
- State management at different context levels:
    - Application
    - User session
    - Request
    - Page
- Integration of HTML/XML content with presentation logic through Java scriptlets and custom tags in a JSP
- Java environment to invoke back-end components such as EJBs through RMI (Remote Method Invocation) and databases through JDBC (Java Database Connectivity)

Distributed Java Components

Two core services provided by the Java platform that overlap all of these layers of the architecture are:

- Java Naming and Directory Interface (JNDI)
- Remote Method Invocation (RMI) protocol

The JNDI service allows you to name and distribute components within the architecture. Any Java object can be stored and retrieved using JNDI; however, you will most often use it for looking up component interfaces to enterprise beans. The components and resources that you look up can be either local or remote.

Look at the case of a distributed enterprise component. The client uses JNDI to look up the corresponding EJB Home interface. This is a special type of interface in Enterprise Java that lets you create, access, and remove instances of Session and Entity Beans. After using the Home interface to gain access to a remote interface of a particular enterprise bean, you can invoke the exposed methods using RMI. The remote interface takes the local method call, serializes the objects that will be passed as arguments, and invokes the corresponding remote method on the distributed object. The serialized

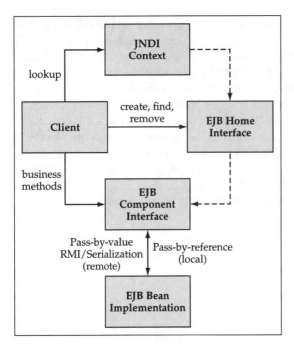

Figure 1.5 Use of JNDI and RMI with EJB Components.

objects passed as arguments are converted back to normal Java objects, and the method invocation continues as normal until the method returns its value, upon which the same process occurs in reverse going back to the remote interface client. This process of using JNDI and RMI with EJB is illustrated in Figure 1.5.

In the case of local Entity Beans, the local Home interface is discovered using a JNDI lookup. This interface lets you create, access, and remove instances of local Entity Beans that you then can access through the corresponding bean's local interface. A method invocation on a local interface is proxied directly to the bean's implementation class and does not go through RMI.

J2EE Access to the Enterprise Information Systems (EIS) Tier

J2EE provides a number of different interfaces and APIs to access resources in the EIS tier. Table 1.2 shows the different resource types and the J2EE interface mechanism.

The use of the JDBC API is encapsulated primarily in the data-access layer or within the Container-Managed Persistence classes of an Entity Bean. Data sources that map connections to a database are defined in JDBC. A client who wishes to access a particular database resource uses JNDI to look up the corresponding data source. The J2EE application server uses this mechanism to provide connection pooling to the different data resources. It is crucial that clients using these connections close them as soon as

Table 1.2 J2EE Interfaces and APIs to Access EIS Tier Resources

EIS RESOURCE	J2EE API	DESCRIPTION
Relational databases	Java Database Connectivity (JDBC)	Database-independent APIs to manage connections, transactions, and all SQL and stored procedure execution.
Legacy and other enterprise applications	Java Connector Architecture	Provides a standard adapter mechanism for integrating enterprise applications.
Email server	JavaMail API	Java API to send and receive email.
Enterprise messaging	Java Message Service (JMS)	A Java messaging architecture that supports both point-to-point and publish/subscribe mechanisms. Also provides for asynchronous processing within J2EE environment.

they are done to prevent bottlenecks. For this reason, a data-access layer should encapsulate all JDBC access.

BEST PRACTICE The logic to access the database connections and close all of the JDBC resources properly, especially during any error conditions, should be implemented in one place and used throughout the application.

The Java Connector Architecture provides a standard way in Java to build adapters to access existing enterprise applications. Another standard interface, the JavaMail API, provides a nice way to access mail server functions.

The Java Message Service (JMS) provides a standard interface to enterprise messaging systems. It is used within the J2EE architecture to provide asynchronous communication with other distributed components in a reliable manner. One other interesting thing to note about JMS is that it is the only mechanism provided in the EJB tier to perform asynchronous processing. Message-Driven Beans, the third type of EJB, are consumers of JMS messages and can be used to perform asynchronous or parallel processing.

As you can see, the J2EE platform provides a wide array of services and components that can be used to build Web applications. The commonly used Model-View-Controller design pattern structures the interaction of these components, particularly on the Web tier. Servlets and JSP naturally fit into the controller and view roles, respectively, within this pattern. Their usage in this pattern is now commonly referred to as the Model 2 architecture. MVC has been used within the paradigm of a thick-client application to tie controls on a screen to their data source within the model. The stateless nature of Web applications, however, does present some interesting challenges to applying this pattern in J2EE. Nonetheless, the MVC pattern still provides the best way to modularize components that handle the user interaction. The next section describes the MVC approach and applies it to the J2EE architecture.

The Model-View-Controller Architecture Approach

The Model 2 architecture is based on the Model-View-Controller design pattern, referred to earlier in this chapter. MVC is a cornerstone of software development best practices, especially in terms of developing the user interface. The pieces of this pattern are defined as follows:

View.   The screens presented to the user

Controller.   A component that controls the flow and processing of user actions

Model.   The application business logic components

The benefit of using the MVC pattern is that you isolate the different portions of an application in order to provide greater flexibility and more opportunity for reuse. A primary isolation point is between the presentation objects and the application back-end objects that manage the data and business rules. This allows a user interface to have many different screens that can be changed to a large degree without impacting the business logic and data components.

BEST PRACTICE Use the MVC, or Model 2, architecture pattern to isolate and modularize screen logic, control logic, and business logic. A generic MVC implementation is a key component of the reference architecture as it provides a flexible and reusable foundation for rapid Web application development.

A view needs to have application data in order to present it to the user. However, views do not contain the definitive source of data. The model contains and manages the definitive source of data for all application objects. Thus, when the model updates its data, it must inform the view that the data has changed. The MVC architecture uses this notification concept of informing the view of any data that has changed so it can rerender the display to the user with the accurate and up-to-date information.

Java Swing uses this pattern throughout all of its GUI components. Each screen widget, such as a *JTable,* has a model behind it, and the GUI widgets are notified when the model has been updated so that it can redraw its display with the new data. A Web application can be thought of in the same way. View objects live in the JSP container, while model objects live in the EJB container. If view objects persist for the life of a user's session within an application, they would need to be notified when the corresponding model objects on the EJB tier are updated.

The controller component isolates how a user's actions on the screen are handled by the application. This allows for an application design to flexibly handle things such as page navigation and access to the functionality provided by the application model in the case of form submissions. This also provides an isolation point between the model and the view. Because the controller component handles the user requests and invokes functions on the model as necessary, it allows for a more loosely coupled front and back end. Interaction between the model and the view is only through an event-based mechanism that informs the view of changes to the model's data.

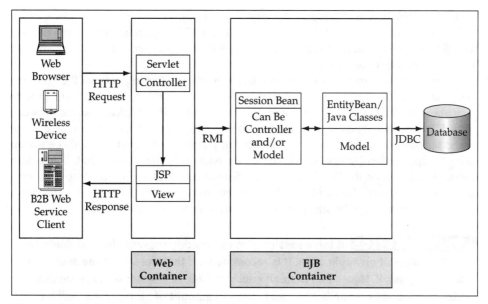

Figure 1.6 MVC Components Mapped to J2EE.

This and the previous section have discussed how some of the MVC patterns apply to the Web architecture. Figure 1.6 gives a complete picture of how objects in the MVC architecture are mapped to the J2EE architecture.

Note that in architectures that do not use Enterprise JavaBeans, the model objects could just as easily live in the JSP container. MVC is only a software pattern and does not restrict where components live in the technical architecture. As you look at different design patterns and architecture considerations, note that model components may actually live in both the JSP and EJB containers in the case of value objects or lightweight business objects. Value objects are primarily objects that act as data structures, and they may be used as a means to transport data from the EJB tier to the Web tier. In some cases, they contain a small amount of validation logic, which qualifies them for the title of "lightweight" business objects. In this sense, they are a part of the model. The rest of the application logic of the model may be found in stateless or stateful components that live on the EJB tier.

Data from the model may be sent to the Web tier either as value objects, XML data, event objects, or any kind of data structure that you can imagine. The MVC architecture is based on an event notification scheme in which, after the data is initially retrieved, updates can be received either to inform the view of the change or provide the new data at the same time. If the new data is not provided, the view or controller is required to go back to the model to get the new data when a change is made. However, does the data need to persist on the Web tier or can it be just temporary for the life of a given transaction, unit-of-work, or screen? This is the topic of a lengthy debate that will be discussed throughout the chapters of this book. A Web application is different from a client-server application in that it presents a page of content to a thin-client browser. It does not need to have data resident on the Web tier any longer at that point. A Web application typically does not rerender screen components or data without going back to the Web tier, in which case the view or controller component can make another call to the application model in order to get the data. This approach makes the data on the Web tier "temporary." It resides there for as long as it is needed, usually to render a given Web page or set of pages.

In any case, performance benefits can be derived from having data on the Web tier. Data that is cached on this tier and that is used throughout the application can save you from invoking methods on the application model. This typically saves network trips, EJB component access, and database processing, all of which can be costly in the grand scheme of things for high-throughput applications. In most cases, this ends up being an application-by-application design decision as to determine what, if any, data should be cached on the Web tier. The *HttpSession* provides a place to store data for a given user's session. This can be easily accessed from the view JSP components. However, you want to keep the size of an individual user session fairly small.

BEST PRACTICE A large session size can quickly degrade the scalability and performance of an application. It is recommended that the size of the session be kept fairly small. How small is small enough? Well, remember that the session size multiplied by a number of users gives an amount of memory that will be consumed on the Web tier. Taking into consideration that this amount is only a portion of the memory needed to run the application, you can get a rough idea of the number of concurrent users that will be supported by a single instance of a JSP container. Multiply this number by the number of JSP container instances in your production cluster, and this gives you a rough limit on the total number of concurrent users your application can support.

Another benefit of the Web tier "temporary" data approach is that of application data shared across users. If multiple users can potentially update a certain object, how do you notify each user session of the change? It is fairly easy to notify the view objects within the session where the update occurred; however, how do you get hold of the other user sessions? Now the scenario is getting a bit more complex. JMS could be used to implement the publish/subscribe mechanism that notifies the view of updates to the model. However, is this the best option for data stored in a session? Well, it would certainly seem to work, but you would have a lot of different JMS clients going in and out of scope as user sessions came and went. This seems like it might be a bit excessive.

NOTE The use of JMS as a publish/subscribe mechanism for updating cached data with changes is actually an excellent approach for systemwide data, and this is discussed in the Business Object Architecture chapter.

As you can see, there are a number of variations on how this pattern can be applied to Web architectures. The common variations will be studied in detail in the User Interaction Architecture chapter. Whether data in the tier containing the View is persistent or temporary, there is tremendous value in isolating the three MVC aspects of an application. The architecture discussed in this book also isolates the front end from the back end. There actually is not a contradiction between the two, but a complementary relationship. All of the same components can exist, but at the high level the distinction between the architecture layers is different. The two overlap in a couple of different ways:

- The User Interaction Architecture includes both the view and controller components.

- In some architecture designs, the controller component may overlap both the user interaction layer and the service-based layer.

- The model includes both the Service-Based Architecture and the Business Object Architecture.

Figure 1.7 shows how the two architectures overlap.

The controller component can have different functions in the Web architecture on the different tiers. A controller component in the Web tier can be used for processing HTTP requests, both form submissions and, potentially, navigation links. A controller component on the EJB tier can control the flow of business object functionality. In some sense, a service-based component that contains workflow type logic implements a "controller" on the EJB side. A benefit of having a controller component on the EJB side goes back to a point discussed earlier about the controller being an isolation point between the View and the Model. This allows the controller components on both tiers to pass data back and forth and act as an intermediary between the view and the

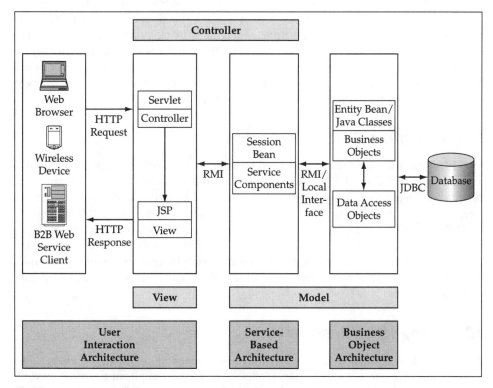

Figure 1.7   MVC and the Business Application Architecture.

model. The component layer can then act as a broker for update events when the model is updated. It is easier to implement this if the update events are represented in a standard fashion, such as an event object, or with objects that implement a standard interface. Value objects, "lightweight" business objects, and actual business objects can all implement standard interfaces in order to enable this. There are many other benefits of this approach that will be discussed in the chapter on the Business Object Architecture.

One option for implementing some of the controller logic is to use a standard base class for all service-based components. The base class could handle communication of update event-type functionality. A data structure that combines object data and update events will be needed to handle this design. If a standard interface is used between the two controller components (or one Web-tier controller and one service-based component, depending on how you look at it), this is made even easier. The benefits of using a standard interface for service-based components is discussed in detail later on, but the data structure needs to include these things, as well as things like error information from the transaction.

Best Practices for Building Business Applications with J2EE

This section summarizes the best practices discussed within this chapter. A corresponding section is used throughout the chapters of this book to break down the key concepts and provide a synopsis of the relevant best practices for J2EE development. At this point, the reference architecture and J2EE technology have only been introduced, so the list of best practices only scratches the surface of what will eventually be covered. The majority of the best practices will be flushed out in the remainder of the book as it goes in-depth into each of the architecture layers. For now, a few key best practices have been highlighted that are summarized here.

Implementing Database Access

In J2EE applications, database access can be implemented either through CMP Entity Beans or with JDBC in BMP Entity Beans or regular Java classes. For performance reasons, a combination of the two approaches may also be used: Entity Beans for transactional updates and JDBC for read-only queries that are used to present data to the user. If JDBC is used, the database logic should be isolated into a separate data-access layer to minimize the impact to the application if either the database schema or vendor changes. The business objects then use the data-access layer to implement the persistence logic. Remember that in the case of CMP Entity Beans, the container implements this layer for you.

Managing JDBC Resources

It is crucial that JDBC resources, such as database connections, be closed properly to prevent resource contention and provide the maximum throughput possible for your application. The logic to access the database connections and close all of the JDBC resources properly, especially during any error conditions, should be implemented in one place and used throughout the application. This logic is typically encapsulated in some type of JDBC utility class that is used by the entire data access layer.

Structuring Your Application Using the MVC Architecture Pattern

The MVC architecture pattern should be used to isolate and modularize screen logic, control logic, and business logic. A generic MVC implementation provides a flexible and reusable foundation for the rapid development of Web applications. J2EE components naturally fit into this pattern to form the Model 2 architecture where a controller servlet processes requests and dispatches them to JSP view components. This forms the basis of the user interaction aspect of the reference architecture. Business logic within the model portion of MVC is implemented using service-based components and business objects within the reference architecture.

Keeping the HTTP Session Size to a Minimum

A large session size can quickly degrade the scalability and performance of high-throughput applications. It is recommended that the size of the session be kept fairly small. Exactly how small depends on the characteristics of your particular application. Early load testing can be done on key architecture scenarios to verify that target concurrent user levels can be adequately supported with any given approach. In general, use the session to store a minimal amount of state needed to maintain future operations. Also remember that data stored in the session is not aware of any simultaneous updates made to the database by other users, so it usually does not make sense to cache global data in the session.

Summary

With J2EE as the development platform, you have a portable, scalable framework on which to build applications. However, the technologies are complex with many potential pitfalls. There is also still a large amount of coding that must be done in order to create a robust application. Each component must be able to manage its data accurately and enforce all of the business rules and constraints. The User Interaction Architecture must be able to drive the user experience, provide dynamic content, process all form transactions, and handle any errors gracefully. To do this all quickly and with great quality, you will use the four guiding principles of design patterns, automation, metadata, and performance considerations to drive the study of advanced J2EE development.

These software development principles applied together can be used to form the foundation of a generic Model 2 architecture implementation. This will be the basis of the reference architecture that will be used to speed the development of quality business applications. Additional services such as error handling will also be added to this foundation. These principles can be equally applied to application components that are built on top of the business logic foundation. The use of proven design patterns, the automation of service components, and the use of metadata to drive business processing are all examples of a robust application design.

The next few chapters look at the composition of each layer of the architecture in detail, apply these principles to the elements of business applications implemented using the architecture, and examine the ramifications of the design decisions on the overall application.

CHAPTER 2

The Business Object Architecture: Design Considerations

The Business Object Architecture is the cornerstone of business application development. The majority of the business logic of a given application is found in this layer. Business object components are the building blocks around which business transactions and processes are built. The other portion of the architecture that makes up the model of the MVC architecture pattern is the Service-Based Architecture. The service-based components typically only provide a transactional or process wrapper around these components. The bulk of the work is still done here within the business object components. This chapter discusses the common elements of business objects and design considerations for their implementation in a J2EE environment. Business objects make up the first layer of the reference architecture that will be discussed and implemented. The central debate within this chapter revolves around two things: options for object persistence to a database and the criteria for using Entity Beans to implement business objects. These design considerations are crucial to the next two chapters, in which the Business Object Architecture is implemented.

One of the core aspects of online transactional applications is managing the persistent state of the business entities. It is the responsibility of the business objects to do this. Typically, business object data is persistent in a database. The responsibility of object persistence can be delegated either to the EJB container or to a separate layer of data-access objects, depending on the business object implementation. Access to read-only data does not necessarily need to go through the business objects (see debate continued below), but all update operations must go through the business objects in order to ensure data integrity, because that is where the business rules and validations exist for a particular object.

Now, the topic of accessing the database outside of the business object model could easily start a lengthy debate between object-oriented purists and those who value every CPU cycle in terms of performance. The opinion of this author is that it is quite all right to do so when the database access is for a read-only operation. If any updates are being made, it is imperative that the business object model be used because this is where the business rules and validations that maintain data integrity exist. As it turns out, a common approach is that of the factory, which ends up being somewhat of a hybrid of the two. It uses the concept of value objects that act primarily as a data structure. The data-access layer then provides a result set as a collection of the value objects. Depending on the implementation of business objects in the architecture, this can be more efficient than always using the business objects themselves. Of course, the most efficient approach is iterating through a JDBC result set, a table of rows read directly from the database. When using this approach, the concept of smart instantiation can be a helpful one if the read-only operation can lead to an update operation. In this case, a database query is executed, and the result set is iterated without using the business object model. However, when it is time for an update operation to occur, a business object is instantiated from the particular row in the result set.

Figure 2.1 shows the high-level components within the Business Object Architecture and how they fit into the overall architecture. Keep in mind that in some implementations, the data objects are not required because the EJB container implements them.

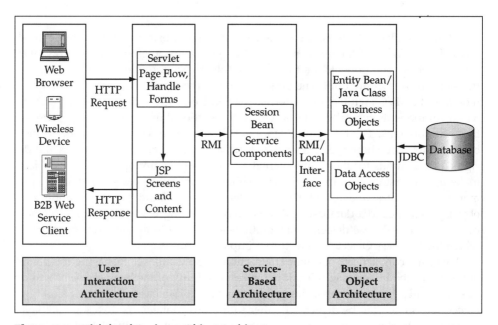

Figure 2.1   High-level Business Object Architecture.

Business Objects in a Banking Application

This book uses a banking application as an example to illustrate the elements and best practices of J2EE applications. In order to determine the business objects within this domain, it is important to first define a *business object*. A business object itself models a business entity. A business entity is loosely defined as something that the business deals with and that has a set of corresponding data and behaviors. Thus, in the banking application, a business object could represent things such as a customer, a bank account, or even an individual transaction on the bank account such as a withdrawal. For the bank application in this book, the business object model consists of four primary entities:

- Customer
- Address
- Account
- Transaction

The overall business object model is shown in the class diagram in Figure 2.2.

In this object model, the Customer has a single Address that is used for correspondence with the bank. The model may have many Accounts, each of which has a defined type such as a checking or savings account. A Transaction object is created

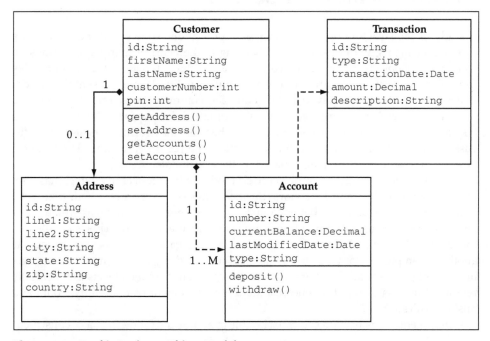

Figure 2.2 Bank's Business Object Model.

each time a deposit, withdrawal, or other transaction affects a particular account. Such transactions might also include things such as a bank fee or accumulated interest. Consequently, instances of `Transaction` are usually created by the `Account` object. This relationship was not noted as a pure aggregation relationship in the object model, however, to show the possibilities for modeling the transaction at a higher level. An aggregated object is owned by another object and shares a similar lifecycle. The bank application could be designed such that when a customer transfers funds from one account to another, it is a single business transaction that affects two different accounts. In this approach, it would not make sense to have the `Account` aggregate the `Transaction` because you would have to choose which of the two accounts is the "owner." In the sample application, however, each account object logs a transaction for this event, so it primarily behaves like an aggregated object in the examples.

> **NOTE** This banking example refers to these objects throughout the study of the Business Object Architecture. Throughout the remainder of the book, you will build services and Web pages on top of these business objects in order to construct a transactional Web site for the bank. This J2EE Web application allows customers to access their accounts, transfer funds, change their addresses, and perform a number of other functions. You also build Web pages to allow administrators of the Web site to perform some basic tasks such as recording transaction adjustments.

Elements of Business Objects

A study of the structure of overall business applications shows that there are many common elements, with business objects being at the heart of many applications. In fact, business objects in general drive many of the characteristics of applications because they are at the foundation of business functionality. They represent the entities that a business deals with day in and day out. The common characteristics of business objects are derived from the concepts of object-oriented development. It is important to take a brief look again at these characteristics because they form the basis of the discussion of how to implement business objects in the J2EE architecture. The business object component structure will be based on these elements.

As defined earlier, a business object itself models a business entity, which has a set of corresponding data and behaviors. Business objects can represent both high-level entities, such as the account that encompasses large amounts of data, as well as low-level entities, such as individual transactions against that account. This is enabled by the fact that business objects can encompass, or aggregate, other business objects. As another example, a `Contract` business object could aggregate many `LineItem` business objects. At each level of the hierarchy, you can view the objects as potentially reusable business objects that encapsulate the management of that entity's data and business rules.

Consequently, business objects must be able to handle the following basic constructs:

- Behaviors, or business methods
- Properties

- Business rules and data validations
- Relationships with other business objects (aggregation, association, and specialization)

Properties

Every business object has data that it must manage. In the case of a `Customer` business object, these properties include the customer's first name and last name. To manage the state of these properties, business objects have methods to set and get the value of each property. Thus, the `Customer` object has a `setFirstName` method and a `getFirstName` method. The state of a business object is made up of the values of all of its properties.

The state of a business object often persists in a relational database. The business object needs to be able somehow to map its data to the schema of the relational database being used. Each property usually maps to a database column in a given table. The simple approach to take (dare I say, keep it simple . . .) is to have the entire set of properties map to the same database table. There are, however, many more complex options to object-relational mapping that can be used as well. These options include mapping a single class to multiple tables as well as mapping inheritance hierarchies to the same table. Object-relational mapping and other persistence design considerations are discussed in detail later in this chapter.

Business Methods

Most business objects have a set of operations, or methods, that implement functionality related to the object. Business methods often change the state of the business object and invoke functionality on other business objects. These changes of state and method invocations on other objects typically become part of a unit-of-work and thus should be included as a part of an overall transaction declared by the application.

Business methods contain the business logic that is associated with the given business entity. For the `Account` object, the methods include operations such as `withdraw` and `deposit`. Other methods may not be exposed to the client and may be used only internally, for example, a `validate` method that gets called when the object's data is about to be set to persist in a database.

Business Rules and Validation Logic

Business objects must enforce the data integrity of the entity they represent. All update operations must go through the business objects for this reason. This includes many levels of validation. The property values must all be validated. For example, the state field in an `Address` component must be a valid state in the United States. This is referred to as field-level validation. Other types of validation occur at the level of the entire business object, going across the different properties of the object. Validations also often go across aggregated objects of a given business component; this type is discussed next.

Relationships with Other Business Objects

Many business objects relate to other business objects in a number of ways. There are three primary categories of relationships: aggregation, association, and specialization.

Aggregation

A business object can contain, or aggregate, another business object. From the earlier discussion of the bank object, the `Customer` component contains an `Address` component. The `Account` component contains zero to many `Transaction` objects. Aggregation can be either a one-to-one (1:1) or a one-to-many (1:M) relationship. In object terms, the aggregated object is stored as a member variable or, in the case of a one-to-many, as a collection of instances. A business object client usually can access data or methods of the aggregated component through the parent, or containing, component. In this example, the `Customer` component may have a `changeAddress` method rather than the client having to get hold of the `Address` object and call an individual method on it in order to change the address. In many cases, the design calls for encapsulation of this type of functionality. You may not want the business object client to be required to have knowledge of the `Customer` underlying object model. Consequently, you may not want to expose the `Address` component to the client, so you'll need to provide a wrapper function on the primary entity. This type of decision is often determined by whether the business entity being encapsulated is meaningful when it stands on its own or whether it really makes sense only as a part of the parent business object.

Aggregated business objects typically share a common lifecycle. For instance, when an object that aggregates other objects is deleted, the aggregated object may also be removed in the same manner. In this example, if an instance of the `Customer` component was deleted from the database, you would also want to delete the aggregated `Address` instance. Otherwise, you would leave an `Address` instance in the database that belongs to a nonexistent customer leading to data integrity problems.

BEST PRACTICE The delete operation of a business object should also encapsulate the deletion of any aggregated objects in order to ensure data integrity.

NOTE Many business applications do not physically delete records from the database in order to keep a history of transactions and entities. Instead, they "inactivate" records through an end date or some other indicator on the record. The same concept applies for this kind of a delete operation. If you inactivate the parent business object, you also want to inactivate the child object that was aggregated.

Likewise, some aggregated objects may not be created until the parent is created. This object creation may happen either immediately after the parent has been created or at some point in the future based on a particular behavior. Aggregated objects that share the same lifecycle boundaries as their parent are often referred to as dependent objects. In the customer example, the corresponding `Address` object should be created at the same time as the customer if the business requirement dictates that all customers must have an address on file. In this case, the customer create operation should also create the address object for that customer.

> **BEST PRACTICE** The create operation of a business object should also encapsulate the creation of any required aggregated objects such as a `Customer` and the corresponding `Address`. Other aggregated objects are created later in the parent lifecycle by corresponding business methods, such as the aggregated `Transaction` object that is created by the `deposit` method on an `Account` object.

Association

Business objects often refer to other business objects that are not aggregated components. They may invoke business methods on other objects or create instances of other business objects that have a different object lifecycle. In these cases, the objects are said to be associated. An example of an association relationship might be between the `Account` and an `InterestRate` object that models a rate of return for a bank account. The account uses the interest rate object to calculate monthly interest; however, there is no aggregation relationship between the two objects.

Specialization

Business objects may specialize or, in object terms, inherit from other business objects. Specialized business objects share the data and behaviors of the inherited business object, although they may override these behaviors and add additional behaviors and properties. One example of this might be the `Account` object. There are different types of accounts, such as a checking account and a savings account. Instead of making the account type a property of `Account`, it could be modeled as the specialized business objects `CheckingAccount` and `SavingsAccount`. These subclasses, or specialized classes, could add additional properties that are specific to the account type as well as additional behaviors that do not exist for a normal account. In other cases, the `Account` may have defined methods that are overridden by the specific account classes because they implement them differently.

Design Considerations

Because the Business Object Architecture is such an integral part of the application architecture, it must be modeled carefully. There are a number of issues to look at in creating the implementation model for business objects. First, look at the issue of business objects maintaining their own state. In most object-oriented viewpoints, it is a given that business objects are stateful, that is, they maintain their instance data across multiple method invocations. However, the concept is worth briefly discussing in order to look at the ramifications of this on the EJB container. Then, look at how to implement your business objects in the J2EE environment. The primary options are as follows:

- Regular Java classes
- Entity Beans
- Stateful Session Beans

NOTE This book will refer to the use of regular Java classes to implement business objects as Java business objects as a shorthand notation throughout the remainder of the chapters. This is not a new concept, but rather simply refers to concrete Java classes that store their state as member variables and contain the business logic related to a particular business entity. These classes are not EJB components and cannot use standard enterprise bean services in and of themselves. However, they can still realize some of the benefits, such as partaking in container-managed transactions, if wrapped by an EJB component.

Stateful versus Stateless Business Objects

Two different approaches to business application development have been used in the past, each with a unique set of advantages and disadvantages.

Stateful.   The object maintains its instance data across business logic method invocations.

Stateless.   The object requires that the instance data be passed in as an argument to business logic methods. No state is maintained within the object itself.

The more object-oriented approach of the two is the concept of stateful business objects that encapsulate both the application data and its particular business logic. All of the object's properties are stored as members of the object, and a given instance of the object represents a particular instance of a business entity. This is the general approach taken with Entity EJB. In fact, any time the state of the business object is changed, it persists in the database as part of an overall transaction. This allows a purer view of the object-oriented world, in which application service components and business methods can modify the state of business objects without being concerned about the persistence of that state. It is automatically taken care of by the Business Object Architecture.

A ramification of the stateful approach is that only one client can use an instance of the business object at a particular time. You cannot multithread operations of a stateful business object, because the member variables can hold the data for only one instance at a time. Partially for this reason, Entity Beans are pooled in an application server and given out to clients as they are requested. However, for each client, the application server must load the state of the object into its member variables before it is safe for the client to use it. Another part of the reason an EJB container pools instances is because Entity Beans are fairly heavyweight components that have a high cost of instantiation.

A straight Java object implementation of stateful business objects would not necessarily need to pool instances because of a lower cost of instantiation, and thus they might not need to be shared among clients. Nonetheless, a straight Java business object approach requires the instantiation of different instances for each client because the multi-threaded limitation still holds true.

This leads to one of the primary advantages of the stateless approach. In general, stateless services usually compare quite favorably to stateful services in terms of scalability and performance. You will see in the discussion of the Service-Based Architecture that stateless services are favored over stateful services partially for this reason. A stateless business object does not need multiple instances to handle multiple clients because it does not store the state of a business object in its member variables. This allows stateless business objects to be multithreaded and saves time on object instantiation and garbage collection, one of the keys to increasing the performance of Java applications.

A stateless business object has the state of a given instance passed into the business methods, usually with a value object that acts as a data structure for the object. It is easy to see why stateful business objects represent the true object-oriented view of the world. Stateless business objects are really like process-oriented objects that deal with a particular entity and the business methods related to it. Business methods of a state-less business object take in the data object, or value object, manipulate the properties on the value object, and perform the business logic. They can then have the data persist in the database typically by passing the modified value object to a data-access object. Some developers find this model works quite well, although it does violate object-oriented theory a bit in terms of encapsulating the data and behaviors of an object in order to accomplish the goal. This technique can be used when performance considerations are taken to the extreme in order to avoid extra object instantiations. However, it is not used as a regular practice.

Object Lifecycle

The fact that an instance of a stateful business object can be used by only one client at a time drives the concept of object lifecycle. An instance of an object is instantiated at some point, initially not containing the state of any given business entity instance. To be used by a client, the object is first given the state of a particular business object instance. These first two steps may or may not happen at the same time. After being used by a client, the business object will at some point either be marked for garbage collection or put back into an object pool to be reused by another client who repeats the process of setting the state and invoking business methods. The Enterprise JavaBeans model handles this lifecycle for you. It manages the creation and instantiation of objects, the pooling of component instances, and the pooling process of handing them out to business object clients with the state of the requested object. This functionality is handled through the EJB Home interface, which also provides APIs to create and remove instances of particular business objects.

Choosing between the Two

So which approach is better? Stateful business objects are widely used in the industry. In fact, the folks who wrote the Enterprise JavaBeans specification felt that stateful

Table 2.1 Stateful versus Stateful Business Objects

STATEFUL	STATELESS
Pure object-oriented view; Enables encapsulation of data and behaviors	Business objects are more process-oriented; no encapsulation of data and behaviors
Higher performance cost	Multithreaded efficient implementation; increased performance
Requires object lifecycle management	Simplified object lifecycle

business objects made sense in the case of Entity Beans. They are inherently stateful, and this fact allows the container to easily provide the service of Container-Managed Persistence. It maps the member variables to columns in a database through the deployment step. The fact that stateful business objects require object lifecycle management was also handled by the Enterprise JavaBeans specification. The EJB container manages the lifecycle of a component, and the client interaction with this lifecycle is handled through the EJB Home interface.

Table 2.1 describes the pros and cons of both business object approaches.

Either approach can and has been used with great success. However, the use of stateful business objects is much more prevalent in the industry due to its adherence to object-oriented theory, primarily the encapsulation of both the data and the behaviors of an entity within an object. These issues are very closely tied in to the implementation model that is used for business objects, which is the next design consideration.

NOTE Stateful business objects are the approach used throughout the remainder of this book. They adhere to the object-oriented theory of encapsulation and are a predominantly used approach. The Entity Bean model fully supports this paradigm, and it can also be easily implemented using regular Java classes.

Implementation Model: Entity Bean, Session Bean, or Java Object

The J2EE architecture provides a number of options for implementing business objects. As in standard Java development, you can always build your business objects as regular Java objects, but in the J2EE architecture, there are also two types of enterprise beans that can be used. The advantage of using an EJB is that a number of additional component services are provided, as well as a standard deployment model if the business object is to be reused across applications or organizations.

Entity Beans are components designed to represent shared instances of persistent data entities within an application. An instance of an Entity Bean typically represents a row in a database, but it is not necessarily limited to this definition. Session Beans are modeled more like process-oriented objects, particularly stateless Session Beans, although stateful Session Beans are a possibility for business object implementation.

Because Session Beans, similar to Entity Beans, provide many component services, they are fairly heavyweight objects and usually have a high instantiation cost within the container. A stateful Session Bean must be instantiated for each client that requires the use of the business object, as opposed to Entity Bean instances, which can be pooled by the container and handed out for the use of each client. For this reason, Entity Beans are around a third faster on some application servers than their stateful Session Bean counterparts when used as stateful business objects. Consequently, this book will consider only Entity Beans and Java objects as the primary alternatives from this point.

Two primary concepts of the business component implementation decision are the persistence model and the transaction model. Take a detailed look at each for the different options.

Object Persistence

Business objects implemented as regular Java classes do not have any built-in framework to manage object persistence. An application framework that automates much of the JDBC processing and ties in to the business object model can make this less of an issue. While the construction of basic JDBC frameworks can be done fairly quickly, the creation of highly optimized JDBC frameworks is not a trivial task. Persistence frameworks that can be used by either BMP Entity Beans or Java business objects are discussed later in this chapter.

Entity Bean Persistence

One of the primary component services provided with Entity Beans is Container-Managed Persistence (CMP). In this option, the container uses a deployment configuration to map a set of beans to their respective database tables in order to automatically manage the selects, inserts, updates, and deletes to the database. The EJB 2.0 persistence model, unlike EJB 1.1, uses an abstract persistence schema.

> **NOTE** The abstract persistence schema used by EJB 2.0 refers to the fact that a bean developer implements only abstract getter and setter methods for both CMP and CMR (container-managed relationships) fields. The container, upon deployment, generates a subclass that implements these abstract methods for all of the properties of the bean. This is vastly different from the EJB 1.1 model, which required public member variables. The EJB 2.0 model allows the container to optimize much of the database access because it has greater control over when to load data and more information about what data was modified. These control points are provided through the implementation of the abstract getter and setter methods. For example, the container can choose either to aggressively load a collection of beans or to wait until a getter method is invoked to load the state of an individual bean. It can also update only those properties of the bean that were modified in a given transaction because it can take note of this during the setter methods.

EJB 2.0 CMP Entity Beans provide the following persistence services:

■ Persistence of each Entity Bean's properties to a single database table (CMP fields).

■ Container-managed relationships between related Entity Beans (CMR fields).

■ Database queries to return individual components or collections of them. This is done both through the use of finder methods on the EJB Home interfaces as well as `ejbSelect` methods within an Entity Bean class.

It is important to note that the EJB specification provides explicit support only for a one-to-one bean to table mapping. It does not specify a standard mechanism for mapping properties of a single Entity Bean to multiple database tables. In terms of more complicated object-relational mapping with Entity Beans, J2EE container vendors and object-relational mapping tools vendors compete to provide more flexible persistence engines built into the Entity Bean component mechanism as a value-added service within their products.

Entity Beans can also manage their own persistence using the Bean-Managed Persistence (BMP) option. In this option, the developer uses the EJB hook methods (`ejbStore`, `ejbLoad`, `ejbCreate`, `ejbRemove`) as placeholders to implement persistence on its own. The object lifecycle is still managed by the container because these hooks are called as determined by the container at various points within a transaction.

Because Entity Beans are fairly heavyweight components, you might not want to use a large number of them in a given transaction. The EJB 2.0 specification attempts to address this by providing local interfaces to access related components in the same JVM (Java Virtual Machine) without the overhead of RMI. For the purposes of this discussion, you will see that local interfaces do provide a slightly more efficient way to use colocated Entity Beans as helper classes that can be used solely for the persistence of data aggregated within a more complex business object.

NOTE An EJB 2.0 component can have a local interface, a remote interface, or both. Because the interface to an Entity Bean can now be either local or remote, these are referred to as *component interfaces* in the specification. Thus, this term is used when no distinction is required between the two.

In EJB 1.1, every component was assumed to be location independent. This means that the component could be colocated in the same JVM or it could reside on a remote server. Thus, every remote call to the Entity Bean was required to go through RMI, which adds a layer of overhead. All method invocations were pass-by-value requiring the arguments to be copied, serialized, and sent through the RMI protocol. Well, in order to efficiently model the concept discussed earlier of aggregated business objects, you would naturally want to colocate them in the same container instance so that the method calls between the two aggregated business objects did not actually have to go over a network. However, the method invocations were still required to go through RMI because of the location independence feature. Local interfaces in EJB 2.0

provide a mechanism through which a component can invoke another EJB that does not go through RMI through its local interface. This is essentially equivalent to a normal method call. However there is still an interface class implementation (the `component` interface), generated by the container, that intercepts and proxies the method invocation. The local component must be resident in the same JVM, and the arguments are now passed by reference. This changes the programming paradigm a bit because developers must be aware that objects passed as arguments to EJB through the local interface can be modified. However, you can now avoid the RMI overhead on these method calls, allowing yourself to build more fine-grained components such as aggregated or dependent objects. Thus, local interfaces should be used wherever possible.

Comparing Container-Managed and Bean-Managed Persistence

Following is a comparison between the CMP and BMP approaches. Using CMP actually has a number of distinct advantages over the BMP approach. The first one is simple; it is one less component service that you are responsible for developing. If you consider things such as database optimizations, object relationships, and concurrency issues, this is a major benefit to application developers. The second reason is that the EJB 2.0 specification's abstract persistence schema has provided containers with the ability to optimize much of the bean's database access. Although the two options might be relatively equal with regards to individual database calls, a CMP Entity Bean usually outperforms a BMP Entity Bean within a transactional application context. An individual database interaction with either a CMP or BMP Entity Bean, or a regular Java class for that matter, exhibits similar characteristics on its own because all of the options execute generally the same JDBC operations. The only noteworthy difference to this may come with containers that use native calls underneath the hood rather than JDBC calls. For the most part, however, this has not taken place in the application server market as products strive to be 100% Java. It is, in fact, the behavior of the component implementation model within a transactional application where you see the differences emerge. For example, consider a finder method invoked on a BMP Entity Bean's Home interface. The finder method itself causes a database lookup to get the primary key. Once a business method is invoked on the component interface, the container calls the `ejbLoad` method to load the state of the instance from the database prior to the bean's business method being executed. Thus, the simple operation of locating an instance of a business object required two database interactions as opposed to one. It should be noted that CMP Entity Beans have the potential to exhibit the same behavior if run in a container that does not optimize database access. However, newer versions of EJB containers are providing much more robust persistence engines, and the amount of optimization being done has greatly increased. EJB containers are now also providing much more control over these types of operations in the deployment configuration so that the application deployer can tune the behavior of Entity Beans. This can make a significant difference in terms of performance, particularly when defined data-access patterns exist.

For all of these reasons, there are few compelling reasons to use BMP Entity Beans as a persistence approach. You get the additional overhead of Entity Beans without deriving many of the benefits. CMP Entity Beans can provide better performance if deployed correctly. As you will see, however, the transaction model and general component overhead can also greatly affect the overall performance of your applications. In particular, the Entity Bean model has the potential to increase the amount of database interaction and disk I/O under a heavy user load, which of course decreases the overall performance and then becomes a factor in the overall decision. One situation in which this can happen is when there are enough concurrent transactions with EJB clients that the entire pool of Entity Bean instances is being used at once. In these cases, the container is often forced to activate and passivate bean instances in order to balance the load and meet the throughput demands being placed on it. Each of these operations adds additional I/O, which can slow down the application. This topic is discussed in detail in the chapter on performance.

Another such example of the component implementation model increasing the number of database interactions is that of finder methods in Entity Beans. A finder method declared on a Home interface can return a collection of Entity Bean component interfaces if the associated database query can return more than one instance. The client can then iterate through the collection of component interfaces invoking methods on each one. Similar to the BMP/CMP comparison scenario, if you say the number of objects found with the query is n, then the number of database interactions used by the Entity Bean model to call the finder and iterate through the collection can actually be $(n + 1)$. If the container is using a lazy-loading approach, this is the number of actual database calls that would be made, which would be horribly inefficient. This results from the following steps that take place:

1. The finder method is called to run the initial query. This returns a list of primary keys to the container that translates into component interfaces.

2. As the collection returned from the finder method is iterated, each method invocation on the Entity Beans can result in another database query (`ejbLoad`) if the state of the instance has not already been loaded into the Entity Bean component. This occurs if either BMP or a lazy-loading CMP implementation is used.

In many early application server implementations, this inefficient behavior was the result. Some application servers now allow some control over this behavior by giving the container a hint to use an aggressive-loading approach. This would populate the Entity Beans on the initial finder method query. This provides a much more efficient database interaction, one that you would expect from a high-performance transactional application. However, this approach is also not without its potential problems. Because Entity Beans are fairly heavyweight components, you can have a large number of instances that are used for a particular query. If more than a few users are hitting this particular data retrieval operation at the same time, you could quickly reach the limit on the pool size for your particular Entity Bean. Once this happens, a pending client request could cause some of the beans that were just retrieved to passivate. This causes another level of overhead to be applied to the application when the client iterates through the list, although managing a pool of shared component instances is one of the EJB container's specialties, so this may be less of an issue.

BEST PRACTICE Do not use Entity Bean finder methods to iterate through a result set of business objects unless you can enforce either a read-only caching strategy or an aggressive-loading approach by the container. For a result set of *n* objects using lazy loading, this can actually cause (n + 1) database interactions. Use a JDBC wrapper component to run the database query and either hold the result set for iteration or return a set of value objects. This limits the operation to one database interaction.

For read-only operations, the client can also easily iterate through the data using a JDBC wrapper component. If transactional update operations are required, a business object can be instantiated from a given row in the result set. This JDBC wrapper can become a generic, smart-instantiation list service that is a part of the Business Logic Foundation. This concept is discussed in full in the next section on building the Business Object Architecture.

Object-Relational Mapping

There are many different approaches to object-relational mapping, which defines how an object's properties map to database tables and columns. As discussed earlier, CMP Entity Beans are limited to persistence to one table. Any object-relational mapping scheme more complicated than a one-to-one table-object mapping is not currently supported specifically by the EJB specification. To implement a more complex approach, you are required to use either Bean-Managed Persistence, vendor-specific persistence mechanisms, or your own Java business objects and JDBC. You have already seen that there are potential performance issues with BMP Entity Beans, so this is not an ideal approach. The one nice thing about using vendor-specific mechanisms here is that it largely does not affect the portability of your code. The mapping between object properties and database columns is done in the deployment step and container-managed relationships abstract the database specifics of foreign key relationships. Thus, your bean's code can operate without specific knowledge of the persistence strategy or database schema. There are a number of object-relational mapping tools that integrate both into EJB and Java components to cause persistence of the business object data in a database. All of these tools, of course, add some overhead to the processing but provide additional flexibility in terms of abstracting the object model from the data model.

It is sometimes best to start with the simple approach and see if that works to some degree of satisfaction. The one-to-one table-object mapping is straightforward and provides a decent level of performance compared to some of the more complicated schemes available. The trade-off comes in terms of the object-oriented design. Assume that for data architecture reasons, the data for a Customer component is actually stored in four different database tables. Conceptually speaking, a customer is a single business entity, and thus you would like to represent it with a single business object. With the one-to-one table mapping, this presents a bit of a problem.

Short of using an object-relational mapping tool, there are some things that you can do to alleviate this type of problem. The primary tool is that of encapsulation. If you use a lightweight business object implementation, you can define "business objects" for each table, although some will be used only for database purposes. These could be called "helper" objects because they really are used only for persistence. The business logic, in this case, is contained within the "super" business objects that aggregate the helper objects. In the banking example, you create a Customer business object and three helper classes, which although technically are business objects in this particular implementation, will be used only by the primary Customer object for the persistence of the additional data to those tables. All of the actual business logic associated with the customer entity resides in the primary Customer object. From the perspective of a business object client, it looks as if there is a single business object that deals with the customer, and that is all it needs to know about. The rest of the database logic is encapsulated within the Customer component. This approach is particularly appealing if you already have code-generation capabilities for business objects based on the data model. You can then generate all of the business objects to deal with persistence and then code business logic in your primary entities.

This approach does have the disadvantage of moving the knowledge of your data model into the business object layer. However, this is the trade-off for simplicity and, in many cases, performance. It might not bring a smile to the face of an object purist, but it is a very commonly used approach. The other model to use is encapsulating this knowledge in the data-access layer. Thus, you would have only one Customer business object and a single data-access object whose data is persistent. Once inside the data access object, the data fields are moved to the appropriate database tables. This removes any knowledge of the data model from the business object, although it is difficult to generate this type of data object through standard code generation. In order to go to this level, you would either need to hand-code these data objects or use an object-relational mapping tool.

Transaction Model

The transaction model used by the different implementations is important to understand. If not used correctly, it can greatly affect the overall performance of the components in an application.

NOTE This section uses the term *transaction model* to cover not only the transaction management service itself (that is, begin transaction, commit/rollback), but also how the component behaves throughout the life of a transaction (that is, how and when it is read from the database, stored back to the database, and so on).

Entity Bean Transaction Model

First, take a look at the model used by Entity Beans. Bean developers can either manage the transaction demarcation themselves using bean-managed transactions, or they can use the container's transaction management service. This second option, called container-managed transactions, relies on the transactional nature of Entity Bean methods to be declared in the deployment process. There are a couple different transaction settings for a method, REQUIRES, REQUIRES_NEW, and SUPPORTS being the primary ones. If a method is declared to require a transaction, the container automatically starts one if the method call is not already part of an overall transaction. Any container-managed operations or Bean-Managed Persistence code sharing the same JDBC data source can participate in the database transaction. The transaction is committed after the highest level method that started the transaction completes, unless any one of the components participating in the transaction invokes the `EJBContext.setRollbackOnly()` method.

Once in a transaction, a client usually makes a request to obtain a particular instance of an object. An Entity Bean client uses a finder method to locate an instance by the primary key or some other defined finder method on the Home interface. This requires a database lookup unless the container has previously cached the primary keys in memory. The container then grabs a free instance of the component from the pool and loads the state from the database through an invocation of the `ejbLoad` method. This must be done before any component-method invocations are processed by the container. Although instances of Entity Beans can be cached by the container, it is important to note that the container must still load the state at the beginning of every transaction in a clustered environment. Why? Because although the container knows that the state has not changed in this application server instance, it may have changed on any of the other server instances in the cluster. Thus, to be safe, it always loads the state from the database before a client can use the object. Thus, there is very little benefit to be gained from caching with regards to Entity Beans. In addition to this, each remote method invocation must go through RMI and serialize all of the arguments in order to make the method call. Thus, it is recommended that in most cases, Entity Beans be exposed through their local interface and fronted with a Session Bean component. This concept is discussed in detail in the Service-Based Architecture chapter. If the Entity Beans do, in fact, require remote access, they should be designed to be coarse-grained so that it is not necessary to make a large number of remote method calls to the component.

With regards to the timing of the persistence methods, it is partly up to the discretion of the container when the `ejbLoad` and `ejbStore` methods are invoked, as long as transactional integrity is maintained. However, the normal case and minimum requirement is to invoke `ejbLoad` at the beginning of every transaction and `ejbStore` at the end of every committed transaction, although these methods have the potential to be invoked more frequently. Once an Entity Bean is loaded for a client in a transaction, the state of the object may be modified, and it is basically used as a cache until that transaction completes. No other client can use that particular instance unless the state is passivated so that it can be restored to complete the transaction. This can happen under periods of heavy transaction volume if all of the beans in a given EJB pool are being used. When an Entity Bean is passivated, the state of the bean is temporarily saved either to disk or to the database in order to ensure transactional integrity and failover. This is something to look out for when sizing the Entity Bean pools in the container, because the additional I/O can start to really affect the overall application performance under heavy user loads.

As EJB container implementations mature, developers are starting to see more optimized database reads and writes within the CMP engine implementations. This includes optimizing the `ejbStore` logic so that only modified fields are updated to the database, or else no update at all takes place in the case where no properties have been modified. Many vendors also offer some level of control over the read and write strategies the container uses regarding its `ejbLoad` and `ejbStore` behavior. These

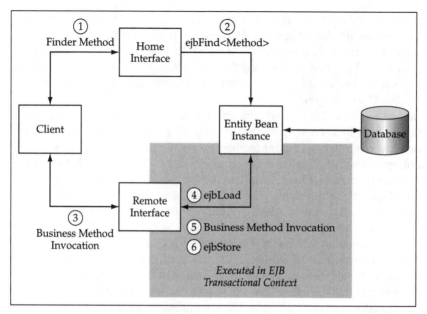

Figure 2.3 Entity Bean Transaction Model: Example of Single Client, Single Transactional Method.

strategies can be adjusted for particular access patterns such as read-only, read-mostly, and updatable entities. However, the majority of business objects in transactional applications fall into the last category, and thus exhibit the same behavior previously described, in which at least one call to `ejbLoad` and `ejbStore` is required at the beginning and end of every transaction. This minimum pattern of database access is, of course, what you would expect from a transactional application and is the same for objects implemented as regular Java classes.

Figure 2.3 illustrates the behavior of this Entity Bean transaction model for a single client invoking a transactional business method. This diagram represents a simple case. Remember that the Entity Bean could also be a part of a larger transaction already started by a Session Bean or another Entity Bean.

In its optimized form, the Entity Bean transaction model is comparable to the Java business object equivalent in which state is loaded at the beginning of the transaction (`ejbLoad`) and saved at the end (`ejbStore`). In nonoptimized or extreme conditions in a clustered environment, Entity Beans can be very database and disk intensive because of the need to manage the free pool and activate and passivate instances in a transactional manner. Other points to consider are that Entity Beans are still fairly heavyweight components and that local interfaces should be used wherever possible to avoid RMI overhead.

If you can model your Entity Beans as coarse-grained components, these issues become less of a consideration, but this has been very difficult to do in practice, especially because Entity Beans using Container-Managed Persistence have a one-to-one object-relational mapping limitation. Most business object interaction also requires multiple method calls. Using only one method invocation takes away many of the advantages of having a stateful business object. EJB 2.0 has addressed many of these issues with local interfaces, although you still must rely on vendor-specific services or third-party object-relational mapping tools to fully address the persistence issues. The next sections compare the Entity Bean transaction model against that of regular Java business objects.

Java Business Object Transaction Model

The transaction model using regular Java classes as business objects depends on the particular implementation. It does not include declarative transactions on the business object itself, although they can participate in existing EJB transactions, particularly those started by a Session Bean. In general, the Java business object approach uses a similar approach to dealing with business objects within transactions with two noticeable differences:

- Instances of Java business objects are not usually pooled; typically, Java objects are instantiated for a particular client from the database to represent an instance of the business entity. Thus, the trade-off is cost of object instantiation versus cost of activation/passivation under heavy user loads.

- Java business objects require participation in a Session Bean transaction, whether it is a container-managed transaction or a bean-managed transaction. In either case, it is recommended to wrap business objects with a Session Bean layer, so there is not much of a trade-off on this point.

Business object persistence within a transaction follows the same pattern under normal circumstances in either option. A business object is either instantiated or grabbed from the pool, and the state of that particular instance is loaded from the database. Methods are invoked on the business objects, and the state is modified. This can happen for a number of business objects in memory at a time within a transaction. Either at different points along the way or when all of the work is completed, each business object can save its data to the database. As long as the data-access objects or Entity Beans being used share the same data source provided by the application server, the business objects can participate in the same overall transaction. This works for either a container-managed transaction declared by a Session Bean or for a user-managed transaction that is executed specifically in the code. The pattern of using Session Beans to declare transactions and wrap the business objects in a service is explored in detail in the chapter on Service-Based Architecture.

One nice benefit provided by the Entity Bean model is that it has a built-in mechanism to handle transaction concurrency. There are different transaction isolation settings that can be used to prevent multiple users from updating the same instance of the same business object at the same time. The strictest setting for Entity Beans, TRANSACTION_SERIALIZABLE, allows only one client at a time to execute a method on a given instance as defined uniquely by the Entity Bean's primary key. Note that, however, this is also the most expensive setting and that a looser setting is more commonly used for better performance. A Java business object implementation is required to implement its own mechanism for transaction concurrency, commonly known as locking. This topic is discussed in detail in the next design consideration about handling transaction concurrency.

Overall Comparison of Entity Beans versus Java Business Objects

So what is the best implementation model to use for business objects? Well, this depends on your particular situation. You have seen that the performance of the Entity Bean model is greatly improved in EJB 2.0, although it still presents potential issues with regard to its behavior under heavy user loads. It is a more heavyweight implementation model when compared to the Java equivalent, although the container pools the Entity Bean instances. Again, the issue is how the container is managing the free pool given the nature of the application and the access patterns it is using. As in most cases, it is best to do a proof-of-concept in the early stages of developing your architecture by performing some basic load tests. This gives you some general benchmarks to consider with regards to meeting your performance requirements. This process is discussed in detail in the Performance chapter. With regard to the straight Java option, keep in mind that there are a number of infrastructure services, such as persistence and transaction concurrency, that you must either build on your own or for which you must use third-party frameworks. Transaction management itself is not really an issue because Java business objects can participate in a transaction declared by a Session Bean service component, but an optimized JDBC framework presents a much bigger challenge. There are a number of JDBC persistence frameworks available including Webgain's TopLink, Thought Inc.'s CocoBase, and the open-source Castor project that will be used in some of the examples in chapter 4. If you have these key services provided in a Java foundation layer and there are strict performance requirements for your application, consider the prospect of using Java business objects. However, Entity Beans can also be an effective solution if you do not have the resources to build these other services and you can mitigate the performance risks. How do you do this? Well, with the emergence of the EJB 2.0 specification and more robust CMP engine implementations from the application server vendors, the J2EE community is seeing higher levels of optimization, more controls over the persistence strategy, and an increased ability to effectively model fine-grained components. Mitigating performance risks with Entity Beans used to be an extremely difficult task under the EJB 1.1 specification, although it is now starting to get a bit easier.

Thus, the two keys points to look at when considering Entity Beans and Java business objects are:

1. Application performance requirements.
2. Ability to develop a Business Logic Foundation layer (or have access to an existing one) to provide key component services.

When you look at point number two, you may ask yourself, "Why would I want to develop or use a separate framework when I have the EJB container to provide many of these services for me?" Well, it really comes down to the first item, performance, and the maturity of the Entity Bean implementation you are using. EJB 2.0 goes a long way toward addressing these key points. However, it still does not include the lightweight persistence option that many people are looking for. The EJB specification group initially looked at the idea of dependent objects with a different implementation model, one that was more lightweight, similar to the search for a more lightweight persistence option. However, in the end, the approach was simply too awkward, and the group settled on the local interface approach. The Java Data Objects (JDO) specification is also out there being addressed separately, outside of the J2EE specification for now, and may provide an eventual solution for this problem. However, within the J2EE specification, the EJB 2.0 abstract persistence schema approach has provided vendors with the ability to create highly optimized containers, so the focus now changes to execution. It is your responsibility as a solution provider to put these containers to the test in your own application environments to see if they meet the challenge.

The major new change introduced in EJB 2.0 was the concept of local interfaces, which explicitly allow you to avoid the overhead of RMI for colocated beans.

NOTE For the most part, Entity Beans will likely have either a local interface or a remote interface because of the difference in programming paradigm (pass-by-value versus pass-by-reference) and the nature of remotely distributed components versus dependent, or aggregated, components.

Although the local interface approach is good, many EJB container vendors have already solved part of the problem of inefficient remote method invocations. Many pre-EJB 2.0 containers, either implicitly under the covers or explicitly through deployment steps, can optimize RMI calls when EJBs are located in the same JVM. With EJB 2.0, you have a standardized method of controlling this behavior. One thing to note is that a JNDI (Java Naming and Directing Interface) lookup is still required to locate a local Entity Bean. This adds some overhead, but can be mitigated through caching of the Home interface. This topic is discussed in detail in the Performance chapter.

The whole discussion of local and remote Entity Beans also begs the question Why would I want to expose the business object (in this case, an Entity Bean) remotely anyway? The architecture described in this book includes a Service-Based Architecture layer in front of the business objects that addresses this issue. However, even for architectures without this formal layer, you can always put the Entity Bean behind a stateless Session Bean component in order to distribute the functionality and manage the transaction.

Look to the additional performance gains that are being realized through the fact that J2EE vendors are focused on providing more robust CMP engines to ensure that the Entity Bean implementation model is a success. A well-optimized CMP engine implementation can make a big difference in the overall performance of an application. J2EE application server vendors are providing much more of this in their products, and they are also allowing more control over some of the optimizations through the deployment step. You have already learned one such optimization with regards to using finder methods for returning collections of Entity Beans. Using the lazy-loading approach, you would end up hitting the database once to return the set of primary keys and then again for each object in the collection. An aggressive-loading approach would populate all of the Entity Beans at the time the finder method was invoked, thus saving potentially numerous database calls depending on the size of the collection. Optimized writes, in which only fields that are modified (if any) are updated as part of the transaction, are another improvement.

With the new specification and more robust implementations, Entity Beans become a very viable option for application development. With either option that you choose, you may want to plan for a potential migration path between Java objects and EJB 2.0 Entity Beans once you see how they behave in your particular application environment, particularly with robust implementations of the EJB 2.0 specification.

Migrating from Java Objects to Entity Beans

A positive aspect of using standard Java classes as business objects is that it does not inhibit you from migrating to Entity Beans at some point in the future. This migration is made even easier if you plan the business object APIs to correspond to functions provided by the Entity Bean model. Because you need to address the same common elements of business objects with either approach, an Entity Bean component wrapper could be added later to an existing Java business object implementation. A business object factory abstraction, which is used to create, locate, and delete instances, can make a migration even easier. These topics are addressed in the next chapters on building the Business Object Architecture. The component wrapper idea follows the same pattern as the Service-Based Architecture, which is to implement the service as a Java object and then wrap it with a Session Bean to take advantage of all of the EJB services. This allows for reuse outside of having you go through the EJB layer.

Comparing Entity Bean and Regular Java Business Object Implementation Models

So, after all of this discussion, what is the verdict? Well, as it stands currently, Java business objects may be better for extremely high-performance applications; however, EJB 2.0 has very closely narrowed the gap and provides a large number of services that you would have to implement yourself otherwise. One of the primary services to implement is object persistence. As you will see through the discussion of building the Business Object Architecture, you can develop a fairly simple, but effective, persistence layer without much trouble. However, it will not have all of the optimization features built in to it as some of the EJB containers would. You can add these features to your own persistence layer, but this can be an intense endeavor. There are also a number of other component services that you need to develop that would otherwise be provided by the EJB container. The next two chapters deal with building the business object foundation and its corresponding services. After going through this exercise and seeing what all is required, you will have a better appreciation for how much work is involved if you choose not to use EJB to implement business objects. At the end of this discussion, there is a table that summarizes these component services and how they can be implemented in either model.

A third hybrid option exists, which is to use a combination of the two. When would you want to do this? One possible situation might be if you want to take advantage of the distribution and transaction management features of Entity Beans for a set of related business objects. This usually happens in a business object hierarchy in which a business object aggregates many smaller business objects. For example, a `Contract` business object might aggregate many `LineItem` business objects. It may be too costly to implement each `LineItem` as an Entity Bean, even with local interfaces. However, they may make sense as Java business objects within a `Contract` Entity Bean. In this sense, you can build more coarse-grained components that encapsulate a larger set of functionality. To do this, you would likely use Bean-Managed Persistence and implement the store and load methods yourself to manage the parent-child business objects. You would also want to design the interfaces of the `Contract` business object to take all of the data needed to perform a given operation, rather than model it as a number of smaller method calls.

Table 2.2 compares the two primary models and the hybrid option at a high level, taking a look at the key aspects of business objects in transactional applications.

When to Use an Entity EJB over a Java Object

Because Entity Beans add some level of overhead, you should use them where there is an advantage to do so. As in many design decisions, it is the cost/benefit analysis that provides the answer to the question. Some possible factors or system requirements that would drive an implementation toward Entity Beans include:

- Coarse-grained component design
- Need to distribute the component directly to remote clients, outside of a service-based component wrapper
- Lack of available or planned component framework, including an optimized JDBC layer for object persistence (that is, use of Container-Managed Persistence and other Entity Bean services)
- Managing transaction concurrency using Entity Bean transaction isolation setting (noting the associated performance implications)
- Desire for industry standard component interfaces and deployment for all business objects

The last bullet point is one that has not been discussed yet but is worth mentioning. There is some value to having business objects implemented as Entity Beans because it provides the basis for an industry-standard component interface. For example, all Entity Beans have a Home interface that is used to locate, create, and delete instances of business objects. A Java-based business object approach would need to create its own object lifecycle mechanism analogous to the features of the Home interface, although it would still not use the exact mechanism. So, is the Java-based approach taking away component reusability? To a large extent, no, this is not a limiting factor. Object lifecycle is but one aspect of a business object. The set of business methods is always application specific. Additionally, reuse can be achieved at the object level just as it can at the component level. In many cases, you can reuse services implemented as EJB components that provide remote access to business object functionality with most of the same benefits. Thus, there is not a distinct argument for wanting to switch based on this reason alone, but it does provide some standardization that is worth mentioning.

Table 2.2 Comparison of Entity Bean and Regular Java Business Object Implementation Models

BUSINESS OBJECT ELEMENT	ENTITY BEAN	JAVA OBJECT	HYBRID: ENTITY BEANS AND AGGREGATED JAVA OBJECTS
Persistence	Container-Managed (explicit support for one-to-one object-table mapping, vendor-specific support for more complex object-relational mapping) or Bean-Managed Persistence	Need other JDBC framework	Need to use BMP and other JDBC framework for aggregate
Transactions	Container-managed or user transactions	Can integrate with Session Bean transactions or use user transactions	Java objects can integrate with Entity Bean transaction
Transaction concurrency	Transaction isolation setting can be used to handle concurrency	Need own mechanism in framework or application	Can use transaction isolation setting as long as parent object is always updated
Performance	Heavyweight component structure; has potential to be database and disk intensive in extreme situations, although generally benefits from CMP engine optimizations	Fairly lightweight compared to Entity Beans	Middle ground between the two primary options
Distribution	Inherently uses JNDI and RMI to provide remote access	Need to explicitly use RMI or, more commonly, wrap with a Session Bean service-based component	Same as Entity Bean (JNDI and RMI)

BEST PRACTICE Perform some amount of load testing early on in your projects to determine if Entity Beans provide an acceptable level of performance in your application environment. As a general rule, you may want to consider using Java business objects instead of Entity Beans for extremely high throughput application components. If performance is acceptable, use Entity Beans to take advantage of a standard component model that provides services such as object persistence and transaction concurrency. Also, use Entity Beans if you want to distribute business objects directly to remote clients. When using either implementation model, consider planning for a migration path between the two. Application requirements or transaction volumes may change. Robust EJB 2.0 container implementations will likely provide a much increased boost from earlier versions; however, test in your environment before making a decision to commit to the Entity Bean model.

Remember that even if you decide not to implement your business objects as Entity Beans, you can still take advantage of many of the EJB container-provided services through the use of the service-based components implemented as Session Beans that sit in front of the business objects in the architecture. For example, the Session Bean façade can declare the transaction using container-managed transactions and distribute the functionality with a service wrapper using JNDI and RMI. This is, in fact, a best practice that is discussed in detail in the chapter on Service-Based Architecture.

Handling Transaction Concurrency

The majority of transactional applications require protection from two users updating the same business entity at the same time. This can result in one user's changes overriding the other's and incorrect updates being made because the data was changing underneath a user during execution of the transaction. In general, there are many possible conflicts when this occurs. Although unlikely, it can happen and must be handled in the application architecture. The concept of handling this potential transaction concurrency is commonly referred to as locking.

There are two general approaches to handling this problem, optimistic or pessimistic locking.

Optimistic Locking

The optimistic locking strategy focuses on preventing the update collision at the time that it may occur. When an update collision is actually caught, the first user to get there is successful, and the second user trying to make an update is informed that the transaction failed because of a previous update. The second user usually is allowed to make a retry attempt after refreshing on the screen the data that was changed during the other user's transaction.

Pessimistic Locking

The pessimistic locking strategy focuses on preventing two users from ever getting to the point at which they could both update the entity at the same time. It prevents users from update collisions by marking each instance that has been opened for update. Any subsequent attempt by a user to open that instance for edit results in a notification that another user has the object open, and the second user typically is only allowed to view the data. Once the original user has released the lock on the object, another user can open it for update.

Choosing a Locking Strategy and Implementation

The optimistic approach is usually the preferred approach if the chances of an update collision are slim. Many business applications have users who are "owners" of particular sets of data. In other cases there is a small group of users who are allowed to update certain sets of data. In these cases, the chance of two users updating the same instance of the same business entity at the same time is fairly slim. If this is the case, the optimistic approach is favored because it typically has less overhead associated with it, mainly because it does not require a separate lock table or threading mechanism. The downside of this approach is that when a collision does occur, the second user has to resubmit the transaction. If optimistic locking is used, it is a good idea to build into the user interface framework the ability to redraw form fields with the data from the previous submission so the user does not have to retype the information before resubmitting the form. In other cases, the business requirements dictate a more conservative approach, and the pessimistic approach should be used when one user opening an object for update should prevent other users from being able to do the same.

Entity Beans provide a container-managed mechanism for implementing the optimistic locking approach through the transaction isolation setting. This deployment setting manages the relationship between different transactions using the same Entity Bean. The strictest setting, TRANSACTION_SERIALIZABLE, allows only one client to execute a method at a time on a given instance of the Entity Bean. An instance is defined uniquely by the primary key class for the Entity Bean. Note that using this technique adds extra overhead to any method defined on your component to be transactional; however, it is a nice service to use that is built in to your EJB. One thing to watch for when using this technique is not to use Entity Beans to model a small set of commonly used reference objects, because this will cause a bottleneck. All transactions will try to invoke methods on these reference objects, and the transactions will be lining up waiting for their turn because method invocation on an instance of the entity is single-threaded. When using this technique, it is also important to mark as transactional only methods that actually require it.

There are two primary drawbacks of using the Entity Bean transaction isolation approach to solve the locking problem. The first of these is that it requires your business objects to be implemented as Entity Beans, which, as discussed earlier, is not the proper approach for all solutions because of the overhead that is incurred by the Entity Bean model. If you have an application that for reasons discussed stands to benefit from using Entity Beans, there is still one more thing to consider. The second drawback is that there is no built-in mechanism to inform users of the fact that another user updated the business entity underneath them. In terms of update conflicts, the likely scenario is that two users would navigate to an update screen for the given business entity. The first user's transaction would be successful; however, the second user would now have updated the entity without knowing that the first update is taking place. There may be a data conflict between the two changes, and the second user needs to be made aware of this. If there is a data conflict and the business rules catch the problem, the error comes back to the second user causing confusion because there was no problem when the user first viewed the data. This drawback of not providing a mechanism to inform the user of semiconcurrent updates may not be a problem for all applications. However, in many cases, it is a system requirement to prevent the second user's update from happening and inform the second user that someone else has updated this entity. The best course of action then usually is to send the second user back to the update screen with the new data for review and resubmission of the transaction if it still makes sense.

This leads to a solution that works both for regular Java classes and can also cause the second transaction to fail in the case of an update collision. A commonly used technique for this is to add an integer property to business objects for which locking is required. This property is retrieved along with the rest of the object's data and sent to the client. In a Web-based application, it might be sent as a hidden HTML field in the form. When the object is updated (that is, the form is submitted), this property is sent back and passed along to the data-access layer. The UPDATE SQL includes this property in the WHERE clause and increments the value by one. If the row in the database is not found, this means that from the time the object was retrieved and displayed on the screen, another user updated that instance of the entity. In the case where the UPDATE statement does not find the row, an Optimistic Lock exception can be thrown. This would also occur in the case in which another user physically deleted the row; however, this is really the same business condition as when another user somehow changed the entity in the time period after the initial data retrieval. By signifying this condition with a particular exception or error, the User Interaction Architecture layer can either react to it in some defined manner, or it can treat it as any other error message. It is best to use a standard property name for all optimistic lock columns so the Business Logic Foundation can handle them generically.

BEST PRACTICE For a lightweight optimistic locking solution, use an integer property with a standardized name on business objects as an optimistic lock column to handle transaction concurrency. The data access objects can generically increment the property's value and include it in the WHERE clause on UPDATE and DELETE statements. If no rows are found from the SQL statement, an Optimistic Lock exception is thrown. Many J2EE containers and object-relational mapping vendors provide support to make implementing optimistic locking quite easy by allowing the developer to designate an optimistic locking column.

A pessimistic locking approach is much more heavyweight than an optimistic solution; however, it provides a solid solution for conservative system requirements. The approach is more complex and usually involves some kind of application lock table in the database. When a user opens an entity for update, an entry is put in the lock table. Another user is prevented from opening the entity for update if a lock entry is found for the given instance. This approach usually requires some application-specific coding in the user interaction layer as well as some extra logic in the data retrieval services;

however, this part can be generalized to some extent. A pessimistic data retrieval service always checks the lock table first and returns an extra indicator denoting that the entity is available for "view-only." Note that this solution does create a potential bottleneck on the lock table in the database for high-throughput applications.

Best Practices for Designing Business Objects

A summary of the best practices for designing the Business Object Architecture is given in this section.

Deciding between Entity Beans and Regular Java Objects as the Business Object Implementation

Entity Beans offer a number of compelling component services for business objects such as Container-Managed Persistence; however, you should load-test early in your development project to ensure that the use of Entity Beans meets the performance requirements of your application. Applications with many fine-grained objects or a large number of business objects in a given transaction should pay particular attention to the widespread use of Entity Beans. Business objects implemented as Java classes provide a more lightweight alternative, although you lose the standard component model and you need to implement the equivalent component services on your own. Many applications also involve a combination of the two. Use Entity Beans where they provide the most value in terms of optimized persistence and standard component deployment and distribution.

Designing Business Objects with a Potential Migration as an Alternative

If you are unsure of the best option, implement the business objects with a potential migration in mind between the two models. Your application requirements or transaction volumes may dictate a change at some point. The interface to business objects can be defined in a similar way for either Entity Beans or Java classes. This includes the use of template methods on Java objects for create and save operations that correspond to the `ejbCreate` and `ejbStore` methods. This approach facilitates any future migrations between the two implementation models.

Configuring the Entity Bean Deployment

In its optimized form, the Entity Bean transaction model is comparable to the Java business object equivalent for which state is loaded at the beginning of the transaction (ejbLoad) and saved at the end (ejbStore). In nonoptimized or extreme conditions in a clustered environment, Entity Beans can be very database and disk intensive because of the need to manage the free pool and activate and passivate instances in a transactional manner. Use a number of load tests to try and determine the optimal pool size for the Entity Beans in your particular application.

Using CMP Entity Beans Instead of BMP Where Possible

CMP Entity Beans should typically be used instead of BMP in order to take advantage of container optimizations and avoid two database hits when using a business object (that is, one on the finder method and another on the ejbLoad operation). BMP can be used to support object-relational mapping strategies not supported by the container or to manage the persistence of dependent Java business objects used within an Entity Bean.

Be Aware of Entity Bean Finder Implementation Strategies

Do not use Entity Bean finder methods to iterate through a collection of objects unless you can enforce either a read-only caching strategy or an aggressive-loading approach by the container. This avoids the $(n + 1)$ database access problem that also appears on a single BMP Entity Bean lookup. Check your application server's documentation for the ability to enforce these strategies or consider the use of JDBC for read-only operations.

Managing Aggregated Business Objects

Create and delete operations of business objects should also encapsulate the corresponding creation and deletion of aggregated objects that share the same lifecycle. This logic can be placed in template methods of your own Java business object implementation or the equivalent Entity Bean hook methods. In the case of cascading deletes, Entity Beans can be configured so the logic is accomplished by the container automatically when the parent object is deleted.

Using EJB Local Interfaces Wherever Possible

In many cases, EJB components do not need to be distributed. Thus, they are typically deployed uniformly throughout a production application server environment. Local interfaces should be used in these cases to avoid RMI and serialization overhead on method invocations. Keep in mind that arguments are passed by reference using local interfaces, so you must be aware that changes to objects passed as arguments are visible to the client.

Considering the Simple Case of a One-to-One Object-Relational Mapping Approach

There is a lot to be said for keeping the object-relational mapping approach simple and using a one-to-one table mapping. This allows for a standard code-generation process to create the data-access objects. Database normalization can still be hidden through encapsulation on primary business objects. EJB 2.0 local interfaces provide an efficient way to access related Entity Beans colocated in the same JVM. If a one-to-one table mapping scheme is used and there are many fine-grained objects in your model, it is important to use a lightweight business object implementation. You should carefully consider using Entity Beans across the board in this type of architecture. A lighter-weight Java object implementation or a combination of Entity Beans and Java objects might be better in this case.

Implementing More Complex Persistence Options

One option for implementing complex database mappings is to encapsulate the logic within the data-access layer. This makes the data-access objects tougher to generate, but this provides a purer approach to business object persistence. You may still be able to generate a majority of the data-access layer and hand-code only the objects for which complex mapping becomes an issue. A variation of this approach is to generate data access objects that map one-to-one for each table and then implement business object save logic that uses the appropriate set of data objects.

Considering the Use of Persistence Tools

For both automation and complex database mapping, it is best to use an object-relational mapping tool or vendor-specific persistence mechanism if you can afford the additional overhead cost in terms of performance. Remember that Entity Beans and Java objects using persistence frameworks are still largely portable even if a vendor-specific mechanism is used at deployment. In all cases, it is best to do a short proof-of-concept with some amount of load testing in order to see if an advanced persistence schema meets your system requirements. While the tools and containers themselves are fairly well optimized, your particular database schema and access patterns will largely define the type of performance realized through this type of an approach.

Using an Optimistic Lock Column for a Lightweight Solution

For a lightweight optimistic locking solution, use an optimistic lock column to detect and notify users of concurrent updates to business objects. If you are using straight JDBC, choose a standardized property name for this column. Persistence frameworks and some J2EE containers already support this mechanism out of the box.

Summary

Business objects are the implementation of business entities in the reference architecture. In most cases, they are implemented as stateful objects that encapsulate both the data and behaviors of a given entity. They manage relationships to other objects and persistence to the database and enforce business rules related to a particular business entity. The implementation model is typically regular Java classes, Entity Beans, or a combination of the two.

With the design considerations and best practices from this chapter in mind, the next two chapters walk through the implementation of business objects in the reference architecture. Implementations are shown for both Entity Beans and regular Java classes as well as a number of different persistence options. Keep in mind that there is no one-size-fits-all approach, so use the guidelines and principles discussed here to choose the best implementation model for your application.

Building Business Objects: Managing Properties and Handling Errors

There are many important design decisions that should be factored into the construction of the Business Object Architecture. One of the primary considerations discussed in the last chapter is the use of Java classes versus Entity Beans. This chapter gets into the basics of building business object components using both regular Java classes as well as EJB 2.0 Entity Beans. Basic elements of business objects such as managing properties and handling errors are discussed in this chapter, while the remainder of the functionality, such as persistence and relationships, are discussed in the next chapter.

Managing Properties

Properties of a business object typically use individual getter and setter methods to manage their values. Most explicit getter and setter methods follow the JavaBeans specification. This specification states that, for example, a String property field1 will have methods defined as:

```
public String getField1();
public void setField1(String value);
```

Many programs that use business objects refer explicitly to these methods in order to get and set property values. A benefit of using this specific naming convention is that the Java language can determine at run time what the properties of a given object are. This allows a business object to have explicit methods for each property but also allows a Java program to discover what the properties are at run time and then invoke the methods to manage the property using introspection.

NOTE The JavaBeans specification is different from the Enterprise JavaBeans specification. It is geared toward GUI components whereas the EJB specification is geared toward business logic and server-side application components. However, with regard to properties and the interface of business objects, the two basically follow the same model. Previously, this was not the case in EJB 1.1 components, but EJB 2.0 components that use Container-Managed Persistence are required to do so. Note that the implementations of Entity Bean accessor methods are declared as `abstract`. An example of this will be discussed in a moment.

Let's take the sample `Account` business object and look at its implementation as both a Java business object and an Entity Bean.

Properties on a Java Object

As a regular Java object, the `Account` business object stores its properties as `private` member variables. The `Account` has properties that include an internal identifier, an account number, and a current balance. With this set of properties, the class might start out looking something like the following using the JavaBeans naming convention:

```
public class Account {

    /*
     * The account internal identifier
     */
    private String id;
    /*
     * The external account number
     */
    private String number;
    /*
     * The account current balance
     */
    private BigDecimal currentBalance;

    /*
     * Default constructor to create a new account
     */
    public Account() {
        currentBalance = new BigDecimal(0);
    }
```

```java
/*
 * Get the account internal identifier.
 */
public String getId () {
    return id;
}

/*
 * Set the account internal identifier.
 */
public void setId (String value) {
    id = value;
}

/*
 * Get the external account number.
 */
public String getNumber () {
    return number;
}

/*
 * Set the external account number.
 */
public void setNumber (String value) {
    number = value;
}

/*
 * Get the account current balance.
 */
public BigDecimal getCurrentBalance () {
    return currentBalance;
}

/*
 * Set the account current balance.
 */
public void setCurrentBalance (BigDecimal value) {
    currentBalance = value;
}
}
```

Code to manipulate these types of business objects is fairly straightforward. A deposit method that adds money to the current balance of the account might look like the following:

```java
/*
 * Deposit money into the account.
 */
public void deposit(BigDecimal value) {
```

```
// Get the current balance and add the new value.
BigDecimal balance = getCurrentBalance();
setCurrentBalance(balance.add(value));
}
```

BEST PRACTICE It is a good practice always to use the getter and setter methods of a given property, even within other methods in that business object. This is the strictest form of encapsulation, in which only the getter and setter methods actually refer to the member variable. The member variables are declared as `private` to help enforce this concept, although use within the class itself requires discipline by the programmer. This technique can be beneficial in many ways. One example of when this comes in handy is the case in which a property does not have an assigned value. If you referred directly to the member variable, your code would get a `NullPointerException` in this case. However, use of the getter method can protect you from this condition by checking for this and initializing the value. This logic can then be implemented and encapsulated in one place, and other methods do not need to worry about this condition. This concept becomes even more powerful when the concept of lazy instantiation is used in getter methods for aggregated objects.

Properties on an Entity Bean

If you are developing a BMP Entity Bean, it is up to you how you want to manage the properties. In most cases, it is recommended to use the same JavaBeans naming convention and implementation approach as was just discussed for regular Java objects. However, a CMP Entity Bean uses abstract accessor methods that implement the JavaBeans naming specification in order to implement the abstract persistence approach. The same `Account` object implemented as an Entity Bean would start to look like the following.

```
public abstract class AccountBean implements EntityBean {

    //
    // Property methods, that is, CMP fields
    //
    public abstract String getId();
    public abstract void setId(String value);

    public abstract String getNumber();
    public abstract void setNumber(String value);

    public abstract BigDecimal getCurrentBalance();
    public abstract void setCurrentBalance(BigDecimal value);

    //
    // EJB methods to follow...
    //
}
```

Note that both the class itself and the accessor methods are declared as `abstract`. This is because the container is responsible for creating a subclass that implements these methods at deployment time. Because the container has control of the implementation of these methods, it can perform the CMP optimizations discussed earlier, such as lazy loading or dirty checking.

Using a Standard Java Interface

Instead of using explicit methods, you can also use a generic property interface. This approach uses a standard Java interface, which can be called `BusinessObject` to retrieve and modify property values. Using a standard interface is a powerful concept in the Java language and one that recurs throughout the study of the overall reference architecture.

> **BEST PRACTICE** Use of a standard interface for business objects is a good technique that can ensure consistency across business objects. In addition to making code more maintainable, this standard interface enables you to automate a number of business object functions and services because you can implement them generically, referring only to the Java `BusinessObject` interface.

By using a standard interface, you can generically refer to a business object without the knowledge of its specific type and method signatures. This concept allows you to create generic services that refer to business objects only by their interface. You can invoke business object methods without knowing what specific business object you are dealing with. This means you can implement a generic update service that calls a standard `setProperty` method and then saves the object to the database. Of course, you still need to discover the exact properties at run time. You could do this by providing the object with metadata that defines the properties and their data types. This sometimes can be easier than dealing with JavaBeans and introspection in application code because you don't need to write code to deal with an unknown method; you already know that the `setProperty` method exists in the standard business object interface. In the case of Entity Beans, you are required to have explicit accessor methods as shown in the last example, although you could also additionally implement a generic interface in order to gain some of the same benefits. The combination of a business object's metadata and a generic property interface can still add value in an Entity Bean scenario by acting as a helper method for easily iterating an object's properties in a standard way. For example, one situation in which this might be helpful is when you are getting all string values from the front end for properties of different data types. A standard property interface that accepts `String` values can hide the work of converting data types to explicit setter methods. The details of this approach and the generic property interface will be discussed as the next section studies the implementation of this concept.

Generic Property Interface for Java Objects

If you define a standard `setProperty` method for Java business objects, you need a way to deal with different Java data types, such as `String` and `BigDecimal`. One alternative is to use strings for everything and then convert to Java data types when you need to deal with the specific properties in your code. The other alternative is to deal with the properties as their normal objects. You can define the `setProperty` method to take an `Object` parameter and then allow either the specific data type or a `String` as an input argument. One reason to do this is based on the fact that data from the front end of an application usually originates in a string format, such as data from an HTTP form submission. If you take this approach, the interface will look something like the following:

```
public interface BusinessObject {

    /*
     * Property management methods
     */
    public void setProperty(String propertyName, Object value);

    public String      getProperty(String propertyName);
    public int         getIntProperty(String propertyName);
    public BigDecimal  getDecimalProperty(String propertyName);
    public Date        getDateProperty(String propertyName);

}
```

The `setProperty()` methods need a property name and a value. The object value can be converted to the `String` representation using either the basic `toString()` method or a defined conversion routine. The latter option is discussed further in the upcoming section on property formatting. The basic getter method, `getProperty()`, returns a `String`. You can also provide some convenience methods so that business object clients are not always required to do data type conversions when they know what type they want to deal with. Thus, methods, such as `getDecimalProperty()` and `getDateProperty()`, that automatically convert from the string to the desired data type, are provided.

This type of data conversion logic is general to all business objects and can be implemented in a base class for all business objects. This allows this logic to be implemented once and reused across all business objects. This may not be enough of a reason alone to use a common base class. However, there are other benefits as well, such as the ability to use superclass methods as templates for common business object behaviors. An example of this is the `save` operation that causes the object's state to persist in the database. You want the `save` operation to invoke any validations that may be required for data integrity. You can implement a `save` method on the common base class that provides this behavior as a template for all specific business object subclasses. As discussed earlier, Enterprise JavaBeans use a similar template concept for their persistence mechanism as well.

With regards to properties, you can put the logic of managing the properties in a common base class. As an added benefit, this also reduces the size of the code base because the specific business objects require very little code to provide basic property manipulation functionality.

Figure 3.1 shows the object design of the business objects using a standard interface and generic property manipulation methods. The specific business object subclasses

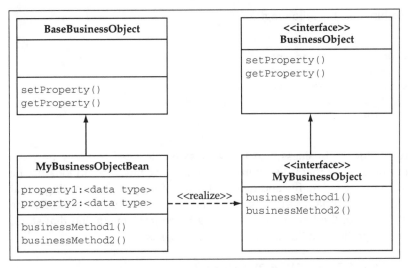

Figure 3.1 Business Object Class Diagram.

inherit from a common base class and implement the standard `BusinessObject` interface.

In order to put the property management logic in the business object base class, you need a generic scheme to store and manipulate property values. One way to implement this is to store the property names and values in one of the Collections data structures, such as a `HashMap`. The `HashMap` would store the name of the property as the key and the property value as the `HashMap` value. The value could be stored either as a `String` in all cases or as the specific object type that represents that property. If the approach of storing the specific object is used, you would need to create wrapper objects for primitive types, such as an `Integer` object to wrap an int value. Another option is to define the member variables and explicit accessor methods as you normally would and then use Java introspection and reflection to implement the generic property methods. This option provides less flexibility in terms of dynamically defining properties, but it does provide a nice, straightforward implementation. In most cases, the properties of a business object are well defined, so this is not much of a consideration. The next section considers the implementation of both approaches, but in the end, the dynamic collection of properties will probably only be used as a solution for flexible value objects. This concept of dynamic value objects will be expanded in the upcoming chapters on the service-based components and the User Interaction Architecture.

Using Metadata to Implement the Standard Interface

The business object base class can use a metadata configuration to define what the set of properties is for a given object. The flexibility of XML can be used as a data structure to define the business object metadata. The `Account` object might require metadata that looks something like the following:

```
<Metadata>
  <BusinessObject name="Account">
    <Property name="id" type="String" />
    <Property name="number" type="String" />
    <Property name="currentBalance" type="Decimal" />
  </BusinessObject>
</Metadata>
```

The constructor for the business object base class would need to know only the name of the business object that is being instantiated. Using this, it could look up the business object in the metadata file and deal with a set of properties accordingly that can be managed by the standard setProperty and getProperty methods. For the setProperty method, the first option discussed is the implementation that stores the collection of properties as a HashMap of String objects.

Storing Properties as a Collection of Strings

A basic implementation of the setProperty method would look like the code that follows. Keep in mind that a more robust version of this method will be shown in the next section using a structured data conversion routine, but for now, the example simply uses the toString method.

```
public void setProperty(String propertyName, Object value)
    throws PropertyException {

    // Ensure that this is a property on this object.
    if (!attributeMetadata.containsKey(propertyName)) {
        throw new PropertyException(propertyName +
            " is not a property of " + bom.getName());
    }

    // Set the property value.
    attributes.put(propertyName, value.toString());
}
```

The corresponding getProperty methods would use the property name as a key value to look up the value in the attributes HashMap. Using these methods, the deposit method on the Account object would now look like this:

```
public void deposit(BigDecimal value)
{
    /*
     * Get the current balance and add the new value.
     */
    BigDecimal balance =
        getDecimalProperty("currentBalance");
    setProperty("currentBalance", balance.add(value));
}
```

The getProperty method would then retrieve properties from the collection using the property name as the key.

Generic Property Methods Using Explicit Accessors

A more conventional approach is to define properties as members and have explicit accessor methods. However, you can still use the generic property methods as a part of the standard `BusinessObject` interface. The `get/setProperty` methods of the generic interface should use introspection to accomplish this. Rather than go through the work of coding the introspection yourself, an open-source utility can be used to make this task very easy. The Jakarta Struts project, which will be looked at in detail in an upcoming chapter, has a set of bean utilities for this purpose.

NOTE The Struts bean utility classes have now been deprecated and moved to the Jakarta Commons Beanutils project, although they are currently still available through Struts.

The primary methods used from this package are the corresponding methods on the `PropertyUtils` class, which generically implement getter and setter functions on classes that follow the JavaBeans naming convention.

```
public static void setProperty(Object bean,
                               String name,
                               Object value)
   throws IllegalAccessException, InvocationTargetException,
       NoSuchMethodException;

public static Object getProperty(Object bean,
                                 String name)
   throws IllegalAccessException, InvocationTargetException,
       NoSuchMethodException;
```

An implementation of the `setProperty` method would look something like the following using the `PropertyUtils` class. Note that this method will be revisited in the next section with a full implementation using a set of data conversion routines.

```
public void setProperty(String propertyName, Object value)
    throws PropertyException {

    // Ensure that this is a property on this object.
    if (!attributeMetadata.containsKey(propertyName)) {
        throw new PropertyException(propertyName +
            " is not a property of " + bom.getName());
    }

    // Validate the data type first because you
    // are going to set the actual member variable.
    PropertyMetadata prop =
        getPropertyMetadata(propertyName);
    String propType = prop.getType();
```

```
try {
    // Validate the data type first.
    validatePropertyDataType(propType,value);

    // Use the utility class to invoke the set method.
    PropertyUtils.setProperty(this,propertyName,
                            value);

} catch (Exception ex) {
    throw new PropertyException(ex.getMessage());
}
}
```

NOTE The `validatePropertyDataType` method will be explained in the next section on field-level validation. Its primary purpose in these examples is to ensure that the proper data type is being sent for the given property.

The getter methods for the different data types do not have to perform any conversion such as would be required from a `String` stored in a generic collection. They can simply return the object value cast to its particular type. For example, a decimal property that would otherwise have been stored as a `String` in a collection and then used to construct a new `BigDecimal` object is now simply returned as the `BigDecimal` object from the getter method. For example, the `getDecimalProperty` method can be implemented as follows:

```
public BigDecimal getDecimalProperty(String propertyName)
    throws PropertyException {

    Object value = null;
    try {
        value =
            PropertyUtils.getProperty(this,propertyName);
    } catch (Exception e) {
        throw new PropertyException(e.getMessage());
    }

    return (BigDecimal) value;
}
```

Metadata and the JavaBeans Property Model

Again, look at the JavaBeans approach compared to the metadata model. The JavaBeans approach uses a standard naming convention to define the set of properties. These properties can be discovered at run time using introspection. If this can be used, why would you want to define a separate metadata mechanism for this purpose? Aside from the convenience, the primary reason is that the metadata can store all of the other aspects of properties needed to build the application, outside of just the property name and data type.

THOUGHT By using XML metadata to define the properties, you can define for each property an entire set of information that can be used to further automate business object functionality. For example, you can add things to the metadata about each property such as an indicator for required fields and primary key fields. This allows you to automatically check that all required fields have a value. You could go beyond this and define the name of a validation class to use to ensure that the property value is valid. There are endless possibilities to what could be defined and used to automate business application functionality, especially with regard to the common characteristics of business applications that show up time after time.

As the study of building the Business Object Architecture continues, you will see things continually added to the business object metadata for the purposes of automation. The overall metadata approach for business objects and the resulting DTD (document type definition) will be discussed in detail in the next chapter.

Comparing Explicit Property Methods and Generic Interface Methods

For many developers, using the generic interface methods (setProperty, getProperty) may seem a bit uncomfortable at first. The generic methods have their drawbacks when compared to the explicit methods. One major drawback is that of compile time type checking on the setProperty method. Because any property value can be passed in as a generic Object argument, this type of edit would not occur until run time. This drawback must be weighed against the benefit gained from having all business objects implement a standard interface. There are also human factors to consider, such as getting your development staff used to the concept of using a generic interface. On the positive side, service components and other business objects can easily access data on the business objects if they implement a standard interface. You can also easily build generic services, such as an update service, that can get and set property values on an object by referring to objects only by their standard interface and not by their specific object type.

One other negative point to make about the generic method approach is that it goes against the JavaBeans specification discussed earlier. Although Java business objects are not required to implement this specification for property methods, it does provide a good standard that is commonly used in the industry. So, which approach is better to use?

THOUGHT Although the business object interface is important, it is not the end goal here in this discussion. The primary objective is to provide a mechanism that generically deals with a set of properties. This mechanism should have some kind of interface that can be used by other business objects and service components. Thus, as long as you can generically store, manage, and validate properties, the specific interface is not so important. This is true for either the JavaBeans explicit getter/setter approach or a generic get/set property approach. A metadata-driven approach can actually be used underneath either business object interface option.

One design that brings the best of both worlds is to actually have both sets of methods available to business objects. A standard interface can still be used as both helper methods and standard hooks for validation and formatting logic. These concepts will be discussed in the next section of this chapter. The explicit accessors in combination with the generic `setProperty` and `getProperty` methods provide the benefits of the JavaBeans interface while still allowing you to manage the properties generically and automate data marshalling and validation.

NOTE The combination of the explicit and generic accessor methods is an interesting concept that will be looked at further in the Entity Bean implementation. In the case of CMP Entity Beans, the explicit accessor methods are required, and they must be defined as `abstract` on the bean.

The combination approach works extremely well if you have code-generation capabilities out of your design models. You can customize your business object templates to generate specific getter and setter methods that follow this pattern based on the data type of the property. This allows clients of the business object to use either method while still achieving the automation of the property management. This logic can still reside in the business object base class, so the core template for the business object subclass is just this set of getter and setter methods. In the case in which only the standard interface is used for properties, the core template of the business object subclass is actually quite empty. To define a business object with properties using this method, you simply need a constructor that indicates the object name and the metadata defined in the configuration. Your core `Account` object (without any business logic added) would consist of the following:

```
public class Account extends BaseBusinessObject {

    /*
     * Default constructor to create a new account
     */
    public Account()
    {
        super("Account");
    }

}
```

Here, the business object base class takes care of looking up the object in the metadata and dealing with the list of properties. The combined approach would add the set of explicit setter and getter methods previously described. In either case, you would now already have a business object that can manage its properties.

Standard Property Interface with Entity Beans

In order for the generic property management implementation to work with Entity Beans, you typically add the explicit accessor methods. The primary reason for this is the fact that Entity Beans require abstract accessor methods for each property in order to use Container-Managed Persistence. This allows the generated container classes to implement the CMP properties specified in the deployment descriptors. The container is not able to access the properties if they are stored as member variables; thus, you are required to use the explicit getter and setter methods to manipulate the properties. The implementation of the get/setProperty methods is the same as the previous example that used the PropertyUtils class to dynamically invoke accessor methods using reflection.

If you wanted to expose the explicit property accessors of the Entity Bean to clients, you would add them to their respective component interface. In most cases, Entity Beans are accessed through a local interface, so the local version of the Account component interface is shown here:

```
public interface AccountLocal extends EJBLocalObject {

    // CMP methods
    public String getId();
    public void setId(String value);
    public String getNumber();
    public void setNumber(String value);
    public BigDecimal getCurrentBalance();
    public void setCurrentBalance(BigDecimal value);

}
```

Remember that there is very little overhead with the invocation of a local interface method, so you are more likely to have a situation in which you would want to have fine-grained access to your component's properties. This is the opposite of how you usually want to deal with a remote component. In these cases, you usually want to avoid the RMI and network overhead by using a bulk getter method that returns a set of the object's properties through a value object or some analogous data structure. Bulk getter methods and value objects are discussed in upcoming sections of this chapter. If you are using the generic property interface, you can create a standard business object interface that extends EJBLocalObject for local access. The specific objects will then extend this standard interface, which can be called EntityLocalBusinessObject. The code for this interface follows:

```
public interface EntityLocalBusinessObject
    extends EJBLocalObject {

    /**
     * Property management methods
     */
    public void setProperty(String propertyName, Object value)
        throws PropertyException;

    public String    getProperty(String propertyName)
        throws PropertyException;
    public int       getIntProperty(String propertyName)
        throws PropertyException;
```

```
public BigDecimal getDecimalProperty(String propertyName)
    throws PropertyException;
public Date       getDateProperty(String propertyName)
    throws PropertyException;

}
```

Note that the methods are essentially equivalent to directly invoking the method on the implementation class, as there is no additional `RemoteException` that can be thrown. The actual `AccountLocal` interface is then implemented as follows:

```
public interface AccountLocal extends EntityLocalBusinessObject
{
}
```

You could also add the explicit accessors to this interface if you want clients of the bean to have the ability to use either option.

Field Validation

Three basic types of validation take place at the individual property level:

- Data type validation
- Required field checking
- Application-specific logic (for example, a valid Social Security number).

Business objects often have these validations coded into either the setter methods or specific validation methods. Separate validation objects are also used in some cases to isolate validation logic. This technique can be helpful either if the validations can be reused across objects or if a business object is getting particularly large, and it helps to move code out to "helper" objects. For business objects that use explicit setter methods, most data type validation is done inherently through compile-time checking because the methods take only specific Java data types. Thus, the business object client can pass only a valid object or primitive type. As far as required field validations and application-specific edits, you must write code to do that either in the setter method or in a validate method of the business object.

In the implementation that uses the standard Java interface and the generic `setProperty` method, you are required to do your own data type validations because a generic `Object` is accepted as an argument. You can define both the data type and the required status of properties in the property metadata. The `setProperty` method can then automatically validate the data type based on the metadata. A general method `validateRequiredFields` can be created that goes through the list of property metadata and validates that each required field has a value.

Using Metadata and Reusable Property Definitions

Much of the property-level validation logic will be redundant. If you use separate validation classes to enforce these edits, you can reuse them across business objects. To do this, you need to know the type of each property. Metadata can be used to define the data types themselves and the name of a corresponding class to use to validate the value. Thus, when you want to validate a given property, you pass it through the appropriate validation class. If a standard interface is used for these classes, you can generically refer to them and plug in new data types very easily.

An interface for the validator class might be as follows:

```
public interface PropertyValidator {

    public void validateProperty(Object value)
        throws ValidationException;
}
```

In the metadata file, you can add the following, which defines the data types and handler classes:

```
<Metadata>
  <PropertyDefinitions>
    <PropertyType name="Decimal"
                  handler="blf.DecimalValidator" />
    <PropertyType name="int"
                  handler="blf.NumberValidator" />
    <PropertyType name="Date"
                  handler="blf.DateValidator" />
  </PropertyDefinitions>
</Metadata>
```

NOTE The prefix `blf` will be used as the package name for the foundation layer classes. This is an acronym for Business Logic Foundation. Any generic class used as a foundation for the applications goes into this package.

In the foundation layer, you can create validation classes that implement this interface for all of the standard data types. As an example, the decimal validator class would look like this:

```
public class DecimalValidator implements PropertyValidator {

    public void validateProperty(Object value)
        throws ValidationException
    {
        // Since this method can be invoked with any
        // object type, you need to check.
        if (value instanceof BigDecimal) return;

        if (value instanceof String) {
            try {
                BigDecimal decimal =
                    new BigDecimal((String)value);
            } catch (Exception e) {
```

```
                throw new ValidationException(value +
                    " is not a valid property value.");
            }
        } else {
            throw new ValidationException(
                "Invalid object type for decimal property.");
        }


    }
}
```

NOTE For the time being, the `PropertyValidator` code examples throw a `ValidationException` to report an error to the client. Later on in this chapter, error and exception handling will be discussed and a more robust mechanism called `ErrorList` will be implemented to handle and report business errors to users.

The logic to invoke validator classes for each property can be embedded into the business object base class. As a part of the validation routine, a `validateProperty-Values` method that loops through each property and calls the validation routine can be invoked. This is illustrated in the following code:

```
public void validatePropertyValues()
    throws ValidationException, PropertyException {

    // For each attribute, validate the property value.
    Iterator iter = attributeMetadata.values().iterator();
    while (iter.hasNext()) {
        PropertyMetadata pmd =
            (PropertyMetadata) iter.next();
        this.validatePropertyDataType(
            pmd.getType(),
            getProperty(pmd.getName()));
    }
}


public void validatePropertyDataType(String type,
                                     Object value)
    throws ValidationException {

    // If no value exists, you can't validate it.
    // Return with no error because either
    // required checks or validation classes will get this.
    if (value == null) {
        return;
    }


    // Look up the property type, get an instance of the
    // validator class based on the metadata, and
```

```
    // validate the value.
    PropertyValidator validator = null;
    try {
        validator = (PropertyValidator)
            CacheList.getInstance().getObject(
                "PropertyTypeCache",type);
    } catch (BlfException ignoreForNow) {}

    if (validator == null) {
        throw new ValidationException("Property type " +
            type + " is not a defined type in " +
            "the metadata.");
    }

    validator.validateProperty(value);
}
```

NOTE There is a reference to a `CacheList` object in this code snippet that obtains a value of the `PropertyValidator`. It would seem like wasteful overhead to create one of these validator classes for each method invocation of `setProperty`, especially because it is a stateless service. A good practice for these types of objects is to cache them and reuse the object instances, because small, temporary objects are a major cause of performance degradation in Java applications. This is the first of many reference-type objects that will be cached in memory. It would be helpful if there was a general-purpose caching mechanism to do this. Thus, in the next chapter, a `CacheList` mechanism will be created for this purpose. This mechanism can be used to store the validator objects.

The last type of field-level validation is put into the category of application-specific checks. These can be coded into the specific business object methods. However, you can also put this logic in the property validator classes used to edit field values. This allows you to define reusable properties, such as a Social Security number property. As the earlier metadata example showed, you can define these custom property types and their corresponding `PropertyValidator` class that should be used for editing their values.

If you created a reusable Social Security property whose value was expected to be xxx-xx-xxxx where x is an integer value between 0 and 9, its validation class might look like this:

```
public class SSNValidator implements PropertyValidator
{

    /*
     * Validate a Social Security number string value.
     */
    public void validateProperty(Object value)
        throws ValidationException
    {
```

```java
        if (!(value instanceof String)) {
            throw new ValidationException(
                "Invalid object type for numeric property.");
        }

        String strValue = (String) value;

        // You are expecting the format xxx-xx-xxxx.
        int size = strValue.length();

        // If it's not the right length, it is invalid.
        if (size != 11)
        {
            throw new ValidationException(strValue +
                " is not a valid property value.");
        }

        // Loop through the characters and ensure that
        // digits and dashes are in the correct positions.
        for (int loop=0; loop < size; loop++)
        {
            if ((loop == 3) || (loop == 6))
            {
                if (strValue.charAt(loop) != '-')
                {
                    throw new ValidationException(strValue +
                        " is not a valid property value.");
                }
            }
            else if (!Character.isDigit(
                                strValue.charAt(loop)))
            {
                throw new ValidationException(strValue +
                    " is not a valid property value.");
            }
        }
    }
}
```

Thus, in some cases, you can combine both data type and application-specific checks in the validator classes. But what if you had an integer property against which you also wanted to perform an application-specific edit, such as validating the numeric value against a valid range? You could create a validator called NumberRangeValidator that extended NumberValidator and called the superclass method before doing the range check. This class might look like the following:

```java
public class RangeFieldValidator extends NumberValidator
    implements PropertyValidator {

    /*
     * Validate the property value against a specific
```

```
 * numeric range.
 */
public void validateProperty(Object value)
    throws ValidationException
{
    int intValue;

    // First, validate that the value is numeric.
    super.validateProperty(value);

    // If numeric, validate that it falls within the
    // given range.

    // Get a common int value.
    if (value instanceof Integer) {
        intValue = ((Integer)value).intValue();
    }
    else if (value instanceof String) {
        intValue =
            (Integer.valueOf((String)value)).intValue();
    } else {
        // You should not ever get here because
        // of superclass validation.
        throw new ValidationException(
            "Invalid object type for numeric property.");
    }

    if ((intValue < 0) || (intValue > 1000))
    {
        throw new ValidationException(value +
            " is not a valid property value.");
    }
}
}
```

Property Value Formatting

There may be times when you want to get a non-`String` property value as a `String`. Perhaps you are retrieving a numeric or date value only to return it to the front end to display to the user. In these cases, you want to format the property values appropriately as a `String`. This formatting often involves converting a Java data type to a specific string format. Many non-`String` properties require additional logic in order to do this correctly. In other cases, there is also a general need to convert the other way, from a `String` to the specific data type. For some data types, this conversion and formatting is fairly straightforward. Integers and decimals have standard conversion routines already provided by Java. For others such as a date field, there is not one standard format or conversion routine. A date can be specified as a string in a number of different ways, often determined by the locale and internationalization. For example, the date of July 14, 1972, could be displayed as '07/14/1972', '1972-07-14', or 'Jul-14-1972' just to name a few options.

NOTE You may be thinking, why would you put a form of presentation logic in your business objects? Well, this property-handling mechanism can also be used to convert values between external formats and internal storage formats. This can be seen as a business object function. This also provides a nice clean implementation to allow the standard `setProperty` interface to take `String` values for any property type. Normally you would not put presentation logic in the business objects, but you will see in the next section that business objects and value objects are closely related. The value objects can definitely use this type of presentation logic, and you may be able to reuse this same property-handling mechanism in a value object base class.

A reusable property mechanism that provides validation has already been created. You can extend this mechanism to include formatting also. In addition to implementing a `PropertyValidator` interface, the property classes can also implement a standard interface called `PropertyHandler`. The implementation classes for these interfaces can be called property handlers now that they provide conversion and formatting routines in addition to validation. Thus, the validation classes can be renamed appropriately and the corresponding property type metadata can be changed to reflect this. The `PropertyHandler` interface can be specified as:

```
/**
 * This interface is used for formatting and converting
 * a property value.
 */
public interface PropertyHandler {

    public Object convertToStringFormat(Object value)
        throws PropertyException;

    public Object convertToObjectFormat(Object value)
        throws PropertyException;

    public String convertToDisplayFormat(Object value)
        throws PropertyException;
}
```

In essence, the primary purpose of this interface is to convert between Java data type objects and their string representations. Note that the conversion methods could be used conversely if a value object or business object base class stored properties as a collection of `String` objects. In most cases however, the conversion to a `String` format happens only for display purposes. Because this mechanism is used in many different scenarios, each `PropertyHandler` takes an `Object`, and the implementations need to deal with different object types.

For simplicity, assume that the application has settled on the date format MM/dd/yyyy to be used throughout the application. The property handler class for dates can now be specified as the following class. Note that this same class implements the `PropertyValidator` and `PropertyHandler` interfaces; thus, you can encapsulate the property manipulation in one implementation class.

```java
package blf;

import java.text.SimpleDateFormat;
import java.util.Date;

/**
 * This class is used to handle date properties.
 */
public class DateHandler
    implements PropertyValidator, PropertyHandler {

    public void validateProperty(Object value)
        throws ValidationException {

        // Since this method can be invoked with any
        // object type, you need to check.
        if (value instanceof Date) return;

        if (value instanceof String) {
            try {
                SimpleDateFormat sdf =
                    new SimpleDateFormat("MM/dd/yyyy");
                java.util.Date myDate =
                    sdf.parse((String)value);
            } catch (java.text.ParseException pe) {
                throw new ValidationException(value +
                    " is not a valid property value.");
            }
        } else {
            throw new ValidationException(
                "Invalid object type for date property.");
        }
    }

    public Object convertToStringFormat(Object value)
        throws PropertyException {

        if (value instanceof String) {
            return value;
        }
        else  if (value instanceof Date) {
            SimpleDateFormat sdf =
                new SimpleDateFormat("MM/dd/yyyy");
            return sdf.format((Date)value);
        } else {
            throw new PropertyException("Invalid date format");
        }
    }

    public Object convertToObjectFormat(Object value)
        throws PropertyException {
```

```
          if (value instanceof String) {
              SimpleDateFormat sdf =
                  new SimpleDateFormat("MM/dd/yyyy");
              try {
                  Date myDate = sdf.parse((String)value);
                  return myDate;
              } catch (Exception e) {
                  throw new PropertyException(e.getMessage());
              }
          }
          else if (value instanceof Date) {
              return value;
          } else {
              throw new PropertyException("Invalid date format");
          }
      }

      public String convertToDisplayFormat(Object value)
          throws PropertyException {

          return convertToStringFormat(value).toString();
      }
  }
```

Effect on *getProperty Method*

The standard `getProperty` method that returns a `String` can be modified to
use these formatting classes to return the proper formatted value. Likewise, if the
`setProperty` method takes a `String`, it can use these classes to convert to the specific Java object. The code for `getProperty` would look like the following code snippet that uses the generic property-handling mechanism:

```
/**
 * The standard getProperty method that returns a string
 */
public String getProperty(String propertyName)
    throws PropertyException {

    // Ensure that this is a property on this object.
    if (!attributeMetadata.containsKey(propertyName)) {
        throw new PropertyException(propertyName +
            " is not a property of " + bom.getName());
    }

    Object value = null;

    try {
        // Get the member variable value as an object.
        Object obj =
            PropertyUtils.getProperty(this,propertyName);
```

```
            // Convert the object to a string using the
            // property-handler mechanism.
            PropertyMetadata prop =
                getPropertyMetadata(propertyName);
            String type = prop.getType();
            value = convertToStringFormat(type,obj);

        } catch (Exception ex) {
            throw new PropertyException(ex.getMessage());
        }

        if (value == null) return null;
        return value.toString();
    }


    /**
     * A helper method to invoke the
     * property-handling mechanism
     */
    public Object convertToStringFormat(String type,
                                         Object value)

        throws PropertyException {

        // If no value exists, you can't convert it.
        if (value == null) {
            return null;
        }

        // Look up the property type, get an instance of the
        // handler class based on the metadata, and
        // convert the value.
        PropertyHandler handler = null;
        try {
            handler = (PropertyHandler)
                CacheList.getInstance().getObject(
                             "PropertyTypeCache",type);
        } catch (BlfException ignoreForNow) {}

        if (handler == null) {
            throw new PropertyException("Property type " + type
                + " is not a defined type in the metadata.");
        }

        return handler.convertToStringFormat(value);
    }
```

Thus, if the sample `Account` Entity Bean had a last-modified date property and the following statement was executed:

```
System.out.println("The account was modified on: " +
    account.getProperty("lastModifiedDate");
```

You would see the following written to standard out:

```
The account was modified on: 07/14/1972
```

NOTE If the property-handling mechanism was used generically as in the preceding example, you need to implement `PropertyHandler` classes for all of the data types. This is not a problem or even a performance issue because of the simplicity. However, it does require the implementation of some primitive implementations in the business logic foundation.

For example, the `StringHandler` class would look like this:

```
public class StringHandler
    implements PropertyValidator, PropertyHandler {

    public void validateProperty(Object value)
        throws ValidationException {

        if (!(value instanceof String)) {
            throw new ValidationException(
                "Invalid object type for numeric property.");
        }
    }

    public Object convertToStringFormat(Object value)
        throws PropertyException {
        return value;
    }


    public Object convertToObjectFormat(Object value)
        throws PropertyException {
        return value;
    }

    public String convertToDisplayFormat(Object value)
        throws PropertyException {

        return convertToStringFormat(value).toString();
    }
}
```

The property-handler implementation for decimals is fairly simple as well. If you are happy with the `toString` implementation of the object, as is the case for `BigDecimal`, you can simply return the object when converting to the external format. Converting to internal format in this case only requires you to construct a `BigDecimal` object, passing the string as an argument.

Effect on `setProperty` Method

Similar to `getProperty`, you could allow the standard `setProperty` method to take `String` representations for non-`String` properties. The `setProperty` method can be modified to use the property-handler class to convert values into the explicit Java data types for Entity Beans and to strings for Java business objects. The code for Entity Bean `setProperty` would be modified as such:

```
public void setProperty(String propertyName, Object value)
    throws PropertyException {

    // Ensure that this is a property on this object.
    if (!attributeMetadata.containsKey(propertyName)) {
        throw new PropertyException(propertyName +
            " is not a property of " + bom.getName());
    }

     // Validate the data type first because you
    // are going to set the actual member variable.
    PropertyMetadata prop =
        getPropertyMetadata(propertyName);
    String propType = prop.getType();

    try {
        // Validate the data type first.
        validatePropertyDataType(propType,value);

        // Use the utility class to invoke the set method.
        PropertyUtils.setProperty(this,propertyName,
            convertToObjectFormat(propType,value));

    } catch (Exception ex) {
        throw new PropertyException(ex.getMessage());
    }
}


/**
 * Helper method to invoke the property-handling mechanism
 */
public Object convertToObjectFormat(String type,
                                    Object value)
    throws PropertyException {

    // If no value exists, you can't convert it.
    if (value == null) {
        return value;
    }
```

```
    // Look up the property type, get an instance of the
    // handler class based on the metadata, and
    // convert the value.
    PropertyHandler handler = null;
    try {
        handler = (PropertyHandler)
            CacheList.getInstance().getObject(
                        "PropertyTypeCache",type);
    } catch (BlfException ignoreForNow) {}

    if (handler == null) {
        throw new PropertyException("Property type " + type
            + " is not a defined type in the metadata.");
    }

    return handler.convertToObjectFormat(value);
}
```

NOTE A corresponding Java business object implementation that stored
properties as a collection of `String` objects would invoke the `convert-
ToStringFormat` method instead within `setProperty`.

Use in Value Conversions

You can also use this mechanism for another purpose. Sometimes the storage format,
or internal format, is different than the input format (or external format). As a con-
trived example, take the Social Security number property. Assume the external format
is 'xxx-xx-xxxx.' However, you don't want to store the extra dashes and waste two
characters, so you will store the SSN as 'xxxxxxxxx.' You can use the property-handler
mechanism to convert between the two. The `convertToObjectFormat` removes
the dashes and the `convertToStringFormat` adds the dashes. The `SSNHandler`
would look like this:

```
public class SSNHandler
    implements PropertyValidator, PropertyHandler
{

    /*
     * Validation method from previous example
     */
    public void validateProperty(Object value)
        throws ValidationException {

        // validation code here...
    }

    public Object convertToStringFormat(Object value)
        throws PropertyException {
```

```java
    // Ensure that you are dealing with a string.
    if (!(value instanceof String)) {
        throw new PropertyException(
            "SSN must be a string value");
    }

    // Make sure the string is the right length.
    String strValue = (String) value;
    if (strValue.length() != 9) {
        throw new PropertyException(
            "SSN must be 9 digits");
    }

    // Construct the display string,
    // adding the '-' characters.
    StringBuffer buffer = new StringBuffer();
    buffer.append(strValue.substring(0,3));
    buffer.append('-');
    buffer.append(strValue.substring(3,5));
    buffer.append('-');
    buffer.append(strValue.substring(5,9));

    // Return the formatted string.
    return buffer.toString();
}


public Object convertToObjectFormat(Object value)
    throws PropertyException {

    // Ensure that you are dealing with a string.
    if (!(value instanceof String)) {
        throw new PropertyException(
            "SSN must be a string value");
    }

    // Convert to a string for convenience.
    String strValue = (String) value;

    // Make sure the string is the right length.
    if (strValue.length() != 11) {
        throw new PropertyException(
            "Formatted SSN must be 11 characters");
    }

    // Construct the string storage format
    // removing the '-' characters.
    StringBuffer buffer = new StringBuffer();
    buffer.append(strValue.substring(0,3));
    buffer.append(strValue.substring(4,6));
    buffer.append(strValue.substring(7,11));
```

```
        // Return the formatted string.
        return buffer.toString();
    }
}
```

Variations on Property-Handling Approach

The SSN property may not come from the front end with the dashes in it. You may have the user type the numbers in directly without the dashes. In this case, you could modify `convertToObjectFormat` to simply pass along the string. However, now you have somewhat of a problem because a client of the business object with this property would not be able to execute the following code:

```
busObj.setProperty("ssn",busObj.getProperty("ssn"));
```

This would fail because the `getProperty` would return the display format ('xxx-xx-xxxx') but the `setProperty` is expecting a different format, one without the dashes. Thus, you can use the `convertToDisplayFormat` method for this purpose. The business object could expose this through a `getDisplayProperty` method on the standard interface. This approach would clearly delineate between getting the property for display and for usage in code. A third option is to have only the value objects use this external conversion, because they are the ones that may be used in the User Interaction Architecture as a data transport. Thus, this is where you would want to have this type of presentation logic.

> **NOTE** If the application architecture uses value objects as a data transport between tiers, you may want to use this property handling mechanism only in the value object base class. As a convenience, it is left in the business object base class so that clients can deal with property values either as `String` objects or their native Java objects. If this still bothers the purist out there, you can always choose to keep this mechanism in the value object class so that the presentation-type logic remains in the User Interaction Architecture.

There are a number of different ways to implement this. You can choose the best one for your application. The concept is a powerful one that can reduce and encapsulate the data conversion code that is often found interspersed throughout an application.

Bulk Getter and Setter Methods

It is sometimes desirable to use a single method invocation to set a number of properties on a given business object. In the case of distributed Entity Beans accessed through a remote interface, the use of value objects is recommended for this purpose because of the transactional and RMI overhead associated with a single remote method invocation. In the case of Java business objects and local Entity Beans, it can also be used as a convenience to shorten the amount of code required to populate the properties of a business object. Often there are different combinations of fields that you want to set on a business object. With explicit setter methods, you would likely have to provide a couple different methods to group the properties or one large method that took all of the values. This would result in an extremely large method signature in the case of primary objects within a design model that may have a lot of properties. With the standard business object interface, you have a generic setProperty method that you can wrap with a method that takes a collection of properties and values. This wrapper method can then invoke setProperty repeatedly. In the case of remote Entity Beans, this is extremely effective because each of the setProperty method invocations would be local as opposed to individual remote method calls.

A bulk setter method like this might look like the following:

```
public void setProperties(Collection propertyNames,
                          Collection propertyValues);
```

If you are using property objects that encapsulate both, you could use a method like this that takes a collection of property objects:

```
public void setProperties(Collection propertyObjects);
```

A more popular technique is the use of setter and getter methods that deal with value objects. Value objects are basically objects used as data structures to hold all of the property values for a given object. This interface might look like this for the Account object:

```
public void setProperties(AccountData accountValueObject);
```

An implementation of this method is shown in the next section on value objects. The code for the AccountData class could also have been listed here, but it would be very similar to the first listing of the Account business object because no business logic has been added to it yet. This comparison brings out an interesting point about value objects and business objects. They share the same core elements: the storage and manipulation of a set of defined properties. Because they have these commonalities, perhaps they should be modeled in a similar way.

Value Objects and Lightweight Business Objects

You have just seen that value objects and business objects have an interesting relationship. They both have the same state, or set of properties, although a value object is used primarily to avoid RMI and network overhead with remote beans by transporting the entire set of object properties at once. By comparison, a business object also contains the business logic and persistence functions of the entity. A primary aspect of the business object that has just been discussed is data validation at the field level. If you are going to use value objects to transport data from the Web tier to the business objects on the EJB tier, do you want to wait until that point to do some of this data validation?

Wouldn't it be better to perform some of this validation before you get to this point so a network trip is not wasted? If the value objects could also perform the field-level validation, this would allow these edits to be performed further up front, and time would be saved in these cases. Now, the value objects are more than just data structures; they have some amount of "smarts" in them. This is the concept of lightweight business objects. You don't want a value object to have all of the logic of a business object because a value object should have a smaller memory footprint and lower instantiation cost. However, it sometimes makes sense to put this extra bit of logic in the value objects.

Same Properties, Same Interface

Because the value objects share the same set of properties, it makes sense that they should share the same interface with respect to property manipulation. In the case of explicit getter and setter methods, this means that the two objects have the same set of methods. In the standard business object interface example, the value objects can have their own standard interface that performs the same property management functions. And why not use the same method signatures so that you don't need to learn a whole new interface? Thus, the value object interface might also look like this:

```
public interface ValueObject {

    /*
     * Property management methods
     */
    public void setProperty(String propertyName, Object value)
        throws PropertyException;

    public String getProperty(String propertyName)
        throws PropertyException;
    public int getIntProperty(String propertyName)
        throws PropertyException;
    public BigDecimal getDecimalProperty(String propertyName)
        throws PropertyException;
    public Date getDateProperty(String propertyName)
        throws PropertyException;

}
```

The value objects can use the same `PropertyHandler` mechanism described earlier for general formatting logic particular to a data type. Methods to retrieve properties as specific data types are provided in the value object interface. However, the `getProperty` method, which returns a `String`, will likely be used by the presentation layer. This is where the formatting logic in the `PropertyHandler` classes is used. Many non-`String` properties, such as date fields, will be formatted as strings in order to be displayed on the screen. Although this general mechanism is also used in the business objects, you normally would not use the presentation logic piece of it in the business object. However, the value object, if used across the architecture as is being discussed here, is in a unique situation in that it lives on both tiers. It can be created within either architecture layer, and it is used to transport data between the two tiers. Thus, general formatting logic particular to a data type can be done using the PropertyHandler mechanism in the value object base class, and additional methods on a value object subclass are a possible placeholder for other presentation logic that can be encapsulated and reused.

As mentioned earlier with regard to bulk getter and setter methods, the business object base class can easily implement a standard method to populate the object from a value object. The properties in the internal value object collection map directly to the properties in the internal business object collection. The method could be implemented as follows for both Java business objects and Entity Beans:

```
public void setProperties(ValueObject value)
    throws BlfException {

    // Get the collection of property metadata objects.
    Iterator iter = attributeMetadata.values().iterator();
    while (iter.hasNext()) {
        // For each one except the key field,
        // set the property from the value object.
        PropertyMetadata prop =
            (PropertyMetadata) iter.next();
        if (!prop.isKey()) {
            String propValue =
                value.getProperty(prop.getName());
            if ((propValue != null) &&
                (!propValue.equals(""))) {
                setProperty(prop.getName(), propValue);
            }
        }
    }
}
```

NOTE The value of key fields is not modified here because their value can be set only at the time the object instance is created. In fact, Entity Beans throw an IllegalStateException if the set method for a primary key field is invoked outside of the ejbCreate method. Thus, properties that are a part of the primary key are only set based on either the create and finder methods in the EJB Home interface or the ejbSelect methods invoked from within a bean.

A Unified Structure for Value Objects and Business Objects

As you have seen, the interfaces and behaviors of value objects and business objects share a common foundation in terms of managing the set of properties that define an object. Thus, you can leverage the value object infrastructure when building the business objects. There are several options for structuring the value objects and business objects:

- Leave the two as separate object hierarchies.
- Have the business object interface extend the value object interface.
- Have the business object implementation classes extend their respective value object implementation classes.

The first option does not allow as much reuse between the two, and thus is not the preferred solution given their core similarities. You can, if you choose, implement options two and three independently. A nice solution might also be to implement both of them together.

By having a common interface hierarchy, you gain some flexibility when dealing with business objects in common services or utilities. There will be cases in which you don't care whether you have the actual business object itself, or the lightweight version of it (that is, the value object), you simply want to access or manage the data associated with that object. The common interface hierarchy allows references to either type of object as a `ValueObject` when you simply want to access the object's set of properties. This modeling also works well to show the relationship between the two types of objects in the application architecture.

The case for putting the implementation classes in a common hierarchy is a little less clear. Because a value object simply manages the properties, you can easily have the business object implementation classes extend their corresponding value classes. In this case, the value object class handles the property management; the business object subclass can extend (and override if necessary) to provide the specific business logic functionality. This works in either the case of a standard property interface or explicit getter and setter methods. However, if this is done, you start to dull the distinction between the two. The business object base class can also include functionality such as persistence and management of aggregated objects. If a common base class is shared, this means that the value objects now have all of this functionality that goes with them, a core set of the business object functionality aside from specific business logic methods. The concept of the value object being a "lightweight" business object gets lost a bit because you want to be able to manage data as a set of thin objects with a small memory footprint. This becomes difficult to do if every value object carries around with it this additional codebase, which may not even be applicable when used in the context of the Web tier.

Thus, you may want to implement only the second option, that is, to have the business object interface extend from the value object interface. The downside of this approach is that the property management functionality is duplicated somewhat between the value object base class and the business object base class. The choice of approach can be different depending on the specifics of the project architecture. For example, smaller applications that may not have an enterprise tier may put all of their logic into the servlet/JSP container. In this case, there is not much need for a pure value object. You may always want to have the actual business object, because you will be modifying and specifying the persistence of the object's state from within the same context in which it is created. Architectures for larger scale implementations have a separate Web tier and enterprise tier, and thus, they may want to distinguish between

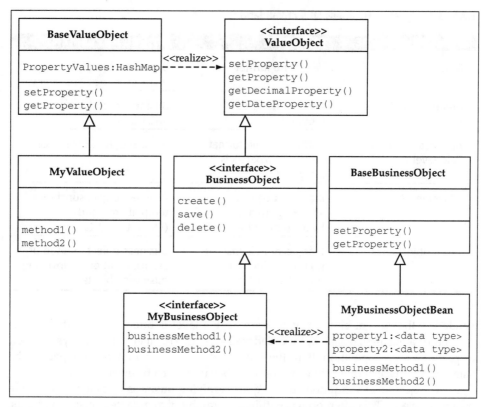

Figure 3.2   UML Representation of Value Object and Business Object Structure.

the two as previously described. Either approach can work quite well depending on the application requirements. For the purposes of the examples in this book, option number two will be used where the value objects and business object share a common interface hierarchy but have separate implementation hierarchies.

Figure 3.2 represents this design in UML (Unified Modeling Language).

Object Validation and Error Handling

Validation at the property level has already been discussed. The remaining sets of validations for a given business object are:

- Object-level validation
- Cross object-level validation

Object-level validation edits require checking multiple property values in an object and applying some business rule. An example of this might be a minimum balance allowed for different account types. A savings account might have a higher minimum balance than a checking account, so this edit would first look at the account type before

Table 3.1 Types of Business Object Validation

VALIDATION TYPE	EXAMPLE	WHERE IMPLEMENTED
Data type	Valid date format	Business object base class `validate, setProperty`
Required field checks	Account number required	Business object base class `validate`
Application-specific field level	SSN must have format xxx-xx-xxxx where x is integer 0–9	`PropertyHandler` class
Object level	If account type is 'checking', minimum balance must be > $100	Business object subclass template method (i.e. `blfValidate`)
Cross-object level	If an account is inactive, no transactions can be posted against it	Business object method or service component invoking business objects

validating the current balance. Validation at this level is often encapsulated in one method of a business object, aptly called `validate`. This method is always invoked as part of a `save` operation. Both the `save` and `validate` methods are part of the standard interface because they are common behaviors of a business object.

Cross object-level validation edits require applying business rules across multiple business objects. This often occurs within a hierarchy of aggregated business objects. An example of this might be a business rule edit that prevents any new transaction objects from being posted against an inactive account. These types of validations are typically implemented in another business method or in a service-based component that uses the business objects, although they can also be a part of the parent object's `validate` method.

Table 3.1 summarizes all of the different types of validation within a business object and where they occur. Note that there is a `blfValidate` method that is referred to for object-level validation. This is a business object subclass method that will be discussed in the next chapter on using the base class as a template for common behaviors.

The `Account` validation example might look like this if you assume that a checking account has a $100 minimum balance and a savings account has a $50 dollar minimum balance.

```
public void validate() throws ValidationException
{
    BigDecimal balance = null;
    try
    {
        // Get hold of the current balance.
        balance = getDecimalProperty("currentBalance");

        // If this is a checking account, compare the
        // balance against its minimum.
```

```
        if (getProperty("type").equals("C"))
        {
            if ((balance.compareTo(
                new BigDecimal("100.00"))) == -1)
            {
                throw new ValidationException(
                    "Minimum balance is not met " +
                    "for checking account");
            }
        }

        // If this is a savings account, compare the
        // balance against its minimum.
        if (getProperty("type").equals("S"))
        {
            if ((balance.compareTo(
                new BigDecimal("50.00"))) == -1)
            {
                throw new ValidationException(
                    "Minimum balance is not met " +
                    "for savings account");
            }
        }
    }
    catch (PropertyException pe)
    {
        throw new ValidationException(pe.getMessage());
    }
}
```

NOTE String literals in these code samples are kept for readability, but in production code, these are often better kept as constants in the case of property names and in resource files in the case of error messages.

There is a new class mentioned in this code snippet that has not been seen yet, the `ValidationException` class. When a business error was encountered, a `ValidationException` was thrown with the error message to be displayed to the user. Luckily, this example had only one possible error condition in it. If more validations had been required, you might have noted the error condition and continued the validation processing so that you could sum up all of the known errors and present the user with the entire list for convenience.

Managing Business Errors

In the case where there are multiple validations, an error list utility would be helpful. This utility class could manage a collection of business errors and integrate them with their message definitions in resource files. This would provide a nice way to simplify these `validate` methods, especially those where multiple validations are taking place.

BEST PRACTICE Use an error utility class to consistently and effectively manage business errors in your application.

This error utility would be able to do the following things:

- Manage a list of business errors and informational messages
- Integrate errors with their user message templates that include run-time data substitution
- Associate errors with particular properties if applicable
- Report whether there are any business errors that warrant a transaction rollback

This error mechanism will eventually integrate with a number of application services, such as transaction management and logging, and possibly even page navigation for the Web front end. The error list utility class should first encapsulate the functions previously defined and then it can be extended and used further within the Business Object Architecture to accomplish the integration goals.

In the foundation layer metadata, a set of error keys that map to user messages in a resource file can be defined. You may also want to define different types of errors that get processed differently. For example, you could use this mechanism to transport informational messages back to the user. On a successful transaction, you might want to show a message that provides a confirmation number. You can use the `ErrorList` utility to track this message, which also has a key and a substitution value. However, you do not want this message to cause the transaction to fail because it is only for informational purposes. If you use this utility to do this, perhaps a better name for it would be `MessageList`, but the name `ErrorList` will be used to convey the idea that it also integrates with error handling and transaction management. Remember that if an actual error is held in the list, you will want to roll back the transaction. Another type of error you might want is a critical type error. In most normal error cases, you want to continue processing and possibly add more errors to the list so you can show the user the entire set at once. But, what if an error is so severe that you don't want to continue processing any longer because it just doesn't make sense? For example, in a `transferFunds` business method, one of the two accounts may not exist. It would not make sense to continue in this condition and check whether there were sufficient funds for the transfer because the transaction couldn't take place anyway. A critical error is closely related to an exception condition, and the error utility may want to immediately throw a `ValidationException` if a critical error is added to the list.

Thus, the basic types of errors to be defined are:

Informational.   Message to be sent to the user that does not affect the transaction

Error.   Message to be sent to the user that eventually causes a transaction rollback

Critical.   Message to be sent to the user that immediately causes a transaction rollback

There may be other levels that might fit in between these that can be created, but these represent the primary distinctions in processing.

The `ErrorList` interface might look like this:

```
public class ErrorList
{

    public void addError(String errorKey;

    public void addError(String errorKey,
                         String arg1);

    public void addError(String errorKey,
                         String arg1,
                         String arg2);

    public void addError(String errorKey, String [] args);

    public boolean isTransactionSuccess();

    public int getNumberOfErrors();

    public void throwExceptionIfErrors()
        throws ValidationException;

}
```

The primary method is `addError`, which takes an array of arguments. The methods that take individual `String` arguments are added for convenience. You also want a convenient method such as the `isTransactionSuccess` method to indicate whether there are any errors in the list that warrant a transaction rollback.

How do you know what type a given error key represents? You can define the error keys in the metadata and provide a type for them, or you can also override the `addError` method and let the client provide the type at run time. A nice solution is to combine the two and give the client the opportunity to override the default type defined in the metadata. To do this, you would add the following method to your `ErrorList` class:

```
public void addError(String errorKey,
                     String [] args,
                     int     type);
```

You can define constants for the different error types for ease of use. The account `validate` example could be rewritten using the error utility as follows:

```
ErrorList error = new ErrorList();

try
{
    // Get hold of the current balance.
    BigDecimal balance =
        getDecimalProperty("currentBalance");
```

```
        // Validations for a checking account
        if (getProperty("type").equals("Checking"))
        {
            // Validate that the balance is above
            // the minimum allowed.
            if ((balance.compareTo(
                new BigDecimal("100.00"))) == -1)
            {
                errorList.addError("CHECKING_MIN_BALANCE",
                                balance.toString());
            }
        }

        // Validations for a savings account
        if (getProperty("type").equals("Savings"))
        {

            // Validate that the balance is above
            // the minimum allowed.
            if ((balance.compareTo(
                new BigDecimal("50.00"))) == -1)
            {
                errorList.addError("SAVINGS_MIN_BALANCE",
                                balance.toString());
            }
        }
    }
    catch (PropertyException pe)
    {
        errorList.addError("GEN_PROPERTY_ERROR",
                        pe.getMessage());
    }
```

You can add the error definitions to the business object metadata. There are three errors in the last code sample that could be defined as follows:

```
<BusinessErrors>
  <BusinessError name="CHECKING_MIN_BALANCE" type="ERROR"
    message="Minimum balance not met for checking account" />
  <BusinessError name="SAVINGS_MIN_BALANCE" type="ERROR"
    message="Minimum balance not met for checking account" />
  <BusinessError name="GEN_PROPERTY_ERROR" type="ERROR"
    message="A general property error occurred: {0}" />
</BusinessErrors>
```

NOTE The easiest substitution format to use is that of `java.text.MessageFormat` because you can use this utility class in Java to do the substitution for you. It simply states that each ordered substitution value with the index x be specified as {x} in the message string.

The `ErrorList` utility needs a data structure to hold each bit of error information. You can define a `BusinessError` class that holds this data for a single error. It really acts only as a data structure with getter and setter methods. Its definition is shown as follows:

```
public class BusinessError {

    private String     errorKey;

    // Default is standard error.
    private int        type = TYPE_ERROR;

    private String [] substitutionValues;

    public final static int TYPE_INFO     = 1;
    public final static int TYPE_ERROR    = 2;
    public final static int TYPE_CRITICAL = 3;

    // Get and set methods to follow...
}
```

The eventual resulting list of these errors for a given transaction can be sent back to the User Interaction Architecture. Within the presentation logic for displaying errors, the error key can be used to look up the error messages from a resource file or configuration service. The corresponding arguments can be substituted into the message and the error list can be displayed to the user.

When to Use Exceptions Instead of Errors

A general rule of thumb to follow regarding the use of exceptions and errors is summarized by the following Best Practice statement.

BEST PRACTICE Use exceptions whenever processing should halt immediately in a given method. Business errors should then be used wherever processing may continue in the case of an error occurring.

An extension to this rule is that the `ErrorList` utility should be used anytime there are multiple edits taking place in a method. It is used to manage a list of errors, and it works well for this purpose. However, how should the business object client be notified if errors have occurred in a given method? You don't usually want to make the `ErrorList` the return argument for a method because business methods usually want to return some result. Rather than create return objects that encapsulate both an `ErrorList` and a return value, you can use the `ValidationException` class to hold the list of errors that occurred.

THOUGHT You can use the `ValidationException` to communicate a list of errors back to a business object client.

If business errors are encountered in a method, you can throw a `Validation-Exception` to notify users of the situation. This takes advantage of the power of exceptions in a programming language, which is the fact that your main body of code can assume that operations are successful. A catch block at the bottom, outside of the main processing logic, can be used to handle the error conditions. To use exceptions for communicating business errors, a method is added to the `ErrorList` utility that creates a `ValidationException` with the list of errors already in it.

```java
public ValidationException createValidationException()
{
        // Add error list to ValidationException.
        ValidationException ve =
            new ValidationException(
                "ValidationException: see error list",
                getErrorList());
        return ve;
}
```

The `ValidationException` class would look like this:

```java
public class ValidationException extends Exception
{
    /*
     * The list of errors that occurred
     */
    protected ArrayList errorList = null;

    /*
     * Default constructor
     */
    public ValidationException(String message)
    {
        super(message);
    }

    /*
     * Construct a validation exception with error list.
     */
    public ValidationException(String message,
                                ArrayList errorList)
    {
        super(message);
        this.errorList = errorList;
    }

    /*
     * Returns the list of BusinessError objects that caused
     * this validation exception
     */
    public ArrayList getErrorList()
```

```
    {
        return errorList;
    }
}
```

You can then use the `throwExceptionIfErrors` method on `ErrorList` to communicate errors to the client. This method automatically creates the exception and throws it if any errors occurred. It can be invoked at the end of all `validate` methods.

```
public void throwExceptionIfErrors()
    throws ValidationException
{

    if (!isTransactionSuccess())
    {
        ValidationException ve = createValidationException();
        throw ve;
    }
}
```

For each business method that requires validation, either you can create an instance of `ErrorList`, or you can give all of the business objects an `ErrorList` by adding it as a member variable to the base class. In this case, you need to add a `clear` method to be able to empty the list of errors so you can start fresh within a given method. You now have all of the tools you need on the `ErrorList` to manage business errors successfully. So that there is an example in which multiple errors can occur, assume also that the account number must start with a 'C' for checking accounts (such as 'C1234') and an 'S' for savings accounts (such as 'S5678'). The `validate` method code would now look like this:

```
public void validate() throws ValidationException
{

    // Create an error list for the validation.
    ErrorList error = new ErrorList();

    try
    {
        // Get hold of the current balance.
        BigDecimal balance =
            getDecimalProperty("currentBalance");

        // Validations for a checking account
        if (getProperty("type").equals("C"))
        {
            // Validate that the account number starts
            // with a 'C'.
            if (!(getProperty("number").startsWith("C")))
            {
                errorList.addError("INVALID_ACCT_NUMBER",
                                getProperty("number"));
            }
        }
```

```
                    // Validate that the balance is above
                    // the minimum allowed.
                    if ((balance.compareTo(
                        new BigDecimal("100.00"))) == -1)
                    {

                        errorList.addError("CHECKING_MIN_BALANCE",
                                            balance.toString());
                    }
                }

                // Validations for a savings account
                if (getProperty("type").equals("S"))
                {
                    // Validate that the account number starts
                    // with an 'S'.
                    if (!(getProperty("number").startsWith("S")))
                    {
                        errorList.addError("INVALID_ACCT_NUMBER",
                                        getProperty("number"));
                    }

                    // Validate that the balance is above
                    // the minimum allowed.
                    if ((balance.compareTo(
                        new BigDecimal("50.00"))) == -1)
                    {
                        errorList.addError("SAVINGS_MIN_BALANCE",
                                            balance.toString());
                    }
                }
            }
            catch (PropertyException pe)
            {
                errorList.addError("GEN_PROPERTY_ERROR",
                                    pe.getMessage());
            }

            // Use the error list utility to automatically throw
            // an exception with the business errors
            // if any occurred.
            errorList.throwExceptionIfErrors();
        }
```

The validate example can be used as a sort of template for all validation methods. You start out by creating an ErrorList instance, applying the validation edits within a try-catch block, and then calling the throwExceptionIfErrors method at the end. The try-catch block is used primarily to catch system exceptions or other general type exceptions. In this example, the PropertyException is thrown if a given property name does not exist for a business object. This is an exception thrown by the business logic foundation layer. It is analogous to a system level exception that you would not normally expect. Note that the code maps this exception to one of the defined business errors. This is a common technique you will want to use for system-level exceptions such as a RemoteException or a SQLException. These exceptions that have technical messages will not make much sense to a user, so they should be wrapped with some kind of meaningful business error that has been defined.

BEST PRACTICE Map system-level exceptions to defined business errors that have more meaningful messages that can be presented to the users.

Note that if you allow a system-level or other run-time exception to be thrown out of a transactional EJB method, the container automatically rolls back the transaction and throws either a RemoteException or a TransactionRolledBack-Exception depending on the transaction context. In these cases, the client needs to handle these exceptions and extract the wrapped exception to determine the cause of failure.

The addError method can automatically throw a ValidationException if a critical level error is added to the bucket. Thus, you can use ValidationException as the primary application-level exception. The other categories of exceptions already mentioned include system-level exceptions such as database failures, resource unavailable, and other run-time Java exceptions. Many of these conditions can be handled in try-catch blocks at the highest level of the application code on the EJB tier, usually the service component. Again, these conditions need to be mapped to one of the defined business errors so that consistent error messages can be provided to the user. You can also provide the option to show or log the actual exception stack trace, which will be of interest to any support staff, but not usually of much interest to the end user. Remember that if you allow EJBException or other run-time exceptions to be thrown out of a transactional method, the container rolls back the transaction automatically. If you use an application exception, such as ValidationException, then you need to explicitly roll back the transaction using EJBContext.setRollbackOnly().

The Application Exception Hierarchy

Currently a ValidationException class is defined that holds a list of business errors. However, you may have other types of application exceptions that have messages you want to display to the user. Thus, you can move the error list member variable to a base class for the application exceptions. There are already two exception classes that can extend from this base class, ValidationException and Property-Exception. The base class can be called BlfException. This also allows you to generically handle exceptions from the business logic foundation if you so choose. The application exception hierarchy now looks like Figure 3.3.

Integrating Business Errors with Transaction Management

Whenever a business error occurs, it means that a validation has failed and any database updates that have already occurred should be rolled back to ensure data integrity.

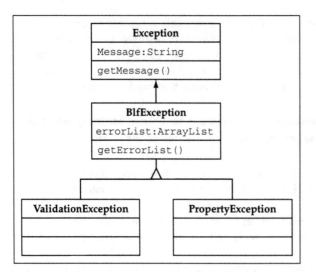

Figure 3.3 Application Exception Hierarchy.

The ErrorList utility uses a standard mechanism for communicating these business errors back to the client, the ValidationException. You can easily integrate this error-handling mechanism into the transaction management service by adding some logic around the call to the validate method. This logic will actually be used in the save template method in the business object base class, which is discussed in the next chapter.

Here is the logic for an Entity Bean business object. The method getEntity-Context is simply a convenience getter method added for the required Entity-Context property of the bean. Remember that you need to explicitly vote to roll back the transaction in the case of an application exception.

```
try {
    // Perform the object validation.
    validate();

} catch (BlfException ex) {
    // If a business error occurred,
    // vote to roll back the transaction
    // and rethrow the exception that
    // has the error list inside to
    // communicate to the client.
    getEntityContext().setRollbackOnly ();
    throw ex;
}
```

If you were dealing with a Java business object, you would need to move this logic back to the Session Bean service component that wrapped the business object, because you would need to access the session context in order to vote for the transaction rollback. When you look at the chapter on the Service-Based Architecture, you will see that there may be cases in which you would want to move this logic out to the highest level of the transaction anyway.

Revisiting Validation in the Property-Handler Mechanism

There is now a mechanism for handling and communicating business errors to the client. Earlier, a set of property-handling classes was created that included validation. In the previous code examples, an exception was thrown with a message to describe the error. In order to simplify the client code and provide consistency across the application, the business error mechanism can also be used in the property-handler classes.

One thing to note in the property-handling classes is the fact that processing usually halts after the first error. Thus, you might not normally be inclined to use the ErrorList mechanism that provides more value for handling multiple errors. However, you still want to be able to use the standard error message and communication mechanism. To do this now, you would need to create the ErrorList, add an error, and then throw the exception. It seems as if it would be nice in this case to have a convenience method for a single error. Thus, the following methods can be added to ErrorList for this purpose.

```
public static ArrayList createSingleErrorList(String errorKey);
public static ArrayList createSingleErrorList(String errorKey,
                                              String arg1);
public static ArrayList createSingleErrorList(String errorKey,
                                              String [] args);
```

The DateHandler class, discussed earlier, that manages date properties might look like this now using these new single error methods:

```
public class DateHandler
    implements PropertyValidator, PropertyHandler {

    public void validateProperty(Object value)
        throws ValidationException {

        // Since this method can be invoked with any
        // object type, you need to check.
        if (value instanceof Date) return;

        if (value instanceof String) {
            try {
                SimpleDateFormat sdf =
                    new SimpleDateFormat("MM/dd/yyyy");
                java.util.Date myDate =
                    sdf.parse((String)value);
            } catch (java.text.ParseException pe) {
                throw new ValidationException(pe.getMessage(),
                    ErrorList.createSingleErrorList(
                        "GEN_PROP_ERR", (String) value));
```

```
                    }
            } else {
                throw new ValidationException(
                    "Invalid object type for date property.",
                    ErrorList.createSingleErrorList(
                                        "INVALID_PROP_TYPE"));
            }
        }


        // Property handler methods to follow...
    }
```

If this same error mechanism is used throughout the code, the front end of the application and the service components become much simpler. This will be illustrated in the upcoming chapters on these topics.

Cross Object Validation

Validation that goes across multiple business objects may reside either in a business object method, a separate validator class, or in a service-based component that uses multiple business objects. This type of validation logic can also use the error list utility.

This case presents some different challenges in terms of integrating the error list with the overall transaction management service. There may be business errors occurring in multiple business objects as well as in a service component. You need a way to merge errors coming from different sources. If all of the components are using `ErrorList`, you can put an `add` method that takes a collection of errors and adds them to the list. This can be defined as:

```
public void addErrors(ArrayList errors);
```

As an example, assume you have the `Customer` object that aggregates an `Address` object. The customer has a PIN number that must be a set of digits but cannot be a set of repeating digits. The address, among other validations, requires that the state be one of the valid fifty United States. The customer validation method might be implemented by using the new `add` method on `ErrorList`:

```
public void validate() throws BlfException
{
    // Initialize the error list.
    ErrorList errorList = new ErrorList();

    try
    {
        /*
         * Validate the PIN value.
         */
        String PIN = getProperty("pin");

        // The PIN digits cannot be all of the same number
```

```
        // (for example, 2222).
        char c = pin.charAt(0);
        int length = pin.length();
        boolean bOtherCharFound = false;
        for (int i = 1; i < length; i++)
        {
            if (pin.charAt(i) != c)
            {
                bOtherCharFound = true;
                break;
            }
        }
        if (!bOtherCharFound)
        {
            errorList.addError("PIN_SAME_NUMBER", pin);
        }

        // Validate the aggregated address object.
        getAddress().validate();

    }
    catch (ValidationException ve)
    {
        // Add any business errors from the address
        // in with your current list of errors.
        errorList.add(ve.getErrorList());
    }
    catch (PropertyException pe)
    {
        errorList.addError("GEN_PROPERTY_ERROR",
                        pe.getMessage());
    }


    // Throw a validation exception if any
    // errors occurred.
    errorList.throwExceptionIfErrors();

}
```

Impact of EJB 2.0 on Exception Handling

There is one small side effect of the introduction of local interfaces into the EJB specification. Method invocations through the remote interface always led to the possibility of a RemoteException being thrown if a system-level error occurred. Well, a local interface is not allowed to throw a RemoteException under any of these conditions. Thus, there is an analogous, but separate, hierarchy of local exceptions that can be thrown from a local method invocation. Applications using the EJB 2.0 specification should be aware of this and handle such cases similarly to their corresponding system-level exceptions.

Best Practices for Implementing Business Objects: Part One

This section summarizes the best practices discussed in this chapter for managing properties and handling errors, two primary elements of implementing business objects.

Use Strict Encapsulation

Use strict encapsulation by always accessing properties through their accessor method in order to avoid conditions in which property values are not initialized. CMP Entity Beans actually force this behavior due to the use of abstract accessor methods on the bean implementation class.

Use a Standard Interface for Business Objects

Have business objects implement a standard interface so that they may be referred to generically throughout application and foundation layer code. Consider the use of a generic property management interface to provide convenient methods for property access. The standard business object interface can extend a standard value object interface so that services can generically refer to either one when no distinction is required.

Consider the Use of Metadata-Driven Components and Reusable Property Definitions

Metadata can be used to define the validation and formatting of property values. A business object base class can provide an extendible foundation that uses the metadata to implement reusable property definitions. This approach or some equivalent mechanism should be used where possible to avoid redundant code and ensure property validation takes place.

Develop a Consistent Approach for Managing Business Errors

A consistent, manageable approach to error handling is an important aspect of business objects in transactional applications. Use a mechanism such as the error list utility discussed in this chapter to manage a list of business errors and communicate them back to clients in a standard way. A standard application exception can be used to communicate a list of errors back to a client. The error list utility should be integrated into the transaction management service to ensure data integrity.

Using Exceptions

Use exceptions when processing should be halted or to communicate a list of errors to a client. Use the error list utility and business errors when multiple validations are taking place or processing should continue in the case of a business error.

Presenting Meaningful Error Messages to the User

Map all system-level exceptions to defined business error codes. Each business error code should have a defined error message that is meaningful to the user. The defined messages can also be used as templates so that run-time values can be added to provide additional information.

Summary

Two primary responsibilities of business objects are to manage the properties of the object and handle any errors that occur. Property management includes providing accessor methods, formatting and converting property values, and validating basic data. In addition to field-level validations, error handling as a whole includes business logic validations at the object level and cross-object level, as well as general exception handling. The approach for all of these responsibilities can be implemented in a similar way for either Java classes or Entity Beans.

These practices provide the basics for building business object components that can manage data and handle errors. The next chapter builds on these concepts to provide a complete business object implementation. The topics of persistence, object relationships, and the use of the template method pattern are discussed next.

Building Business Objects: Persistence, Relationships, and the Template Method Pattern

This chapter first discusses the persistence implementation used by the business objects. It then looks at how object relationships are implemented, in particular, aggregated objects that are managed by their parent object. The Template Method pattern will also be applied to the business object hierarchy in order to execute common business logic that is customized for each object. A primary example of this is the `save` template that is executed before the object is saved to the database.

Object Persistence

This section discusses four different options for implementing business object persistence:

- JDBC (Java Database Connectivity) using explicit data objects
- JDBC using a metadata-driven approach
- Use of persistence frameworks and object-relational mapping tools
- CMP Entity Beans

The first three options can be used with either Java business objects or BMP Entity Beans. The fourth option is limited to persistence that is invoked through the container's Entity Bean mechanism. Keep in mind that persistence vendors are likely to have products that work with both Java classes and Entity Beans, so the distinction between options 3 and 4 can be viewed as the use of the Entity Bean CMP specification to invoke the persistence service as opposed to Java Data Objects (JDO) or some other specification.

Keep in mind that if you use a Java business object implementation, you must implement your own persistence layer or else use a third-party solution. Even if you use Entity Beans, you may still want to use your own collection and database query services for efficiency. The JDBC utility class referred to in these chapters can be used in either approach to perform regular database queries outside the scope of business objects. For collections or lists of objects, there is a section in this chapter on collection services. For now, however, the focus is on single business objects and their persistence in a database.

JDBC in Explicit Data Objects

In this option, you can add methods to the standard business object interface to deal with object persistence. As discussed earlier, the actual database logic is isolated in a set of objects called the data-access layer. The actual implementation of the persistence methods on the business object (for example, `insert`, `update`, and `delete`) will delegate their responsibilities to the corresponding data-access object. A typical pattern for implementing this logic involves populating a value object with the property values and passing it as an argument to the corresponding data-access method. The data object methods could take the individual property values as arguments, but it is usually easier to wrap them all in a value object, especially if value objects are used throughout the Business Object Architecture. Assume for the persistence examples that the properties of the `Account` object (for example, ID, account number, and current balance) are all stored in the same table named 'account.'

The persistence methods of the `Account` object might look like this:

```
public class Account
{

    public void insert() throws PersistenceException
    {

        // Construct a value object from the property values.
        AccountData valueObject = new AccountData();
        valueObject.setId(generateNewAccountId());
        valueObject.setNumber(getNumber());
        valueObject.setCurrentBalance(getCurrentBalance());

        // Delegate the persistence to the data-access object.
        AccountDataObject dataObject
                = new AccountDataObject();
```

```
        dataObject.insert(valueObject);
    }


    public void update() throws PersistenceException
    {
        // Construct a value object from the property values.
        AccountData valueObject = new AccountData();
        valueObject.setId(getId());
        valueObject.setNumber(getNumber());
        valueObject.setCurrentBalance(getCurrentBalance());

        // Delegate the persistence to the data-access object.
        AccountDataObject dataObject
                = new AccountDataObject();
        dataObject.update(valueObject);
    }


    public void delete() throws PersistenceException
    {
        // Construct a value object from the property values.
        // You need only the key value to delete the instance.
        AccountData valueObject = new AccountData();
        valueObject.setId(getId());

        // Delegate the persistence to the data-access object.
        AccountDataObject dataObject
                = new AccountDataObject();
        dataObject.delete(valueObject);
    }


}
```

The actual data object methods construct the proper SQL statement, marshal the property values, and execute the statement. As an example, the `update` method would look like this:

```
public int update(AccountData account)
    throws PersistenceException
{

    Connection conn = null;
    Statement stmt = null;
    PreparedStatement pStmt = null;
    int result = 0;

    try
    {
        // Obtain a database connection from
        // a defined data source named 'txDataSource'.
        InitialContext ctx = new InitialContext();
```

```
            DataSource ds =
                (DataSource) ctx.lookup("txDataSource");
            conn = ds.getConnection();

            // Create a prepared statement to update
            // your object to the database.
            pStmt = conn.prepareStatement("update account " +
                "set number = ?, balance = ? where id = ?");
            pStmt.setString(1, account.getNumber());
            pStmt.setBigDecimal(2,
                    account.getCurrentBalance());
            pStmt.setString(3, account.getId());

            // Execute the statement.
            result = pStmt.executeUpdate();

        }
        catch (SQLException sqlEx)
        {
            throw new PersistenceException("SQLException" +
              " occured in account update. Message=> " +
              sqlEx.getMessage());
        }
        catch (Exception ex)
        {
            throw new PersistenceException("General exception"
                + " occured in account update.  Message => "
                + ex.getMessage());
        }
        finally
        {

            if (pStmt != null)
            {
                try {
                    pStmt.close();
                } catch (SQLException sqlEx) {
                    sqlEx.printStackTrace();
                }
            }
            if (conn != null)
            {
                try {
                    conn.close();
                } catch (SQLException sqlEx) {
                    sqlEx.printStackTrace();
                }
            }
        }

        return result;

    }
```

Best Practices for Using JDBC within an Application

If you choose to use straight JDBC code within your application, there are a few best practices that are important to consider. The first of these is to isolate the JDBC logic in one place.

Isolating JDBC Access

One reason to isolate JDBC access is to ensure that resources are properly managed. For example, database connections are pooled by the application server and can be accessed in J2EE application servers through the JDBC data source. It is important that these resources be closed and returned to the pool immediately after being used by enterprise components. Any resources that are left open can cause resource contention among transactions and lead to degradations in scalability. Thus, it is a good practice to isolate the actual JDBC code in one place so that it can be implemented correctly and handle all error conditions appropriately.

BEST PRACTICE Isolate the JDBC logic to execute a SQL statement in a common utility class. This prevents every application developer from having to write this common logic and ensures that all resources are closed properly.

A JDBC utility class can be created that provides methods to execute prepared statements. This utility can be used in the data object methods to actually perform the JDBC operations. The logic to marshal the data and construct the proper prepared statements is done in the particular data object, but the execution of the query or statement is delegated to the utility class. A core method used to execute a PreparedStatement within the JDBCUtility follows:

```
public int executePreparedStatement(String sql,
                                    ArrayList args)
    throws ValidationException
{

    int result = 0;
    try
    {
        // Obtain a database connection from
        // a defined data source named 'txDataSource'.
        InitialContext ctx = new InitialContext();
        DataSource ds =
            (DataSource) ctx.lookup("txDataSource");
        conn = ds.getConnection();

        // Create a prepared statement from the given SQL.
        pStmt = conn.prepareStatement(sql);

        // Loop through the arguments and set them in
        // the prepared statement according to object type.
        int count = 1;
```

```java
        Iterator iter = args.iterator();
        while (iter.hasNext())
        {
            Object arg = iter.next();
            if (arg instanceof String)
            {
                pStmt.setString(count,
                                (String) arg);
            }
            if (arg instanceof BigDecimal)
            {
                pStmt.setBigDecimal(count,
                                    (BigDecimal) arg);
            }
            //
            // and so on for the other data types...
            //
            count++;
        }

        // Execute the statement.
        result = pStmt.executeUpdate();

    }
    catch (SQLException sqlEx)
    {
        throw new PersistenceException("SQLException " +
            " occured in account update. Message=> " +
            sqlEx.getMessage());
    }
    catch (Exception ex)
    {
        throw new PersistenceException("General execption"
            + " occured in account update.  Message => "
            + ex.getMessage());
    }
    finally
    {

        if (pStmt != null)
        {
            try {
                pStmt.close();
            } catch (SQLException sqlEx) {
                sqlEx.printStackTrace();
            }
        }
        if (conn != null)
        {
            try {
```

```
                     conn.close();
                } catch (SQLException sqlEx) {
                     sqlEx.printStackTrace();
                }
            }
        }


        return result;
    }
```

This method takes a SQL prepared statement string and a collection of arguments to be put into the prepared statement. It takes care of obtaining the connection, creating the prepared statement, and setting all of the property values. It wraps all of this logic in a try-catch block and closes all of the resources in a `finally` clause. In order to deal with the different data types, it uses the `instanceof` operator to determine what type of object each argument is. This small example only uses Strings and BigDecimals, but the complete implementation would simply be expanded to check for all possible data types.

The account data object `update` method that uses this utility would become much simpler. In fact, it would be responsible only for creating the SQL and passing the correct arguments from the object's property values. Because the JDBC logic is implemented in one place, the rest of the data objects now become simpler, and they will have a smaller code base than if this logic was duplicated. It can also ensure that exception conditions are handled properly in one place, and this does not have to be implemented everywhere. This also makes your testing easier because this utility gets used quite often.

The account data object `update` method would now look like this:

```
public int update(AccountData account)
    throws ValidationException
{

    // Create an instance of a database utility class.
    JDBCUtility dbutil = new JDBCUtility();

    // Populate a collection of arguments
    // to go into the prepared statement.
    ArrayList args = new ArrayList(3);
    args.add(account.getNumber());
    args.add(account.getCurrentBalance());
    args.add(account.getId());

    // Use the utility to execute the SQL update.
    // The utility populates the prepared statement
    // based on the object type of the argument.
    return dbutil.executePreparedStatement(
        "update account set number = ?, balance = ? "
      + "where id = ?", args);

}
```

Externalizing the SQL from the Code

The data-access object for the `Account` business object has the update SQL string directly in the `update` method code. This works fine; but what if you need to change the column names in your database? You will need to go into the data-access object code to make the change, recompile the application, and redeploy it to the application server. In some organizations, the database schemas are relatively stable, and this does not often become an issue. In other organizations and also in many software development projects, the database schemas are often being changed quite frequently. Thus, it can be beneficial to externalize the SQL from the data-access objects so that it does not need to be hard-coded into the application.

BEST PRACTICE Externalize the SQL from the Java code to minimize impacts to the application if the database schema changes. The SQL strings could be stored in a resource file or in the XML metadata and then referenced from the application. This approach also makes it fairly easy to determine impacts to the application if the database schema changes because the SQL is all in one searchable repository.

It would be fairly easy to modify the `executePreparedStatement` method on `JDBCUtility` to take a SQL identifier rather than the actual SQL string itself. The SQL identifier could be used to look up the actual SQL string from a metadata file. This allows you to simply make the change in the configuration file rather than in the code itself.

JDBC Using a Metadata-Driven Approach

Now that the majority of the JDBC logic is encapsulated in a utility class, the primary responsibilities of the data-access object are to generate the correct SQL string and map the property values to the database columns. If the business objects are configured using metadata, as was described in the last chapter, you can accomplish both of these tasks by using the metadata and a bit of extra logic in the business object base class.

To do this, you need to add the database information to the business object metadata. You need to know the corresponding database column names for each property. You also need to know what the key fields are in order to construct the `WHERE` clause for `UPDATE` and `DELETE` statements. At the business object level, you need to know what database table this object is stored in.

The business object metadata will now look like this:

```
<Metadata>
  <BusinessObject name="Account" table="account">
<Property name="id" dbname="id" type="String"
        required="true" key="true" />
```

```
<Property name="number" dbname="number" type="String"
        required="true" />
<Property name="currentBalance" dbname="balance"
        type="Decimal" required="true" />
  </BusinessObject>
</Metadata>
```

The property metadata can now do the mapping between object properties and database columns. Previously, this knowledge was hard-coded into the data access method. Given the set of column names and an indicator of which one is the key field, you can generate INSERT, UPDATE, and DELETE SQL strings for the object. The logic to do this can be done generically in the business logic foundation, because it is entirely driven by the metadata.

The metadata is stored in memory in an object called BusinessObject-Metadata. Because the SQL strings are the same every time, you can put the logic to create the SQL at this level. That way, it needs to be generated only once and can then be shared by all business object instances of the same type. Thus, BusinessObject-Metadata has the following methods:

```
public String getSelectSQL();
public String getInsertSQL();
public String getUpdateSQL();
public String getDeleteSQL();
```

These methods construct the SQL string based on the metadata. As an example, in the case of update, it creates a StringBuffer starting out with UPDATE <tablename> SET and then iterates through the property list adding <columnName> = ? for each property. Finally, a WHERE clause is added based on the key field indicated by the property list.

You can now implement a generic update method in the business object base class. It will not have very much logic in it. It will simply instantiate a JDBCUtility class and invoke the update method passing the business object itself as an argument. The generic update method on JDBCUtility will implement the following logic:

1. Obtain the UPDATE SQL string from the business object metadata.

2. Iterate through the property metadata and map between property names and database columns, setting the property value in the prepared statement. (Note that the order of the property metadata must be the same for the SQL generation and execution. Using ordered collections in the implementation of the metadata classes takes care of this.)

3. Invoke the generic executePreparedStatement logic of the JDBCUtility that is already encapsulated.

You now have a metadata-driven persistence layer that works with any business object configured according to the metadata schema previously shown. This is a very powerful utility that you can use in the development of the Business Object Architecture if you want to write your own persistence.

NOTE There are also other ways to accomplish the same goal of automating the business object persistence functions. One popular way is to code-generate each of the data access objects for each business object based on the same set of metadata. Either method works just fine. There are a number of development tools that use code generation to build data-access objects given a database, object model, or set of metadata. The metadata-driven utility classes previously described are nice if you do not have one of these code-generation utilities available to you. One other minor benefit of this approach is a smaller code base due to repetitive code blocks being eliminated through isolation in one place. However, the generated data objects may be slightly faster due to their explicit nature, which requires slightly less processing to determine data types, and so on.

Using Persistence Frameworks and Object-Relational Mapping Tools

Before deciding to use you own JDBC persistence solution, keep in mind that it is fairly easy to build a simple persistence layer to use with the business objects. Either a metadata-driven approach or code generation can be used to rapidly implement one-to-one object to table data objects. The difficult part is building a persistence layer that is both highly optimized and uses more complex object-relational mapping schemes. Optimization techniques such as preventing unnecessary updates, updating only modified fields, and using aggressive- and lazy-loading strategies can greatly affect the overall performance of an application. These things are not trivial to implement. Outside of using Entity Beans, there are a handful of products available, both commercial and open source, that can be used for this purpose. For the examples in this book, a popular open-source package called Castor is used.

NOTE Castor is a part of the ExoLab project. Examples in this book are based on version 0.9.3.9. Castor can be found on the Internet at http://castor.exolab.org/.

Persistence as a Component Service

Most Java-based persistence packages, including Entity Beans, use a similar approach. After looking at the Entity Bean approach next, it will be evident that the two business object implementations are actually quite similar in nature. A deployment configuration is used to map object properties to database tables and columns. The persistent objects are required to implement the JavaBeans naming convention for properties so that reflection can be used to access them at run time. A layer of abstraction is usually placed over the persistence functions, so that in most cases, an application developer does not explicitly control when the persistence events are invoked. A factory or query mechanism is usually used to locate object instances. The save, or update, to the database is usually triggered by the container committing the transaction. The abstract approach allows the tools to use different optimization strategies underneath the covers such as aggressive or lazy loading. Object creation and deletion is, however, still an explicit event that is invoked by the application developer. A standard interface is used to provide callback methods for persistence events. This allows the application code to be informed of the event and react to it, if necessary. For example, these interfaces include notification methods for the object being loaded from the database and stored to the database. This is analogous to the `ejbLoad` and `ejbStore` methods on the `EntityBean` interface.

Persistence Using Castor

The Castor project provides data-binding from Java objects to SQL tables, XML documents, and a number of other sources. This chapter looks only at the SQL mapping functionality, which is implemented in the `org.exolab.castor.jdo` package. An object using Castor for persistence must implement the `Persistent` interface. This standard interface has the callback methods for persistence events. In addition to the notification methods described earlier, this includes a method to give the object a reference to the Castor `Database` object. The `Database` object represents the connection to the database and is used to add Java objects to the persistence engine for a given transaction. It has methods to create, update, and remove `Persistent` objects. Existing objects are located using the `OQLQuery` class. This class is used to implement a subset of the object query language as defined by the Object Management Group (OMG) 3.0 Object Query Language (OQL) Specification. OQL is used to select objects from the database. The basic structure of OQL is similar to SQL, except that OQL refers to objects and properties rather than tables and columns. For a full description of these classes, please refer to the production documentation available on the OMG Web site.

Because persistent objects must implement a Castor-specific interface, a version of the business object base class, called `CastorBaseBusinessObject`, is created specifically for the Castor implementation. This base class, as well as all of the foundation classes related to Castor, is put in the `blf.castor` package of the reference architecture. The application business objects now implement both the `Business-Object` interface and Castor's `Persistent` interface. A basic outline of the base class, `CastorBaseBusinessObject`, is shown here:

```
package blf.castor;

import org.exolab.castor.jdo.Database;
import org.exolab.castor.jdo.Persistent;
import blf.*;

public class CastorBaseBusinessObject
    implements Persistent, BusinessObject {

    protected HashMap attributeMetadata;
    protected BusinessObjectMetadata bom;
    protected ErrorList errorList;
    protected String objectName;
    private   Database _db;
```

```java
public CastorBaseBusinessObject(String objectName) {
    try {
        bom =
            MetadataManager.getBusinessObject(objectName);
        attributeMetadata = bom.getPropertyMap();
        this.objectName = objectName;

    } catch (BlfException be) {
        be.printStackTrace();
    }
}

public CastorBaseBusinessObject(String objectName,
                               ValueObject valueObject) {
    try {
        bom =
            MetadataManager.getBusinessObject(objectName);
        attributeMetadata = bom.getPropertyMap();
        setProperties(valueObject);
        this.objectName = objectName;

    } catch (Exception e) {
        e.printStackTrace();
    }
}

//
// Implementation of business object methods to follow,
// that is, standard property management methods, and so on
//

//
// Castor JDO callbacks
//
public void jdoPersistent( Database db ) {
    _db = db;
}

public void jdoTransient() {
    _db = null;
}

public Database getDatabase() {
    return _db;
}

public Class jdoLoad(short accessMode) {
    return null;
}

public void jdoBeforeCreate( Database db ) {
}
```

```
        public void jdoAfterCreate() {
        }

        public void jdoStore(boolean modified){
        }

        //
        // Rest of JDO callbacks to follow...
        //
}
```

NOTE In this code snippet, you see that no real work is being done in the persistence callbacks. One reason for this is that the create methods cannot be overloaded as is the case with `ejbCreate` methods on Entity Beans. In the next section on object creation and instantiation, you will see that some of these lifecycle events for Castor business objects are handled by the business object factory mechanism. This pattern will be used to abstract the persistence mechanism and simplify its integration into the Business Object Architecture. Once the Entity Bean implementation is discussed, you will see the persistence callbacks being used to implement business logic template methods.

The `Account` business object using Castor as an object-relational mapping tool then extends `CastorBaseBusinessObject` and implements the JavaBeans convention for properties. The basic code for the `Account` object is shown here:

```
package bank.castor;

import blf.*;
import org.exolab.castor.jdo.Database;
import org.exolab.castor.jdo.Persistent;
import java.math.BigDecimal;
import java.util.Date;

public class Account extends CastorBaseBusinessObject
    implements java.io.Serializable, Persistent, BusinessObject
{

    private String id;
    private String number;
    private String type;
    private BigDecimal currentBalance;
    private Date lastModifiedDate;


    public Account() {
        super("Account");
    }
```

```java
public Account(ValueObject values) {
    super("Account",values);
}


public String getId() {
    return id;
}
public void setId(String value) {
    id = value;
}

public String getNumber() {
    return number;
}
public void setNumber(String value) {
    number = value;
}

public String getType() {
    return type;
}
public void setType(String value) {
    type = value;
}

public BigDecimal getCurrentBalance() {
    return currentBalance;
}
public void setCurrentBalance(BigDecimal value) {
    currentBalance = value;
}

public Date getLastModifiedDate() {
    return lastModifiedDate;
}
public void setLastModifiedDate(Date value) {
    lastModifiedDate = value;
}


//
// Business methods to follow...
//
}
```

The deployment configuration to map the account's properties to the database is shown here. In this case, it maps all of the properties to a single table named 'account.' Note that the 'field' and 'sql' types have different values in some cases to properly map between SQL data types and Java data types. The `mapping.xml` file for the example is as follows:

```
<!DOCTYPE databases PUBLIC
  "-//EXOLAB/Castor Mapping DTD Version 1.0//EN"
  "http://castor.exolab.org/mapping.dtd">
<mapping>
  <class name="bank.castor.Account"
         identity="id">
    <description>Account</description>
    <map-to table="account" />
    <field name="id" type="string" >
      <sql name="id" type="varchar"/>
    </field>
    <field name="type" type="string">
      <sql name="type" type="char" dirty="check" />
    </field>
    <field name="number" type="string">
      <sql name="number" type="char" dirty="check" />
    </field>
    <field name="currentBalance" type="big-decimal">
      <sql name="balance" type="decimal" dirty="check" />
    </field>
    <field name="lastModifiedDate" type="date">
      <sql name="last_modified_date" type="date"
           dirty="check" />
    </field>
  </class>
</mapping>
```

Entity Bean Container-Managed Persistence

The abstract persistence approach used by EJB 2.0 CMP has already been discussed. It follows a very similar pattern to the Castor business object implementation. A common base class for Entity Beans, called `EntityBaseBusinessObject`, which implements the `EntityBean` interface, is created. Rather than having explicit property members, abstract accessor methods are declared on the business object subclasses that adhere to the JavaBeans property specification. The shell of the base class is shown here:

```
package blf.entity;

import blf.*;
import javax.ejb.*;


public class EntityBaseBusinessObject implements EntityBean {
```

```java
protected HashMap attributeMetadata;
protected BusinessObjectMetadata bom;
protected ErrorList errorList;

protected EntityContext myContext;


public EntityBaseBusinessObject(String objectName) {
    try {
        bom =
            MetadataManager.getBusinessObject(objectName);\
        attributeMetadata = bom.getPropertyMap();
    } catch (BlfException be) {
        be.printStackTrace();
    }
}

public EntityBaseBusinessObject(String objectName,
                               ValueObject valueObject) {
    try {
        bom =
            MetadataManager.getBusinessObject(objectName);
        attributeMetadata = bom.getPropertyMap();
        setProperties(valueObject);
    } catch (BlfException be) {
        be.printStackTrace();
    }
}

//
// Entity Bean callback methods
//
public void ejbActivate() {
}

public void ejbPassivate() {
}

/**
 * Creates a new instance of the business object
 * and generates a new unique object identifier
 *
 */
public String ejbCreate()
    throws CreateException, BlfException {

    blfCreate(null);
    return null;
}

public void ejbPostCreate() throws BlfException {
```

```java
        blfPostInsert();
    }

    public String ejbCreate(ValueObject initialValues)
        throws CreateException, BlfException {

        try {
            blfCreate(initialValues);
        } catch (BlfException be) {

            // NOTE: This should be called only if
            // the create was done in a transactional
            // context. Your architecture always has
            // business objects wrapped with a
            // transactional service object, but
            // you may want to check here first
            // if there is a transaction running.
            getEntityContext().setRollbackOnly();
            throw be;
        }
        return null;
    }

    public void ejbPostCreate(ValueObject initialValues)
        throws BlfException {

        blfPostInsert(initialValues);
    }

    public void ejbLoad() {
    }

    public void ejbRemove() {
    }

    public void ejbStore() {
    }

    public void setEntityContext (EntityContext newContext) {
        myContext = newContext;
    }

    public void unsetEntityContext() {
        myContext = null;
    }

    public EntityContext getEntityContext() {
        return myContext;
    }
}
```

NOTE In this implementation, there are not business logic template methods for all of the entity callbacks, as is the case with `ejbCreate` which calls a template method `blfCreate`. You could easily add hook methods for all of these, or you can always override any of these methods in the subclass if you want to implement functionality at these points.

The `Account` Entity Bean extends this base class and declares the accessor methods as abstract.

```
package bank.entity;

import java.math.BigDecimal;
import java.sql.Date;
import blf.entity.*;
import blf.*;

public abstract class AccountBean
    extends EntityBaseBusinessObject {

    public AccountBean() {
        super("Account");
    }

    //
    // Property methods, that is, CMP fields
    //
    public abstract String getId();
    public abstract void setId(String value);

    public abstract String getNumber();
    public abstract void setNumber(String value);

    public abstract String getType();
    public abstract void setType(String value);

    public abstract BigDecimal getCurrentBalance();
    public abstract void setCurrentBalance(BigDecimal value);

    public abstract Date getLastModifiedDate();
    public abstract void setLastModifiedDate(Date value);

    //
    // Business methods to follow...
    //
}
```

The `ejb-jar.xml` standard deployment file is used to define the CMP fields.

```
<!DOCTYPE ejb-jar PUBLIC '-//Sun Microsystems, Inc.//DTD
    Enterprise JavaBeans 2.0//EN'
    'http://java.sun.com/j2ee/dtds/ejb-jar_2_0.dtd'>
```

```
<ejb-jar>
  <description>
      <![CDATA[Bank Sample Application]]>
  </description>
  <display-name>Bank Sample Application</display-name>

    <entity>
      <description>
        <![CDATA[Models a bank account]]>
      </description>
      <ejb-name>Account</ejb-name>
      <local-home>bank.entity.AccountLocalHome</local-home>
      <local>bank.entity.AccountLocal</local>
      <ejb-class>bank.entity.AccountBean</ejb-class>
      <persistence-type>Container</persistence-type>
      <prim-key-class>java.lang.String</prim-key-class>
      <reentrant>False</reentrant>
      <cmp-version>2.x</cmp-version>
      <abstract-schema-name>Account</abstract-schema-name>
      <cmp-field>
        <field-name>id</field-name>
      </cmp-field>
      <cmp-field>
        <field-name>type</field-name>
      </cmp-field>
      <cmp-field>
        <field-name>number</field-name>
      </cmp-field>
      <cmp-field>
        <field-name>currentBalance</field-name>
      </cmp-field>
      <cmp-field>
        <field-name>lastModifiedDate</field-name>
      </cmp-field>
      <cmp-field>
        <field-name>customerId</field-name>
      </cmp-field>
      <primkey-field>id</primkey-field>
      <ejb-local-ref>
        <ejb-ref-name>Transaction</ejb-ref-name>
        <ejb-ref-type>Entity</ejb-ref-type>
        <local-home>bank.TransactionLocalHome</local-home>
        <local>bank.TransactionLocal</local>
        <ejb-link>Transaction</ejb-link>
      </ejb-local-ref>
    </entity>
```

The specific mapping from the bean's properties to database tables is done in a vendor-specific manner in another XML deployment descriptor.

Business Object Creation and Instantiation

It is a good idea to abstract the particular persistence mechanism you are using from your business object client code. Enterprise JavaBeans enforce a similar abstraction through the use of the Home interface. The EJB Home interface is used to create new instances of enterprise beans, discover existing instances, and delete existing instances. In the case of Castor, the Object Query Language (OQLQuery) object is used to discover existing instances and the Database object is used to add and remove instances. If you were using Java business objects, you could create an analogous factory object that was used to access and create business objects. There are a couple benefits to this approach. The primary reason is to simplify the code that uses your business objects. For example, the service components can use an EJBFactory class to handle the JNDI lookup of the Home interface and the invocation of the finder method. In the case of Castor, you can create some standard methods that encapsulate the use of OQL to look up existing objects. This speeds up the development of the service components by factoring out redundant code. It also allows you the opportunity to optimize these steps if you choose to do so. For example, in some cases, you can cache the Home interface and save yourself a JNDI lookup. This technique will be discussed in detail in the Performance chapter. Another benefit of this approach is that it isolates the client code as much as possible so that there is less of an impact if you choose to change your persistence implementation. Finally, you can also standardize the error handling for cases for which an existing business object is not found.

BEST PRACTICE Whether you are using Entity Beans or regular Java business objects, use a factory method (Erich Gamma et al. 1995) abstraction to create and discover instances of business objects. This simplifies the client code and provides a hook for potential future optimizations such as caching EJB Home interfaces. You can create a BusinessObjectFactory utility class to do this. In the case of EJBs, the BusinessObjectFactory can use the EJB Home interface to look up the Entity Bean. In the case of Java business objects, you can instantiate and populate the proper business object within the BusinessObjectFactory.

Figure 4.1 represents the object model for this pattern.

NOTE This pattern as shown can be used to create both EJB, Java, and Castor business object implementations. Three implementation classes, EJBFactoryImpl, JavaFactoryImpl, or CastorFactoryImpl, can either implement the same interface or extend from a common base class. This can be helpful if a project uses both Java business objects and Entity Beans or if there is consideration for future migrations between the different options. This additional flexibility may not be required on projects in which a clear direction has been set on the business object implementation model.

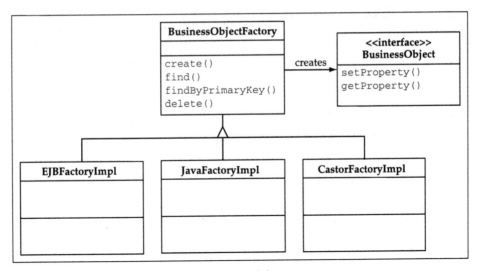

Figure 4.1 BusinessObjectFactory Object Model.

The business object factory can also help automate some common steps in components that update or create business objects. On both insert and update operations, you will often have data that you want to use to populate the business object coming from the User Interaction Architecture. One common data structure used for this is the value object. Thus, you can overload your factory method for creation to take a value object, and the BusinessObjectFactory can populate it using the setProperties(ValueObject valueObject) method. Another common operation you need to perform is to create an existing instance, represented by a value object, into a business object instance that you can use. This function can also be provided by the BusinessObjectFactory.

The factory methods are sometimes used to invoke Template Methods for insert and update operations. The Template Method pattern, described later in this chapter, is a complimentary technique that is used with the object factory to automate common steps while also providing extensibility for object specific logic.

The methods for the base factory might look like this:

```
/*
 * Create a new instance of a business object.
 */
public static Object create(String objectName)
    throws BlfException;

/*
 * Create a new instance of a business object with initial
 * values.
 */
```

```
public static Object create(String objectName,
                               ValueObject initialValues)
    throws BlfException;

/*
 * Discover an instance of a business object
 * with the given key object.
 */
public static Object findByPrimaryKey(String objectName,
                                   Object keyObject)
    throws BlfException;

/*
 * Discover an instance of a business object using
 * the given query and arguments.
 */
public static Object find(String objectName,
                          String queryId,
                          ArrayList args)
    throws BlfException;
```

Each method takes the business object name as an argument. In the business logic foundation, this equates to the name of the object in the metadata. In the case of Entity Beans, this can then be mapped to the JNDI name. It is a good idea to make the JNDI name and the metadata name the same if you are using the foundation layer with Entity Beans. In the case of Java objects, the factory uses the metadata to determine the business object class name so that it can instantiate the object. In the EJB implementation, it uses a JNDI lookup to find the Home interface and call the appropriate method.

Creating New Instances

The `create` methods for a Castor implementation will now be discussed. To create a new object instance, you add a method to your business object interface, `create`, that sets any initial values and creates any generated key fields values for the new instance. Thus, the factory `create` methods would look like this:

```
public class CastorFactoryImpl extends BusinessObjectFactory {

    /*
     * Create a new instance of a business object.
     */
    public static BusinessObject create(String objectName,
                                        Database db)
        throws BlfException {

        return create(objectName, null, db);
    }

    /*
     * Create a new instance of a business object
```

```java
 * with initial values.
 */
public static BusinessObject create(String objectName,
        ValueObject valueObject, Database db)
    throws BlfException {

    // Obtain the business object metadata.
    BusinessObjectMetadata bom =
        MetadataManager.getBusinessObject(objectName);

    // Determine the business object class name.
    String busObjectClass = bom.getBusObjClass();

    // Use a helper method to create an instance
    // of the given class.
    BusinessObject instance =
        createObjectInstance(busObjectClass);

    // Invoke the business object create template method.
    if (valueObject != null) {
        instance.create(valueObject);
    } else {
        instance.create();
    }


    try {
        // Add to the persistence engine.
        db.create(instance);
    } catch (PersistenceException pe) {
        throw new BlfException(pe.getMessage());
    }

    // Invoke the postCreate business object method.
    if (valueObject != null) {
        instance.postCreate(valueObject);
    } else {
        instance.postCreate();
    }

    // Return the newly created instance to the client.
    return instance;
}

/*
 * Helper method to create an instance of a class and
 * cast to BusinessObject interface
 */
private static BusinessObject createObjectInstance(
    String className) throws BlfException {
```

```
        BusinessObject busObject = null;
        try {
            busObject = (BusinessObject)
                (Class.forName(className)).newInstance();
        } catch(Exception e) {
            throw new BlfException(e.getMessage());
        }
        return busObject;
    }
}
```

The new business object `create` method looks like this:

```
public void create() throws BlfException {
    create(null);
}


public void create(ValueObject initialValues)
    throws BlfException {

    // If initial values were supplied, populate
    // the properties from the value object.
    if (initialValues != null) {
        setProperties(initialValues);
    }


    // From the business object metadata (bom), get the
    // key field and check to see if you need to automatically
    // generate a key value.
    PropertyMetadata prop = bom.getKeyField();
    if (prop.isAutogen()) {

        // Use primitive algorithm - value of
        // current milliseconds.
        String keyValue = getNextKeyValue();
        setProperty(prop.getName(),keyValue);
    }


    // Call the template method for preinsert logic.
    if (initialValues == null) {
        blfPreInsert();
    } else {
        blfPreInsert(initialValues);
    }
}
```

There is now a fair amount of logic in the process. This accomplishes the goal of encapsulating the process of object creation and simplifying the business object client logic.

NOTE This example also needs to implement a unique primary key generation mechanism in the `getNextKeyValue` method. There has been much written about this topic, so this section won't go into detail, but a few thoughts on the topic are appropriate. If you don't mind locking in on a database, database sequences can work well. Otherwise, your factory implementation can grab a block of numbers to allocate in the case of sequential numeric key values. The blocks can be centrally defined by a database table. This avoids going to the database for the purpose of getting a key value on every create operation. Most persistence tools also support a variety of mechanisms for primary key generation. Castor supports a 'max' key value, UUIDs, and database sequences in addition to a few other popular techniques. You can specify the usage of these techniques in the `mapping.xml` configuration file.

The business object interface now looks like this with regards to persistence:

```
public interface BusinessObject extends ValueObject {

    /*
     * Persistence methods
     */

    // The create methods are invoked by BusinessObjectFactory.
    // They do not need to be invoked directly by business
    // object clients, but they do need to be in the standard
    // interface so they can be referred to in the factory.
    public void create() throws BlfException;
    public void create(ValueObject initialValues)
        throws BlfException;
    public void postCreate() throws BlfException;
    public void postCreate(ValueObject initialValues)
        throws BlfException;

    // A template method for saving an object.  This method
    // is invoked directly by business object clients.
    public void save() throws BlfException;

    // This method is invoked by the BusinessObjectFactory
    // to remove an instance.
    public void delete() throws BlfException;
}
```

One thing to note is that the save method does not actually trigger the update to the database in the case of Castor business objects and Entity Beans. As mentioned earlier, this event is triggered by the transaction being committed. The save method, however, acts as a template method for business logic, which is discussed in the next section. It encapsulates any validation and presave logic that you want executed before the object is saved to the database.

NOTE There is a bit more flexibility when you use standard Java objects rather than Entity Beans in regard to object creation. Regular Java classes can be instantiated in memory and populated throughout the course of a transaction without touching the database until the end. You can create the instance, generate key field values, and call additional business methods to populate other properties of the object before invoking the actual database INSERT operation. Persistence engines like the Entity Bean model can cause a SQL INSERT after the ejbCreate method concludes. From this point, additional business methods that update object properties require that the ejbStore method be used when the transaction commits. This can be inefficient if you want to perform additional logic to populate other properties when creating this object. In the Java model, you can wait and perform one INSERT when you call save as opposed to the Entity Bean model which might require an INSERT and UPDATE operation to accomplish the same thing.

Finding Existing Instances

The lookup methods to find existing business object instances are a bit simpler than the creation methods. In the case of regular Java objects, they can simply use utility methods on the JDBCUtility object to query the database and instantiate the populated business object. For the Castor objects, however, these methods can encapsulate basic object queries used to locate existing instances. A query in OQL is very similar to a SQL query. For example, the query to locate an Account object by its primary key is as follows:

```
SELECT a FROM Account a WHERE id = $1
```

The dollar signs represent placeholders for run-time values to be bound to the query. Remember that the WHERE clause in OQL queries refers to actual property names rather than database columns. OQL queries automatically take care of database joins when the WHERE clause refers to associated objects. As an example, the Account object has a 'customer' property that links it back to the owner of the account. The query to obtain the collection of accounts for a given customer would then be as follows:

```
SELECT a FROM Account a WHERE customer = $1
```

This query would take the primary key property of the customer as an argument.

Find by Primary Key

From these examples, you can see that these queries can easily be generated if you have the information in the business object metadata. Thus, you have the findBy-PrimaryKey method on the CastorFactoryImpl class. This is a static method, so you pass in the Database instance being used by the transaction in order to create the query object. This is needed on all of the persistence methods that use Castor.

```
/*
 * Discover an instance of a business object with the
 * given key object.
 */
public static BusinessObject findByPrimaryKey(
    String objectName, Object keyObject, Database db)
    throws BlfException {

    // Obtain the business object metadata.
    BusinessObjectMetadata bom =
        MetadataManager.getBusinessObject(objectName);

    try {
        // Create the arguments for the
        // OQL string.
        Object [] args = new Object[2];
        args[0] = bom.getBusObjClass();
        args[1] = bom.getKeyField().getName();

        // Create a standard OQL string
        // to look up by primary key.
        String oqlString = MessageFormat.format(
            "SELECT b FROM {0} b WHERE {1} = $1", args);

        // Create the query and bind the
        // arguments.
        OQLQuery busobjOql = db.getOQLQuery( oqlString );
        busobjOql.bind( keyObject );
        QueryResults results = busobjOql.execute();

        // There should be only one object found.
        if ( results.hasMore() ) {
            Object obj = results.next();
            return (BusinessObject) obj;
        } else {
            throw new ObjectNotFoundException(objectName,
                                              keyObject);

        }

    } catch (PersistenceException pe) {
        pe.printStackTrace();
        throw new BlfException(pe.getMessage());
    }
}
```

This method took the query by primary key example discussed earlier and parameterized it into an OQL string template. From the business object metadata, this method fills in the name of the business object and the key field property name. The run-time argument is bound to the query, and it is executed. A singular object is returned to the client, or an `ObjectNotFoundException` is thrown if no object is found. This exception is a subclass of `BlfException` and is used as a standardized way to report this condition. Usually, a search by primary key assumes the existence of an object, so you can regard this as an error condition. The `ObjectNotFoundException` code is shown here:

```
package blf;

public class ObjectNotFoundException extends BlfException {

    public ObjectNotFoundException(String objectName,
                                   Object keyObject) {
        super(objectName + " object not found");

        // Map to a standard application error.
        setErrorList(ErrorList.createSingleErrorList(
            "OBJ_NOT_FOUND", objectName, keyObject.toString()));
    }
}
```

You can then customize the definition of the `OBJ_NOT_FOUND` error message for your application. A basic definition might be defined as follows:

```
OBJ_NOT_FOUND=The {0} object with primary key {1} was not found.
```

NOTE You can see how the `findByPrimaryKey` factory method could also easily be implemented using straight JDBC as well. You could easily generate the SQL just like you generated the OQL. The reference architecture isolates this type of logic in the `JDBCUtility` class.

This example assumed that the object had an object identifier as a primary key field. In most cases, this is the recommended approach for managing objects; however, you may have objects with a more complicated key structure. In lieu of a primary key object, you could use a value object to represent the key structure for the `findByPrimaryKey` method. You could also easily create a specific `PrimaryKey` base class to represent a key object. If you look at what that class would contain, it would have a set of properties that it would need to manage. This is the same thing that a value object does, and it has already been implemented. It generically manages a set of properties. You could use it for this purpose rather than create a bunch of specific key classes for the business objects. Now, if you were using Entity Beans, you would still need that type of artifact (that is, a primary key object with explicit properties) in order to use the component correctly. For the Java implementations, this is not necessary and the standard value object suffices. This approach may make the object purist a bit uncomfortable, and there may be a yearning for creating a subclass of `PrimaryKeyObject` that extends `ValueObject`. This is certainly an option. However, it requires you to convert value objects that come from the front end to a subclass in order to use them for this purpose. This is applicable, of course, only if you are using a value object approach to transport data between tiers. This topic will be discussed in detail in the next chapter on Service-Based Architecture. The eventual decision to have a specific primary key class is purely a design preference, and either choice works well. For the examples in this book, all of the objects have a single object identifier as a primary key.

A General Find Method

You would also like to be able to define different queries for a business object so that you can look up the object by non–key fields or combinations of values. This is analogous to additional finder methods being added to an EJB Home interface. The unique queries for a particular business object are defined by the WHERE clause portion of the SQL or OQL. According to the same principle of isolating JDBC and SQL from the application code, you can define these queries in the business object metadata.

As an example, say you want to look up an account based on the account number. The account number is an external identifier sometimes given as input data from the user as opposed to the primary key identifier in the database. You can define the following in the metadata:

```
<BusinessObject name="Account"
                busObjClass="bank.castor.Account"
                valueObjClass="bank.AccountData" >
   <Property name="id" type="String"
             required="true" key="true" autogen="true" />
   <Property name="number" type="String"
             required="true" />
   <Property name="currentBalance" type="Currency"
             required="true" />
   <Property name="lastModifiedDate" type="Date" />
   <Property name="type" type="String" required="true" />
   <Collection name="byCustomer"
               query="where customer = $1" />
   <Collection name="byNumber" query="where number = $1" />
</BusinessObject>
```

A <Collection> tag was added that defines a WHERE clause for the particular query. The collection has the name 'byNumber' so that you can refer to it in the call to the factory method. The factory appends this query to the base SELECT string, runs the query, and returns the populated business object. For queries that return multiple instances, there are a few options as to how you can handle these cases. You can throw an exception if more than one business object is found. You can also add an additional method to the BusinessObjectFactory such as findCollection, which returns a collection of business objects. This type of operation may be better handled by a collection service if you don't want to deal with all of the results as business objects. Some operations are geared more toward running queries and possibly instantiating business objects from the results. This concept will be discussed in detail in the section on object collection services later in this chapter.

For the example, imagine you have an account search function in your application. It might use the factory as follows to get a handle to an instance of the Account business object identified by the particular account number:

```
ArrayList args = new ArrayList(1);
args.add(accountData.getProperty("number"));
Account account = (Account)
    BusinessObjectFactory.find("Account",
                               "byNumber",
                               args,
                               getDatabase());
```

This code snippet takes an account value object and uses the account number property as an argument to the query. The 'byName' string references the collection defined in the metadata. The number of arguments must match up with the number of references in the query's WHERE clause. The factory could return a `null` if not found or throw an exception if more than one customer record is found in this case.

You can also create a `findCollection` method that returns a collection of business objects. An example of this would be if you want to retrieve the accounts for a given customer. The `byCustomer` query was defined in the metadata that selects the accounts by customer. The following code snippet takes a customer value object and uses the identifier as an argument to the query. The factory returns a collection of business objects that matched the query.

```
ArrayList args = new ArrayList(1);
args.add(customerData.getProperty("id"));
Collection accountList =
    BusinessObjectFactory.findCollection("Account",
                                         "byCustomer",
                                         args);
```

The code to implement these two general find functions follows. The primary work is done in `findCollection`. The individual `find` method simply delegates the call to `findCollection` and throws an exception if more than one object is found. This typically is considered an error condition, since the application using the `find` method expects a single object in return. If no object is found, a `null` is returned. On the other hand, a search on some set of nonprimary key fields does not necessarily imply the existence of objects, so the application code can be allowed to directly handle this condition. Here is the code from `CastorFactoryImpl` for these methods.

```
/*
 * Discover an instance of a business object using the
 * given query and arguments.
 */
public static BusinessObject find(String objectName,
    String queryId, ArrayList args, Database db)
    throws BlfException {

    Object obj = null;

    // Run the collection query and then
    // pick off the first element. There
    // should be only one object
```

```
    // in the result set.
    Collection coll =
        findCollection(objectName,queryId,args,db);
    if (coll.size() > 1) {
        throw new BlfException("Multiple Objects Found",
            ErrorList.createSingleErrorList(
                "MULTIPLE_OBJECTS_FOUND", objectName));
    }
    Iterator iter = coll.iterator();
    if ( iter.hasNext() ) {
        obj = iter.next();
    } else {
        return null;
    }

    return (BusinessObject) obj;
}


/*
 * Discover a collection of business objects using the
 * given query and arguments.
 */
public static Collection findCollection(String objectName,
    String queryId, ArrayList args, Database db)
    throws BlfException {

    // Obtain the business object metadata.
    BusinessObjectMetadata bom =
        MetadataManager.getBusinessObject(objectName);

    // Create the result collection.
    ArrayList results = new ArrayList();

    try {
        // Create the arguments for the
        // OQL string.
        Object [] objArgs = new Object[1];
        objArgs[0] = bom.getBusObjClass();

        // Create a standard OQL string
        // to look up with the given WHERE clause.
        StringBuffer buffer = new StringBuffer(
            MessageFormat.format(
                "SELECT b FROM {0} b", objArgs));
        buffer.append(' ');
        buffer.append(bom.getQuery(queryId));

        // Create the query and bind the
        // arguments.
        String oqlString = buffer.toString();
        OQLQuery busobjOql = db.getOQLQuery( oqlString );
```

```
                int endLoop = args.size();
                for (int loop = 0; loop < endLoop; loop++) {
                    busobjOql.bind( args.get(loop) );
                }

                // There should be only one object found.
                QueryResults queryResults = busobjOql.execute();
                while ( queryResults.hasMore() ) {
                    results.add(queryResults.next());
                }

        } catch (PersistenceException pe) {
            throw new BlfException(pe.getMessage());
        }

        return results;
    }
```

BusinessObjectFactory and Entity Beans

One big advantage to using a factory for Entity Beans is that it greatly simplifies the
process of obtaining a component interface to the EJB. You can encapsulate the context
and JNDI lookup operations and simply provide the business object interface. If you
are using a standard business object interface as discussed in this chapter, you can have
it extend the `EJBLocalObject` interface so that it can also act as an EJB component
interface. The interface hierarchy is shown in Figure 4.2.

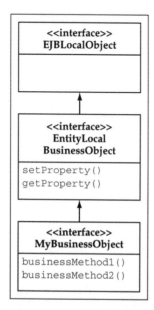

Figure 4.2 EJB Business
Object Interface Hierarchy.

Because this is encapsulating the EJB lookup process, you can also make the process more efficient. JNDI operations can be relatively expensive if used for every business object lookup in a transaction. Thus, the factory can cache the EJB Home interface in order to save a JNDI lookup for each client that obtains a business object. This gives a significant boost to performance for applications that have a large number of business objects involved in a given transaction. This concept is explained fully in the chapter on Performance. This concept also applies to the service components implemented as Session Beans, although there is a slightly different interface for this because the factory operations have a different meaning when referring to stateless components as opposed to specific business object instances.

The factory methods map up directly to the EJB Home interfaces required for Entity Beans. The `create` method and `ejbCreate` methods correspond directly. The `create` interface that takes a value object can be implemented as an override of the `ejbCreate` method that takes the same argument. The `findByPrimaryKey` method is the same, and the `find` method would map up to the specific additional finder methods that are added to the EJB Home interface.

Finding Existing Instances

This section discusses locating an Entity Bean business object by its primary key. The first thing that `EJBFactoryImpl` must be able to do for all of its operations is to obtain hold of the EJB Home interface. This logic can be isolated to a single method so that it can cache the home interfaces later on if you need to do some performance optimizations. It has everything needed to do this except the actual EJB Home interface class itself, which is required in the `narrow` operation. Thus, this class name needs to be added to the business object metadata. As an example, here is the `Account` metadata with the addition in bold:

```
<Metadata>
  <BusinessObject name="Account" busObjClass="bank.Account"
          valueObjClass="bank.AccountData"
          ejbHomeClass="bank.entity.AccountLocalHome">
    <Property name="id" dbname="id" type="String"
            required="true" key="true" autogen="true" />
    ...
    <Property name="type" dbname="type" type="String"
            required="true" />
  </BusinessObject>
</Metadata>
```

NOTE The EJB factory implementation always returns the local interface. Based on previous design discussions, local Entity Beans are used most of the time. The implementation, however, could be easily extended to deal with both local and remote beans.

Here is the `getHomeInterface` method in the EJB factory:

```
/*
 * Helper method to get the EJBHome interface
 */
```

```
public static EJBHome getHomeInterface(String objectName,
            BusinessObjectMetadata bom) throws BlfException
{
    EJBHome home = null;

    try {
        // Get a naming context.
        InitialContext jndiContext = new InitialContext();

        // Get a reference to the Interest Bean.
        Object ref  = jndiContext.lookup(objectName);

        // Get hold of the Home class.
        Class homeClass =
            Class.forName(bom.getEJBHomeClass());

        // Get a reference from this to the
        // Bean's Home interface.
        home = (EJBHome) PortableRemoteObject.narrow(
                                    ref, homeClass);

    } catch (Exception e) {
        throw new BlfException(e.getMessage());
    }

    return home;
}
```

That takes care of getting the Home interface, but it still needs to invoke the findByPrimaryKey method. Well, to do this generically, you won't know the specific home interface class ahead of time, so you have to be able to invoke this method on the fly using reflection methods. You couldn't make a generic base interface for all the business objects because, although you could create a common set of arguments (such as a generic value object as a key structure), each method needs to return the specific business object home interface. Thus, it is probably safer to use reflection methods to accomplish this. The findByPrimaryKey method that has a single key property would look like this:

```
/*
 * Discover an instance of a business object with the given
 * key object.
 */
public static Object findByPrimaryKey(String objectName,
                                    Object keyObject)
    throws BlfException {

    // Obtain the business object metadata.
    BusinessObjectMetadata bom =
        MetadataManager.getBusinessObject(objectName);

    // Get the home interface.
    EJBLocalHome home = getHomeInterface(objectName, bom);
```

```
    // Invoke by findByPrimaryKey method.
    PropertyMetadata keyProp = bom.getKeyField();
    EJBLocalObject busObject = null;

    try {
        // Define the parameter types.
        Class[] parameterTypes = new Class[1];
        if (keyProp.getType().equals("String")) {
            parameterTypes[0] =
                Class.forName("java.lang.String");
        }
        if (keyProp.getType().equals("Number")) {
            parameterTypes[0] =
                Class.forName("java.lang.Long");
        }
        //
        // and so on for the other data types...
        //

        Object[] args = new Object[1];
        args[0] = keyObject;

        // Get a handle to the finder method and invoke it.
        Class homeClass = home.getClass();
        Method findByPK =
            homeClass.getMethod("findByPrimaryKey",
                                parameterTypes);
        busObject = (EJBLocalObject)
            findByPK.invoke(home, args);

    } catch (InvocationTargetException ite) {
        Throwable t = ite.getTargetException();
        if (t instanceof BlfException) {
            throw (BlfException)t;
        } else if (t instanceof FinderException) {
            throw new ObjectNotFoundException(objectName,
                                              keyObject);
        } else {
            throw new BlfException(ite.getMessage());
        }
    } catch (Exception e) {
        throw new BlfException(e.getMessage());
    }

    return busObject;

}
```

To handle objects with multiple key fields, you can extend this logic to implement this method:

```
public static Object findByPrimaryKey(String objectName,
                ValueObject keyObject) throws BlfException;
```

The second argument would be a subclass of ValueObject, or alternatively, you could have this method take a subclass of a PrimaryKeyClass that you created.

The AccountLocalHome interface also had a few finder methods defined specific to the Account bean. They were findByNumber and findByCustomer, which were analogous to the previous examples using the Castor persistence framework. Again, you can see the similarity of the two approaches. Rather than using OQL, J2EE uses an EJB QL to define a portable query language for enterprise beans. EJB QL is also very similar to SQL. These two queries are defined in the ejb-jar.xml deployment descriptor as follows:

```
<entity>
  <description>
    <![CDATA[Models a bank account]]>
  </description>
  <ejb-name>Account</ejb-name>
  ...
  <query>
    <query-method>
      <method-name>findByNumber</method-name>
      <method-params>
        <method-param>java.lang.String</method-param>
      </method-params>
    </query-method>
    <ejb-ql>
      <![CDATA[SELECT OBJECT(a) FROM Account a
               WHERE a.number = ?1]]>
    </ejb-ql>
  </query>
  <query>
    <query-method>
      <method-name>findByCustomer</method-name>
      <method-params>
        <method-param>java.lang.String</method-param>
      </method-params>
    </query-method>
    <ejb-ql>
      <![CDATA[SELECT OBJECT(a) FROM Account a,
               IN (a.customer) AS c WHERE c.id = ?1]]>
    </ejb-ql>
  </query>
</entity>
```

There are a few options with regard to exposing these finder methods. The first option is to allow the business object client to use the factory's helper method to get the EJB's Home interface. The client can then invoke the finder methods directly. A second option would be to implement a find method on EJBFactory that used reflection to invoke the finder method. This continues the theme of abstracting the persistence layer, similar to what was done with the findByPrimaryKey method. In either case, you will want to keep the getHomeInterface method public so that clients can use it to invoke any static business methods available on the home interface.

Creating New Instances

To create new object instances, the EJBFactoryImpl can call the create method on the Home interface for a given Entity Bean. Just like calling the finder method, it will use Java reflection to invoke the method. Because a database INSERT is normally executed by the container at the end of the ejbCreate method for CMP beans, you want to make sure you provide the ability to provide all of the initial values so that you can avoid an UPDATE of this row in the same transaction. Thus, you should always provide an additional create method that takes a set of initial values. You can use the generic value object structure to hold these properties. Thus, for the Account Entity Bean, the local home interface includes these methods:

```
public interface AccountLocalHome extends EJBLocalHome
{
  public AccountLocal create ()
    throws CreateException, BlfException;

  public AccountLocal create (ValueObject initialValues)
    throws CreateException, BlfException;

  public AccountLocal findByPrimaryKey(String id)
    throws FinderException;

  //
  // Additional finder methods
  //
  public AccountLocal findByNumber(String number)
    throws FinderException;

  public Collection findByCustomer(String customerId)
    throws FinderException;
}
```

The factory method to invoke the create methods follows. This code shows the EJBFactoryImpl method that takes the initial values. The first method without arguments is just a simpler version of this one.

```
/*
 * Create a new instance of a business object
 * with initial values.
 */
public static Object create(String objectName,
                            ValueObject valueObject)
    throws BlfException {

    // Obtain the business object metadata.
    BusinessObjectMetadata bom =
        MetadataManager.getBusinessObject(objectName);
```

```
// Get the home interface.
EJBLocalHome home = getHomeInterface(objectName, bom);

EJBLocalObject busObj = null;

try {
    // Define the parameter types.
    Class[] parameterTypes = new Class[1];
    parameterTypes[0] =
        Class.forName("blf.ValueObject");

    Object[] args = new Object[1];
    args[0] = valueObject;

    // Get a handle to the finder method and invoke it.
    Class homeClass = home.getClass();
    Method createWithInitValues =
        homeClass.getMethod("create", parameterTypes);
    busObj = (EJBLocalObject)
        createWithInitValues.invoke(home, args);

} catch (InvocationTargetException ite) {
    Throwable t = ite.getTargetException();
    if (t instanceof BlfException) {
        throw (BlfException)t;
    } else {
        throw new BlfException(ite.getMessage());
    }
} catch (Exception e) {
    throw new BlfException(e.getMessage());
}

return busObj;
}
```

One interesting thing to note about this code sample is the catch block for
InvocationTargetException. Because it is using reflection to invoke the method,
any exception that occurs is wrapped with this exception. You want the Blf-
Exception with its list of errors to be the actual exception thrown back to the client
so that the error handling works as it normally does.

And finally, you have the ejbCreate implementation on the Entity Bean base
class, which delegates its work to its corresponding method, blfCreate. The method
getEntityContext is simply a convenience getter method added for the required
EntityContext property of the bean.

```
public String ejbCreate(ValueObject initialValues)
    throws RemoteException, CreateException, BlfException
{
    try {
        blfCreate(initialValues);
    } catch (BlfException be) {
```

```
            // NOTE: This should be called only if
            // the create was done in a transactional
            // context. Your architecture always has
            // business objects wrapped with a
            // transactional service object, but
            // you may want to check here first
            // if there is a transaction running.
            getEntityContext().setRollbackOnly();
            throw be;
        }
        return null;
    }

    public void blfCreate(ValueObject initialValues)
        throws BlfException, RemoteException
    {
        // If initial values were supplied, populate
        // the properties from the value object.
        if (initialValues != null) {
            setProperties(initialValues);
        }

        // From the business object metadata (bom), get the
        // key field and check to see if you need to automatically
        // generate a key value.
        PropertyMetadata prop = bom.getKeyField();
        if (prop.isAutogen()) {

            // Generate the new key value and set the
            // property.
            String keyValue = getNextKeyValue();
            setProperty(prop.getName(),keyValue);
        }

        // Call the template method for preinsert logic.
        blfPreInsert();
    }

    public void ejbPostCreate(ValueObject initialValues)
        throws RemoteException
    {
        blfPostInsert();
    }

    // Template method - Base class implementation is empty.
    public void blfPreInsert() throws BlfException {
    }

    // Template method - Base class implementation is empty.
    public void blfPostInsert() {
    }
```

There are a couple of things to note in this bit of code:

- It explicitly votes to roll back the transaction if the ejbCreate fails due to an application exception thrown during validation. In most cases, the Entity Beans are wrapped by a transactional Session Bean, although you can optionally vote to roll back the transaction if you catch the exception in the Session Bean. This code snippet shows how to create a self-contained component that makes no assumptions about the transactional context of the client. In either case, make sure that the home interface create methods are declared to be transactional.

- To set the initial values, it reuses the same bulk setter method (setProperties) that takes a ValueObject.

- In the ejbCreate and ejbPostCreate, it invokes the template methods blfPreInsert and blfPostInsert, which can be optionally implemented by the specific business object subclasses.

Delete Operations

The delete operation should also be invoked through the business object factory. These method implementations are fairly straightforward and follow a similar pattern as did their predecessors. Like some of the earlier methods, the delete methods take the object name and key object as parameters. They then invoke the corresponding remove method on either the EJB Home interface or the persistence engine interface.

Aggregated Objects

Business objects often aggregate other business objects. In object designs with good encapsulation, it is the responsibility of the parent business object to manage instances of child objects. For example, refer back to the bank's object model. The Account object may aggregate zero-to-many Transaction business objects that represent different types of account transactions such as deposits, withdrawals, and fees incurred against an account. Thus, when the deposit method on the Account object is invoked, it is the responsibility of the Account object to create a new Transaction instance and have its state persist in the database. If the Account is required to calculate total deposits for a given month, it may need to iterate through all of its Transaction instances and sum up the total of all deposit-type transactions.

Managing Aggregated Objects

The parent object is often responsible for the following actions:

- Providing accessors (get and set methods) and maintaining referential integrity
- Cascading validation and persistence (a 'save' template) within a transaction
- Cascading deletes

The EJB implementation of container-managed relationships (CMR) is discussed first. Other Java persistence frameworks such as the Castor examples handle the concept of aggregated objects in a similar manner. The EJB 2.0 specification provides component services to manage the aspects of aggregated objects described earlier, including local interfaces as a lightweight mechanism to communicate between the components.

Access Methods

Just as Entity Beans define get and set methods for CMP fields, they also define accessor methods for aggregated business objects. These properties are defined as CMR fields in the `ejb-jar.xml` deployment descriptor. Most containers offer get methods that use the concept of lazy instantiation to make using the parent object more efficient. This means that the object does not instantiate the aggregated objects until the get method is invoked, that is, until it is needed. Otherwise, instantiating an `Account` object just to manipulate the account type would also mean instantiating all of its aggregated `Transaction` objects.

As an example, take the `Customer` object, which aggregates a single `Address` object. The `CustomerBean` is defined to have an address property with the following methods for this one-to-one relationship:

```
public abstract CustomerLocal getCustomer();
public abstract void setCustomer(CustomerLocal customer);
```

The `Customer` object also has zero-to-many aggregated `Account` objects. In this relationship, the `Account` object has a customer property that points back to its owner. For this one-to-many relationship, accessors are defined that use collections. In practice, the set method that takes a collection is rarely used. Typically, the client gets the collection and then adds or removes objects from it. The accessor methods follow:

```
public abstract Collection getTransactions();
public abstract void setTransactions(
                        Collection transactions);
```

The code to implement these accessor methods on an Entity Bean is supplied by the container in its generated subclasses.

THOUGHT If you want the business object clients to be able to access the aggregated components, you need to define these methods in the local interface as well. For convenience, you can also define standard get and set methods for related objects in the base class and the standard business object interface. This allows you to deal with aggregated objects in a generic manner, similar to the way properties are handled. You can also add these relationships to the business object metadata to verify that you are dealing with a valid relationship.

You can add the get and set relationship methods to the version of the standard business object interface for Entity Beans. This interface now looks like this

```
public interface EntityLocalBusinessObject
    extends EJBLocalObject {

    /**
     * Template methods
```

```
    */
    public void save() throws BlfException;

    public void delete() throws BlfException;

    public void validate() throws BlfException;

    /**
     * Property management methods
     */
    public void setProperty(String propertyName, Object value)
        throws PropertyException;

    public String getProperty(String propertyName)
        throws PropertyException;
    public int getIntProperty(String propertyName)
        throws PropertyException;
    public BigDecimal getDecimalProperty(String propertyName)
        throws PropertyException;
    public Date getDateProperty(String propertyName)
        throws PropertyException;

    public void setProperties(ValueObject valueObject)
        throws BlfException;
    public ValueObject getValueObject();

    /**
     * Relationships management methods
     */
    public void setRelationship(String cmrName,
                               EntityLocalBusinessObject object)
        throws BlfException;
    public void setRelationship(String cmrName,
                               Collection coll)
        throws BlfException;
    public EntityLocalBusinessObject getOneToOneRelationship(
                                               String cmrName)
        throws BlfException;
    public Collection getOneToManyRelationship(String cmrName)
        throws BlfException;
}
```

You can add a <Relationship> tag to the metadata to define the relationship. The account metadata for Entity Beans might look like the following:

```
<BusinessObject name="Account"
               valueObjClass="bank.AccountData"
               ejbHomeClass="bank.entity.AccountLocalHome">
  <Property name="id" type="String" required="true"
           key="true" autogen="true" />
  ...
  <Property name="type" type="String" required="true" />
```

```
    <Relationship name="transactions" multiplicity="many" />
</BusinessObject>
```

The name of the relationship should be the same as the name of the CMR field. This metadata defines the relationship in the similar manner to what you must do in the ejb-jar.xml deployment descriptor. As another example, the Customer object has two different relationships that would be defined as follows:

```
<BusinessObject name="Customer"
                valueObjClass="bank.CustomerData"
                ejbHomeClass="bank.entity.CustomerLocalHome">
   <Property name="id" type="String" required="true"
             key="true" autogen="true" />
    ...
   <Relationship name="address" multiplicity="one" />
   <Relationship name="accounts" multiplicity="many" />
</BusinessObject>
```

The standard get and set methods on EntityBaseBusinessObject are fairly straightforward. They can be treated basically like any other property, although you get to ignore the formatting and validation aspects. These methods would be implemented as follows:

```
public void setRelationship(String cmrName,
                       EntityLocalBusinessObject object)
    throws BlfException {

    try {
        // Invoke the CMR set method.
        PropertyUtils.setProperty(this,cmrName,object);

    } catch (Exception ex) {
        throw new BlfException(ex.getMessage());
    }

}


public void setRelationship(String cmrName,
                        Collection coll)
    throws BlfException {

    try {
        // Invoke the CMR set method.
        PropertyUtils.setProperty(this,cmrName,coll);

    } catch (Exception ex) {
        throw new BlfException(ex.getMessage());
    }

}
```

```java
public EntityLocalBusinessObject
          getOneToOneRelationship(String cmrName)
    throws BlfException {

    try {
        // Invoke the CMR set method.
        Object obj =
            PropertyUtils.getProperty(this,cmrName);
        return (EntityLocalBusinessObject)obj;

    } catch (Exception ex) {
        throw new BlfException(ex.getMessage());
    }
}

public Collection getOneToManyRelationship(String cmrName)
    throws BlfException {

    try {
        // Invoke the CMR set method.
        Object obj =
            PropertyUtils.getProperty(this,cmrName);
        return (Collection)obj;

    } catch (Exception ex) {
        throw new BlfException(ex.getMessage());
    }
}
```

Cascading Save and Validation Operations

Whenever you save a parent object that aggregates another business object, you want to validate and save any instantiated child objects as well. In the Entity Bean model, all updates to aggregated objects are also saved because all Entity Bean methods and object creations can be defined as transactional. However, if you are using dependent Java objects, you also want to trigger their persistence to the database when the Entity Bean is being saved. You can perform this logic in the `ejbStore` method. If you are using the relationship metadata approach described earlier, you can also automate this process. This concept can be used for object validation as well as persistence. This technique will be discussed in detail in the next section when the `save` template is discussed.

Cascading Deletes

A similar concept applies also to delete operations. EJB 2.0 allows you to define cascading deletes as a deployment property of Entity Beans that have container-managed relationships. This means that any aggregated objects will also be deleted when the parent object is removed. If you are using dependent Java objects, you would be responsible for this yourself, although you could use a similar pattern to the one described above for updates and validation.

The Account and Transaction Example

The withdraw and deposit methods on AccountBean each create a Transaction object to record the corresponding event. They use the getTransactions method to obtain the collection of transaction objects in order to add a new one. The code for the withdraw method follows. It is overloaded to allow a transaction description to be supplied.

```
public void withdraw(BigDecimal value)
    throws BlfException {

    withdraw(value,null);
}

public void withdraw(BigDecimal value,
                     String transactionDescription)
    throws BlfException {

    // Ensure that this account will not be
    // overwithdrawn.
    BigDecimal currBalance =
        getDecimalProperty("currentBalance");
    if (currBalance.compareTo(value) < 0) {
        throw new ValidationException("Insufficient Funds",
            ErrorList.createSingleErrorList(
            "INSUFFICIENT_FUNDS",currBalance.toString())));
    }

    // Remove the amount from the balance.
    setProperty("currentBalance",
                currBalance.subtract(value));

    // Create a record of the transaction.
    TransactionData transData = new TransactionData();
    transData.setProperty("type","W");
    transData.setProperty("amount",value.negate());
    if (transactionDescription == null) {
        transData.setProperty("description",
                              "Normal Withdraw");
    } else {
        transData.setProperty("description",
                              transactionDescription);
    }
    TransactionLocal transaction = (TransactionLocal)
        EJBFactoryImpl.create("Transaction",transData);
    Collection coll = getTransactions();
    coll.add(transaction);

    // Invoke the save template.
    save();
}
```

Object Collection Services

The previous example dealt with a collection of `Transaction` business objects in order to add one to the `Account`. This is just one case of many in which you end up dealing with a list of business objects in an application. In other situations, the circumstances could be different. You may need to deal with these collections outside of the scope of an individual business object or within a service component. Or in many other cases, it may be for a read-only operation, or else you may need to go through the collection and update only some subset of the list. These types of operations are so common that it makes sense to provide a utility to easily manage collections of objects. An `ObjectList` JDBC utility class can be created that provides a consistent way to implement these operations more efficiently than might normally be done throughout an application.

Whether the business objects are implemented as Java classes or Entity Beans, business objects are usually more heavyweight than just a data structure such as a value object. Thus, the `ObjectList` can provide a collection of value objects that can be iterated. If you are only going to read the list, this becomes especially important for Entity Beans because of the potential performance issues. Even if you are only going to update a subset of the list, you might want to get the list as value objects and then only instantiate the respective business objects when you determine an update is necessary.

> **BEST PRACTICE** Managing a list of objects for data retrieval or for selective updates is a common operation in business applications. Consider the use of a utility class that consistently and effectively manages collections of objects for you. If Entity Beans are used as the business object implementation, you can also use the collection utility to get a list of value objects and have it instantiate corresponding Entity Beans for any transactional updates.

Implementing the `ObjectList` Utility

Sometimes you want the entire set of an object from the database, but in most cases, you want a specific collection. Earlier in the section on finder methods in the `BusinessObjectFactory` interface, a mechanism was discussed in the reference architecture through which a named collection was defined in the business object metadata. These collections were tied to a defined SQL or OQL WHERE clause. This same mechanism can be used to define the collections for the `ObjectList` utility. As an example, assume that you wanted to retrieve active accounts for a customer. You could define another `Account` collection for this as follows:

```
<Collection name="activeByCustomer"
  query="where customer_id = ? and last_modified_date > ?" />
```

> **NOTE** `ObjectList` is a JDBC wrapper utility, so it needs the database column and table names specified in the business object metadata in order to generate the correct SQL. This was otherwise not required in the reference architecture metadata for Entity Beans or other persistence framework options. Also note that the query is defined using regular SQL and Java's `PreparedStatement` format of question marks as placeholders for run-time bindings.

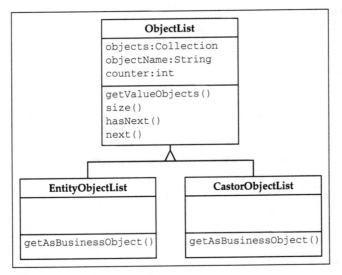

Figure 4.3 `ObjectList` UML Model.

The `ObjectList` utility can be constructed for a given object type. You can then use it to retrieve various defined collections of the corresponding value objects. It can hold a retrieved list until a new collection is retrieved. You can provide an interface similar to `Iterator` for navigating the list. You also want to have a method that can be used to get the current object as a business object; however, this will be implemented differently based on your particular business object implementation model. Thus, subclasses of `ObjectList` can be created, such as `EntityObjectList`, that add a `getAsBusinessObject` method. The overall object design for this utility is shown in Figure 4.3.

The code for `ObjectList` is shown next. The `getValueObjects` method is used to retrieve the collection. It returns the collection but also stores it to be potentially iterated using the `hasNext` and `next` methods. A `getSelectAllSQL` method is used on the business object metadata class that returns the 'select `field1`, `field2`, . . . from `tableName`' for the object. The complete SQL string for the query is formed by appending the WHERE clause for the collection to this string.

```
public class ObjectList {

    // The collection of objects
    protected ArrayList collection = null;
    // The business object metadata
    protected BusinessObjectMetadata bom = null;
    // The name of the object in the list
    protected String objectName = null;
    // An index of the current object
    // being iterated
    protected int counter = 0;
```

```java
// The size of the list
protected int collectionSize = 0;

/*
 * Constructor for a given object
 */
public ObjectList(String objectName) {
    this.objectName = objectName;
    try {
        bom =
            MetadataManager.getBusinessObject(objectName);
    } catch (Exception ex) {
        ex.printStackTrace();
    }
}

/*
 * The default constructor should not be used.
 */
private ObjectList() {
}

/*
 * Get the entire list of objects for this type.
 */
public Collection getValueObjects() throws BlfException {
    return getValueObjects(null, null);
}

/*
 * Get a named collection of value objects.
 */
public Collection getValueObjects(String queryId,
                                  ArrayList args)
    throws BlfException {

    try {
        JDBCUtility dbutil = new JDBCUtility();
        if (queryId == null) {
            // If no query defined, get the entire list
            collection = dbutil.getValueObjects(objectName,
                                bom.getSelectAllSQL());
            collectionSize = collection.size();
        } else {
            // Build the SQL string
            // core select + defined query (where clause)
            StringBuffer buffer =
                new StringBuffer(bom.getSelectAllSQL());
            buffer.append(' ');
            buffer.append(bom.getQuery(queryId));
            String sql = buffer.toString();
```

```
            collection = dbutil.getValueObjects(objectName,
                                            sql , args);
            collectionSize = collection.size();
        }
    } catch (Exception e) {
        throw new BlfException(e.getMessage());
    }

    return collection;
}


/*
 * Returns an indicator of whether there
 * is another object in the list
 */
public boolean hasNext() {
    if (counter > (collectionSize - 1)) {
        return false;
    }
    return true;
}


/*
 * Return the next object in the list.
 */
public ValueObject next() {
    return (ValueObject) collection.get(counter++);
}


/*
 * Return the size of the list.
 */
public int size() {
    return collectionSize;
}


/*
 * Accessor for business object metadata
 */
protected BusinessObjectMetadata getMetadata() {
    return bom;
}
}
```

The EntityObjectList subclass then just adds the getAsBusinessObject method. The code for this class is as follows:

```
public class EntityObjectList extends ObjectList {

    public EntityObjectList(String objectName) {
        super(objectName);
    }
```

```
public Object getAsBusinessObject() throws BlfException {
    if (counter == 0) {
        throw new BlfException("You need to invoke next()"
          + "before you can invoke getAsBusinessObject().");
    }

    ValueObject valueObj = (ValueObject)
        collection.get(counter - 1);
    String keyProperty =
        getMetadata().getKeyField().getName();
    Object obj = EJBFactoryImpl.findByPrimaryKey(
                        valueObj.getObjectName(),
                        valueObj.getProperty(keyProperty));
    return obj;
    }


}
```

The primary code used from JDBCUtility follows:

```
public ArrayList getValueObjects(String object,
                                 String sql)
    throws BlfException {
    return getObjects(object,sql,emptyArgs,true);
}

public ArrayList getValueObjects(String object,
                                 String sql,
                                 ArrayList args)
    throws BlfException {
    return getObjects(object,sql,args,true);
}

public ArrayList getObjects(String object,
                            String sql,
                            ArrayList args,
                            boolean createValueObjects)
    throws ValidationException {
    ArrayList results = new ArrayList();
    try {
        // Determine the collection class name.
        BusinessObjectMetadata bom =
            MetadataManager.getBusinessObject(object);
        HashMap attributeMetadata = bom.getPropertyMap();
        String objectClassName = null;
        if (createValueObjects) {
            objectClassName = bom.getValueObjClass();
        } else {
            objectClassName = bom.getBusObjClass();
        }
```

```
        // Invoke a generic method that executes a
        // prepared statement with arguments.
        rs = executePreparedStatementQuery(sql, args);
        while (rs.next()) {
            // Use the common interface for the two:
            // value objects and business objects.
            ValueObject valueObject = (ValueObject)
              (Class.forName(objectClassName)).newInstance();
            Iterator propertyIterator =
                attributeMetadata.values().iterator();
            while (propertyIterator.hasNext()) {
                PropertyMetadata prop =
                  (PropertyMetadata)propertyIterator.next();
                String columnName = prop.getDBName();
                // Not all properties are stored
                // in the database.
                if (columnName != null) {
                    // Call a generic method that uses
                    // the common value object interface to
                    // set the property value.
                    setField(rs, prop.getName(),
                            prop.getDBName(),
                            prop.getType(),
                            valueObject);
                }
            }
            results.add(valueObject);
        }
    } catch (Exception e) {
        throw new BlfException(e.getMessage());
    }
    close();
    return results;
}
```

Using ObjectList

There will likely be cases in which you simply want to retrieve a list of objects for display to the user. You can use `ObjectList` for this purpose, but you can also use it if you potentially need to update some of the objects and don't want to incur the overhead of using a collection of Entity Beans. As an example, assume you are using Entity Beans to implement the business objects and you want to assess a fee to customers if the total of all their account balances is less than $1,000. This is a contrived example, but it could be anything that requires some business logic that you might not do directly in a SQL query. Thus, you can use `ObjectList` to run the previous search example of active accounts by customer. You then want to iterate through the collection, calculate the total balance of all the accounts, and if it is less than $1,000, assess a fee to one of the accounts. To do this, the `getValueObjects` method is invoked to run the query and create the list of value objects. You can then iterate through the collection and, after calculating the total, use the `getAsBusinessObject` method to obtain a handle to that particular Entity Bean if you want to perform an update. The code to do this is as follows:

```
EntityObjectList eol = new EntityObjectList("Account");
ArrayList args = new ArrayList(2);
args.add(customerId);
args.add(cutoffDate);
eol.getValueObjects("activeByCustomer",args);

BigDecimal total = new BigDecimal(0);
while (eol.hasNext()) {
    ValueObject valueObj = eol.next();
    total = total.add(
        valueObj.getDecimalProperty("currentBalance"));
}

if (total.compareTo(new BigDecimal(1000)) < 0) {
    AccountLocal account = (AccountLocal)
        eol.getAsBusinessObject();
    account.withdraw(new BigDecimal(10), "bank fee");
}
```

Using EJB Select Methods

If you know that you want to deal with a number of business objects within a given Entity Bean, you can also use an `ejbSelect` method to retrieve a collection of objects. EJB Select methods can be used only within a bean implementation class; however, they avoid the need to use JNDI and the Home interface in order to locate other beans. A powerful aspect of these select methods is that they can return any object within the same JAR file. The container implements these methods in a similar manner to EJB finder methods.

As an example, assume there is an administrative function to mark all customer transactions as fraudulent after a certain date. The corresponding method would be invoked once it was determined that a customer's PIN number, or analogous credentials, had been compromised and money was withdrawn from accounts. From the perspective of the `Customer` object, the select method should return all transactions after a given date for any of the customer's accounts. The select method can be defined for the customer Entity Bean in the `ejb-jar.xml` file as follows:

```
<query>
    <query-method>
      <method-name>
          ejbSelectTransactionsByTypeAndDate
      </method-name>
      <method-params>
        <method-param>java.lang.String</method-param>
        <method-param>java.lang.String</method-param>
        <method-param>java.util.Date</method-param>
```

```
        </method-params>
      </query-method>
      <ejb-ql>
        <![CDATA[SELECT OBJECT(t) FROM Customer c,
            IN (c.accounts) as a, IN (a.transactions) as t
            WHERE c.id = ?1 and t.type = ?2 and
                t.transactionDate > ?3]]>
      </ejb-ql>
    </query>
```

On the `CustomerBean` implementation, the select method is defined as abstract. The `markWithdrawalsAsFraud` business method is defined and added to the `CustomerLocal` interface as well. This method executes the query for the customer and marks all of the `Transaction` objects as fraudulent.

```
//
// Select method
//
public abstract Collection
    ejbSelectTransactionsByTypeAndDate(String id,
            String type, java.util.Date transactionDate)
    throws FinderException;


//
// Business method
//
public void markWithdrawalsAsFraud(
        java.util.Date beginDate) throws BlfException {
    try {
        Collection coll =
            ejbSelectTransactionsByTypeAndDate(getId(),
                                    "W",beginDate);

        Iterator iter = coll.iterator();
        while (iter.hasNext()) {
            TransactionLocal transaction =
                (TransactionLocal) iter.next();

            // Instead of a fraud indicator, you will update
            // the transaction description.
            String description =
                transaction.getProperty("description");
            String fraudDescription = description +
                                    " - FRAUD";
            transaction.setProperty("description",
                                    fraudDescription);
        }
    } catch (Exception e) {
        throw new BlfException(e.getMessage());
    }
}
```

Database Queries

Thus far, you have only seen database queries that access a single table. This is because examples have always been referencing collections of a single object. There are many cases in application development where a join query is required to efficiently access the data. Object purists may argue that you should always use the object model when accessing data. Although there are many benefits to doing this, it becomes quite inefficient for data retrieval operations when it traverses large table structures. The general rule is to always use business objects when performing transactional updates because they contain the validations to maintain data integrity. However, as you have seen for read-only operations, you can use query mechanisms instead of objects if the associated risks can be mitigated. The EJB Select methods can return CMP fields; however, they are somewhat limited in that they can only return single CMP fields for beans within a given JAR file. A meaningful query often needs more widespread data to be useful. Thus, this section looks at the option of using JDBC queries for this purpose.

BEST PRACTICE Always use business objects for transactional updates to ensure data integrity and avoid redundant business logic validation code. Straight database queries can be used for read-only operations if they are more effective at traversing large table structures. However, this should be done only if you can mitigate the risk of having database names permeate throughout the application code.

One of the primary risks of using queries directly in your application is that the column names can start to appear all over the code if not managed well. This can be a maintenance nightmare if the database schema changes or even if a few column names change. Thus, if you are going to use database queries, try to adhere to the following guidelines, many of which have already been mentioned during the discussion of object persistence:

- Externalize the SQL in a metadata or configuration file.

- Isolate all JDBC code in utility class to ensure proper management of database resources (`JDBCUtility` has generic methods to execute a `PreparedStatement`).

- Map the result set rows to some kind of value object; this can isolate or eliminate references to database names in application code.

The first two points have already been discussed; it is the third point that is of interest here. How can you avoid referencing the database column names in your code? If you move the result set fields to the value object structure, you need to be able to map between the database column names and the logical property names. You have this information in the metadata; however, it is organized by business object, and the majority of these database queries will be join queries. Currently, the value object structure also assumes that all properties belong to the same business object.

There are a couple of options to address this issue. You can create either a subclass of `BaseValueObject` or another implementation of the `ValueObject` interface that allows for properties from different objects. This class could be called `ResultSetValueObject` to clearly note that this is not strict object data. You could put logic in it to reference metadata from multiple objects, although you would likely need to add direct access to properties in the metadata classes to support this. Aside from using application metadata, another option is to use the logical property names as aliases in the SELECT statement. The SQL would be defined as follows in this case:

```
Select fieldName1 propertyName1, fieldName2 propertyName2, ...
From tableName1, tableName2, ...
```

The `JDBCUtility` could then look at the `ResultSetMetaData` to put the property values into a generic `ResultSetValueObject` according to the logical property name (from the result set column name due to the alias) and its data type (from the `ResultSetMetaData`).

The Base Class as a Template

The Template Method design pattern can be applied to the business object base class to provide a template for common business behaviors. A primary example of this is business validation logic. In the last chapter, validation routines were developed to perform edits on individual fields and the object as a whole. You want these validation methods to be executed when the object is saved to the database in order to preserve data integrity. You can define a `save` method on the business object that acts as a template for this validation. The `save` method in the base class can invoke a generic validation method that performs required field checking and data type checking using the `PropertyHandler` mechanism. The application-specific edits that occurred in the previous `validate` method examples can then reside in the business objects subclasses and be invoked as a part of the `save` template.

If you are implementing business objects as regular Java classes, it is also a good idea to build the interface so that it easily maps to the Entity Bean interface methods. This would be helpful to enable any future migrations from Java business objects to Entity Beans. This can be accomplished without much extra effort because many of the hook points will be the same between the two models. Enterprise JavaBeans provide hook methods that get called prior to insert, update, and delete operations. The business object base class can provide a corresponding set of template methods. Table 4.1 shows the mapping between the business object interface templates methods and those of the Enterprise JavaBeans specification.

Table 4.1 Template Methods of Business Object Interface and Entity Beans

OPERATION	BUSINESS OBJECT INTERFACE TEMPLATE METHODS	ENTITY BEAN INTERFACE METHODS
Create	`blfPreInsert,` `blfPostInsert`	`ejbCreate,` `ejbPostCreate`
Save	`blfPreSave, blfValidate`	`ejbStore`
Delete	`blfPreDelete`	`ejbRemove`

The Save Template

The save template is used typically for the following purposes:

- Property and object-level validation integrated with transaction management
- Manipulation of aggregated objects
- Presave logic

NOTE In the case of CMP Entity Beans and other persistence frameworks, the save method is not actually doing the work of causing the object to persist in the database. This is taken care of by the respective EJB container or framework when the transaction commits. Rather, the save template is used to execute application code prior to saving the object to the database.

Some of the validation aspects of this template have already been touched on. The last item, presave logic, is a helpful one. Many applications have standard fields that get updated on each transaction. Other applications have business logic to execute each time an entity is updated. There are a number of possibilities. One common occurrence is standard auditing fields. The Account object has a lastModifiedDate property. This property should always reflect the last date that the object was updated. You can have this automatically occur in the presave template method. The Account implementation has this code:

```
public void blfPreSave() throws BlfException {
    // Set the audit date to today's date.
    setProperty("lastModifiedDate",new Date());
}
```

As a part of the save template, this method always gets invoked and you do not need to code this multiple times in every business method.

The implementation of the save method is now shown. This implementation is common among the different business object implementation models.

```
public void save() throws BlfException {

    // Initialize the error list for the business object.
    getErrorList().clear();

    // Call the presave template method.
    blfPreSave();

    try {
        // Perform all of the object validation.
        validate();
    } catch (BlfException be) {
        getErrorList().addErrors(be.getErrorList());
    }
```

```
        // Throw a validation exception if any
        // errors occurred.
        errorList.throwExceptionIfErrors();
}


/**
 * Validation template for business object
 */
public void validate() throws BlfException {

    validateRequiredFields();
    validatePropertyValues();
    blfValidate();
}


/**
 * Helper method to validate
 * (checks all required fields)
 */
protected void validateRequiredFields()
        throws ValidationException {

    Collection allFields = attributeMetadata.values();
    Iterator iter = allFields.iterator();
    while (iter.hasNext()) {
        PropertyMetadata prop =
            (PropertyMetadata)iter.next();
        if (prop.isRequired()) {
            String value = null;
            try {
              value = getProperty(prop.getName());
            } catch (PropertyException ignore) {}
            if ((value == null) || (value.equals(""))) {
                getErrorList().addError("REQ_FIELD",
                                        prop.getName());

            }
        }
    }
}


/**
 * Helper method to validate
 * (iterates through all properties
 * and runs the property validation routines)
 */
protected void validatePropertyValues()
        throws BlfException {

    Iterator iter = attributeMetadata.values().iterator();
    while (iter.hasNext()) {
```

```
        PropertyMetadata pmd =
            (PropertyMetadata) iter.next();
        try {
            validatePropertyDataType(pmd.getType(),
                            getProperty(pmd.getName())));
        } catch (ValidationException ve) {
            getErrorList().addErrors(ve.getErrorList());
        }
    }
}


// Base class implementations are empty.
// Implemented by subclasses
public void blfValidate() throws BlfException {
}

public void blfPreSave() throws BlfException {
}
```

The save method first calls the validate method. The validate method invokes other base class methods that perform required field checking and individual field value edits. Both of these generic routines go through the list of property metadata objects and perform the appropriate edit. In the case of property value checking, each value is sent through its corresponding PropertyHandler validation class. The last thing the validate method does is call a method called blfValidate.

NOTE The blf prefix is used to correspond to the ejb prefix found in front of the EJB template methods (that is, ejbCreate). BLF stands for Business Logic Foundation, the name of the foundation layer.

The blfValidate method has a default implementation in the base class that does nothing, but its purpose is to provide a hook that specific business object subclasses can implement to provide object level validation logic. If there are no edits at this level to perform, the subclass is not required to implement the method, and the validate return will go on as normal.

BEST PRACTICE Use the Template Method pattern to implement common behaviors in the business object base class. A primary example of this is the save method, which can call a hook method to perform data validation, specific object validation, and any presave logic implemented in the subclass.

Managing Aggregated Objects

If there is a hierarchy of related objects, it would be nice to invoke the save method on the parent object and have it deal with all of the child objects as well. This can be done either with specific code in the blfPreSave methods of the business object subclasses, or it can be addressed at the foundation level generically by the base class. In the latter option, the base class can go through each relationship defined in the metadata and, using the standard accessor methods, iterate through each aggregated object and invoke its `save` method. This can be implemented as shown here:

```
/**
 * Helper method to save (iterates
 * through all aggregated objects and
 * invokes the save routine)
 */
protected void saveAggregatedObjects()
    throws BlfException {

    Collection coll = bom.getRelationships();
    Iterator iter = coll.iterator();
    while (iter.hasNext()) {
        RelationshipMetadata relation =
            (RelationshipMetadata) iter.next();
        if (relation.isAutoSave()) {
            if (relation.isMultiple()) {
                Collection relatedColl =
                    getOneToManyRelationship(
                                relation.getName());
                Iterator relatedIter =
                    relatedColl.iterator();
                while (relatedIter.hasNext()) {
                    try {
                        BusinessObject busObj =
                            (BusinessObject)
                                relatedIter.next();
                        busObj.save();
                    } catch (BlfException be) {
                        getErrorList().addErrors(
                                be.getErrorList());
                    }
                }
            } else {
                try {
                    BusinessObject busObj =
                        getOneToOneRelationship(
                                relation.getName());
                    busObj.save();
                } catch (BlfException be) {
                    getErrorList().addErrors(
                                be.getErrorList());
                }
            }
        }
    }
}
```

NOTE You might notice that an `autoSave` indicator was added to the relationship metadata. This is used as a performance optimization so this feature can be turned on or off for specific relationships.

Entity Beans, as well as many other persistence frameworks, do not indicate whether an aggregated component has already been loaded from the database. Thus, iterating through aggregated objects may cause the container to load objects that were not even used in order to invoke the `save` method. In many cases, the object graph is small, or it is known that the objects are already instantiated, so this concept can be used without additional, unnecessary overhead. Optionally, an indicator could be added as an argument to the `save` method as to whether it should be a "deep" save operation. As the implementation is currently shown, you can configure this behavior in the metadata. For example, if you wanted to have the `Customer` component automatically run the save template on its accounts, but not on the address, the relationships would be defined as follows:

```
<BusinessObject name="Customer" >
  ...
  <Relationship name="address" multiplicity="one"
                autoSave="false" />
  <Relationship name="accounts" multiplicity="many"
                autoSave="true" />
</BusinessObject>
```

Save Template for Entity Beans

At first glance, you might think to use the `ejbStore` template method provided by the container to invoke the save template logic. However, this method only throws an `EJBException` or `RemoteException`, and there is no way to override it and throw an application exception. The EJB specification explicitly defines how application exceptions are handled when thrown out of business methods, but `ejbStore` is a container-invoked callback, and it treats all exceptions the same. If you could throw the `ValidationException` out of this method, it seems as if it still might behave as you intended, but there is no way to do so given the `ejbStore` method signature. The intent here was that only system-level exceptions would occur in these container-invoked callback methods. You will see later that `ejbCreate` and `ejbRemote` do not fall into this category because they are invoked directly as a result of a client invoking the `create` or `remove` methods on the Home interface. They are still classified as business methods.

Thus, the save logic needs to be explicitly invoked at the end of Entity Bean business methods or service components that use the bean. You also need to consider transaction management if the Entity Beans can be invoked directly from a client. In this case, the transaction begins and ends with the Entity Bean business method so you need to vote for a rollback if a business error occurs. In many cases, you can wrap the Entity Beans with a Session Bean, and you can move this logic out to the Session Bean just as you will need to do for Java business objects. For the time being, however, consider the case in which you must manage the transaction in the business object. Every business method like this will have a similar pattern: an encompassing try-catch block and a `save` method invocation at the end. Consider, for example, a `convertToCheckingAccount` method on the `Account` Entity Bean. It changes the account type and account number accordingly and then calls the `save` method to verify that all business validations have been met. Once the account is converted to a checking account, the minimum balance requirement changes, and it may not meet the requirement. If a business exception such as this occurs, a `BlfException` is thrown from the `save` method and is caught by this business method. The transaction is then set to roll back in the catch block of this exception.

```
public void convertToCheckingAccount()
    throws BlfException {

    try {
        // Change the account type
        setProperty("type","C");

        // All account numbers start
        // with their type, for example, Cxxxxx.
        // Change the account number
        // accordingly.
        setProperty("number",
            "C" + getProperty("number").substring(1));

        // Invoke the save template
        // in case a minimum balance is
        // not met, and so on.
        save();

    } catch (BlfException be) {
        // If a business error occurred,
        // vote to roll back the transaction
        // and rethrow the exception that
        // has the error list inside to
        // communicate to the client.
        getEntityContext().setRollbackOnly ();
        throw be;
    }
}
```

The Create Template

The create template actually appeared earlier in the discussion of the business object factory. It is implemented by the base class method `blfCreate`, which is triggered by a `create` operation on the factory. It has both `pre` and `post` creation methods. In the Entity Bean implementation, these can be triggered by `ejbCreate` and `ejbPostCreate`. In the case of the Castor business objects, this flow was controlled directly from the object factory's `create` method.

The blfPreInsert method is often used to set properties that have application-defined initial values. The blfPostInsert method can be used to create any aggregated objects that have a dependent lifecycle. As an example, your Customer component can take a customer value object that also contains address data. The create template can then be used to insert the Address object as well. The code for this method is shown here. It uses the Castor implementation, although any object factory could be substituted here.

```
/**
 * Template method called from create
 */
public void blfPostInsert(ValueObject initialValues)
    throws BlfException {

    //
    // Create the aggregated address.
    //
    CustomerData custData = (CustomerData) initialValues;
    AddressData addrData =
        (AddressData) custData.getAddress();
    Address address = (Address)
        CastorFactoryImpl.create("Address",
                                 addrData,
                                 getDatabase());
    setAddress(address);
}
```

Also note that the save template can be used from within the create template as well in order to run the same business validations and presave logic. In many cases, the same logic is still applicable to an insert operation. For example, you want to run validations when you create an Address to ensure you have a valid state and zip code, and so on. The blfPreInsert method is currently used to default the country, in case one is not specified. It can also be used to invoke the save method to run the validations. The code for this is shown here.

```
/*
 * This method is called by the create new instance
 * template in the business object base class.
 */
public void blfPreInsert() throws BlfException {
    //
    // Default the country to the USA.
    //
    setProperty("country","USA");

    // Run the validations.
    save();
}
```

The Template Method for Application-Specific Logic

The template pattern can be used for application-specific logic as well as common foundation logic. If an object model for an application has an inheritance hierarchy in which a common process is altered based on the specific subclass, the template method can provide a nice flexible solution. In the `Account` examples thus far, a `type` property was used to designate what type of account the object represents; however, you could also have implemented this using specific subclasses for checking and savings accounts. If there was a common business behavior that differed in some steps between the two, you could implement the business method as a template in an application account base class.

As an example, take account close-out as a process that differs for checking and savings accounts. The close-out process at a high level is as follows:

1. Issue a money order to withdraw the remaining balance.

2. For checking accounts, send an email to ask customer to tear up old checks and thank the customer for banking with you. For savings accounts, send an email to thank the customer for banking with you.

3. Send the final statement.

4. Inactivate the account in the database.

The `Account` base class would have the following methods:

```
public void closeOut()
{

    issueMoneyOrder();
    sendCustomerEmail();
    sendFinalStatement();
    inactivateAccount();

}


public void sendCustomerEmail()
{
    // Do nothing here; subclases will implement.

}
```

The `CheckingAccount` object would have the following method implementation:

```
public void sendCustomerEmail()
{

    String message = "Please tear up old checks. " +
        " Thank you for banking with us.";
    sendEmail(message);

}
```

The `SavingsAccount` object would have the following method implementation:

```
public void sendCustomerEmail()
{

    String message = " Thank you for banking with us.";
    sendEmail(message);
}
```

Although this example is oversimplified, the concept is a powerful one when used appropriately. One thing to watch out for, however, is forcing the use of this pattern. If your business entities are not modeled very well by inheritance, it is not a good idea to force the issue so that you can use this pattern. Inheritance is a strict form of object reuse compared to delegation, so you want to make sure that your object design fits the application requirements well.

Overall Business Object Metadata Approach

The generic foundation layer for business objects has been using XML metadata to define the aspects of the business objects as well as other important pieces of information. This section takes a look at the entire definition of the XML metadata now that all of the pieces are defined.

The Metadata XML DTD

The metadata DTD (document type definition) is as follows:

```
<?xml version="1.0" encoding="UTF-8"?>
<!--
    Business Logic Foundation Metadata DTD
 -->


<!--
    A set of business logic foundation metadata.
    This is the top level element.

 -->
<!ELEMENT Metadata ( BusinessObject*, PropertyDefinitions*,
DatabaseQueries?, BusinessErrors?, CacheList? )>


<!--
    The definition of a business object, which includes
    its properties, relationships to other business objects,
    and defined collections.

 -->
```

```
<!ELEMENT BusinessObject ( Property+, Relationship*, Collection*  )>
<!ATTLIST BusinessObject
    name          CDATA    #REQUIRED
    busObjClass   CDATA    #IMPLIED
    valueObjClass CDATA    #IMPLIED
    table         CDATA    #IMPLIED
    ejbHomeClass  CDATA    #IMPLIED>


<!--
    A property of an object.  The property type is required and
    refers to a type defined within the PropertyDefinitions element.

 -->
<!ELEMENT Property EMPTY>
<!ATTLIST Property
    name            CDATA   #REQUIRED
    dbname          CDATA   #IMPLIED
    type            CDATA   #REQUIRED
    required        (true|false) "false"
    key             (true|false) "false"
    autogen         (true|false) "false">

<!--
    A relationship from the containing object to another. This
    can be a 1-1 or a 1-M relationship. The name is a reference
    to another business object. The autosave attribute defines
    whether the save template is automatically applied to these
    aggregated objects.

 -->
<!ELEMENT Relationship EMPTY>
<!ATTLIST Relationship
    name            CDATA   #REQUIRED
    multiplicity    (one|many) "one"
    autoSave        (true|false) "false">

<!--
    A named collection of the object.  This defines, in
    essence, a 'where' clause for SQL, OQL, or EJB QL,
    depending on the business object implementation that is
    being used.
    Collections can be used to locate business objects using
    BusinessObjectFactory or to locate sets of value objects
    using ObjectList.  The name is any unique name you choose.

 -->
<!ELEMENT Collection EMPTY>
<!ATTLIST Collection
    name            CDATA   #REQUIRED
    query           CDATA   #REQUIRED>
```

```
<!--
    A collection of property definitions
  -->
<!ELEMENT PropertyDefinitions ( PropertyType* )>

<!--
    A PropertyType defines a category of properties
    that use a specific handler class for validation
    and formatting.

  -->
<!ELEMENT PropertyType EMPTY>
<!ATTLIST PropertyType
    name            CDATA   #REQUIRED
    handler         CDATA   #REQUIRED>


<!--
    Database queries are defined SQL queries to be
    used by the DatabaseQuery utility class. They
    are defined here to externalize the SQL from
    the application.

  -->
<!ELEMENT DatabaseQueries ( Query* )>


<!--
    A defined SQL query

  -->
<!ELEMENT Query EMPTY>
<!ATTLIST Query
    name            CDATA   #REQUIRED
    sql             CDATA   #REQUIRED>

<!--
    A set of business errors

  -->
<!ELEMENT BusinessErrors ( BusinessError* )>

<!--
    Business errors are defined error codes that have
    a type defined as warning, error, or critical errors.
    They have a defined user message that acts as a
    run-time template with substitution values.

  -->
<!ELEMENT BusinessError EMPTY>
<!ATTLIST BusinessError
    name            CDATA   #REQUIRED
    type            CDATA   #REQUIRED
    message         CDATA   #REQUIRED>
```

```
<!--
    A set of defined caches used by the CacheList
    utility class

 -->
<!ELEMENT CacheList ( Cache* )>

<!--
    A named cache that can be accessed by the
    CacheList utility.  A subclass of ObjectCache
    can be used as the implementation of
    ObjectCache foundation class itself.

 -->
<!ELEMENT Cache EMPTY>
<!ATTLIST Cache
    name            CDATA   #REQUIRED
    class           CDATA   #REQUIRED>
```

There are efforts underway to standardize both the metadata XML formats and the methods used to access the metadata. One format now commonly supported by modeling tools is XML Metadata Interchange (XMI), a standard XML format used to represent UML models. Ideally, you would either use the XMI format itself or build a utility to convert from the XMI format to our own. This would allow you to automate this portion of the development process using UML design models and development tools such as Rational Rose.

The XMI DTD is very verbose and thorough so that it can encompass all of the information from a UML model. A small portion of an XMI document for your Account object might look like this:

```
<?xml version="1.0" encoding="UTF-8"?>
<!DOCTYPE XMI SYSTEM "uml13.dtd">
<XMI xmi.version="1.0">
  <XMI.header>
    <XMI.metamodel xmi.name="UML" xmi.version="1.3"/>
  </XMI.header>
  <XMI.content>
    <Model_Management.Model xmi.id="xmi.1"
        xmi.uuid="-106--106-25-11--7e352540:e17838870b:-7fed">
      <Foundation.Core.ModelElement.name>Bank Example Model
      </Foundation.Core.ModelElement.name>
      <Foundation.Core.ModelElement.isSpecification
          xmi.value="false"/>
      <Foundation.Core.GeneralizableElement.isRoot
          xmi.value="false"/>
      <Foundation.Core.GeneralizableElement.isLeaf
          xmi.value="false"/>
      <Foundation.Core.GeneralizableElement.isAbstract
          xmi.value="false"/>
      <Foundation.Core.Namespace.ownedElement>
```

```
<Foundation.Core.Class xmi.id="xmi.2"
 xmi.uuid="-106--106-25-11--7e352540:e17838870b:-7fec">
  <Foundation.Core.ModelElement.name>Account
  </Foundation.Core.ModelElement.name>
  <Foundation.Core.ModelElement.isSpecification
        xmi.value="false"/>
  <Foundation.Core.GeneralizableElement.isRoot
        xmi.value="false"/>
  <Foundation.Core.GeneralizableElement.isLeaf
        xmi.value="false"/>
  <Foundation.Core.GeneralizableElement.isAbstract
        xmi.value="false"/>
  <Foundation.Core.Class.isActive xmi.value="false"/>
  <Foundation.Core.ModelElement.namespace>
    <Model_Management.Model xmi.idref="xmi.1"/>
  </Foundation.Core.ModelElement.namespace>
  <Foundation.Core.Classifier.feature>
    <Foundation.Core.Attribute xmi.id="xmi.3">
      <Foundation.Core.ModelElement.name>currentBalance
      </Foundation.Core.ModelElement.name>
      <Foundation.Core.ModelElement.visibility
            xmi.value="public"/>
      <Foundation.Core.ModelElement.isSpecification
            xmi.value="false"/>
      <Foundation.Core.Feature.owner>
        <Foundation.Core.Class xmi.idref="xmi.2"/>
      </Foundation.Core.Feature.owner>
      <Foundation.Core.StructuralFeature.type>
        <Foundation.Core.DataType xmi.idref="xmi.4"/>
      </Foundation.Core.StructuralFeature.type>
    </Foundation.Core.Attribute>
    ...
  </Foundation.Core.Namespace.ownedElement>
 </Model_Management.Model>
 </XMI.content>
</XMI>
```

BEST PRACTICE Use a metadata format that allows your design models to be the original source of the metadata. Either build your metadata parser to read the XMI format or use a conversion utility to create your own XML format from XMI, which is generated by development tools from the design models.

Accessing the Metadata from the Application

The foundation layer would be quite inefficient if it needed to read and parse the XML metadata file from disk every time you needed to reference it. A better approach is to parse the file once and cache the metadata in memory. To do this, you need an object

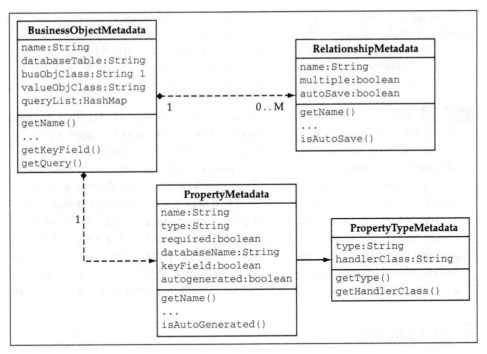

Figure 4.4 Metadata Class Diagram.

structure to hold the data and provide easy access to the information. Some of the previous code samples have referenced the BusinessObjectMetadata class that stores object-level information from the metadata, such as the database name. This class aggregates a collection of PropertyMetadata objects used to define each of the properties of the business object. Each property has a type, which references a global list of property definitions. These are stored as PropertyTypeMetadata objects. The BusinessObjectMetadata also aggregates a collection of Relationship-Metadata objects.

Figure 4.4 shows the entire object model for the metadata in a UML class diagram. You will need two different caches to store this information:

- Business object metadata cache: A collection of BusinessObjectMetadata objects keyed by object name. Each of these objects contains its respective list of PropertyMetadata and RelationshipMetadata objects.

- Property type metadata cache: A collection of PropertyTypeMetadata objects keyed by type name.

You can use the general-purpose cache mechanism, which is discussed in the next section of this chapter, to store the metadata objects in memory. However, you probably want to wrap the general cache interface with a MetadataManager interface for convenience because the metadata will be used so often throughout our business logic foundation.

Likewise, the business object base class will refer to the metadata so often that it is probably best to add a member variable that references its particular `Business-ObjectMetadata` object. Going even one step farther, you can add a member variable that references the property list within that object, because there will be numerous occasions on which you will wish to iterate through this collection.

NOTE Way back during the discussion of implementing properties for a business object, the properties could have been stored as a collection of `Property` objects that held both the metadata and the property value. This would have allowed the business object to hold only one collection as opposed to the current design, which has both a collection of property values and a collection of property metadata objects. However, having these two separated is coming in handy now for performance reasons. Because the property metadata is read-only, it can be shared across all business objects. Thus, you don't need to make a copy of the property metadata objects for each new business object instance. You simply give each business object a reference to the same shared object. This would have been a bit more difficult if the property objects had both metadata and instance values.

Data Caching

Disk and database I/O are usually the most expensive operations that an application performs. You can perform hundreds or perhaps thousands of CPU instructions in the time that it takes to do one database query using JDBC. Thus, for high-performance applications, you should look to cache data that is fairly static and used often throughout an application. In the effort to build the Business Object Architecture, you have already come across a number of places where you would like to cache data in memory of the application server. There are two types of caches for metadata, the business object metadata and the property type metadata. There also is the option of caching EJB Home interfaces encapsulated within the `BusinessObjectFactory`. Once you get into developing actual applications, there likely will be a number of application objects and lookup tables that can be cached to give the application a performance boost.

Cache Implementation Options

There are two primary options for caching data within a J2EE application server:

- Java singleton class
- Stateless Session Bean

The singleton pattern (Erich Gamma et al. 1995) is typically used to ensure that an in-memory cache is not duplicated within a given JVM. This pattern provides a static getter method that lazily instantiates a single static member within a synchronized block to ensure that only one instance of the cache object is created. The cache object is usually some type of collection that holds the objects to be stored. In many cases, this is a very effective implementation for a cache because it has almost no overhead associated with accessing the cache. A HashMap lookup is about the only operation required to access a cached object given its key.

On some application servers, however, there is an issue with using a regular Java singleton. The class loaders on some servers tend to drop and reload classes at different intervals. This will occur on some implementations while it may not on others. You can test for the occurrence of this on your platform fairly easily by putting some debug statements in the data loading method. After doing this, run your application under a load test and see how often, if at all, this happens in your environment. If the class loading does not reoccur, then this approach will likely work quite well for you.

The other primary option for caching data is to use the same pattern wrapped by a stateless Session Bean. This approach can be used if the class loading issue becomes a problem. This is also a nice implementation if you wish to distribute your cache to a remote client. These benefits, however, come at the cost of the additional RMI overhead and possibly a network trip to access the cache. Nonetheless, this is almost assuredly more efficient than a database query to get the same data. One additional benefit of using an EJB for the cache implementation is that the management of your cache component lifecycle is handled by the application server. This ensures it is highly available and pooled according to the particular client load. It is up to the server's discretion whether it should make multiple instances available to EJB clients. This may not be desirable for extremely large caches because of the memory consumption involved. However, for most normal size caches, this usually does not become a problem.

Designing the Cache Objects

With either implementation, you are building a type of singleton cache. There are already three caches to be implemented, and it is almost a certainty that you will want to cache application data. Should you build separate caching objects for each one of these caches? You can do this; however, this would lead to a large number of components being deployed by the server in the case of a Session Bean cache. It would also add a large number of objects to the code base if you created specific objects for each cache. You probably don't need to do this. Each cache object will basically follow the same singleton pattern that uses a HashMap to store the objects by a given key. You can create an encompassing `CacheList` object that manages these caches and stores each one of them in a master HashMap keyed by their cache name. The caches themselves can be implemented using an `ObjectCache` class that wraps the HashMap collection.

NOTE HashMap is not a synchronized class, so if you need to protect your cache with synchronized access, you should create a `SynchronizedObjectCache` class that uses a hashtable. If the cache data is loaded all at once when the cache is initialized, this usually is not an issue because clients are only reading data. If data can be added to the cache during the life of an application, then this becomes a consideration, although the normal implementation pattern usually involves a cache "refresh" that reloads the entire set of data within a synchronized block. One last issue to consider regarding this topic is to ensure that your cached objects are thread-safe because they will likely be accessed by multiple clients at a time. Remember that the caches are not making copies of the data. They give all clients a handle to the same object. There have been some problems, for example, with caching XML documents using some earlier Document Object Model parser implementations that were not thread-safe. In these cases, you would want to move the data into a thread-safe data structure, such as strings in a hashtable.

The general cache mechanism should be able to manage a number of caches, thus each method will require a cache name. You can expose the basic put and get operations on the CacheList itself so that the entire cache does not always need to be returned to the client. In the Java singleton implementation, this would not be an issue. However, in the stateless Session Bean model, this would cause unnecessary overhead for simple lookup operations because it would need to serialize an entire cache object rather than just the requested object. Exposing the access methods on the primary CacheList object allows you to define an interface that will work with either the Java singleton or Session Bean implementation.

The caches are implemented by a simple wrapper around HashMap, which is called ObjectCache. They expose the put and get operations for that particular cache. The CacheList utility stores a collection of these identified by a cache name. The CacheList class will look something like this:

```
/*
 * CacheList is a utility to manage a set of object caches.
 * It stores a HashMap of cache objects keyed by a cache name.
 */
public class CacheList
{

    // The singleton instance
    public static CacheList instance = null;

    // The "master" cache - a collection of caches
    // keyed by cache name
    private HashMap caches;

    /*
     * Default constructor that initializes the
     * master collection
     */
    public CacheList()
    {
        caches = new HashMap();
    }

    /*
     * The singleton static accessor
     */
    public static CacheList getInstance()
    {
```

```java
    if (instance == null)
    {
        synchronized (CacheList.class)
        {
            if (instance == null)
            {
                instance = new CacheList();
            }
        }
    }
    return instance;
}

/*
 * Return an object within the named cache
 * identified by the key.
 */
public Object getObject(String cacheName, Object key)
{
    ObjectCache cache = getCache(cacheName);
    return cache.get(key);
}


/*
 * Store an object in the named cache with the given key.
 */
public void putObject(String cacheName,
                      Object key,
                      Object value)
{
    ObjectCache cache = getCache(cacheName);
    cache.put(key, value);
}


/*
 * Return the named cache.
 */
public ObjectCache getCache(String cacheName)
{
    ObjectCache cache = null;

    // Check to see if the cache has already
    // been created.
    Object obj = caches.get(cacheName);

    // If not, go ahead and create it putting
    // it in the 'master' cache.
    if (obj == null)
    {
        cache = new ObjectCache(cacheName);
        caches.put(cacheName,cache);
```

```
        }
        else
        {
            cache = (ObjectCache) obj;
        }

        return cache;
    }

}
```

The caches need a method to load all of their data. This method will be called initially and also when a refresh operation is needed. You can add a method `loadData` that is responsible for loading all of the data into the cache. The default implementation on `ObjectCache` will not do anything because it is a general all-purpose cache. However, you can create subclasses of `ObjectCache` that implement this method to load specific data. For example, you may have a cache of the fifty states keyed by their two-letter abbreviations. This cache could be implemented as follows using the `loadData` method:

```
public class StateCache extends ObjectCache
{

    /*
     * Construct the superclass giving the object name.
     */
    public StateCache()
    {
        super("States");
    }

    /*
     * Standard cache method to load the data
     */
    public void loadData()
    {
        // Note that you could easily load from a JDBC or
        // other data source, but you will simply add
        // some values for the example.
        put("CA", "California");
        put("IL", "Illinois");
        put("VA", "Virginia");
    }

}
```

You can add the definition for each named cache into the metadata so the first call to `CacheList` automatically instantiates and loads the data for the state cache. You can add a cache list section in the metadata file such as the following:

```
<CacheList>
  <Cache name="States" class="bank.StateCache">
</CacheList>
```

The getCache method in CacheList is now a bit more complicated. It is implemented as follows in order to account for the metadata and the initial loading of data into the cache:

```
/*
 * Return the named cache.
 */
public ObjectCache getCache(String cacheName)
    throws BlfException
{
    ObjectCache cache = null;

    // Check to see if the cache has already
    // been created.
    Object obj = caches.get(cacheName);

    // If not, go ahead and create it putting
    // it in the 'master' cache.
    if (obj == null)
    {
        // Look up in the metadata to see if there is a
        // defined class for this cache. Note that you
        // can't do this for the cache metadata itself.
        CacheMetadata cacheMetadata = null;
        if (!(cacheName.equals("CacheTypeCache")))
        {
            cacheMetadata = (CacheMetadata)
                getObject("CacheTypeCache", cacheName);
        }

        // If you have defined metadata for this cache,
        // use it to instantiate the proper object.
        // Otherwise, use the standard ObjectCache.
        if (cacheMetadata == null)
        {
            cache = new ObjectCache(cacheName);
        }
        else
        {
            // Construct the cache implementation class and
            // call the loadData method to initialize its
            // data.
            try
            {
                String cacheImplClass =
                    cacheMetadata.getImplClass();
                cache = (ObjectCache)
(Class.forName(cacheImplClass)).newInstance();
                cache.loadData();
            }
            catch (Exception e)
            {
```

```
                    throw new BlfException(e.getMessage());
            }
        }

        // Store the new cache in the 'master' cache.
        caches.put(cacheName,cache);
    }
    else
    {
        // If the cache already exists, simply return
        // the handle to it.
        cache = (ObjectCache) obj;
    }

    return cache;
}
```

Lookup Tables

In addition to providing methods for loading data, there is another reason you may want to have subclasses of `ObjectCache`. A subclass can allow you to extend the functionality if you want to provide more specific types of caches. One such case that recurs in almost all business applications is the lookup table. A lookup table is a collection of codes and values that are commonly used as drop-down lists on a Web page. The previous state cache really can be implemented as a lookup table. If you create a subclass of `ObjectCache` called `LookupCache`, you can add methods that are commonly used against lookups such as validating that a value exists in the list of lookup values. If the cache is used heavily in the presentation logic, you might also add methods to create a drop-down list from the `LookupCache`, although it might be better to isolate this type of logic in a set of HTML utility classes. Going back to the validation example, the `Address` business object could use this cache to validate that the state given is a valid one. To implement this in the caching mechanism, the `LookupCache` might be implemented like this:

```
public class LookupCache extends ObjectCache
{

    /*
     * Construct the cache with the given name.
     */
    public LookupCache(String cacheName)
    {
        super(cacheName);
    }

    /*
     * Override the put method to use strings
     * instead of object.
     */
```

```
public void put(String code, String value)
{
    collection.put(code,value);
}

/*
 * Override the get method to use strings
 * instead of object.
 */
public String get(String code)
{
    return (String) collection.get(code);
}

/*
 * Check to see whether a given code exists
 * as a key in this lookup cache.
 */
public boolean isValidCode(String code)
{
    return collection.containsKey(code);
}

}
```

The isValidCode method was added as a convenience to perform valid value edits in a business object against this cache. The validate method of the Address business object could invoke this method to ensure a valid state was given. The code for this is as follows:

```
public void blfValidate() throws BlfException {
    ErrorList errorList = new ErrorList();
    try {
        // Validate the state.
        StateCache states = (StateCache)
            CacheList.getInstance().getCache("States");
        if (!states.isValidCode(getProperty("state"))) {
            errorList.addError("INVALID_STATE",
                            getProperty("state"));
        }

        // Other validations here...

    } catch (PropertyException pe) {
        errorList.addError("GEN_PROPERTY_ERROR",
                        pe.getMessage());
    }
    errorList.throwExceptionIfErrors();
}
```

Configuration Cache

Another common occurrence of something you would like to cache in an application is the configuration parameters. Most applications have a set of configuration properties, usually stored in a Java properties file, that control how an application is set up to run. These can be referred to quite often, and it would be very inefficient to have to read and parse the properties file each time you wanted to use a configuration parameter. Another subclass can be created called `ConfigurationCache` to hold these parameters. It would override the `put` and `get` methods to deal with strings as a convenience, and also implement a `loadData` method that read the application's configuration properties file and loaded the values into the cache. The other important part about this is to have a special named cache for the purpose of storing configuration parameters that all application components use when necessary. In order to simplify this for application components, you may want to create a wrapper class that uses the `CacheList` underneath but always refers to the specific named configuration cache. This prevents the possible mistake of referring to the wrong name and simplifies the API for this purpose.

The primary code for `ConfigurationCache` is shown here. The properties file was named `BlfConfiguration.properties`.

```
public class ConfigurationCache extends ObjectCache {

    /*
     * Construct the superclass giving the object name.
     */
    public ConfigurationCache() {
        super("Config");
    }

    /*
     * Standard cache method to load the data
     */
    public void loadData() {

        try {
        PropertyResourceBundle blfProperties =
            (PropertyResourceBundle)
                PropertyResourceBundle.getBundle(
                                    "BlfConfiguration");

        if (blfProperties == null) {
            System.out.println("Error getting " +
                    "BlfConfiguration.properties file.");
        }

        Enumeration enum = blfProperties.getKeys();
        while (enum.hasMoreElements()) {
            String key = (String) enum.nextElement();
            put(key,blfProperties.getString(key));
        }
```

```
        } catch (MissingResourceException e) {
          System.out.println("Error getting " +
                    "BlfConfiguration.properties file.");
        }

    }

}
```

The convenience wrapper class to access configuration properties is shown here:

```
public class ConfigurationManager {

    public static String getString(String key)
        throws BlfException {

        return (String)
            CacheList.getInstance().getObject("Config",key);
    }
}
```

Configuration parameters include things such as the level of debug output to write to the log, what log files to use, and other similar application level parameters that control the flow or define application resources. For example, the location of the business object metadata file could be specified in the configuration properties.

CacheList Object Model

The caching implementation is summed up by Figure 4.5.

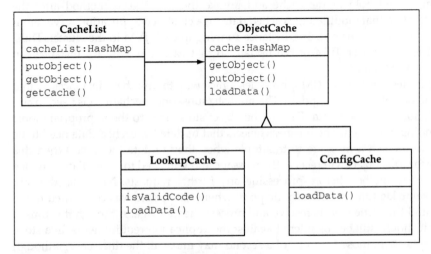

Figure 4.5 Object Model for Caching Mechanism.

When to Cache Data

Although data caching provides a great performance boost when used for frequently accessed data, there are drawbacks and design considerations that should be taken into consideration before you decide to cache a set of data. Two primary things to consider are the amount of memory that is consumed in order to cache these objects and the rate at which the data changes. As the entire cache mechanism consumes more and more memory, there is less memory available for application objects, which can also slow an application down because the JVM will be forced to collect garbage more often. The other issue to consider is that frequently changed data will require a large amount of effort to keep up to date in the cache, which will also consume resources.

Good candidates for cached data exhibit the following characteristics:

- Fairly static or read-only data

- Used frequently or predictably by the application

- Small volumes of data

Data that does not meet one or more of these characteristics may be better accessed through a database. Any data that is modified through transactional updates is usually better off being handled by an RDBMS that specializes in that exact thing. Remember that this is not trying to implement a database here, it is only trying to provide a simple mechanism to speed access to commonly used, static data.

Refresh Mechanism

Notice that the criteria didn't entirely limit data caching to read-only data. There are cases in which data remains static for the majority of the time but can be changed during the course of an application's uptime. If it is not updated very frequently but is still used quite often, it may still be beneficial to cache this data. In these cases, you need a way to make a live update to the cache. In a single JVM environment, this is trivial. You would simply get hold of the cache and invoke the `loadData` method after the update operation that modified the cached data. In a clustered application server environment, you have a `CacheList` instance running in each JVM in the cluster. Thus, you need to notify each JVM of the update so that each `CacheList` instance can obtain the correct data.

The Java Message Service (JMS) provides a nice way to link these instances so that they can all be notified of an update. The publish/subscribe mechanism is used to create a topic for the cached data. Each cache object subscribes to the appropriate topic corresponding to its data. The business objects that update the cached data need to be modified to publish a message to this topic when they update the data. When this occurs, each cache object will receive the message and will need to immediately invoke the `loadData` method before processing any further requests. Note that this still provides some lag time in between the point where the update was committed to the database and the cache objects receive and process the message. Although this time is minimal, it should still be considered against the application requirements. In a stock market application, those fractions of a second may make all the difference, although in many applications this brief time interval would be acceptable.

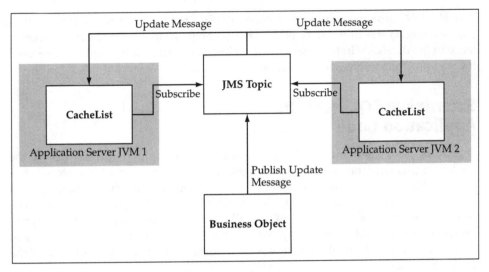

Figure 4.6 Using JMS as a Cache Refresh Mechanism.

Figure 4.6 illustrates this approach. It shows how different cache objects in the cluster subscribe to the same topic, which receives messages posted from the corresponding business objects making the update.

In J2EE 1.3, JMS is required to be implemented by certified application server products, although many of the JMS implementations built into the application server products are currently not industrial-strength messaging engines. However, they are more than powerful enough to support the refresh mechanism due to the low volume of updates that you should have based on the data caching criteria.

BEST PRACTICE Cache frequently used data that is fairly static to speed application performance. Use a consistent, extensible cache mechanism that can be implemented either as a Stateless Session Bean or as a Java singleton class. If the cached data can be updated and the application needs the latest data, consider the use of a JMS solution for notifying caches across a cluster to refresh their data.

Best Practices for Implementing Business Objects: Part Two

This section summarizes the best practices discussed in this chapter for implementing persistence, relationships, and the Template Method pattern in business objects.

Isolate and Encapsulate JDBC Logic

Isolate any JDBC logic to execute a SQL statement in a common utility class. This prevents every application developer from having to write this common logic and ensures that all JDBC resources are closed properly. The implementation of regular Java business objects and BMP Entity Beans can use the JDBC utility for object data persistence in the database. In the case of CMP Entity Beans, this utility might still be used for read-only operations such as executing join queries.

Externalize SQL from the Application Code

If JDBC is used, externalize the SQL from the Java code to minimize impacts to the application if the database schema changes. The SQL strings could be stored in a resource file or in the XML metadata and then referenced from the application. This approach also makes it fairly easy to determine impacts to the application if the database schema changes, because the SQL is all in one searchable repository. Enterprise JavaBeans enforce this concept by placing the EJB QL in the bean's deployment descriptor. Each finder method then uses the defined query that is abstracted out of the application code.

Always Use Business Objects for Transactional Updates

Always use business objects for transactional updates to ensure data integrity and avoid redundant business logic validation code. Straight database queries can be used for read-only operations if they are more effective at traversing large table structures. However, this should be done only if you can mitigate the risk of having database names permeate throughout the application code. This risk is addressed in the next best practice.

Minimize Use of Database Names in Code

One of the primary risks of using queries directly in your application is that the database column names can start to appear all over the code if not managed well. This can be a maintenance nightmare if the database schema changes or even if a few column names change. Map the result set rows to some kind of value object with logical property names in order to isolate or eliminate references to database names in application code.

Use a Business Object Factory Abstraction

Use a factory method abstraction to create and discover instances of business objects. This simplifies the client code and provides a hook for potential future optimizations such as caching EJB Home interfaces. A common interface or base class can be used to create implementations for each type of business object. For example, an EJB factory, a Castor object factory, and a regular Java business object factory can be used respectively for the different business object implementations. They can all share a common interface that is used to invoke the `create` and `delete` templates on the business objects. The `find` method on the factory interface encapsulates the logic necessary to look up an object. In the case of Entity Beans, this prevents the developer from having to use JNDI and the EJB Home interface every time an Entity Bean is needed. The factory should still expose the underlying artifacts through getter methods so that they can be used if necessary. For example, the EJB factory should provide a method to get the Home interface of a bean so that any static business methods may be invoked.

Use an Object Collection Service

Managing a list of objects for data retrieval or for selective updates is a common operation in business applications. Consider the use of a utility class that consistently and effectively manages collections of objects for you. If Entity Beans are used as the business object implementation, you can also use the collection utility to get a list of value objects and have it instantiate corresponding Entity Beans for any transactional updates. Within an Entity Bean, `ejbSelect` methods are used to retrieve other Entity Beans deployed from the same JAR file. Use Entity Bean finder methods only if you can mitigate the $(n + 1)$ performance issue through CMP implementation strategies such as aggressive loading.

Use the Template Method Pattern for Common Business Behaviors

The Template Method pattern is an excellent mechanism for providing extensible business object foundation classes that implement the common behaviors of business objects. A primary example of the use of this technique is the `save` method, which can call a hook method to perform data validation, specific object validation, and any presave logic implemented in the subclass. A `create` template method can be used to initialize object values and create any aggregated objects with a shared lifecycle. A `delete` template method can be used to perform any predelete functionality. These template methods map directly to the Entity Bean hook methods for an easy migration path between a straight Java implementation of the business objects and an EJB implementation. The Entity Bean base class becomes merely a component wrapper of the Java implementation that is used to take advantage of the many EJB component services. The Template Method pattern is also very powerful when used for application-specific functionality that has slight variations for different implementations.

Consider Metadata-Driven Business Objects Derived from Design Models

Business objects that use metadata to configure properties, collections, and relationships provide a powerful foundation for component development. EJB uses this concept extensively to configure persistence and other services through the deployment descriptor. The concept can be extended even further as a part of a reference architecture to automate property management, relationship management, and many other functions. If you choose to take this approach, use a metadata format that allows your design models to be the original source of the metadata. Either build your metadata parser to read the XMI format or use a conversion utility to create your own XML format from XMI that is generated by development tools from the design models. A configurable business object foundation that uses metadata derived from a design model is a very powerful concept that can be used to automate business object development.

Use a Consistent, Extensible Caching Mechanism to Improve Performance

Cache frequently used data that is fairly static to speed application performance. Use a consistent, extensible cache mechanism that can be implemented either as a stateless Session Bean or as a Java singleton class. If the cached data can be updated and the application needs the latest data, consider the use of a JMS solution for notifying caches across a cluster to refresh their data. Keep in mind, however, that databases are very good at what they do and that any caching mechanism should not try to replace the database. If there are large volumes of data or if the data is updated frequently, using the application database is likely to be just as efficient as a caching solution, if not more efficient.

Summary

Two primary responsibilities of business objects are to manage database persistence and relationships to other business objects. The Template Method pattern actually helps to augment both of these functions in a consistent, extensible manner. There are a number of options for implementing persistence including explicit JDBC, a metadata-driven JDBC approach, third-party persistence frameworks, and CMP Entity Beans. No matter what approach is taken, a business object factory should be used to abstract the creation, deletion, and discovery of business objects. This simplifies the client code and isolates the rest of the application from the implementation model to the extent possible. Each of the factory operations should trigger the corresponding `create`, `save`, or `delete` template methods. These methods ensure that the proper validations and business logic take place during these persistence events. This business logic typically includes managing aggregated objects and executing standard audit logic on database saves, although the possibilities are endless.

These practices round out the implementation of business object components in J2EE. The business objects contain the majority of the business logic in a given application and are at the core of the reference architecture. They are used to do the majority of the work in the next architecture layer, which contains process-oriented objects called service components. The design of these service-based components is the topic of the next chapter.

The Service-Based Architecture: Design Considerations

Stateless, service-based components have been a core element of business applications for quite some time. Before J2EE application servers came into existence, transaction-processing monitors such as BEA Tuxedo used stateless services to distribute functionality and manage transactions, somewhat similar to how Enterprise JavaBeans provides these types of infrastructure services. The Enterprise JavaBeans model is built around components. Software components can sometimes be viewed as wrappers around either an individual object or a set of related objects. Thus, the EJB model is based on an object-oriented programming paradigm. The prior transaction-processing model was based on services, which can be viewed as global functions such as in a procedural programming language. These services typically could be either stateful or stateless, although stateless was the recommended choice for scalability and performance. A primary reason for this is the fact that a stateful service consumes resources that could be shared across multiple clients in between different client requests. The other problem with the stateful approach is the potential issue of users who walk away from their desks during the use of a client-server application. This leaves the stateful service hanging there, consuming resources until the session or application times out. Thus, stateless services were often the solution that formed the basis of many of these applications.

You can use the concept of a service within the J2EE architecture as a primary option for distributing and managing business functionality. So why would you want to regress to a model more accustomed to procedural programming languages rather than use the newer paradigm of object-oriented development? Well, this is not really an accurate way to look at it. Using service-based components is not really a complete regression into the past although it does take advantage of the many benefits that come with using this proven design pattern in the architecture. If you go back to the loose definition of a component, you see that a service really provides an interface into the service's functionality, remotely distributing a particular method of the primary object within the component. Most likely the component encapsulates a set of related objects; this is often the case, because service-based components in the architecture will use business objects to do the bulk of the work. In this sense, components in the EJB tier build on each other, at different levels encapsulating larger and larger sets of functionality. You have already seen how business objects themselves exhibit this characteristic in the case of aggregated business objects. Based on this view, you can look at each of these components as building blocks in your application architecture. This allows for great levels of reusability across a portfolio of related applications, and it will be discussed in full detail in later chapters on reusability and the strategic architecture.

Many service-based components are actually nothing more than workflow managers that invoke business methods across multiple Entity Beans or business objects. Consequently, the implementation of these service-based components is actually quite object-oriented underneath the covers. It is primarily the exposure to the client that is still modeled as a stateless service, a single method call that holds no state across invocations. These stateless services are much more scalable and provide a higher level of throughput than their stateful equivalents. Enterprise JavaBeans containers are no exception to this rule. The nice part about this model in the J2EE architecture is that it fits nicely into the Web-based application design. The Web tier contains a primary mechanism, which is called the HttpSession, to maintain state in an application. For this reason, there is seldom need to use stateful Session Beans to maintain state. Most J2EE application servers already provide high-availability clustering with failover on the Web tier, but they have been slower to do so with stateful Session Beans. A different viewpoint may be taken, however, for Java Swing-based applications. A thick-client application might likely use a stateful Session Bean to maintain a connection with the server and make repeated method invocations based on user events. However, in a thin-client application, this happens much less frequently because the state is maintained on the Web tier, and invoking stateless service-based components to access business functionality is a much more natural fit to the architecture.

Service-based components represent the business processes and transactions of a given application. They often implement a single unit-of-work, although they may also be combined with other services as a portion of a larger transaction. Extending the building block view of the world, the same concept that applied for business objects also applies to service-based components. Some services are smaller and have meaning individually, but they can also be used as a step in a larger workflow or service that gets used somewhere else in the application, perhaps even across applications in a particular business. Take an order processing system on an electronic commerce Web site as an example. One service in the back-end system might be named PurchaseNew-Product. This service would be invoked when an existing customer purchases a new product on the Web site. However, when a customer comes to the Web site for the first time and makes a purchase, you can't invoke this service yet because the customer does not exist. Thus, in one transaction you would like to invoke the services `Create-NewCustomer` and `CreateNewBillingAccount` first, and then invoke the `PurchaseNewProduct` service. One design for implementing this would be to create a "master" service that controls the flow of invoking these services. In the correct order and within a single transaction, the master service would create the new customer record, create an account for the customer in the system, and then process the new purchase order. In this manner, services can be used as building blocks for other services. Service-based components can encapsulate different levels of functionality as they go up or down in this hierarchy. Keep in mind that all applications and businesses are unique, and different levels of reusability will be achievable; however, the architecture and component design should always take these things into account to provide for the possibility of extending the functionality. Businesses often change their models and processes, so the building blocks can also get shuffled around and extended, as is often the case. Figure 5.1 illustrates how, in this example, services are being reused as building blocks within an application.

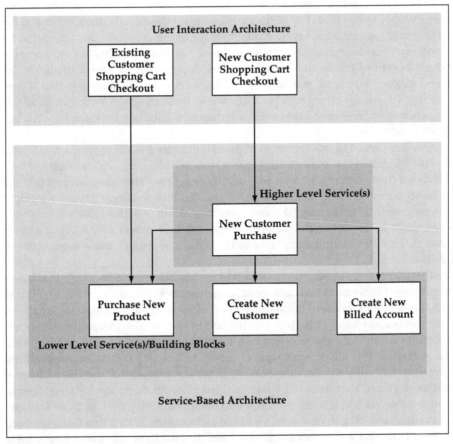

Figure 5.1 Services as Building Blocks in an Order Processing System.

It is important to note that not all architectures have a service layer. Many designers and architects implement the functionality found in the services as a business logic method on one of the primary business objects involved in the transaction. In many cases, this works just fine, and there is nothing wrong with doing this. However, there are many benefits to adding a service-based layer in between the user interaction layer and the business objects layer. The primary benefits of this design are based on two different thought patterns. The first of these is based on the ramifications of the overall software architecture and how these services fit nicely into the Web-based application architecture. The second basis point is that the study of businesses and business applications shows that business processes or transactions naturally fall out of the model. There are numerous transactions in a typical business involving the same business entities. This is the case in the recurring example of the bank account that can be a part of many different interactions with a customer. In some cases, business entities might even act or react differently based on which process they are currently involved in.

The first basis point deals with the rationale of the services layer in terms of software architecture. It is based on a number of things including flexibility, reusability, and the efficient use of Enterprise Java services. A primary benefit to note is that it isolates the business object layer from the user interaction layer. It provides a wrapper that limits what the front end needs to know about the back end. It simplifies the front end greatly because the only things that it must do are package up the data for the service and invoke the correct service component. No knowledge of the business object model or its interfaces is required to have access to the business functionality. This isolation point is a primary benefit of the Model-View-Controller design pattern. This also allows the back-end functionality to be reused across different client applications. It also allows the client to drastically change its behavior without affecting the back end at all. To summarize this in Enterprise Java terms, it reduces the coupling between the Web tier and the EJB tier.

A secondary benefit of this reduced coupling is increased performance. Invoking an Enterprise JavaBeans component can mean a network trip between the Web tier and the EJB tier if the two tiers are physically distributed. This pattern usually reduces the interactions between the presentation layer and the business logic layer to a single remote method call. There may be some cases in which it is better to invoke multiple services remotely. However, the majority of cases will be covered by a single service invocation. Thus, this architecture layer reduces the amount of unnecessary network and RMI overhead.

Another point to make about this model in terms of software architecture is that it provides an excellent way to take advantage of Enterprise Java services, such as distribution and transaction management, through the most efficient type of Enterprise JavaBean, the stateless Session Bean. This gives you the best of both worlds in a sense, the performance and scalability of a stateless service combined with the container-provided infrastructure services that allow you to quickly build and deploy enterprise applications.

After examining the architecture in depth, it will be argued that there is additional benefit to be gained from creating a standard interface for these service components. This allows the creation of a generic front-end component that invokes these services. You can also easily plug in new services to the architecture. Taking this thought a step further, you can also implement a common base class for these services if you want to provide common hooks for application-level security, logging, or audit trail features.

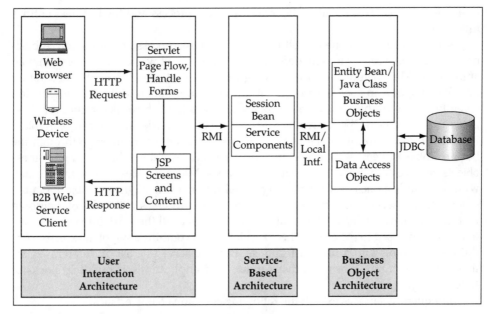

Figure 5.2   High-level Service-Based Architecture.

Consequently, the rationale for the Service-Based Architecture can be summed up by the following points:

- Reduces the coupling between the Web tier (User Interaction Architecture) and the EJB tier (Business Object Architecture)
- Limits the number of remote method calls and RMI/network overhead
- Distributes business functionality through a standard, service-based interface
- Utilizes the most efficient Enterprise JavaBean, the stateless Session Bean, to take advantage of container-managed services such as distribution and transaction management
- Is used to coordinate multiple business objects in a transaction; manages workflow between entity business methods
- Provides the potential for a common base class to generically manage application-level security, logging, and audit trail functions

Thus, there are many benefits to encapsulating business process functionality in a stateless Session Bean. Figure 5.2 shows the high-level components within the Service-Based Architecture and how they fit into the overall architecture.

Elements of Service-Based Components

A study of business applications shows that business processes are what drive business functionality within an application. They represent the meaningful interactions or events that occur between a business and its customers. They are often transactions or units-of-work that are crucial to the integrity of the process and the business entities involved.

A service-based component itself models a business process or transaction. A business process here can be loosely defined as any element of work to be done within an application. This includes services ranging from transactions initiated by a customer on a Web page to any service required to provide information to the user interaction layer. In these examples, the data access and updates to the business entities are delegated to the Business Object Architecture. Note that data retrieval itself can be invoked from the service component. However, any update functionality must go through the business objects. Because much of the work of a service is done through the business objects, services can come in all sizes and shapes. Many services will be fairly small with the simplest ones executing a single method on a single business object. On the other extreme, services can model complex business processes with rules of their own that invoke many business objects and must coordinate all the work into one transaction that is exposed to the client. These services must combine any potential error conditions or failures into a unified response. Because services exist at different levels, they can also be reused across other services and applications as building blocks of functionality.

Consequently, services exhibit the following common characteristics:

- Are used to model a business process or transaction
- Use reusable business objects to update business entity data
- Coordinate one or more business objects in a transaction
- Are categorized as read-only or update services

Services Model Business Processes and Transactions

Primary business functions in an application that are accessed by a client are modeled as service-based components. These functions can represent an overall process or an individual transaction. The service-based component is used to distribute and manage the transaction provided by the service object. It provides a single interface for the client to use to invoke the transaction and isolates the front end from the back end.

Examples of business processes include the recurring bank example. A customer moving money from a checking account to a money market might invoke the `TransferFunds` service. A customer of a Web-based retailer might be invoking the `PurchaseNewProduct` service to buy a product from an Internet storefront.

Services Use Reusable Business Objects

Service-based components often contain very little code because they use business objects to do the majority of the work. Simple services usually invoke only a single method on a business object. This is a result of the fact that either a single business entity is affected or the business object actually aggregates related business objects that are included in the transaction. Complex services or processes do require the service component to contain business logic or rules that define how the service will use the business objects.

The `TransferFunds` service in the bank example instantiates two instances of the `Account` object and invokes the `withdraw` method on one and the `deposit` method on the other. The service itself would not modify the account entities; it would use the business objects to do so. Likewise, the `CreateNewCustomer` service for a Web-based retailer would use the `Customer` object to create a new instance of a customer in the database.

A single business object might get used in ten, twenty, or even a hundred different processes or transactions within an application. The different services use the business object in different contexts, often invoking different business methods on the object. In a given process, the business rules or logic may differ as to how the business object is manipulated. It is important to note that all updates to business entity data must go through the business objects themselves rather than be updated directly through the service component. Although there is nothing technically from preventing this, it exposes places in the architecture where updates are allowed without going through the proper data validation and business edits.

One of the primary responsibilities of the service component is to move the data received from the interface to the different business objects involved in the transaction. Services must be able to instantiate particular instances of business objects from the data passed into the method. Likewise, any updated business object data or error information that results from the transaction must be returned from the business objects and marshaled back into the form expected by the client.

Coordinating Multiple Business Objects in a Transaction

One of the primary aspects of a service-based component is that it can encapsulate a subset of functionality in a system. To do this, it is often necessary to instantiate and invoke multiple business objects within a process or transaction. Any update methods invoked on these business objects are usually coordinated into an overall transaction. Session Bean EJB components allow you to do this by declaring a transaction and then having all of your business objects share in that same transaction.

The `TransferFunds` service example uses multiple instances of the same business object, `Account`, to perform the work of the transaction. The two method invocations, `withdraw` and `deposit`, must be executed as part of a single overall transaction to ensure data integrity. In this case, even more importantly, a single transaction is required to ensure that the bank doesn't lose money on the deal, which could happen if the `withdraw` is successful, but the `deposit` is not. This is just as applicable for services that invoke multiple types of business objects, such as when a new customer comes in to open an account. A `CreateNewCustomer` service would use the `Customer` object to create the customer record and the `Account` object to create a new account.

Service Categories: Data Retrieval and Update

Services can be categorized either as data retrieval or update services. It is sometimes helpful to distinguish between the two for modeling purposes and to understand the overall purpose of services in the application architecture. Services that simply retrieve data may not be viewed necessarily as a business process or transaction; however, they are essential services in order to provide application functionality to a client. From a modeling perspective, they provide information to a customer or client. Often they involve complex logic to provide different views or calculations that involve data presented to the user.

Data retrieval services are not required to use the business objects in most cases. For straight database access, the data-access objects can be invoked directly for better performance. However, in update services, any time an actual update is going to occur, a business object must be instantiated from the data and the proper business method called to perform the update. An example of a data retrieval service is `GetAccount-Transactions` for the banking Web site. This service returns a list of transactions for a given account and time period for a customer who went onto the bank's Web site to see if a deposit was posted against his or her account.

Update services are designated such that they are marked as transactional when deployed as Enterprise JavaBeans. They may involve one or more business objects in the update and are usually coordinated into an overall transaction by the service component. Most of the examples thus far, such as `TransferFunds` and `ChangeAddress`, have been update services.

Although it occurs much less frequently, there is another type of service that doesn't necessarily fit nicely into either category. This type of service often performs some kind of calculation or data validation and returns a result that does not persist in the database. A service that performs a what-if kind of analysis or calculation and returns a result might be an example of this kind of service. Most of these types of services have the result or scenario persist in the database and are thus considered update services; however, there can be cases in which there is no database update. For purposes of categorization, any service that does not perform a database update can be considered a data retrieval service. Although this does not fit the definition of a data retrieval service perfectly, it does to a degree fit the spirit of the definition. In these cases, most likely the service returns a result, or piece of data, that is given back to the client for the purpose of supporting the User Interaction Architecture or another larger service that is reusing this service as a building block. In this sense, it is in fact "retrieving" a piece of data for the front end.

Design Considerations

The Service-Based Architecture is primary a design concept and pattern implementation within the overall software architecture. The components themselves typically contain a small amount of code, but they act as an important isolation point between the front end and back end of any application. Nonetheless, there are still a few design issues to take into consideration when implementing a Service-Based Architecture.

The Enterprise Java Implementation

Based on the earlier discussions, stateless Session Beans are a perfect fit for implementing service-based components in J2EE.

> **BEST PRACTICE** Implement service-based components as stateless Session Beans to take advantage of Enterprise Java services such as distribution and transaction management while maximizing scalability and performance.

The service method defined for the component in the remote interface should be marked as transactional for all update services. This method begins and ends the transaction and is required to mark the transaction for rollback if any unhandled application exception conditions are caught out of business object methods. To do this, all service methods should have an overall try-catch block that catches any application exceptions, executes `EJBContext.setRollbackOnly` in these conditions, and gracefully handles the situation. Remember that the EJB container is required only to fail a transaction when this method is called. An application exception being thrown does not necessarily cause the transaction to roll back in all application servers; thus, it is better to do this explicitly in the service component code (or business object code based on the approach to error handling).

Remember that these services are stateless, so member variables of the service component should be used only for data that is shared across all clients that will access the service. Any data should be held using local variables in the method or objects that are instantiated within the service.

Using the Session Bean as a Wrapper

Because services can be reused across other services, it may be desirable to invoke a service without going through the Enterprise JavaBeans distribution method. RMI and JNDI add an amount of overhead that can be avoided if you are already within another service and would like to invoke a service. Thus, it is better to use the Session Bean artifact as a wrapper only around the actual service object implementation. Figure 5.3 illustrates how a remote client invoking a service will go through the EJB wrapper while the server-side component would like to invoke other services directly by invoking their methods. This technique still allows the services to share the same transaction if desired.

The Session Bean in this type of design is merely a required artifact that is used to engage the container-managed services of transaction management, distribution, and so on. The code to actually implement the business logic of the service is housed in a regular Java object called by the Session Bean. The interface to the actual implementation object would be similar to the remote interface provided by the EJB to the client. The interface itself is discussed in the next design consideration topic.

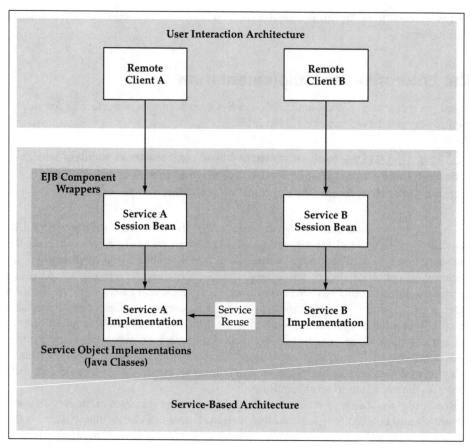

Figure 5.3 Session Bean as a Component Wrapper to Service Implementation Objects.

BEST PRACTICE Put the actual workflow and transaction logic of the service in a Java class. This implementation of the service can then be wrapped by the Session Bean to engage the container-managed services of transaction management, distribution, and so on. This allows services to be reused within other services more efficiently because you have the option of avoiding another EJB method invocation. Optionally, you can use a local interface of the Session Bean, which is slightly less efficient but avoids the RMI and serialization overhead.

The common logic to invoke the service implementation object, handle errors, and manage the transaction can be implemented in a standard Session Bean in the foundation layer. Although there is not much to this, it will still be helpful to implement this in a foundation Session Bean that can be called BlfService. If you isolate the logic that just invokes the service implementation object in a separate method, you can make this a template method that can be overridden by subclasses. This allows you to create specific subclasses with different deployment properties while reusing the basic transaction management logic in the `BlfService` base class. You may want to do this, for example, if you don't need a transactional context for a service. Because you need to choose a transactional setting for `BlfService`, you need to deploy different instances if you want to have a transactional service and a nontransactional service. Note that you could also deploy the same code twice with different JNDI names and different transactional settings, something to the effect of `BlfTransactionalService` and `BlfNonTransactionalService`. However, there may be other types of deployment settings for different application service components, and this concept allows you to do that easily while still reusing foundation functionality.

Impact of the Business Object Implementation

The actual implementation model used by the business objects in the overall architecture has little bearing on the design of the Service-Based Architecture. However, there are a few points worth noting in regard to this topic. The fact that a services layer exists at all helps to make this implementation choice less important for the overall architecture. The services layer allows you to change the business object implementation model with little impact to the User Interaction Architecture.

THOUGHT The service-based components allow for a potential migration between either Java-based business objects to Entity Beans or vice versa. Based on the criteria defined in the Business Object Architecture, different applications favor different solutions. For example, if Entity Beans were chosen as a business object implementation and system performance became a problem, the back end could be ported to regular Java classes without affecting any of the clients or User Interaction Architecture.

If Entity Beans are used as the business object implementation, the Session Bean service components implement the Facade pattern (Gamma et al. 1995) to the Entity Bean business object components. This is a recommended pattern when you use Entity Beans. It prevents a large number of remote method invocations on the Entity Bean component using RMI. In EJB 2.0 containers, the Session Bean service component can, and usually should, invoke Entity Bean business objects using their local interfaces. Figure 5.4 illustrates the component interaction in this case.

The Java Interface to the Service Component

Java interfaces provide a very powerful mechanism that not all programming languages have the luxury of using. The Enterprise JavaBeans specification dictates that both the Home and Remote interfaces are actual Java interfaces. A powerful aspect of

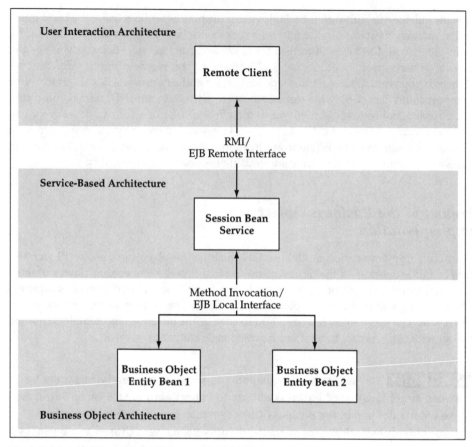

Figure 5.4 Services Using EJB 2.0 Entity Bean Business Objects.

interfaces is that they allow the client to deal with different implementation types without having any knowledge of the actual implementation. The client deals only with the interface class. Because they are similar to a class, Java interfaces can also extend from other interfaces.

THOUGHT The design of the interface to the service-based components is perhaps the most important decision to make in this portion of the architecture.

The interface is the piece of the service-based component that is exposed to the client. It dictates the form and data structure that the front end is required to create in order to invoke the service component. It also will drive what type, if any, of data marshaling is required in the service component itself in order to take input data and then instantiate and populate business objects. Likewise, it dictates how and in what form any data and error information that results from the service is returned to the client.

There are two basic choices that drive the design of the interface. The first question is do all service components have their own interface that takes specific data required for the transaction, or is there a decision to use a standard interface with a generic data structure that can be used for all services? Second, what data structure is used in either case to transport the data remotely from the client to the service and then back again?

Explicit versus Generic Interfaces

Similar to the business objects, the generic interface referred to here can be implemented using a Java interface. However, there are a number of advantages to creating specific interfaces based on the functionality of the service. It allows the reader of the interface to determine exactly what data is required. It also simplifies the data-marshaling process because data is probably already typed and organized based on business object. For example, a `ChangeAddress` service might take a customer identifier and an `Address` value object as arguments. This is the required data for the service component to do its job. It can instantiate the correct instance of the `Customer` object based on the identifier and invoke the `changeAddress` method by passing in the `Address` value object. The method signature might look like the following:

```
public void changeAddress(String customerId,
                          AddressData address);
```

These are good reasons to choose unique interfaces over a generic one. However, if you look back at the guiding principles for building effective software architectures, you see that automation and metadata-driven components are keys to creating a foundation for rapid application development. These principles are very applicable to the Service-Based Architecture. A generic service interface that is standardized across all service-based components allows you to automate the invocation of service components and data packaging that is required in the front end within the User Interaction Architecture. A standard interface allows the front end to generically call the service components given only the name of the service to invoke. This is metadata that can be configured based on the user event that occurred. A standard interface also implies that a standard data structure is used to pass data back and forth. A major responsibility of the front end of a Web-based application is to package data coming from the `HttpServletRequest` into a usable form for the service components. A standard interface allows for a level of automation in terms of data packaging in the front-end components. Finally, a standard service interface allows for easy component integration into the architecture by providing a standard way to plug-in services.

To implement a standard interface for your services with a Session Bean component wrapper, you need to create a standard Java interface for the EJB and for the implementation class. These interfaces should have corresponding method signatures so that the Session Bean can delegate the service request to the implementation class. Figure 5.5 shows a UML representation of the service components and their interfaces.

The Choice of Data Structure

The second issue to decide upon for your services is the data structure. This is even more important for the standardized service interface because it drives the automation

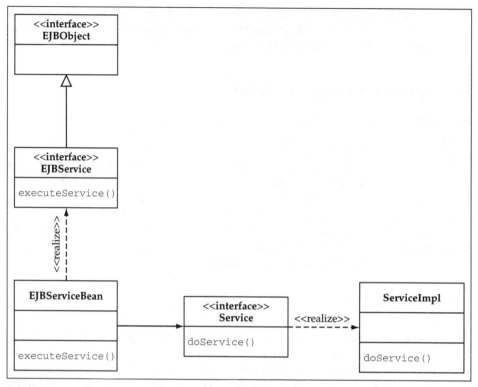

Figure 5.5 UML Representation of Service Component Interfaces.

and data marshaling steps that will occur for all service components. The choice of data structures includes:

- Individual Java data types and objects (that is, date, int, string, and so on)
- Value objects
- XML data
- Argument (or parameter) list: A collection of name and value pairs (for example, java.util.HashMap)

There are not necessarily right or wrong answers on this list. For unique method signatures for each service component, the likely choice is the appropriate set of Java objects and primitive data types to represent the data for the service. For a standardized service interface, the selection of data structure largely depends on the remainder of the architecture decisions surrounding this component in the user interaction and business object layers of the architecture.

Value Objects

If the Business Object Architecture uses value objects throughout to retrieve data from the data-access layer and to populate instances of business objects, then a collection of value objects might be the right choice for a generic service-based interface. You still want to handle value objects generically, so you can require that value objects implement a standard Java interface as mentioned in the discussion on the Business Object Architecture. One challenge with using value objects is that there are different types of objects to transport and there are often multiple objects coming into services; thus, the interface needs to handle a collection of value objects of different types. This requires the service objects either to do object casting and typing in order to determine how to handle different sets of object data or to assume some set of indices that represent different objects. Take, for example, a service that takes a `Customer` and an `Address` object. A generic interface would require a collection of objects, thus, the client and service would need to agree upon the fact that the 0th index in the collection contains a `Customer` object and the 1st index in the collection contains an `Address` object. This approach requires an agreed upon contract for the service beyond just the method signature, because it assumes an ordering of value objects within the collection. The number of cases in which indices are required can be reduced through the use of aggregated value objects. In this example, the `Address` object can be aggregated by the `Customer` and accessed using a `getAddress` method. However, cases that include disparate objects and in which aggregation is not appropriate will still require an agreement on the ordering. In any case, the value object approach will require the front end to have the knowledge of mapping form fields to object properties in order to initially populate the value objects. If an agreed upon order of objects is used, it will also need to know in what order to put the value objects in the collection. Finally, one big benefit of this approach mentioned earlier is that it easily handles multiple instances of objects, a requirement that often occurs in transactional business applications. The next option, a single argument list, needs to do some additional work in order to deal with this type of situation.

Argument List

A collection, equivalent to a Java HashMap, of name and value pairs is the simplest choice because it mirrors the `HttpServletRequest` itself coming from the front end. Both objects have a flat naming space in which to provide attributes and their values, although the `HttpServletRequest` allows for multiple parameter values for the same parameter name. For this reason, the choice of a HashMap-type structure reduces the complexity of the data packaging to be done in the front end. Note, however, that a copy must be made of the name and value pairs from the `HttpServlet-Request` object into a separate HashMap object because it would not make sense to send this servlet-based object to the EJB tier. The limitation of the HashMap approach that is often encountered is that it does not work well for multiple instances of objects or hierarchies of object data. Both value objects and XML data structures provide easy solutions for aggregated objects and collections of objects. These patterns occur quite often, as many update screens deal with a master-detail, or parent-child, relationship. Two very simple examples of this might be `Customer-Address` or `Purchase-Order-LineItem`. Data from both the parent and the set of child objects would likely appear on the same Web page to be updated, and you would want to transfer their data together to the service. Now, this of course is not impossible using a collection of name-value pairs; it just gets to be a bit more difficult to handle when there are multiple instances of objects, and even more complex when the multiple instances go down a couple levels. In these cases, the XML and value object approaches provide much simpler solutions. However, it is important to note that no matter what option is chosen, in a Web-based application, you will be starting from a flat name space of name and value pairs, because this is what HTTP and the `HttpServletRequest` object are based on. You are allowed to have multiple values for a given HTTP parameter name. However, you also want to be able to ensure their correct order and association with object instances in a given form.

You must also consider how data is returned from a service. In a data retrieval service, you will often want to return a collection of object instances, the equivalent of a result set. This would be a little tricky, but not impossible to do, using a flat namespace of name and value pairs.

XML

XML is a very popular data structure that is generic enough to store any type of object data including hierarchies of objects. This works very well for generically handling objects aggregated within other objects. XML data is typically used for data transfer between applications. However, it can also be used to transfer data to and from the service components. This type of data structure adds some amount of overhead for XML parsing, but might be a good choice if the front end is driven by XSL stylesheets that expect XML data as input. If XSL transformations are to be used to generate much of the Web page content in an application, an XML interface for service components makes a lot of sense. Another reason might be if these services are also to be deployed as Web services using SOAP (Simple Object Access Protocol). Web services based on SOAP, as well as many other B2B interactions, send data across HTTP requests as XML. Thus, if your services are based on XML interfaces, only a simple translation within the User Interaction Architecture is required to wrap these services as Web services.

Evaluating Data Structures

Table 5.1 summarizes the advantages and disadvantages of each data structure for use as a standardized service interface.

So which then is the best choice of data structure for the service component interface? Well, there is no clear-cut winner, and the choice, again, depends on the rest of the architecture decisions. However, the focus in this book is on both value objects and argument lists throughout the implementation examples. The integration of value objects with the Business Object Architecture all the way through to the data-access layer presents a strong value proposition (no pun intended). Imagine the ease of creating data retrieval services if the data-access objects return collections of value objects. Even if the data-access layer returns the equivalent of a result set, it would be easy to write a generic routine to create value objects from a data retrieval service component. In this regard, value objects provide a modest amount of data marshaling while using a data structure that can be used pervasively throughout the architecture. Additionally, not all of the input data to a service maps directly to an object property, so an argument list will be quite helpful for many services. This argument list can implement the same value object interface (`get`/`setProperty`); however, it will not be tied to the

Table 5.1   Evaluation of Data Structures for Service Interface

DATA STRUCTURE	ADVANTAGES	DISADVANTAGES
Individual Java objects and data types	Cannot be used for a generic interface	Efficiently represents service data
Argument list (HashMap of name and value pairs)	Maps directly from `HttpServletRequest` form fields	Requires complex solution for hierarchies of objects and result sets
Value objects	Integrates well with Business Object Architecture	Requires a generic collection of value objects that must be typed and handled
XML	Most flexible data structure; handles hierarchies and collections of objects well; integrates with XSL on the front end	Slowest data structure due to XML parsing and number of objects required to represent tree structure

metadata for a single business object. In terms of performance, either kind of value object compares quite favorably to an XML data structure.

Although it is true that XML parsing adds overhead, especially for large data sets, it is still worth consideration for certain architectures. If you consider that HTML is nothing more than a subset of XML, it seems quite natural to send XML to the front end. If your project team has a skillset in XSL, it is even more of a reason to consider it. As previously mentioned, it integrates well into a Web service model, although it is also true that any service can be wrapped to provide an XML interface. This would be required, for example, with service components that return a set of value objects. In fact, in a robust architecture, value objects would know how to transform themselves in and out of XML, so this would not likely be an issue. Nonetheless, XML deserves consideration for a generic interface because of its great flexibility and ease of handling hierarchies and multiple sets of objects. In terms of automation, it is quite easy to create generic routines to transform objects and results sets into XML and then back again.

THOUGHT The flexibility and self-describing nature of the XML data structure provide a mechanism that is quite tempting to use within highly automated foundation architectures. It is the performance aspect that must be kept in mind, especially for large amounts of data.

XML parsers are becoming more efficient; however, they still use a large number of objects underneath the covers in order to implement DOM (Document Object Model) functionality. SAX (Simple API for XML) parsers are effective for handling XML data in a service component. However, the DOM allows you to create an XML representation in memory, which is needed for so many application services. The DOM represents a tree structure that introduces a large number of additional objects on each XML tree that is parsed or created. Performance degradation can sometimes be worse than linear for larger XML documents because of the time needed to create and navigate the large tree structures. The XPath lookups can be especially time-consuming if the document grows in size, which many business applications demand.

The more types of client devices that access the business services, the more likely that XML is a solid choice for the format of data. A standard interface that needs to interact with many different devices lends itself to XML. As mentioned earlier, HTML itself is merely a form of XML. Web services operate using XML data, and wireless clients can use a variant called Wireless Markup Language (WML). In all of these cases, the user interaction layer would simply need to use different translations of the same XML data coming from the service for the particular device. Many content management tools are based on this concept of storing content as XML and using different stylesheets, or transformations, for the particular view of the data or for the particular device.

If performance engineering can be done to the XML parser as well as other parts of the application to a degree that is acceptable for the application requirements, the XML data structure choice is a powerful one for automated, configurable foundation components. In many other cases, the use of value objects is highly effective due to its better performance and integration with the Business Object Architecture.

> **BEST PRACTICE** Service components with specific interfaces for different functions work well in many software architectures. Use a standard interface for service-based components in order to enable highly automated front-end components. Choose the generic data structure that best fits your needs for this interface. XML data is the most flexible choice for automated components. However, it performs the worst, especially for large amounts of data. For many cases, a collection of value objects that implement a standard value object interface works well. For simpler architectures that do not involve many hierarchies or collections of objects, an argument list containing name and value pairs can also work quite well.

Integrating Service-Based Architecture with the Business Object Architecture

There are a few aspects of the Business Logic Foundation that should be shared or integrated between the Service-Based Architecture and the Business Object Architecture. The most fundamental of these is error handling. There should be a uniform approach to error handling across these two layers. Any business errors or exceptions that occur within the service components should use the same error-handling framework that is used by the business objects. Additionally, the service components are responsible for aggregating all of the business errors that may have occurred across business components during a transaction and presenting them uniformly to the user interaction layer.

The other aspect of error handling that can be integrated in relation to the service components is transaction management. A method on the service component will often be the point where you want to initiate a transaction. Thus, the highest-level service component in a transaction will typically start and end the transaction, usually through a declarative step in the deployment of the Session Bean. Any error that occurs in a business object or the service component itself should cause the transaction to fail. It would be very helpful to be able to automate this step through the use of the error-handling framework from within either a business object or a service component.

The other major integration point between the service components and the business objects is the data. This has been discussed through the different interface options for the service components. Data sent into the service must be used to instantiate and populate business objects. Value objects used throughout the architecture provide an excellent way to do this. However, the options also include simple argument lists all the way up to XML data. These approaches can be done just as easily by adding marshaling methods on the business objects, although they come with their own set of costs and benefits.

Best Practices for Designing Service-Based Components

A summary of the best practices for designing the Service-Based Architecture is given in this section.

Implementing Service-Based Components

Implement service-based components as stateless Session Beans to take advantage of Enterprise Java services such as distribution and transaction management while maximizing scalability and performance.

Using the Session Bean as a Component Wrapper

Implement the actual workflow and transaction logic of the service in a regular Java class. This implementation of the service can then be wrapped by a Session Bean to engage the container-managed services of transaction management, distribution, and so on. This allows services to be reused within other services more efficiently because you have the option of avoiding another EJB method invocation. It also follows the general design principle of implementing objects as normal and then packaging them as EJB components when it is advantageous to do so. As an alternative, you could also invoke other services within a service using a Session Bean local interface. This is slightly less efficient than a pure method call, but it does avoid RMI and serialization overhead. One thing to be aware of with this approach is that it may introduce both a remote and local interface for the service component. If this fact is not considered during the design phase, it could potentially cause problems later on because the programming paradigm switches between pass-by-reference and pass-by-value.

Designing the Service Interface

Service components with specific interfaces for different functions work well in many software architectures. Use a standard interface for service-based components in order to enable highly automated front-end components. Choose the generic data structure that best fits your needs for this interface. XML data is the most flexible choice for automated components. However, it performs the worst, especially for large amounts of data. For many cases, a collection of value objects that implement a standard value object interface works well. For simpler architectures that do not involve many hierarchies or collections of objects, an argument list containing name and value pairs can also work quite well.

Summary

Service-based components represent the business processes and transactions of a given application. They often implement a single unit-of-work, although they may also be combined with other services as a portion of a larger transaction. They make up an important layer in the reference architecture because they simplify the front-end logic and isolate the business object implementation model. Service components provide Web-tier components with a standard interface to invoke that encapsulates the overall transaction and manages the workflow between multiple business objects or Entity Beans. The implementation model for service components is typically a stateless Session Bean as a wrapper around a Java implementation object.

With the design considerations and best practices from this chapter in mind, the next chapter walks through the implementation of service-based components in the reference architecture. Services from the bank application are implemented that build on the business objects implemented in earlier chapters. A service component foundation class is also constructed for the Session Bean wrapper. This foundation is used to standardize error handling and the invocation of service implementation objects.

CHAPTER

6

Building Service-Based Components

As discussed earlier, the service component layer in the architecture is largely a design pattern in your application. Implementation of service components does not require a large degree of foundation code, although the amount of actual business logic will vary. Many services will be simple and elegant, although in some applications there may also be complex services that implement intricate business processes. In many cases, the service components act as a workflow manager between business objects.

The Actual Service Interface

For the specific interface of the `TransferFunds` service example, the two account identifiers and an amount to transfer are required as arguments. Thus, the interface looks like this:

```
public interface TransferFunds extends EJBObject {

    public void executeService(String accountId1,
                               String accountId2,
                               BigDecimal amount)
        throws BlfException, RemoteException;
}
```

For the `ChangeAddress` service, it might look like this:

```
public interface ChangeAddress extends EJBObject {

    public void executeService(String addressId,
                               String line1,
                               String line2,
                               String city,
                               String state,
                               String zip,
                               String country)
          throws BlfException, RemoteException;
}
```

Using a standard service interface, you need a generic way to encompass the data for these services as well as any others that you can imagine. As concluded in the design consideration discussion, value objects, and sometimes their implementation as straight argument lists, provide an efficient and flexible mechanism to transport data. Note that the data in these two service examples falls into two categories:

- Object data
- Service arguments

The address fields sent to `ChangeAddress` all map directly to object properties. This type of data is well suited for value objects since it corresponds directly to an object. However, some data sent to a service is simply a service argument. For example, the dollar amount in `TransferFunds` does not map directly to any object property. It will, of course, affect the current balance property of the account, but it does not correspond directly. It is an argument to the business logic that will add or subtract from a given account's balance. Thus, it might be nice to have a data structure that supports both.

THOUGHT Use a service data structure that explicitly supports an argument list as well as a collection of value objects so that both types of data can be easily handled.

An Implementation for Argument Lists

It would simplify things if the argument list class implemented the same `ValueObject` interface. Consequently, you can create a new implementation of `ValueObject` called `ArgumentList`, that does not associate properties with any specific business object metadata. It is required to store everything as a collection of strings because it won't know the data type. Specific get methods can still be used to extract argument values as different data types. The basic code for this class is as follows:

```
public class ArgumentList implements ValueObject {

    /*
     * Collection of string argument values. You can't deal
```

```
 * with specific types because you don't have the metadata.
 */
protected HashMap attributes;

/*
 * Default constructor
 */
public ArgumentList() {
    attributes = new HashMap();
}

/*
 * Property management methods
 */

public void setProperty(String propertyName, Object value)
    throws PropertyException {

    attributes.put(propertyName,value.toString());
}

public String getProperty(String propertyName)
    throws PropertyException {

    return (String) attributes.get(propertyName);
}

public BigDecimal getDecimalProperty(String propertyName)
    throws PropertyException {

    String value = (String)attributes.get(propertyName);
    BigDecimal decimal =
        (BigDecimal) convertToObjectFormat("Decimal",value);
    return decimal;
}

public Date getDateProperty(String propertyName)
    throws PropertyException {

    String value = (String)attributes.get(propertyName);
    Date myDate =
        (Date) convertToObjectFormat("Date",value);
    return myDate;
}

public Object convertToObjectFormat(String type,
                                    Object value)
    throws PropertyException {

    // If no value exists, you can't convert it.
    if (value == null) {
```

```
        return value;
    }

    // Look up the property type, get an instance of the
    // handler class based on the metadata, and
    // convert the value.
    PropertyHandler handler = null;
    try {
        handler = (PropertyHandler)
          CacheList.getInstance().getObject(
                            "PropertyTypeCache",type);
    } catch (BlfException ignoreForNow) {}

    if (handler == null) {
        throw new PropertyException("Property type " +
          type + " is not a defined type in the metadata.");
    }

    return handler.convertToObjectFormat(value);
  }
}
```

NOTE Another alternative for implementing argument lists is to create specific value object definitions in the metadata. In this option, the argument lists are really just instances of `BaseValueObject`. You can then use the specific named value object in the metadata, just as you would for a particular business object, when you want a specific argument list. This adds a bit to the metadata for all of the services, but provides a nice alternative if you want the ability to deal with setter methods specific to data types rather than deal with everything as a string.

A Unified Service Data Structure and Interface

It would be nice to have one standard interface you can use for all services. This requires a data structure wrapper that can hold the following items:

- Argument list
- Collection of value objects
- Error list

Optionally, you can also store both the input and output data in a service data structure if you want a nice way to hold on to both for comparisons or for other purposes. You can wrap all of these things in a single `ServiceData` class to simplify the standard interface. It is a simple wrapper class that could look like this:

```
package blf;

import java.util.*;
```

```
/**
 * A data structure for services
 */
public class ServiceData  {

    // The name of the service
    private String serviceName;

    // The argument list
    private ValueObject argumentList;

    // A collection of input value objects
    private ArrayList inputData;

    // A collection of output value objects
    private ArrayList outputData;

    // A list of errors or messages
    private ErrorList errors;

    /**
     * Construct the data structure for a particular service.
     */
    public ServiceData(String serviceName) {
        this.serviceName = serviceName;
        // Instantiate what you typically need.
        // Most services have input data, output data,
        // and potential for error messages, although
        // you could have used lazy instantiation for these.
        inputData = new ArrayList();
        outputData = new ArrayList();
        errors = new ErrorList();
    }

    /**
     * Get the service name.
     */
    public String getServiceName() {
        return serviceName;
    }

    /**
     * Get the argument list.
     */
    public ValueObject getArgumentList() {
        return argumentList;
    }

    /**
     * Set the argument list.
     */
```

```java
    public void setArgumentList(ValueObject value) {
        argumentList = value;
    }


    /**
     * Get the collection of input value objects.
     */
    public ArrayList getInputData() {
        return inputData;
    }


/**
     * Add an individual input value object.
     */
    public void addInputData(ValueObject valueObject) {
        inputData.add(valueObject);
    }


    /**
     * Get an individual input object.
     */
    public ValueObject getInputData(int index)
        throws BlfException {
        if (index > (inputData.size() - 1)) {
            throw new BlfException("Service Data does not have "
                + index + " objects.");
        }
        return (ValueObject) inputData.get(index);
    }


    /**
     * Get the collection of output value objects.
     */
    public ArrayList getOutputData() {
        return outputData;
    }


    /**
     * Add an individual output value object.
     */
    public void addOutputData(ValueObject valueObject) {
        outputData.add(valueObject);
    }


    /**
     * Get an individual output object.
     */
    public ValueObject getOutputData(int index)
        throws BlfException {
        if (index > (outputData.size() - 1)) {
            throw new BlfException("Service Data does not have "
```

```
                    + index + " objects.");
        }
        return (ValueObject) outputData.get(index);
    }

    /**
     * Get the error list.
     */
    public ErrorList getErrorList() {
        return errors;
    }

}
```

Thus, this class holds everything needed for both update and data retrieval services. The Java interface for services then can be defined as follows:

```
package blf;

import java.rmi.RemoteException;

public interface BlfServiceObject {

    public void doService(ServiceData data)
        throws BlfException, RemoteException;
}
```

BEST PRACTICE Consider the use of a standard interface for service components. This approach enables the reference architecture to automate the invocation of services to a large extent. Services can be generically invoked through their interface, and standard data structures allow for the automated creation of input data. A standard service data structure can be used to store arguments and object data as input as well as the corresponding output data and error information from the service.

The Session Bean as a Component Wrapper to the Service

The `BlfServiceObject` interface is used for the actual implementation objects. As discussed earlier, you can use a standard foundation Session Bean as an EJB component wrapper to take advantage of container-managed services such as transactions and security. The remote interface to this EJB component mirrors the service implementation interface. This component will be called `BlfService`. It is defined as:

```
package blf;

import javax.ejb.EJBObject;
import java.rmi.RemoteException;
```

```
public interface BlfService extends EJBObject {

    public ServiceData executeService(ServiceData data)
        throws BlfException, RemoteException;
}
```

The implementation of the foundation service component is quite simple. It uses a new utility called `ServiceObjectFactory`, similar to `BusinessObject-Factory`, to obtain a handle to the service implementation object. It uses the service name stored in `ServiceData` to determine what actual service is being invoked. The mapping between the service name and the implementation class can be added to the overall business object metadata. As an example, you can define the following service definitions in the metadata:

```
<Service name="ChangeAddress"
        class="bank.entity.ChangeAddressServiceImpl" />
<Service name="TransferFunds"
        class="bank.entity.TransferFundsServiceImpl" />
```

NOTE This is an implementation of the Command pattern (Gamma et al. 1995) on the EJB tier. The name of the service is used to locate and execute an object that implements a standard command interface, in this case the `BlfService-Object` interface. The Command pattern certainly is not required here, but it does provide a key benefit. It provides a nice mechanism that allows the service objects to be implemented as Java classes so that they can be reused outside of the context of an EJB. This can prevent unnecessary overhead caused by an additional EJB when you are already in the context of a Session Bean.

A common base class for all services is `BlfServiceBean`. It provides the transaction management functionality shared by all service components. It can act either as a Command pattern to invoke service implementations or as a Template Method pattern for specific deployments of service components. The code for `BlfServiceBean` is as follows:

```
package blf;

import java.rmi.RemoteException;
import javax.ejb.*;

public class BlfServiceBean implements SessionBean {

    /**
     * EJB context variable
     */
    protected SessionContext myContext;


    public ServiceData executeService(ServiceData data)
        throws BlfException, RemoteException {
```

```
        try
        {
            // This method is implemented by the base class to
            // run the Command pattern to execute service.
            // This method can also be implemented by
            // specific services implemented as
            // Session Bean subclasses.
            doService(data);

            // If errors are logged in the service itself
            // (for example, in the ServiceData object),
            // throw an exception to roll back
            // and get the errors sent back to the client.
            if (!(data.getErrorList().isTransactionSuccess())) {
                throw new BlfException("Service Error");
            }

        }
        catch (BlfException be) {

            // Integrate errors from the service into
            // your overall list.
            be.addErrors(data.getErrorList().getErrorList());

            // Vote to roll back the transaction.
            getSessionContext().setRollbackOnly();

            // Throw the same exception to communicate the
            // error list that may be inside.
            throw be;
        }
        catch (Exception e) {

            // Vote to roll back the transaction.
            getSessionContext().setRollbackOnly();

            // Map the exception to a general
            // application error.
            throw new BlfException("General error: ",
                ErrorList.createSingleErrorList(
                        "GEN_EXCEPTION_ERR", e.getMessage())));

        }

        // Return the service data object.
        return data;
    }

    /**
     * This method can be overriden by a subclass if you want to
     * deploy a specific service
     * (different transactional context, and so on).
     */
```

```java
public void doService(ServiceData data)
    throws BlfException, RemoteException {

    // Obtain an instance of the service object
    // implementation for this service and invoke
    // passing the service data as a parameter.
    BlfServiceObject bso =
        ServiceObjectFactory.getServiceObject(
                                    data.getServiceName());
    bso.doService(data);
}


// Empty implementation for EJB container methods
public void ejbCreate() {}
public void ejbPostCreate() {}
public void ejbRemove() {}
public void ejbActivate() {}
public void ejbPassivate() {}

/**
 * Set the EJB session context.
 */
public void setSessionContext(SessionContext sc) {
    myContext = sc;
}

/**
 * Get the EJB context object.
 */
protected SessionContext getSessionContext () {
    return myContext;
}

}
```

There are several interesting things to note about this code:

- The primary method, executeService, consists only of a try-catch block to invoke the service and manage the transaction. This topic is briefly revisited in the next section.

- The executeService method needs to integrate any errors occurring directly in the service object with any business object errors that may have occurred. It does this by adding any errors from the ErrorList in the ServiceData object to the application exception thrown out of the service. The application exception thrown out to the client is then guaranteed to have the complete list. Note that to avoid duplicate errors using this approach, the service object should add errors to the ErrorList in ServiceData and then, if it wants to halt execution immediately, throw a blank BlfException without errors because they will automatically be added in by the base class.

- General exceptions are caught and mapped to a generic application error. This should happen only in the case of system-level exceptions.
- The main work is done in `doService`, which mirrors the `BlfService-Object` interface. The base class implementation of this method uses the Command pattern to invoke the corresponding service implementation. This method can be overridden by a subclass and deployed as an additional Session Bean in order to use different deployment settings than the standard `BlfService` deployment.

BEST PRACTICE Wrap service components with a stateless Session Bean to manage the transaction and distribute the service. Use a common base class to standardize the service error handling and integration with EJB transaction management. Command pattern logic can be used to easily invoke services implemented as regular Java objects while subclasses using the Template Method pattern can be used in order to have specific EJB deployments of a service.

Figure 6.1 describes the UML model of the service components. As discussed, note that `BlfServiceBean` can be used as a Command pattern to invoke services or as a Template Method pattern to rapidly deploy specific service components.

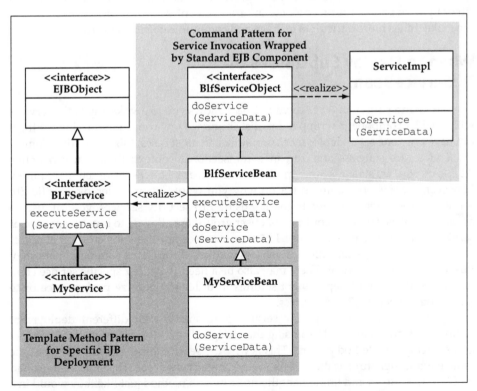

Figure 6.1 Class Diagram of Service Component Implementation.

Transaction Management Revisited

As alluded to earlier in the business object chapters, transaction management is often done at the level of the service component. This occurs for a number of reasons. The most common include leveraging Session Beans as the most efficient EJB component regardless of the business object implementation as well as the fact that many services require coordination between multiple business objects in a transaction. In the business object chapter, there was an example of a call to `EJBContext.setRollbackOnly` in the catch block after the save template within an Entity Bean business method. To simplify things in the architecture, you probably want to remove this logic from business methods because it confuses things when you want to roll back the transaction in the service component. You could check to see whether the transaction has already been voted for rollback; however, the simplest thing might be to have the business objects just throw the application exception containing the business errors and always have the service component be the one to roll back the transaction. As long as you access your business objects through a service, this pattern works quite well. Any business objects that are invoked directly and originate transactions still need to include their own try-catch block in business methods to catch application exceptions and call `setRollbackOnly`.

Remember that the application exception is rethrown to the client to communicate the error list. This is done because the EJB container is required to preserve any application exceptions for the client. System or other unhandled run-time exceptions are wrapped either by a `RemoteException` or a `TransactionRolledBackException` and can make things more difficult to manage and communicate business errors.

When to Deploy Subclasses of BlfServiceBean

The Command pattern in `BlfServiceBean` allows you to invoke any of the services with an EJB component wrapper for distribution. However, being a single EJB, it can have only one set of deployment properties. In most cases, this works fine. Almost all services are stateless and run in a transactional context; thus you can define `BlfService` as stateless and mark `executeService` as transaction required. However, there is one common reason why you would want to deploy specific EJB service components—security. If you are using EJB security services, you can use an access control list (ACL) to control what user groups are allowed to invoke a particular service. A singular deployment of `BlfService` does not allow the creation of different security privileges for different services invoked through the command pattern of this foundation component. There may also be a need to deploy specific service components with different deployment settings in order to optimize performance or to refer to other specific J2EE resources.

If you want to deploy specific service components with different deployment settings, it is quite easy to do so using this design. The `doService` method can also act as a Template Method pattern. This is why the service logic is isolated and has the same method signature as the `BlfServiceObject` interface. The subclasses extend `BlfServiceBean` and implement the `doService` method just like they would in a separate service implementation class. You can then deploy this new bean with a specific set of deployment properties.

The following example illustrates how to use `BlfService` as a template and deploy a specific subclass. The service that requires the use of EJB security is a common example.

```
public class MySecureServiceBean extends BlfServiceBean {

    /**
     * This method overrides the base class implementation
     * and is invoked by the executeService method.
     */
    public void doService(ServiceData data)
        throws BlfException, RemoteException {

        // Do the work of the service here, just like in
        // a Java object implementation, or else call an
        // implementation object.
    }
}
```

Responsibilities of the Service Component

There are a few general responsibilities that most services undertake. For update services, these responsibilities usually fall into the following general outline:

- Instantiating business objects from input data
- Invoking methods on the business objects
- Managing the transaction and handling errors

For data retrieval services, the outline consists of the following responsibilities:

- Executing queries based on input data
- Formatting the results into output data

Instantiating Business Objects

The first responsibility of the update service is to get a handle to the proper instances of the business object that is going to perform the work of the transaction. This requires instantiating the right set of business objects or creating new ones based on the input data sent to the service. When an existing instance of a business object is instantiated, it usually has the current state already set from a trip to the database. Services then often invoke methods on the business objects, passing in data that was sent to the service.

In the case of data entry screens such as a change of address, the service may want to set all or most of the properties of a given object. In this example, the correct instance of the `Address` object is instantiated and all of the address fields, such as city and state, are populated on the business object from the form data. The service would then invoke the `save` Template Method to perform validations and have the data persist in the database. In a more transaction-based service such as an account transfer, the withdraw and deposit methods are called on the Account objects, but only a few key data fields, such as the transfer amount, are passed to the method.

In architectures in which specific interfaces are used for each service, the method for doing this will be determined on a case-by-case basis. For architectures that use a standard service interface, you can automate the majority of this process using the business object metadata.

THOUGHT In a highly automated architecture, you want the instantiation and population of business objects to be as easy as possible. In most cases, this can be accomplished with a single line of code. This sticks to the goal of keeping the service components simple and elegant.

Populating from Value Objects and Argument Lists

This process can be done very easily using the business object metadata. In fact, methods have already been defined on the business object that populate themselves based on a value object such as setProperties. The popular choice of value objects as a data structure does provide a nice, efficient way to implement this process. As previously discussed, value objects that implement the same setProperty and getProperty interfaces simplify this even further. The business object method simply can iterate through the list of property metadata objects, get the property from the value object, and set the property on itself. This code for the setProperties method was shown in an earlier chapter on property manipulation.

Aggregated objects are sent either as aggregated objects within the value objects, similar to the business objects, or as separate value objects in an overall collection sent to the service. It can become fairly complex to deal with value objects in an aggregated hierarchy in your architecture because your User Interaction Architecture will often be constructing and populating them based on form data from the front end. It may be simpler to have the front end move the data to a specific object and have the service components map this data to the appropriate business object hierarchy. This, in fact, is a major benefit of having a service layer in the architecture. It prevents the front end from having to deal with all of the knowledge of the business components. It simplifies things by providing a single interface that takes the data and interacts with the proper business components. Taking this argument further, this thought would support sending all of the form data as a single argument list (in essence, a value object acting as a HashMap), rather than separated into different value objects, so that the front end doesn't even need to know what object a given piece of data belongs to. This approach breaks down because of complexities with a single namespace. If you need to process form data about two (or more) Account objects, you need to send two identifier fields and two amount fields. You can deal with this in HTTP form submissions as multiple occurrences of the same parameter, or you can create a naming convention to separate them (amount1, amount2 . . .). Either way, this logic is best left in the User Interaction Architecture because it deals with specifics of the Web page construct. Thus, you find that a collection of value objects can be a happy medium between the two approaches.

THOUGHT A collection of value objects as a data transport provides a compromise between isolating front-end knowledge from the back end, and vice versa. It isolates logic to deal with multiple object instances on the front end. It minimizes the required back-end knowledge to be the association between a form field and an object. This can be eliminated by using a single argument list (that is, a value object that is really a HashMap for all parameters), as long as namespace conflicts do not become a problem, such as with multiple object instances.

XML Data as an Option

You could also create similar methods to populate a business object that takes a string of XML data. If XML is used as the data structure for the service, this logic is slightly more complicated and perhaps a bit less efficient. Nonetheless, it provides a powerful, flexible mechanism to deal with application data. Because XML is self-describing data, the process becomes easier if it is driven by traversing the XML document and then setting properties as they are encountered. The first thing that must be decided on is the representation of business object data in XML. A common approach is to use an element to define the object itself and subelements to define properties of the object. The Account object might look like this:

```
<Account>
    <Number>C123456789</Number>
    <Type>Checking</Type>
    <CurrentBalance>1259.78</CurrentBalance>
</Account>
```

Another option is to use XML attributes to define properties of the object. In this case, the example would look like:

```
<Account number="C123456789"
         type="Checking"
         currentBalance="1259.78" />
```

In either case, aggregated objects would be represented by a child element underneath the <Account> tag. The attribute-based approach uses less overhead for Document Object Model (DOM) parsers because the data structure uses fewer objects. If a Simple API for XML (SAX) parser is used, attributes are nice because they are given to the document handler method at the same time as the element tag.

Instantiation and Population Mechanism

The actual tools to do this have already been discussed, so now it just needs to be put together in a simple example. You can use the BusinessObjectFactory mechanism created in an earlier chapter to look up or create the business object. The bulk set method that takes a value object, setProperties, does the population of property values. Thus, this process is quite simple in terms of the code.

```
// addressData is your Address data object.
String addressId = addressData.getProperty("id");

// Use BusinessObjectFactory to locate components.
Address address = (Address)
    BusinessObjectFactory.findByPrimaryKey("Address",
                                    addressId);

// Set all of the properties from the input data (value object).
address.setProperties(addressData);
```

NOTE You can simplify this even further because you know which property is defined as the key field in your metadata. Thus, you could implement a `findByPrimaryKey` method on the factory that takes a `value` object without even having to code specifically for the `id` field.

Invoking Business Object Methods

Different services require different business method invocations to do the job. For many services, the particular methods are specific to the transaction. However, there are also many update services that simply take form data and save it. For these, you can use the general `save` method. If the business objects are modeled such that the object validation is automatically invoked on a save, the only thing you need to do here is populate the business object and call `save` in order to fulfill the duties of the service. Because there are so many general form-based applications that are like this that don't have additional logic in the service, this pattern tends to recur. It can actually be parameterized and implemented as a generic update service that follows this pattern. This topic will be addressed in full detail later in this chapter in the "Building Generic, Reusable Services."

Managing the Transaction and Handling Errors

The last major responsibility of an update service is to manage the transaction and handle any error conditions. The foundation for the service components, `BlfService-Bean`, handles most of this responsibility. The only additional thing to be aware of is error conditions that could occur in the service itself.

Business Errors in the Service

Almost all services can generate business errors on their own. Even simple services can encounter conditions such as the instance of the business object is not found. More complicated services that implement business rules and logic will have normal validations and edits that can trigger business errors. You can reuse the `ErrorList` utility created earlier for the business object foundation within the service layer. Remember that the `ServiceData` object that is available to the service contains an instance of

`ErrorList`, so you should use that for any business errors in the service. The base class will take care of integrating any errors logged here to the overall error list sent back to the client. If you want to terminate execution of a service immediately, remember to just throw a blank `BlfException` because the errors from the service data are automatically added to any errors from the business objects. If you use the `throw-ExceptionIfErrors` within the service, you get duplicate errors from the service under the current implementation.

Update Service Examples

A good place to start is to look at some simple update service objects. The `Transfer-Funds` example is fairly straightforward. First, the explicit implementation of this service is shown that uses a unique interface. Next, the same service implemented is shown using the standard interface and foundation class.

Explicit Transfer Funds Service Implementation

If you implemented a `TransferFunds` service component with a specific interface that used Entity Bean business objects, the Session Bean would look like this:

```
public class TransferFundsBean implements SessionBean
{
    public void executeService(String fromAccountId,
                               String toAccountId,
                               BigDecimal amount)
        throws BlfException, RemoteException {

        try
        {
            // Use Entity BusinessObjectFactory to locate
            // components.
            Account fromAcct = (Account)
                EJBFactoryImpl.findByPrimaryKey("Account",
                                                    fromAccountId);
            Account toAcct = (Account)
                EJBFactoryImpl.findByPrimaryKey("Account",
                                                    toAccountId);

            toAcct.deposit(amount);
            fromAcct.withdraw(amount);

        }
        catch (BlfException be) {

            // Vote to roll back the transaction.
            getSessionContext().setRollbackOnly();
```

```
                // Throw the same exception to communicate the
                // error list that may be inside.
                throw be;
        }
        catch (Exception e) {

                // Vote to roll back the transaction.
                getSessionContext().setRollbackOnly();

                // Map the exception to a general
                // application error.
                throw new BlfException("General error: ",
                    ErrorList.createSingleErrorList(
                        "GEN_EXCEPTION_ERR", e.getMessage())));
        }

        // Standard Session EJB methods to follow
    }
```

Transfer Funds Implementation with Standard Interface

The version of `TransferFunds` that uses the standard interface and base class is simplified somewhat in that the transaction management is handled by the foundation
component. In fact, you do not need to create any additional EJB artifacts if you use the
standard `BlfService` deployment. The code for `BlfServiceBean`, which was
described earlier in the chapter, invokes this service object. You need only to create the
Java service object implementation. In this service, there are three data fields that fit
more into the category of service arguments than object data. The identifiers match up
to the account objects, but there are no other equivalent properties. As discussed
earlier, the amount argument does not correlate directly to a property value. Thus, the
argument list in the `ServiceData` is used to hold these values. The code for this
implementation is:

```
public class TransferFundsServiceImpl
    implements BlfServiceObject {

    public void doService(ServiceData data)
        throws BlfException, RemoteException {

        // Get the input data from the argument list.
        ValueObject args = data.getArgumentList();
        String fromAccountId = args.getProperty("fromAccount");
        String toAccountId = args.getProperty("toAccount");
        BigDecimal amount = args.getDecimalProperty("amount");

        // Use Entity BusinessObjectFactory to locate
        // components.
        Account fromAcct = (Account)
            EJBFactoryImpl.findByPrimaryKey("Account",
                                            fromAccountId);
```

```
    Account toAcct = (Account)
        EJBFactoryImpl.findByPrimaryKey("Account",
                                        toAccountId);

    // Perform the transfer by depositing the amount
    // into the to account and withdrawing from
    // the from account.
    toAcct.deposit(amount);
    fromAcct.withdraw(amount);
    }
}
```

Note that in this service, if a business error occurs in either Account object, such as insufficient funds, a ValidationException (a subclass of BlfException), which is caught by the try-catch block in BlfServiceBean, will be thrown. It is BlfServiceBean that deals with the transaction rollback.

Change Address Service

The TransferFunds example was more of a transaction-based service. The next example is a service that would process a data entry form like a ChangeAddress. This service takes all of the properties of an address, such as if they came from a form on a Web page, as an address value object and updates the address in the database. This service requires that the address already exist. These types of services are quite simple given the ability to easily instantiate and populate business objects.

Java Business Object Implementation

The code looks like this for an implementation that uses Java business objects and an underlying JDBC framework:

```
public class ChangeAddressServiceImpl
    implements BlfServiceObject {

    public void doService(ServiceData serviceData)
        throws BlfException, RemoteException {

        AddressData addressData =
            (AddressData) serviceData.getInputData(0);
        String addressId = addressData.getProperty("id");

        // Use Java BusinessObjectFactory to locate components.
        Address addr = (Address)
            JavaFactoryImpl.findByPrimaryKey("Address",
                                             addressId);
        addr.setProperties(addressData);
        addr.save();
    }
}
```

All service objects that take form data and use it to update an object follow this pattern. Note that the save method invocation automatically invokes the property-level validation as well as object-level validation implemented in the blfValidate Template Method.

Entity Bean Business Object Implementation

The version of the ChangeAddress service that uses Entity Bean business objects is identical to the straight Java version except that it uses the EJB version of Business-ObjectFactory.

What If the Address Object Doesn't Exist?

A general error condition almost every service needs to deal with is the nonexistence of a particular business object. This can occur if faulty data is sent into a service or if an application user deletes an entity while another user was viewing that object's data. This condition can happen in service components as well as in business object methods; thus, you should have a general error-handling mechanism for this. The Business-ObjectFactory classes need to be able to report this error condition, so the logic is encapsulated in these factory implementations. For Entity Beans, a FinderException is thrown from the finder method on the Home interface. In the case of JDBC or other persistence frameworks, you need to code logic into the foundation classes to notify clients when no objects are found in a given result set.

To be able to handle all implementation models, you can create a subclass of BlfException called ObjectNotFoundException that maps to a standard busiess error. The exception code could take an object name and key object to automatically create an error list containing the standard business error for "object not found."

```
public class ObjectNotFoundException extends BlfException {

    public ObjectNotFoundException(String objectName,
                                   Object keyObject) {
        super(objectName + " object not found");

        // Map to a standard application error.
        setErrorList(ErrorList.createSingleErrorList(
                "OBJ_NOT_FOUND",
                objectName,
                keyObject.toString()));
    }


}
```

As an example, EJBFactoryImpl would throw this exception on a find method. Remember that reflection is used to generically call a method on a Home interface, so the EJB `FinderException` actually comes wrapped in an `InvocationTarget-Exception`. The target exception could also be a `ValidationException` from a failed edit, so you need to check what kind of exception it was. Looking back at the implementation of `findByPrimaryKey` in `EJBFactoryImpl`, you can examine the highlighted code to deal with these cases:

```
public static Object findByPrimaryKey(String objectName,
                                      Object keyObject)
    throws BlfException {

    // Obtain the business object metadata.
    BusinessObjectMetadata bom =
        MetadataManager.getBusinessObject(objectName);

    // Get the Home interface.
    EJBLocalHome home = getHomeInterface(objectName, bom);

    // Invoke by findByPrimaryKey method.
    PropertyMetadata keyProp = bom.getKeyField();
    EJBLocalObject busObject = null;

    try {
        // Define the parameter types.
        Class[] parameterTypes = new Class[1];
        if (keyProp.getType().equals("String")) {
            parameterTypes[0] =
                Class.forName("java.lang.String");
        }
        if (keyProp.getType().equals("Number")) {
            parameterTypes[0] =
                Class.forName("java.lang.Long");
        }
        //
        // and so on for the other data types...
        //

        Object[] args = new Object[1];
        args[0] = keyObject;

        // Get a handle to the finder method and invoke it.
        Class homeClass = home.getClass();
        Method findByPK =
            homeClass.getMethod("findByPrimaryKey",
                                parameterTypes);
        busObject = (EJBLocalObject)
            findByPK.invoke(home, args);

    } catch (InvocationTargetException ite) {
        Throwable t = ite.getTargetException();
        if (t instanceof BlfException) {
            throw (BlfException)t;
```

```
        } else if (t instanceof FinderException) {
            throw new ObjectNotFoundException(objectName,
                                             keyObject);
        } else {
            throw new BlfException(ite.getMessage());
        }
    } catch (Exception e) {
        throw new BlfException(e.getMessage());
    }


    return busObject;


}
```

Thus, you do not need to specifically code for this exception case in every service component. Just by using the `BusinessObjectFactory` class, the exception with the correct error gets thrown out to base service class without any additional work by the developer. Now, if you want to execute different logic based on this condition, you will need to catch this exception within the service code and then react accordingly. For example, in some services, you may want to go ahead and create an entity if one does not exist. Thus, you would do something like this:

```
try {
    // Use Java BusinessObjectFactory to locate components.
    Address addr = (Address)
        JavaFactoryImpl.findByPrimaryKey("Address",
                                         addressId);
    addr.setProperties(addressData);
    addr.save();
} catch (ObjectNotFoundException onfe) {
    // Perform exception case logic ...
}
```

The Castor Implementation of Change Address

If you are using a persistence framework, such as Castor, there may be some slight modifications required to plug the business object components into the service. With Castor, an instance of the `Database` class is used for all persistence events such as select and update operations. Thus, the `Database` object for the service needs to be made available to the implementation classes. One way to do this is to create a base class for the service implementation objects that creates the `Database` and closes it at the end of the service. Since this will be standard logic, it makes sense to implement it once and extend it to each service. Remember, this is a base class for the `BlfServiceObject` implementation classes. This is different from the `BlfServiceBean` base class used for the Session Bean itself. The `CastorBaseService` class is shown here:

```
public abstract class CastorBaseService
    implements BlfServiceObject {
```

```java
// The Castor persistence engine
private Database db = null;

/**
 * Helper method to get the persistence database engine
 */
protected Database getDatabase() {
    if (db == null) {
        try {
            // Get the Castor database properties
            // out of the configuration.
            String castorConfigFile =
                ConfigurationManager.getString(
                                    "castorConfigFile");
            String databaseName =
                ConfigurationManager.getString(
                                    "databaseName");
            String transactionManagerName =
                ConfigurationManager.getString(
                                    "transactionManager");

            // Create the Castor database object
            // for persistence and add it to
            // the service data so it can be
            // used by the service implementations.
            PrintWriter writer =
                new Logger(
                        System.out).setPrefix("BlfService");
            JDO jdo = new JDO();
            jdo.setLogWriter( writer );
            jdo.setConfiguration( castorConfigFile );
            jdo.setDatabaseName( databaseName );
            jdo.setTransactionManager(
                            transactionManagerName );
            db = jdo.getDatabase();

        } catch (PersistenceException pe) {
            pe.printStackTrace();
        } catch (BlfException be) {
            be.printStackTrace();
        }
    }
    return db;
}

/**
 * Helper method to close the persistence engine
 */
protected void closeDatabase() throws BlfException {
    // Close the database.
    try {
```

```
                    if (db != null) {
                        db.close();
                    }
                } catch (PersistenceException pe) {
                    throw new BlfException(pe.getMessage());
                }
            }


            /**
             * An implementation of the standard service interface
             * that acts as an adapter for Castor-based services
             */
            public void doService(ServiceData serviceData)
                throws BlfException, RemoteException {

                // Instantiate the persistence database engine.
                getDatabase();

                // Invoke the Template Method to execute the subclass
                // implementation of the service.
                doCastorService(serviceData);

                // Close the persistence database engine.
                closeDatabase();

            }


            /**
             * The template method that subclasses must implement
             */
            public abstract void doCastorService(ServiceData data)
                throws BlfException, RemoteException;
        }
```

In order to maintain the Command pattern and also implement the template logic of maintaining the database, a new Template Method was created called `doCastor-Service`. Specific service implementations that use Castor implement this method rather than the `doService` method. This was done to provide the template function-ality of creating the `Database` object, invoking the application-specific logic, and then closing the database.

The Castor implementation of the `ChangeAddress` service then extends the `CastorBaseService` class and implements the `doCastorService` method. The `doService` method invoked directly by `BlfServiceBean` now implements the Castor database template described earlier and uses the `doCastorService` method as the application hook. The `ChangeAddressServiceImpl` uses the `getDatabase` method as an input to the object factory because it is needed for Castor persistence events.

```
    public class ChangeAddressServiceImpl extends CastorBaseService
        implements BlfServiceObject {
```

```
public void doCastorService(ServiceData serviceData)
    throws BlfException, RemoteException {

    AddressData addressData = (AddressData)
        serviceData.getInputData(0);
    String addressId = addressData.getProperty("id");

    // Use CastorObjectFactory to locate components.
    Address addr = (Address)
        CastorFactoryImpl.findByPrimaryKey("Address",
                            addressId,getDatabase());
    addr.setProperties(addressData);
    addr.save();

    serviceData.addOutputData(addr.getValueObject());
    }
}
```

NOTE Aside from the structural changes, the Castor implementation of `ChangeAddress` is still almost identical to the Java and Entity Bean versions. The only difference, again, is the usage of the object factory.

Updating Multiple Business Objects

Many data-entry-type services update more than one business object. Take for example, an `UpdateCustomer` service that updates both the customer entity and the corresponding address. This service might be used from a Web page that lets customers update all of their personal information as well as their contact information. The code for this service using Java business objects would look like this:

```
public class UpdateCustomerServiceImpl
    implements BlfServiceObject {

    public void doService(ServiceData serviceData)
        throws BlfException, RemoteException {

        // Get hold of the input value objects.
        CustomerData customerData =
            (CustomerData) serviceData.getInputData(0);
        AddressData addressData =
            (AddressData) serviceData.getInputData(1);
        String customerId = customerData.getProperty("id");

        // Use Java BusinessObjectFactory to locate components.
        Customer customer = (Customer)
            JavaFactoryImpl.findByPrimaryKey("Customer",
                                        customerId);
```

```
customer.setProperties(customerData);
Address address = customer.getAddress();
address.setProperties(addressData);

// Save all changes to customer and aggregated address.
customer.save();
    }
}
```

NOTE This service could also have been implemented where the address data was aggregated within the customer value object.

Remember that from the study of aggregated objects in the business object chapters, the `save` template can be used to invoke `save` on all aggregated objects, as is the case in this example. If business objects in different hierarchies were updated (that is, non-aggregated objects), then you would have needed to invoke `save` separately on each of the business objects.

The New Customer Service

The bank application also has an application service that creates a new customer in the system. There is a link on the bank home page that allows a visitor to open an account with the bank. This link takes users through a series of screens to capture their name and address information, the type of account they want to open, as well as an initial deposit amount that will be wire-transferred into the account initially to meet the minimum balance requirement. You can create a `NewCustomer` service that processes all of this information to create the new customer, and the new account and to make the initial deposit. This service needs to perform the following tasks:

1. Create a new customer entity

2. Create a new aggregated address entity for the customer

3. Create an account

4. Deposit the initial amount into the account

This service takes input data for three different objects: customer, address, and account. Rather than use three separate value objects and define indices for them in the input collection, you can also implement the value objects to model the same relationships as the business objects. Thus, the customer value object can aggregate a single address and a collection of account value objects. The implementation of the `CustomerData` value object that does this is shown here:

```
package bank;

import blf.*;
import java.util.Collection;
import java.util.ArrayList;
```

```
public class CustomerData extends BaseValueObject
    implements java.io.Serializable {

    // Aggregated address
    private AddressData address = null;

    // Aggregated accounts
    private Collection accounts;

    /**
     * Default constructor
     */
    public CustomerData() {
        super("Customer");
    }

    /**
     * Aggregated address data
     */
    public AddressData getAddress() {
        if (address == null) {
            address = new AddressData();
        }
        return address;
    }
    public void setAddress(AddressData value) {
        address = value;
    }

    /**
     * Aggregated account data
     */
    public Collection getAccounts() {
        if (accounts == null) {
            accounts = new ArrayList();
        }
        return accounts;
    }

    public void setAccounts(Collection coll) {
        accounts = coll;
    }
}
```

The amount for the initial deposit is sent in the argument list because it does not directly correspond to an object property value. In essence, it actually does end up being the current balance because the initial value is 0, but you want to set this value through an invocation of the deposit method to ensure that any other business logic is executed. The code for the Entity Bean implementation of the NewCustomer service is as follows:

```
public class NewCustomerServiceImpl
    implements BlfServiceObject {
```

```
public void doService(ServiceData serviceData)
    throws BlfException, RemoteException {

    // Get hold of the input value objects.
    CustomerData customerData =
        (CustomerData) serviceData.getInputData(0);

    // Use EJB factory to create the customer.
    // This also creates the address,
    // which is aggregrated in the value object.
    CustomerLocal customer = (CustomerLocal)
        EJBFactoryImpl.create("Customer",customerData);

    // Create the account for this customer.
    // The account type and initial deposit
    // amount are given as input.
    // The account ID and number are generated
    // by the business object.
    Collection inputAccounts = customerData.getAccounts();
    if (inputAccounts.isEmpty()) {
        throw new BlfException("Missing Account Data",
            ErrorList.createSingleErrorList(
                "GEN_SERVICE_ERROR",
                "Missing Input Account Data Object"));
    }
    Iterator iter = inputAccounts.iterator();
    // There will only be one account in the
    // input data collection.
    AccountData accountData = (AccountData) iter.next();
    AccountLocal account = (AccountLocal)
        EJBFactoryImpl.create("Account",accountData);

    Collection accounts =
        customer.getOneToManyRelationship("accounts");
    accounts.add(account);

    // Make the initial deposit.
    ValueObject argumentList =
        serviceData.getArgumentList();
    BigDecimal amount =
        argumentList.getDecimalProperty("amount");
    account.deposit(amount, "Initial Deposit");

    // Save all changes to the customer and aggregated
    // address and account.
    customer.save();

    // Return the objects as output data.
    CustomerData outputData =
        (CustomerData) customer.getValueObject();
```

```
        outputData.setAddress((AddressData)
            customer.getAddress().getValueObject());
        ArrayList outputAccounts = new ArrayList(1);
        outputAccounts.add(account.getValueObject());
        outputData.setAccounts(outputAccounts);
        serviceData.addOutputData(outputData);

    }
}
```

Invoking Services within Services

One of the benefits of isolating the service implementation objects (BlfService-Object) is that you can easily reuse existing services as building blocks within larger services. You do not need to go through the additional overhead of the JNDI lookup and EJB component invocation.

As an example, assume you have a Withdraw service that simply subtracts from the current balance of an account. Again, the Withdraw service takes an argument list because it requires an amount value that does not map directly to an object property. The code for the Withdraw service is quite simple because its main purpose is to expose the withdraw business method through the service infrastructure. The code is shown here:

```
public class WithdrawServiceImpl implements BlfServiceObject {
    public void doService(ServiceData serviceData)
        throws BlfException, RemoteException {

        ValueObject argumentList =
            serviceData.getArgumentList();
        String accountId =
            argumentList.getProperty("accountId");
        BigDecimal amount =
            argumentList.getDecimalProperty("amount");

        // Use Java BusinessObjectFactory to locate components.
        Account account = (Account)
         JavaFactoryImpl.findByPrimaryKey("Account",accountId);
        account.withdraw(amount);
        account.save();
    }
}
```

Assume the bank Web site also has a link that allows the user to obtain a money order. This new service, IssueMoneyOrder, will use a utility class to invoke a legacy application to generate and mail a money order to the customer's address. The service, however, also needs to debit the account for the amount of the money order. To do this, the Withdraw service can be reused as a building block for the new service. Although this example is fairly simple and the reuse value is small, many services in business applications become quite complex, and there can be significant value added from using this technique. The `IssueMoneyOrder` takes a customer ID, account ID, and an amount in the argument list. The customer's address on file is used for security purposes. The code for this service is as follows:

```
public class IssueMoneyOrderServiceImpl
    implements BlfServiceObject {

    public void doService(ServiceData serviceData)
        throws BlfException, RemoteException {

        ValueObject argumentList =
            serviceData.getArgumentList();
        String customerId =
            argumentList.getProperty("customerId");
        String accountId =
            argumentList.getProperty("accountId");
        BigDecimal amount =
            argumentList.getDecimalProperty("amount");

        // Reuse the Withdraw service as a building block.
        // This service takes a subset of the argument list,
        // so you can simply pass on the same service data.
        BlfServiceObject service =
            ServiceObjectFactory.getServiceObject("Withdraw");
        service.doService(serviceData);

        // Use Java BusinessObjectFactory to locate components.
        Customer customer = (Customer)
            JavaFactoryImpl.findByPrimaryKey("Customer",
                                             customerId);
        Address address = customer.getAddress();
        if (address == null) {
            serviceData.getErrorList().addError(
                    "NO_ADDR_FOR_CUSTOMER",customerId);
        } else {
            // Use a legacy utility to actually create
            // and mail the money order.  This utility takes
            // the dollar amount and address object.
            BankUtils.createAndMailMoneyOrder(amount,address);
        }
    }
}
```

BEST PRACTICE Reuse services as building blocks whenever applicable to implement larger services. If all the logic is a part of the same transaction, invoke the service implementation directly without going through an unnecessary EJB method invocation.

Combining Error Data from Embedded Services

In the `IssueMoneyOrder` service, any errors that occurred within the `Withdraw` service, such as insufficient funds, would be thrown as a `BlfException` all the way out to the service foundation for the transaction. This works just fine as it is automatically handled and communicated back to the client. However, imagine a situation in which you want to invoke a service within a service and add any errors that came back to the overall list, and then continue on with the original service to finish any validations so that a complete list of errors can be returned back to the user. In the money order example, you could check for both a valid address on file as well as sufficient funds and return both errors in case both validations fail.

To combine errors from an embedded service, you simply need to wrap the service invocation with a try-catch block and add the errors using the `addErrors` method on the `ErrorList` utility. The code snippet that invokes the `Withdraw` service is rewritten as follows to do this:

```
// Reuse the Withdraw service as a building block.
// This service takes a subset of the argument list,
// so you can simply pass on the same service data.
try {
   BlfServiceObject service =
      ServiceObjectFactory.getServiceObject("Withdraw");
   service.doService(serviceData);
} catch (BlfException be) {
   serviceData.getErrorList().addErrors(
                             be.getErrorList());

}
```

The `addErrors` method on `ErrorList` is quite simple. It simply adds an ArrayList of business errors to its existing list. The code for this method is as follows:

```
public void addErrors(ArrayList errors) {

   // Add all of the errors list argument
   // to your current error list.
   Iterator iter = errors.iterator();
   while (iter.hasNext()) {
      getErrorList().add(iter.next());
   }
}
```

Earlier you added a similar method to `BlfException` so that a method can also catch an exception, add some errors to it, and then rethrow that exception with the overall list of business errors. This provides another mechanism to ensure that an overall error list can be maintained and communicated to the client.

Data Retrieval Services

Thus far, the examples were within a category defined as update services. These components were primarily defined by the fact that they modified, or had the possibility to modify, the state of the database through business objects. The other major category of services, which includes almost everything else, is the data retrieval service. The primary function of these services is to return a specific set of data to the client. The most common usage of these services is to populate a Web page with data within the User Interaction Architecture.

Responsibilities of the Data Retrieval Service

Earlier, the primary responsibilities of these two types of services were defined. This section reviews them and studies the primary tasks within a data retrieval service.

Executing Queries Based on Input Data

The majority of data retrieval services have input arguments used to define the set of data to be returned to the client. There are, of course, instances in which this is not the case. Usually this involves returning some kind of reference data that is not particular to any user or business entity, such as a service that would return the list of fifty states from a reference table in the database. However, most services use application data to narrow the result set, for example with a service called `GetAccountList`, which returns a list of accounts for a particular customer.

The input data for queries usually comes in the form of an argument list. This occurs because query parameters usually include only one or two fields from an individual object or else fields from multiple objects or tables. In the `GetAccountList` example, the argument list would consist only of a customer identifier, although more complex services would require a number of arguments. Thus, you can use the argument list inside of the `ServiceData` class to hold the input data. The code to do this is similar to what was seen at the beginning of the update services.

```
// Get hold of the input data.
ValueObject argumentList =
    serviceData.getArgumentList();
String customerId =
    argumentList.getProperty("customerId");
```

Remember that the `ArgumentList` implementation is interchangeable with the value objects because it also implements the `ValueObject` interface. Thus, if your client already has a particular value object, it is usually not necessary to convert it into an `ArgumentList` object. In this case, the client would only have to ensure that the value object is placed in the argument list holder in `ServiceData`.

In the Business Object Architecture chapters, different options were evaluated for executing database queries. Much of the prior focus was on retrieving individual business objects using the `BusinessObjectFactory` or collections of objects using

`ObjectList`. This covers some of the basic data retrieval services needed; however, many services will require data from multiple tables and object structures. Thus, a strategy is needed to handle these cases because they will occur quite frequently in all but the most basic business applications. The set of options for executing database queries now includes:

- Use of business objects
- Object list (collections of value objects)
- Straight database queries

Formatting the Results into Output Data

The current `ServiceData` class holds a collection of `ValueObject` implementations. All of the query options need to be able to convert their data into one of the value object implementations to work with this interface. The business objects already have a `getValueObject` method, and `ObjectList` deals with collections of value objects, so these are already taken care of. The database query strategy needs to include a new implementation of `ValueObject` called `ResultSetValueObject`. This is done to differentiate a result set "row" from your regular value object, which maps to an object's properties. It also makes sense to differentiate this from `ArgumentList`, because although there is not much difference in functionality, `ArgumentList` represents a collection of arguments versus a set of database fields from a result set. Thus, the `ValueObject` class diagram now looks like Figure 6.2.

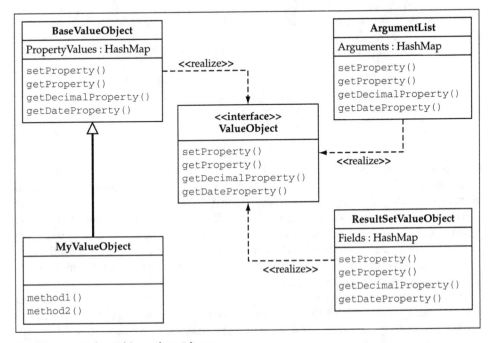

Figure 6.2 Value Object Class Diagram.

Some Example Data Retrieval Services

This section will look at some data retrieval services. The Web page that invokes the `UpdateCustomer` service shown earlier needs a data retrieval service to return the customer and address data to display on the page. Thus, a `GetCustomerData` service is created.

GetCustomerData Using Business Objects

The tools to do this using business objects have already been discussed. The code is as follows:

```
public class GetCustomerDataServiceImpl
    implements BlfServiceObject {

  public void doService(ServiceData serviceData)
      throws BlfException, RemoteException {

      // Get hold of the input data.
      ValueObject argumentList =
          serviceData.getArgumentList();
      String customerId =
          argumentList.getProperty("customerId");

      // Use Java BusinessObjectFactory to locate components.
      Customer customer = (Customer)
          JavaFactoryImpl.findByPrimaryKey("Customer",
                                            customerId);
      Address address = customer.getAddress();

      // Put results in output data.
      serviceData.addOutputData(customer.getValueObject());
      serviceData.addOutputData(address.getValueObject());
    }
  }
```

This service first gets the input data, the customer identifier, out of the argument list. It uses the `BusinessObjectFactory` implementation to get the business object and then invokes the `getValueObject` method to get the data in the form you need it to transport back to the remote client. The address data for this customer is easy to retrieve because the `Customer` business object aggregates the `Address` object, so you can just call `customer.getAddress()`. Remember that you do not need to code for the condition when the object does not exist in the database, because the factory implementations throw an `ObjectNotFoundException` in this case.

Business objects provide the safest way to access data because the business object model already encapsulates the mapping between object data and the database. It knows the underlying database table and column names, as well as the relationships between objects such as between the customer and address in this example. Using business objects is also the slowest method in most cases because it requires individual database SELECTs for each instance, in addition to the fact that business objects are relatively heavyweight objects compared to the other alternative, the value object.

GetCustomerData Using Database Queries

Another alternative is to use a straight database query to select this data. In the GetCustomerData example, you can reduce the number of database calls from two to one. In more complex data models with large object hierarchies, the number of database calls can be drastically reduced using this technique. It has already been argued that for performance and practicality reasons, you do not need to use the object model to retrieve data as long as you do not make any transactional updates. Because data retrieval services do not update the database, it is safe to use a database query mechanism if it makes sense rather than always use the business objects.

Remember, you want to do this only if you can mitigate the associated development risk. For example, if the database column names permeated throughout the application code and the data model changed, you have caused a major headache for the maintenance developer. Earlier in the business object chapter, three goals were defined for mitigating this risk, including externalizing the SQL from the application, isolating the JDBC code, and mapping database column names to logical property names as soon as possible.

BEST PRACTICE If you are going to use straight database queries in your application for performance reasons, mitigate the development risk by externalizing the SQL from the application, isolating the JDBC code in a reusable utility to ensure that resources are properly managed, and mapping the database column names to properties as soon as possible to ease code maintenance.

There are a couple of options for doing this. The first, and most basic option, is to use the data retrieval service as the encapsulation mechanism for the database query. Your GetCustomerData implementation could use JDBCUtility to execute the specific SQL query, get the fields out of the result set, and put them into the proper value object instances to be returned. This would isolate the SQL and the mapping between the database columns and property names within the service component. You could also externalize the SQL string and move it out to your metadata to meet your first goal. This strategy can work well as it meets all three of your goals, noting that it isolates the database column names to within the service component. While this would work fine, you may want to take this further and make the exposure of the database column names even more fine-grained so that you can use a database query as a standalone component.

To do this, you can create a DatabaseQuery class that encapsulates the mapping between columns and properties so that this utility can be used from anywhere within a service or business object component. The DatabaseQuery utility has a few options for doing the property mapping. One interesting technique that was briefly described in the business object chapter is to use aliases as the logical property names in the SQL for the query. This takes the following form:

```
Select fieldName1 propertyName1, fieldName2 propertyName2, ...
From tableName1, tableName2, ...
```

The database utility can then retrieve the fields out of the result set by their logical property names rather than their column names. This puts the mapping knowledge in the query itself in the metadata, so it is fairly self-contained. The one missing piece of this approach is the data type of each property. You could get this information from the `ResultSetMetaData`, although this introduces a second source of metadata for your application, the database itself. Remember that you don't want to use the straight `toString` version of the result set objects because of the property-handler mechanism, which standardizes how different data types are converted and presented to the user. Thus, if you don't mind using the `ResultSetMetaData` to determine the field types, this provides a nice approach. You can fairly easily write a generic routine to do this logic given the foundation that already exists with `JDBCUtility`. Another option is to create specific value objects for each result set. These value objects can be defined in your metadata to provide the database mapping and data type information. The specific value objects would be implementations or specializations of `Result-SetValueObject`, which implements the same `ValueObject` interface. This adds quite a bit of data, some of which is redundant, to the application metadata but does provide a nice explicit way to implement database queries and their result sets.

Either implementation option works nicely. As an example, you can use the first alternative, using aliases in the SQL queries and the `ResultSetMetaData` to run the query. First, you need to create a `DatabaseQueryMetadata` class to store the queries defined in the metadata in the `CacheList`. The metadata class can simply hold the query name and SQL string. You can also add a method to the `Metadata-Manager` to access this metadata. For the get customer service, the metadata would look like:

```
<DatabaseQueries>
  <Query name="getCustomerData"
         sql="select first_name firstName, last_name lastName,
    cust_number customerNumber, pin, line_1 line1, line_2 line2,
    city, state, zip, country from customer c, address a
    where c.id = ? and c.address_id = a.id" />
</DatabaseQueries>
```

NOTE You notice that not all of the fields in the SELECT statement have an alias. These fields happen to have the same logical and physical name, so an alias is not necessary. The result set column name is already equal to the logical property name.

The `DatabaseQueryMetadata` objects used to store this data can be put in a special cache named DatabaseQueryCache. You can then add the `getDatabaseQuery` method to `MetadataManager` to access this data. This class now looks like this:

```
public class MetadataManager {

    public static BusinessObjectMetadata
      getBusinessObject(String objectName) throws BlfException
    {
```

```
            BusinessObjectMetadata bom = (BusinessObjectMetadata)
                CacheList.getInstance().getObject(
                              "BusinessObjectCache",objectName);
            return bom;
        }

    public static DatabaseQueryMetadata
        getDatabaseQuery(String queryName) throws BlfException
    {
        DatabaseQueryMetadata qm = (DatabaseQueryMetadata)
            CacheList.getInstance().getObject(
                          "DatabaseQueryCache",queryName);
        return qm;

        }

    }
```

The JDBCUtility can use this class to map the query name into the appropriate SQL string. In the last chapter, there was a general utility method on JDBCUtility that executed a prepared statement with a generic collection of arguments. You can use this method, executePreparedStatementQuery, to execute the query and give the result set. From this point, you iterate through the ResultSetMetadata and set the property values on the ResultSetValueObject. Remember that the column names in the ResultSetMetadata are actually the logical property names because of the aliases used in the query string. Based on the data type for each column from the ResultSetMetadata, you can use the corresponding property handler to format the data correctly. This is particularly important for data retrieval services because the data often goes directly back to the client for presentation to the user. The relevant JDBCUtility code is shown below:

```
    public ArrayList getResultSetObjects(String queryId,
                                         ArrayList args)
        throws BlfException {

        ArrayList results = new ArrayList();
        try {
            DatabaseQueryMetadata qm =
                MetadataManager.getDatabaseQuery(queryId);
            String sql = qm.getSQL();

            rs = executePreparedStatementQuery(sql, args);
            ResultSetMetaData metadata = rs.getMetaData();
            while (rs.next()) {
                ValueObject valueObject =
                    new ResultSetValueObject();
                for (int i=1; i <= metadata.getColumnCount();
                    i++) {

                    int columnType =
                        metadata.getColumnType(i);
                    Object obj = rs.getObject(i);
```

```
                            if (obj == null) {
                               valueObject.setProperty(
                                    metadata.getColumnName(i),"");
                            } else {
                                if ((columnType == Types.CHAR) ||
                                    (columnType == Types.VARCHAR)) {
                                    valueObject.setProperty(
                                            metadata.getColumnName(i),
                                            obj.toString());
                                }
                                if (columnType == Types.DATE) {
                                    valueObject.setProperty(
                                        metadata.getColumnName(i),
                                        convertToStringFormat(
                                                    "Date",obj));
                                }
                                if (columnType == Types.DECIMAL) {
                                    valueObject.setProperty(
                                        metadata.getColumnName(i),
                                        convertToStringFormat(
                                                    "Decimal",obj));
                                }
                                if (columnType == Types.INTEGER) {
                                    valueObject.setProperty(
                                        metadata.getColumnName(i),
                                        convertToStringFormat(
                                                    "int",obj));
                                }
                            }
                        }
                        results.add(valueObject);
                    }
            } catch (Exception e) {
                throw new BlfException(e.getMessage();
            }
            close();
            return results;
        }


    public Object convertToStringFormat(String type,
                                        Object value)
        throws PropertyException {

        // If no value exists, you can't convert it.
        if (value == null) {
            return null;
        }


        // Look up the property type, get an instance of the
        // handler class based on the metadata, and
        // convert the value.
```

```
        PropertyHandler handler = null;
        try {
            handler = (PropertyHandler)
                 CacheList.getInstance().getObject(
                              "PropertyTypeCache",type);
        } catch (BlfException ignoreForNow) {}

        if (handler == null) {
            throw new PropertyException("Property type " +
              type + " is not a defined type in the metadata.");
        }

        return handler.convertToStringFormat(value);
    }
}
```

This method actually does most of the work to implement this technique. Because it will be a commonly used service, it would be nice to have a wrapper class to use for readability. This clearly delineates in the code when this type of retrieval option is being used. The simple `DatabaseQuery` class is used for this purpose.

```
public class DatabaseQuery {

    public static ArrayList runQuery(String queryId,
                                     ArrayList args)
        throws BlfException {

        ArrayList results = null;
        try {
            JDBCUtility dbutil = new JDBCUtility();
            results = dbutil.getResultSetObjects(queryId,args);
        } catch (Exception e) {
            throw new BlfException(e.getMessage());
        }

        return results;
    }
}
```

Now you have a mechanism you can use within your data retrieval services that performs straight database queries while isolating all of the logic within a `Database-Query` class and the application metadata. You can create a different implementation of the `GetCustomerData` service called `GetCustomerQuery` to get the customer and address data for a particular customer using the `DatabaseQuery` approach.

```
public class GetCustomerQueryServiceImpl
    implements BlfServiceObject {

    public void doService(ServiceData serviceData)
        throws BlfException, RemoteException {

        // Get hold of the input data.
```

```
            ValueObject argumentList =
                serviceData.getArgumentList();
            String customerId =
                argumentList.getProperty("customerId");

            // Use Java BusinessObjectFactory to locate components.
            ArrayList args = new ArrayList(1);
            args.add(customerId);
            ArrayList results =
                DatabaseQuery.runQuery("getCustomerData",args);

            // Put the results, if any, in the output data.
            if (results.size() > 0) {
                serviceData.addOutputData(
                                (ValueObject)results.get(0));
            }
        }
    }
}
```

GetAccountList Service Using ObjectList

Database queries can, of course, also be used for queries with multiple result set rows. If your query retrieves data for a single object, you can use the object collection service, ObjectList, to run the query. This utility returns a collection of value objects. Take the service GetAccountList, which returns the collection of accounts for a particular customer. The collection, as seen earlier, is already defined in the metadata:

```
<BusinessObject name="Account" busObjClass="bank.Account"
        valueObjClass="bank.AccountData" table="account"
        ejbHomeClass="bank.entity.AccountHome">
  <Property name="id" dbname="id" type="String"
        required="true" key="true" autogen="true" />
  ...
  <Property name="customerId" dbname="customer_id"
        type="String" />
  <Collection name="byCustomer"
            query="where customer_id = ?" />
</BusinessObject>
```

The service code to use ObjectList and this defined object collection looks like this:

```
public class GetAccountListServiceImpl
    implements BlfServiceObject {

    public void doService(ServiceData serviceData)
        throws BlfException, RemoteException {

        // Get hold of the input data.
        ValueObject argumentList =
```

```
            serviceData.getArgumentList();
        String customerId =
            argumentList.getProperty("customerId");

        // Use ObjectList to get the collection of accounts.
        ObjectList accountsListObj = new ObjectList("Account");
        ArrayList args = new ArrayList(1);
        args.add(customerId);
        ArrayList accountList =
            accountsListObj.getValueObjects("byCustomer",args);

        // Put the results in the output data.
        Iterator iter = accountList.iterator();
        while (iter.hasNext()) {
            serviceData.addOutputData(
                            (ValueObject)iter.next());
        }
    }
}
```

NOTE Because the list of accounts is the only data to be returned in this service and you already have the value objects in an ArrayList, you could add a setOutputData method on ServiceData, which sets the entire output data collection. You could optionally use this method rather than have to iterate through the collection and add each one individually.

GetAccountList using Castor

The last example can be implemented using a persistence framework, such as Castor, with the following slight modifications. The collection is defined using OQL as follows:

```
<Collection name="byCustomer" query="where customer = $1" />
```

The service implementation is the same except that it uses CastorObjectList, which extends ObjectList.

```
public class GetAccountListServiceImpl
    extends CastorBaseService implements BlfServiceObject {

    public void doCastorService(ServiceData serviceData)
        throws BlfException, RemoteException {

        // Get hold of the input data.
        ValueObject argumentList =
            serviceData.getArgumentList();
        String customerId =
            argumentList.getProperty("customerId");

        // Use ObjectList to get the collection of accounts.
        CastorObjectList accountsListObj =
            new CastorObjectList("Account",getDatabase());
```

```
ArrayList args = new ArrayList(1);
args.add(customerId);
Collection accountList =
    accountsListObj.getValueObjects("byCustomer",args);

// Put the results in the output data.
Iterator iter = accountList.iterator();
while (iter.hasNext()) {
    ValueObject valueObj = (ValueObject)iter.next();
    serviceData.addOutputData(valueObj);
}
    }
}
```

Is the Data Retrieval Service Mechanism Needed?

Now that the structure of a data retrieval service component has been shown, is it really needed within an application? Why can't you just use the DatabaseQuery or ObjectList mechanism from within a JSP or an action class in the User Interaction Architecture? This would save the overhead of going through an EJB component, albeit the most efficient type, the stateless Session Bean. Well, the technical answer to this question is no (see the following note). You are not required to have a data retrieval component wrapper to perform these functions, and you can invoke the collection and database query utilities directly from a JSP or other Web component if you wish.

> **NOTE** There should have been an asterisk by the "no" answer. You do not need a data retrieval component wrapper if the physical tier on which the User Interaction Architecture resides has a direct path within the hardware and network architecture to the database. This tends to be the case in most architectures, even if the logical tiers are split onto different physical machines. If this was not true, then yes, you would need to remotely invoke a data retrieval service on the EJB tier.

So, why would you want to have this design in your application? Well, you may not need to create a data retrieval service component for every query, but it does make sense in many cases for the following reasons:

- The standard service interface plugs in to the automated User Interaction Architecture. A data retrieval service can be automatically invoked as a result of a user action in the front end.

- The data retrieval examples shown here are fairly simple. They take data directly from the database and return it. However, many services require application logic to perform calculations or manipulations on the data before it is returned to the client. A service component is a great place to isolate and encapsulate this logic.

- Services can be chained together, a topic that will be explored later in this chapter. Thus, you can chain together an update service followed by a data retrieval service to return updated data to the User Interaction Architecture through one remote service call.

■ Later in the study of the User Interaction Architecture, you will see that JavaServer Pages can quickly become unmanageable if too much code is placed within the HTML and other presentation logic. Putting this logic in a data retrieval service helps to create a cleanly defined application with maintainable code.

All of this said, if you need to squeeze every ounce of performance you can out of your application, you can always run your database queries directly from a Web component to get around an EJB invocation. This comes down to a design decision and its trade-offs for your particular application. Try to design everything as cleanly as possible and then go back later and optimize if necessary.

In some cases, more data is returned from a query than is displayed on a given Web page at a time. You may want to allow the user to scroll through this data, one page at a time. This can be done by saving the last key values and running another retrieval service for each page request. However, a disconnected result set of value objects does not always meet your applications needs. In these cases, you will not want to use the data retrieval service as it has been described here. Instead, you may want to use a stateful Session Bean or some other mechanism to maintain the connected result set to scroll and fetch rows between page requests. Just be aware of the potential ramifications if you are going to take this approach.

Building Generic, Reusable Services

A concept that can be used to automate and simplify the development of business applications is generic, reusable services. One common function that you can automate within the Business Logic Foundation is the basic data entry form that retrieves data and allows the user to update it. If the data is contained within a single object, or perhaps even an object hierarchy, you can use a generic update service to do the actual update with the form data. You will see this concept through the entire architecture once you look at the User Interaction Architecture and forms processing. However, for the time being, the focus is on the update and data retrieval service aspect of this.

If you go back and look at the `ChangeAddress` service, all services that update a single business object will follow the same steps. These basic steps are:

1. Obtain the key value from the input data.

2. Use the `BusinessObjectFactory` to obtain the instance of the business object.

3. Set the property values from the input data.

4. Call the `save` method.

If you parameterize the object name and key value, you can build a generic implementation of these steps to create a foundation service called `BlfUpdate` that updates a particular business object. How can you do this? Well, the reference architecture has positioned you to do this through the design of the Business Object Architecture. There is a generic factory interface that locates a business object based on the object name and a key value (or key object for multiple key fields). The business objects implement a standard interface so that you can generically invoke the `setProperties` and `save` methods. This is just one example in which you can utilize the power of Java interfaces. Thus, the generic `BlfUpdate` service, in this case for Entity Bean implementations, is implemented as follows:

```
public class BlfUpdateServiceImpl implements BlfServiceObject {

    public void doService(ServiceData serviceData)
        throws BlfException, RemoteException {

        // Get hold of the input values.
        ValueObject argList = serviceData.getArgumentList();
        String objectName = argList.getProperty("objectName");
        String keyValue = argList.getProperty("keyValue");
        ValueObject valueObject = serviceData.getInputData(0);

        // Use Entity BusinessObjectFactory to locate objects.
        EntityBusinessObject busObj = (EntityBusinessObject)
          EJBFactoryImpl.findByPrimaryKey(objectName,keyValue);
        busObj.setProperties(valueObject);
        busObj.save();
    }
}
```

There are a couple of things to note about this code snippet:

- The service takes two arguments in the argument list, object name and key value. These are the two values needed to parameterize the specific `ChangeAddress` service. These values are passed to the `BusinessObjectFactory` to locate the correct instance.

- The business objects are referred to by their common interface, `EntityBusinessObject`. This is the standard business object interface, which contains the methods `setProperties` and `save`. In the case of Entity Beans, this interface extends `EJBLocalObject`.

This concept reduces the amount of overall code and increases the overall quality of the application by using standard foundation components to implement basic functionality. You could also apply this same concept to simple data retrieval services that use either `ObjectList` or `DatabaseQuery` to retrieve data from the database. On an application level, there may also be recurring patterns in the business logic that could be parameterized into generic, reusable services such as these.

BEST PRACTICE Build and use generic, reusable services whenever appropriate to realize the benefits of automation, rapid application development, and increased code quality and maintainability.

Implementing the Controller Pattern in Services

All of the services you have seen thus far provide a single function to the application. For example, `UpdateCustomer` is there to take data for a particular customer and update the state of the object. This service is not used to perform other functions related to the customer entity such as creating a new account or getting the list of accounts for this customer. This is beneficial for a couple of reasons. Each service is explicit and easily understandable. You know from the name of the service what function is being provided, and the service code for each is simple and readable.

Should you build all services in this fashion? Well, not necessarily. You will see an implementation of the controller pattern (of the MVC architecture) within the User Interaction Architecture in the next chapter. However, you can also implement this pattern on the EJB side as well in the service components. There are a number of different ways this can manifest itself.

Object-Centric Services

Another way to design services is to create a service component that provides a number of functions, usually for the same set of objects or data. For example, you could create a `CustomerController` service that performs all of the functions mentioned earlier for the customer entity. The particular function invoked within the service could be based upon a particular argument passed into the service in the argument list. It sometimes makes sense to build services in this fashion because there is a lot of common code shared among services that deal with the same business entities. For example, the `CustomerController` component could implement the logic to get the input arguments and obtain a handle to the correct `Customer` instance at the top of the service. All business functions would execute this code, but then the particular business methods or operations that are invoked would depend on the arguments passed into the service. These types of service components can be partitioned by read-only and update services, or you can group all of the functions together in one component.

Workflow-Type Services

Once you have built up a library of services for your application or business domain, you will start to realize opportunities to reuse some of the lower-level services as building blocks in higher-level services. This concept, discussed earlier in this chapter, provides another mechanism for implementing more coarse-grained services while realizing the benefits of reuse at the same time. Services like this typically control the flow between the different functions based on business logic and input parameters. They use the technique of invoking services within services that was shown earlier to avoid the EJB overhead on each service invocation. You can also easily pass along the same `ServiceData` object to each service along the way. This actually is easier than creating new input for each service because you can share the same `ErrorList` and you can also keep adding to the output data as you go. This idea of adding to the output bucket is useful for services that want to return data from multiple building block services.

Service Chaining

This topic was referred to earlier in the discussion of the merits of the data retrieval service. This concept extends from the Command pattern that was used to implement services as well as the idea just discussed of passing the `ServiceData` along as a bucket for errors and output data throughout the master service. Because each service implementation object implements the `BlfServiceObject` interface, which takes a `ServiceData` object and returns a `ServiceData` object, it is easy to chain services together. To do this, you can use the output of one service as the input for the next service in the chain until you reach the end. At that point, you simply return the `ServiceData` back up to the service foundation base class for return to the client. In some sense, this creates an assembly line of service components that act on input data, perform business logic, and add to the collection of output data.

As an example, in the bank application, users may go directly from the transfer funds screen to a list of their accounts with current balances to see the net result of the transaction. From the transfer funds form in the User Interaction Architecture, you would invoke the `TransferFunds` update service. If you returned back to the client at this point, you would eventually want to invoke the `GetAccountList` data retrieval service so that you have the current account data, which lists the customer's accounts with their current balances, to present on a screen. If you chain these services together, you can execute the account transfer and then run the data retrieval service to get the new account information for presentation to the user. This saves an EJB invocation and possibly a network trip by chaining the services together from one remote invocation. This technique requires that all of the input data needed for both services be sent in the initial service invocation. In this case, you will likely have all of the input data you need for both services. The input data consists of a customer identifier, a from and a to account, as well as a dollar amount. At the end of the `TransferFunds` service, the object has been updated, and there is no output data yet. Then the `GetAccountList` service, which fills the output data with the account objects, is executed.

> **NOTE** If your next Web page only displays the form data that was just updated, such as in a `ChangeAddress` form, the update service itself should populate the output data with the state of the object at the end of the service. This saves the overhead of a separate `GetCustomerData` service invocation. This pattern tends to occur frequently; thus, you can parameterize the generic `BlfUpdate` service to populate the object into the output data. In the example, more data is returned than was actually sent into the service; thus, it is necessary to chain the services together.

There is one design consideration to be aware of when using the service chaining technique. In the account transfer example, you may want to commit the transaction after the account transfer has completed. If something fails in the data retrieval service, you may not want to fail the first service, which successfully transferred the funds. The data retrieval is an after-the-fact kind of thing that really is not relevant to the update transaction. Thus, you could not chain the invocation of the two service implementation objects within the same EJB method using container-managed transactions. A container-managed transaction encompasses an entire business method declared in the component interface. In the reference architecture, this usually is the `execute-Service` method of `BlfServiceBean`. Thus, if you want unique transactions between services in a chain, you need to implement one of the following two options:

- Use a wrapper Session EJB called `BlfServiceChain` to control the invocation of multiple instances of `BlfService`. Each invocation of `BlfService` works just as it did before with each instance requiring its own transaction. The master EJB in this case, what controls the chaining, `BlfServiceChain`, should not specify a transaction context so that a single transaction context is not carried throughout the entire chain.

- Use bean-managed transactions within the service component to start and end transactions in between each invocation of the service implementation objects. This type of logic can be put into the service base class or within specific service implementations.

As mentioned in the second option, you could build the logic to chain the services and manage the user transactions in the service base class. To do this, you would define the chain of services in the metadata. This metadata might look like this:

```
<ServiceChain name="accountTransferAndView">
    <Service name="TransferFunds" beginTransaction="true"
                                  endTransaction="true" />
    <Service name="GetAccountList" />
</ServiceChain>
```

In this metadata example, you define whether to start and end a transaction around each service, with the default being false. This flexibility is added into the chaining definition because you may have blocks of services in a chain that should be included in individual transactions. This flexibility is not always possible using EJB container-managed transactions because you can specify only one transaction setting for the service component across the whole application.

Best Practices for Implementing Service-Based Components

This section summarizes the best practices discussed in this chapter for implementing service-based components in the reference architecture.

Consider the Use of a Standard Service Interface

The use of a standard interface for service components enables the reference architecture to automate the invocation of services to a large extent. Services can be generically invoked through their interface, and standard data structures allow for the automated creation of input data. A standard service data structure can be used to store arguments and object data as input as well as the corresponding output data and error information from the service. Services that explicitly take input data as arguments also work quite well but provide less opportunity for automation of the service invocation and creation of input data.

Use a Common Base Class

Wrap service components with a stateless Session Bean to manage the transaction and distribute the service. Use a common base class for the Session Bean to standardize the service error handling and integration with EJB transaction management. The base class should enclose the actual service logic within a try-catch block that handles application exceptions and maps system-level exceptions to defined business errors with user-friendly messages. The implementation of the service can be structured to use the base class in two different ways. The Command pattern can be implemented within the base class to easily invoke services implemented as regular Java objects. This promotes the use of process-oriented objects that can be used outside the context of an EJB. The other option is to implement subclasses of the common base class that use the Template Method pattern to wrap the service in the try-catch block. This approach is used to enable specific deployments of Session Bean components that may have different EJB deployment configurations.

Reuse Services as Building Blocks

Services can be fine-grained segments of business logic or they can implement entire business processes. Design and implement your services as building blocks whenever applicable so that lower-level services can be reused to implement larger services. Integrate any errors returned from other services into the original service error-handling mechanism. If the services are all part of the same transaction, invoke service implementations directly without going through unnecessary EJB method invocations. Optionally, local interfaces to Session Bean components can also be used for this purpose, but be aware that local interface method invocations are pass-by-reference.

Build Generic, Reusable Services

Build and use generic, reusable services whenever appropriate to realize the benefits of automation, rapid application development, and increased code quality and maintainability. These types of services become a part of the Business Logic Foundation of your application. A generic update service is an example of a common pattern that can be easily automated. Look for data retrieval patterns and other common business logic in your application for other possibilities.

Implementing Data Retrieval Services

Use data retrieval services to isolate and encapsulate logic to retrieve data for presentation to the user. Data retrieval services also provide a good isolation mechanism for straight database queries if you are using them in your application for performance reasons. Keep the JDBC best practices that were discussed in earlier chapters in mind. These practices include externalizing the SQL from the application, isolating JDBC code in a reusable utility, and mapping database column names to logical property names as soon as possible to ease code maintenance. A data retrieval service typically should not return value objects that refer to database column names.

Summary

Service components are typically implemented as process-oriented objects wrapped by a Session Bean for transaction management and distribution. They typically act as workflow managers between multiple Entity Beans or business objects, although they range from fine-grained transactions to the implementation of entire business processes. In fact, services often become building blocks for the construction of larger services. A common base class and service interface provide the structure needed to automate the development and integration of services into the reference architecture. Generic services can also be built to implement common patterns such as basic update and data retrieval services. Service components can also be used to implement the controller pattern on the EJB tier.

Session Beans as a front to Entity Beans is a common pattern in J2EE. Services are the realization of this concept, and Session Beans are a natural fit for their implementation in the reference architecture. Service components manage the workflow of business processes and coordinate the transaction between multiple business objects. They are an important part of the reference architecture used to provide an interface to the business logic. Service components simplify the design and implementation of the Web-tier components that are the topic of the next chapter.

The User Interaction Architecture: Design Considerations and an Overview of Jakarta Struts

In this study of the J2EE architecture, the first step was to look at building business object components to model the business entities. In the last chapters, service components were constructed that sit on top of the Business Object Architecture to implement the business transactions and processes of an application. The last layer, which then finally sits on top of the Service-Based Architecture, is what was defined as the User Interaction Architecture. This layer provides users with the ability to access and engage these services, or in other words, it handles all of the interaction with the user. The importance of this layer then goes without saying; the services that were just created are of no use to anyone if application users or other systems cannot access those services. Technically speaking, there are actually a few ways to access services without going through the User Interaction Architecture. These include scheduled batch jobs that run in the production environment or components of other applications running within the same application server domain that have the ability to directly perform a JNDI lookup and invoke your EJB service components. In fact, this is the only manner in which some service components are accessed. However, the majority of services are consumed through applications deployed to end users or external systems. Thus, the focus here is primarily on end users accessing an application through a Web interface; a brief look at external system-to-system access through a Web services type model is also provided.

In a Web application, the majority of the User Interaction Architecture is running within the JSP container on the application server. Components running within this tier are referred to as Web components. The job of these Web components is to handle all of the interaction with the user, or in more general terms, the client, of the application services. What does this job consist of? Well, the basic flow at a high level can be broken down into the following steps:

1. Process the user request.

2. Invoke any applicable application services (that is, service-based components).

3. Generate a response with the appropriate content.

For a browser-based application, the definition of these steps can be refined slightly to be the following:

1. Process the HTTP requests (form submission or HTML link).

2. Invoke any applicable application services (that is, service-based components).

3. Generate the next appropriate Web page with HTML/XML content.

Already, you can see that the basic responsibilities map directly to the Model-View-Controller pattern that will be used to effectively build this architecture. The controller handles the request and the model represents the application services and business objects underneath, while the view renders the dynamic content into Web pages presented to the user. This pattern is at the core of the design considerations and the implementation of the Web components. The rationale for this is to separate the presentation logic, the flow control, and the back-end business logic. The service layer already encapsulates the business logic and provides an access point that the Web components can invoke. The remainder of this isolation of functionality is implemented through the design of the User Interaction Architecture, which uses a central controller servlet that abstracts the flow of the application and dispatches requests to the appropriate Web components. The use of the MVC pattern in the J2EE architecture is now commonly referred to as the JSP Model 2 architecture. Its use has become widespread and has become almost a standard for designing Web applications in Java. There are a number of MVC framework implementations throughout the industry. One of the leading ones is an excellent open-source implementation called Jakarta Struts.

NOTE Struts can be found on the Web at `http://jakarta.apache.org/struts`. This book is based on the final release of version 1.0.

The User Interaction Architecture is crucial to the development process for a number of reasons. The first reason is one that has been touched on already, the fact that it provides the user's view into an application. It is the user's window into all of the underlying functionality provided by the service and business object components. In addition to creating the basic Web page representation of these services, many of the other supplemental application requirements, such as security and personalization, are funneled through the user interface. Different user groups typically have diverse views into the same functions with different security privileges and data access rights. Additionally, as mobile computing grows in popularity, the demand for access to these application services from wireless devices grows with it. When moving beyond browser-based clients, the basic responsibilities of the Web components remain the same, but the flavor of XML content can vary (for example, HTML, WML, and so on) and a slightly different set of challenges await regarding the different user interfaces.

A second reason to take note of this layer stems from the vast number of responsibilities required to interact with a user and the many types of components used to implement them. For example, there are JavaServer Pages components to create the HTML content, action components to process specific user events, session objects to maintain state, and tag libraries to encapsulate presentation logic. Additionally, many Web applications integrate with content management and personalization products to meet the needs of their users. Thus, there are many different types of components in this layer as opposed to the service and business objects, which are the primary components in their respective architecture layers. Along with this list of components comes a host of options in terms of designing and implementing these responsibilities. Mixed in with these choices, there are a number of places where decisions can be made that greatly affect scalability and code maintainability.

Thus, these next few chapters will carefully study the elements of user interaction and guidelines for their implementation. Note that the focus here is not on Web design, but on integrating business functionality into the Web site. The end goal is the front-to-back integration of the Web architecture through the three software layers. To accomplish this, the general development principles can be applied to automate the common elements of the user interface and integrate service component functionality into the user's Web application experience.

Elements of the User Interaction Architecture

Almost all Web-based applications share a number of common characteristics. These elements of the User Interaction Architecture are derived from basic aspects of user interfaces applied to the HTTP protocol and HTML interface. The common elements include:

- Application presentation (HTML/XML over HTTP) including both static and dynamic content
- Access to business functions and services
- Screen flow, or page navigation
- Forms processing
- Error handling
- State management

Application Presentation

As stated earlier, the User Interaction Architecture provides the window, or view, into the application and its functionality for the user. In Web-based applications, this involves generating both static and dynamic HTML/XML content over HTTP. Static content can include text, images, or other multimedia files. The majority of the static content is usually processed by the Web server that is used in conjunction with the J2EE application server. In many architectures, the Web server is used to serve any pages that might be completely static, such as help text pages, as well as page fragments that are included in an overall Web page, such as image files. The Web server acts as a proxy for any request for a dynamically generated page. This request is forwarded through to the application server and processed by a Java servlet or JSP. The majority of Web pages in business applications fall into this category. They contain application data selected from the database as well as content based on business rules, user preferences, and security requirements.

For the sample banking application, the corporate information pages can be static content stored on the Web server as regular HTML files. The majority of the HTML content is created through JavaServer Pages that integrate application data and business functions into the presentation. This content includes pages such as a list of the user's accounts with current balances and a form page that allows the user to transfer funds between accounts. Other banking applications might include dynamic content ranging from personalized home pages to a list of special promotions based on marketing information and that particular customer's characteristics.

Access to Business Functions and Services

Any application that acts as more than purely an informational Web site requires access to the application's business services and functions. These services are invoked based on the particular user events, or HTTP requests, that are generated from the application's presentation. The context and form data from these user events are used to invoke the Service-Based Architecture with the proper data to execute the business services. The results of the service are then displayed appropriately back to the user as either confirmation or error messages within the next page displayed. Which particular page is determined through the next common element, page navigation.

In the banking application, the majority of pages invoke services to access application data for presentation or to update data based on a form submission. For example, the `TransferFunds` and `ChangeAddress` services are invoked from their corresponding Web pages. The view accounts page invokes the `GetAccountList` service to retrieve the account data to create the HTML table for presentation to the user.

Screen Flow, or Page Navigation

Similar to any user interface application, Web-based applications have a defined navigation path between Web pages based on user events, business rules, and security privileges. Navigation between pages can be triggered from a browser by a user when an HTML link is clicked or when an HTML form is submitted. A design model describes the flow between pages in the user interface; the design model represents the page entities and the conditions upon which the control is passed between them. This page flow can vary at run time and often depends on the success or failure of an application service that was invoked. For example, it is quite common for applications to navigate a user back to the same page when a form submission fails due to business errors. In these cases, the lists of errors are often displayed along with the populated form so that the user can retry the submission after correcting the data.

In the banking application, the user has links on the main page to go to a view accounts page, a transfer funds request form, and an address change screen among others. After a successful funds transfer, the user is sent to the accounts list page so that the net result of the transaction can be seen in the update balances. If the transfer fails for some reason, such as the user entering a dollar amount beyond the balance of the from account (that is, insufficient funds), the transfer funds form page is redisplayed with the submitted data as well as an error message to inform the user of the problem.

Forms Processing

A core element of business applications is the processing of HTML form submissions. Form data must be used by the User Interaction Architecture to invoke the proper application service. This responsibility includes taking the input data out of the HTTP request and packaging it appropriately so that it can be sent to the service's component interface.

A basic form in the bank application is the form with the address fields for the `ChangeAddress` service. There are also more complex variations on form handling that typically occur in business applications. These include multipage forms, sometimes referred to as wizards, because they guide the user incrementally through a large amount of data entry. The link on the bank's home page to open a new account takes the user through a number of sequential forms to capture personal information about the customer as well as what type of account the user wishes to open. Some multipage forms within applications save information to the database after each intermediate form, whereas others aggregate the input data from each form until the end of the sequence when all of the data is used to invoke an application service. Other variations on form submissions include functions such as an intermediate validation that simply runs the form data through the business edits and reports any errors thus far without actually saving the information to the database yet. This can be helpful for applications that have large amounts of data entry to large transactions, such as a lengthy tax form.

Error Handling

An element of user interaction that is closely related to forms processing is error handling. This element of the architecture is dealt with as its own topic both because of its importance and for the fact that errors sometimes occur outside of forms processing. For example, a system failure may occur when a user clicks on the View Accounts link if the application database is unavailable. These type of errors are usually pretty rare but still need to be handled gracefully. The vast majority of errors that occur within an application are the result of incorrect data being entered into forms submissions, such as the insufficient funds example.

The two primary aspects of error handling are error detection and error reporting back to the user. Some basic edits such as data type validation can be handled on the client side with a small amount of JavaScript running within the browser, although this should be done with caution to avoid compatibility problems between different Web browsers. The majority of data validation that occurs within the User Interaction Architecture can be done on the server within the Web container. The error-handling mechanism used here should integrate into what is used by the Service-Based Architecture in order to seamlessly report any errors that occurred within the business logic of the application. Typically, the entire list of errors that occurred in a given transaction is reported back to the user at once so that all of the corrections may be made. A helpful feature is to have the screen tie the errors back to the form field that caused the error, if applicable. This is usually done through some notation or color scheme on the fields within the Web page. This enables users to rapidly understand the problem and resolve the error so that they can resubmit the form.

State Management

Because HTTP is a stateless protocol, the application must maintain state between page requests. There are two general options for doing this, maintaining context on the client or on the server. Context that is maintained on the client is typically done through hidden input fields in an HTML form or parameters added to a URL link. Both of these parameter types are created by the JSP that generates the HTML content for the page. The technical implementation of managing state on the server is much more complex than this due to failover requirements, but fortunately for developers, the underlying infrastructure for this service is provided by the application server and the servlet API. An HttpSession object is available within a servlet or JSP to store Java objects for that particular user's session. The responsibility of the User Interaction Architecture is to use the session object wisely to manage the state of the application and store data across page requests when appropriate. One advantage of storing state on the server is that the user is not able to view the data. This means that application users cannot simply go to the View Source function on their browsers and see any hidden fields that might be in the HTML. For parameters in a URL, it is even easier because they appear directly in the browser. Thus, using state management on the server can be helpful if you want to manage state through internal identifiers, control parameters, or other such information that you might not wish the user to have access to. This topic will be explored in more detail in the design considerations section of this chapter.

In the bank application, the state management service is used in a number of places. A prime example is the new account wizard that takes a user through a number of pages to sign up for an account. This particular application does not save the data to the application database after each intermediate form. Thus, it must store the input data within the HttpSession object until the final form is submitted and the data is sent to the corresponding application service. E-commerce Web sites that have a shopping cart use state management to remember the list of items until the actual purchase is made upon checkout. In addition to these types of scenarios, there is the basic element of state management that remembers which customer is being dealt with from page to page. Something as simple as this is needed so that when the user clicks on the View Accounts link, the application knows the customer identifier to use to query the database for a list of accounts.

User Interaction in Web Services

In the Web services model, the client of your application is actually another system, or application, rather than an end user sitting at a graphical interface. This actually makes interacting with a Web service client a bit simpler because it reduces the elements of the architecture to a subset of what you have just listed here. A Web service is basically an HTTP-based mechanism for invoking component functionality. Thus, the primary aspects of user interaction for Web services are:

- Processing XML data and generating a response over HTTP
- Error handling
- Access to the business functions and services

The Web component in this case is generally a wrapper around one or more of the business services provided by the Service-Based Architecture. Typically, the data is sent as XML, as is the case with services based on SOAP (Simple Object Access Protocol). This protocol has quickly gained momentum as a standard for exchanging data and invoking Web services over a heterogeneous, distributed environment such as the Internet. Thus, the primary responsibility here is marshaling data from the HTTP or SOAP request and using it to invoke an application service. Some amount of basic data validation usually occurs within this layer, including the DTD or XML schema validation done by the XML parser. Again, the error-handling mechanism is integrated with that of the business service, and any errors are reported back appropriately in the response to the client.

Design Considerations

As was mentioned earlier, the User Interaction Architecture is largely based on the Model-View-Controller (MVC) pattern. This architecture pattern can be used to structure the elements of the User Interaction Architecture such that portions of functionality are isolated in order to provide greater flexibility, reuse, and ease of maintenance.

The Controller Architecture

The controller component can be thought of as the hub of the MVC architecture with the model and view components acting as the spokes. The controller is the entry point into the application for all HTTP form submissions. It invokes the components within the model to access business logic and data as necessary, and it controls the flow back to the appropriate view for the user. In Web architectures, the controller component is usually implemented as a Java servlet. The controller servlet can become the single entry point for all HTTP requests in some application architectures, processing both form submissions and HTML links. In these cases, the anchor tags in an HTML page all point to the aliased URL of the controller servlet that determines the next appropriate view component to be used to render the page for the user.

Because the general request-handling logic of the controller servlet makes up a foundation that all Web applications are built on, it must be extremely extensible and flexible. The primary way in which this is done is through a number of abstractions. The controller architecture is designed with a balance of two things in mind:

- The desire to have robust, automated front-end processing
- A flexible and extensible foundation to handle all types and sizes of applications

The user interface is simply the most dynamic part of an application. There are many, many variations on pages and their associated logic, and this foundation must provide a way to support all of them, even if the involvement in the complex cases is minimal. A key design goal has been to automate as much of the processing as possible. This occurs to a larger degree for the more standard, repeatable patterns that occur within the User Interaction Architecture. However, the more complex, unique pages require greater extensibility to implement their specific logic.

BEST PRACTICE Use a generic MVC, or Model 2, implementation as the foundation for the User Interaction Architecture. The Jakarta Struts project provides an excellent, readily available implementation that you can use for this purpose. This approach automates much of the front-end processing while providing a flexible and extensible foundation to meet all types of application requirements. This also adheres to a key design principle that permeates the reference architecture. This principle is to make the normal case as simple as possible through automation and configuration but give the application the ability to override automated, configurable elements when necessary for complex cases.

The primary element of flexibility within the controller architecture is the delegation of specific request handling to action classes.

Action Classes

As stated earlier, it is essential that the controller component be configurable and flexible. For this reason, the controller usually delegates the request to a handler class to be processed. Handler classes are commonly referred to as action classes. The action classes are written specifically for each application to perform the requested action. These action classes can implement a standard interface, again using the Command pattern, so that the controller can determine which action class to use at run time and then generically invoke it. The implementation of the action class should be a stateless, thread-safe object so that instances can be pooled for performance optimizations.

The responsibilities of the action classes include preparing current or future pages for presentation to the user. This includes accessing data and business functionality and then preparing the results for inclusion into page content. The controller servlet needs to make this data available to a JSP that it dispatches the request to. This is usually done through putting the data in either the request or session scope so that the JSP has access to it. This concept is discussed further in the section on state management.

Controller Architecture.   The term "controller architecture" is used to describe the combination of the controller servlet and the action class components invoked to handle specific application requests. This combination is a key part of the User Interaction Architecture. The next section will abstract key aspects of Web-based user interaction and define eight core responsibilities of the controller architecture. These design steps are taken so that the core responsibilities can be automated to the extent possible and partitioned correctly within the controller architecture.

Overall Controller Logic

The controller architecture has eight core responsibilities that make up the basic flow of processing. These eight responsibilities are:

1. Determine the user event and the appropriate action to take.
2. Create the event object.
3. Invoke the action class.
4. Perform any application validations and handle errors.
5. Invoke application services and handle errors.
6. Manage the user context.
7. Determine the next page.
8. Forward the request to the next page.

As you see, some of these steps can be omitted for simple events such as pure page navigation events, but this list outlines the overall core of the controller architecture's responsibilities.

Abstracting HTTP Requests

The HTTP requests that the controller receives are specific to the user interface environment in which they live, in this case, a Web application. Thus, you would not want to forward this request directly to a service component or business object because these components are independent of the user interface. A primary responsibility of the controller servlet is to abstract the protocol-specific nature of an HTTP request by translating the user action into a business event. The business event is represented by an object or set of objects that hold the appropriate data from the request as well as any other parameters that define the particular user event. The data structure used for this can be either application specific or a common data structure that is a part of the business logic foundation. The reasoning for this choice largely resembles the discussion in the previous chapters on the choice of data structure for the Service-Based Architecture. Thus, the common choices include an argument list and value objects. In fact, it can be advantageous to use the same structure chosen for the service interface to avoid unnecessary data conversions and object instantiation. The downside of making this choice is that you sacrifice some flexibility; thus, the business event and the service invocation are kept as different abstractions. They can potentially be implemented together, but they are abstracted separately for design purposes. Looking ahead in this chapter to the Struts discussion, you will see that the Struts implementation of the event object is very Web-centric. Thus, it is not ideal to use on both the Web tier and the EJB tier. However, there is a strong value proposition for using a single value object structure across the entire architecture. Subclasses that implement the standard `ValueObject` interface can be created of the Struts event object, and thus they can be used seamlessly across the entire architecture as long as the service code refers only to the `ValueObject` interface. If the Web-centric nature of the Struts event objects bothers you, or if you need the flexibility to map between the event and service data abstractions, you can always implement the event objects and value objects separately. This topic will be discussed in detail in the next chapter on building the user interaction components.

User Events

Abstracting the key elements of request processing is at the core of making the architecture flexible and extensible. The first abstraction is the user event, a representation of what the user did on the page. A user event can be a form submission on a page or the click of an HTML link. The user event is a driver for a number of things including:

- The event object to create
- The action class to use to process this request
- The next page to navigate to depending on the success or failure of the action

BEST PRACTICE Abstract the HTTP request as a user event to isolate the specific protocol being used from as much of the front-end logic as possible. The user event can then be used to drive the other key abstractions in the controller architecture. These include the action, the service, and the next Web page. By abstracting these key elements of user interaction, a good portion of the front-end processing can be automated and defined through metadata.

The result of the action class usually involves invoking an application service. The service itself was abstracted because the action class can decide what service to invoke. This may depend on the input data and may need to be determined at run time. By having the event, action, and service abstractions, a loose coupling is created in the front end, thus giving the flexibility that is needed to cover both simple and complex scenarios. Figure 7.1 illustrates the relationships between the abstractions of the user interaction layer.

The controller typically determines the event that occurred through one of the following mechanisms:

- A specific HTTP parameter
- The request URL
- A portion of the URL path

The event directly determines what event object is created and what action class is used to handle the request. It is a key determinant of the next Web page, but it is not the only factor. The mapping between events and these other abstractions is defined in application metadata. As you will see later in this chapter, Struts uses an XML configuration file to define metadata for the controller.

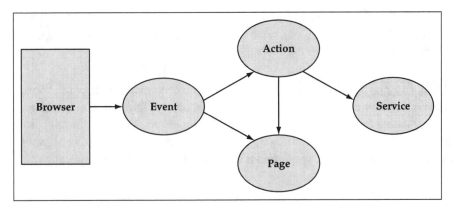

Figure 7.1   User Interaction Abstractions.

CORE RESPONSIBILITY ONE The first core responsibility of the controller architecture is to determine the event and action based on the request and application metadata. This drives what event object will be created to capture the user event.

Mapping between Events and Actions

In many cases, there is a one-to-one mapping between events and actions. The transfer funds event is one example of this. The only time the transfer funds action is used is when the actual transfer funds event (transfer funds form submission) is executed. In other situations, you may have a single action that is used to process multiple events. The arguments for designing your user interaction this way are similar to those discussed in the previous chapter on the Service-Based Architecture. Many times there is common logic, especially around common business entities, that can be encapsulated in the same action class. This prevents a large proliferation of action classes in your code base because of the potential for large numbers of user events defined in application Web pages. You will see an example of this in the new customer wizard set of pages that process a bank application for a new customer. These pages don't invoke the application service until the final page of the wizard, so request handling for this entire user process is captured in the `NewCustomerAction` class.

Pure Navigation Events

It is important to note that not every event is required to have an action. Many events are simple navigation events in which the user just goes from one page to another. If there is no setup or other presentation logic to execute prior to processing the JSP, there is no need to have an action class. You can simply define the next page to navigate to in the metadata. This might occur when you click on a link to go to the transfer funds form. There is no setup work required for this page prior to the JSP, so no action is defined for the event in the metadata. In this case, it is only linked to a navigation element within the metadata.

Mapping Input Data to Event Objects

After the controller first determines what user event occurred, it can then create the appropriate objects to represent the business event.

CORE RESPONSIBILITY TWO The second core responsibility of the controller architecture is to create and populate event objects from the request data. A generic library function is usually used to implement this. Although the specific event object to create is determined by the metadata, the actual mapping between input data and event object properties is usually determined by the application.

If the service data structure is used as the event object, there are some ramifications to this choice, most of which pertain to the flexibility of naming data elements. A data element has many names throughout the application such as its database column name and the business object property name. These are not required to be the same and are mapped either in the EJB deployment descriptor or application metadata. On the front end, there is also a name for the input field on the HTML form and the bean property. In order to maintain flexibility and isolation between the application layers, you may not want to require that all these names be the same. There is indeed an argument to be made for keeping it simple and using a single common name throughout all of these layers, but naming conventions and standards often prevent this from happening anyway. There is also the potential for name collisions if multiple objects are involved in the same form.

In most cases, it is realistic to make the HTML input field name be the same as the event property or argument name. The JSP architecture is actually geared toward this paradigm because it provides a <jsp:setProperty> tag that is based on the fact that the form field names match the bean's property names. This enables it to automatically populate the Java objects when requested. Another option is to add logic within the controller architecture to map the input data to event objects. Some amount of mapping logic is required if you want the event object to be more than just a single list of properties (that is, an `ArgumentList`). This occurs in the case of multiple object instances as well as different business objects used within the same form. Thus, in more complex applications, there may be a recurring need for this type of functionality.

If you use an object structure such as value objects to abstract the HTTP request, the data mapping at this level requires consideration of three things:

- Mapping between HTML form input fields and property names
- Mapping between form fields and their particular value object
- Mapping between form fields and the particular instance of the value object

This level of mapping allows you to handle almost any scenario of mapping between form data and objects. Some of the more common scenarios follow. Figure 7.2 shows the simple case in which all of the form data maps to one value object.

Figure 7.3 illustrates an example in which a single form maps to multiple value objects.

Figure 7.4 shows a more complex example in which a single form has data from multiple instances of the same value object.

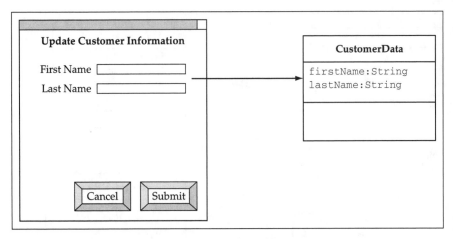

Figure 7.2   Simple Form Scenario: One Value Object.

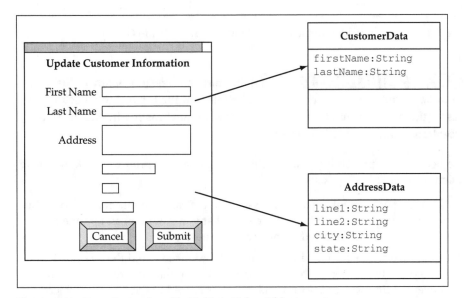

Figure 7.3   Form Scenario with Multiple Value Objects.

Invoking the Action

The action class uses the Command design pattern. All actions implement a standard interface, which takes the event object as an argument as well as the `HttpServlet-Request` and `HttpServletResponse` objects from the servlet API. This follows the general rule of extensibility discussed earlier because the application developer is not limited to the automated processing configured through metadata. There is still the option to use the servlet request and response objects directly when necessary for complex cases. This principle of declaration combined with extensibility is a very important one throughout the reference architecture foundation.

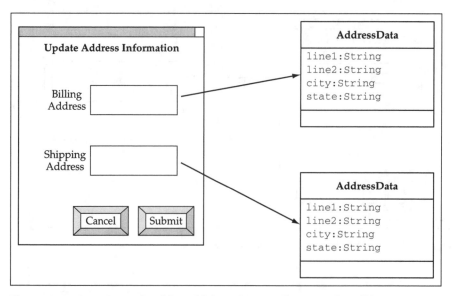

Figure 7.4 Form Scenario with Multiple Instances of Same Value Object.

CORE RESPONSIBILITY THREE The third core responsibility of the controller architecture is to delegate the handling of the request to an action class if there is an action to invoke. This is true in most cases with the notable exception of pure navigation events.

The next core responsibility is to execute any validations prior to invoking the application service. This step exists for two reasons:

- You may not be invoking a service yet, as in the case of a multipage form. Thus, you need to execute validation here so that any mistakes on an intermediate page can be communicated to the user and resolved.

- You may want to do some preliminary validations to avoid the overhead of a remote EJB invocation in the case of basic data validation errors. This is the concept of lightweight business objects as discussed in the Business Object Architecture chapter. The event objects or corresponding value objects can be used for this type of validation.

CORE RESPONSIBILITY FOUR The fourth core responsibility of the controller architecture is to perform any validations before invoking an application service. This can be done out of necessity if no service is used in the action class or as an optimization to prevent unnecessary network trips to the EJB tier.

You can place action class validations into two categories:

- Data-driven validations
- Application-specific validations

The bank's new customer wizard has examples of both of these types of edits. The customer and address information goes through basic data validations while the initial deposit must be checked against the minimum balance requirements for the specified account type. The application-specific edits are usually coded in a validation method of the value/event object or in the action class directly.

> **NOTE** The phrase "value/event object" is used in this section to describe the event object, the value object, or the combination of the two if they happen to be implemented as the same object structure.

Data-driven edits can be handled by the value/event object foundation layer and its associated metadata. An interesting difference between validation in the business objects and value objects is the number of properties that are actually validated. A business object must validate all of its properties before having its data persist in a database in order to maintain data integrity. However, a value object is only a first line of defense used to catch data entry errors. Thus, you want to validate only those properties that were passed from the front end. In some cases, you must validate only input data because some properties may not exist yet. This occurs in the case of a new customer. Neither the customer nor the address entity exists at the time the user is entering data into the Web page, thus the user can't possibly have a valid `id` or `lastModifiedDate` property. This can be handled automatically by the value/event object infrastructure. Each object can keep track of which properties were modified. When the `validate` method is called from the action, only those properties that were set based on request data are validated.

Invoking the Application Service

The first thing to consider regarding invoking an application service is the data and how it is passed to the service interface. In some cases, you are working with existing services and you need to map your event data to a given service data structure. In other cases, you are creating new functionality and have the liberty to define both during development. The manner in which this is done also depends on whether your event objects and service data structure are implemented separately or together. If you separate the two, you have more flexibility and a loosely coupled architecture. However, you also introduce the need to do an additional data mapping.

There are many straightforward screens that fall into the simple mapping scenarios described earlier. For these screens, a simple argument list is the best choice to capture the input data and invoke the service. Remember that the `ArgumentList` object used by `ServiceData` also implements the generic `ValueObject` interface, so you can use these two interchangeably to some degree. The decision was made, however, to provide only one argument list to work with for a given transaction. Many business applications tend to have a number of screens that cannot be categorized as simple because they deal with aggregated objects or have multiple instances of objects. For these cases, value objects provide a nice solution to capture the data. Again, you should also look at using value objects as a standard across the board because of the strong value proposition they provide in terms of integrating with the rest of the architecture.

THOUGHT A key differentiator for using value objects is that they are lightweight data structures that integrate well with service components, business objects, and database query mechanisms. A consistent, flexible implementation of a value object enables front-to-back automation within the architecture.

A nice feature of value objects is that the business objects automatically know how to get their data in and out of value objects using the application metadata. The power of this is illustrated in a generic update service that can be written once and used for any business object. You also have a number of database query services that can create result sets of value objects. The value object is a lightweight data structure that can be used across the tiers to easily integrate all facets of the architecture. This provides a strong case for using them here to take event data and use it to invoke the application service. Because you can integrate value objects throughout the architecture, this enables greater automation across the tiers through configuration. By doing this, the business logic foundation can provide basic data maintenance functions (read, insert, update, and delete) for a given object with hardly any custom code except the HTML to create the Web page. This is a very powerful concept that enables the rapid development of Web applications. This has been a core concept of many development environments, tools, and products for some time; however, this can be implemented while maintaining the flexibility of building applications with straight Java code.

If you use the service data structure for the event object, then the step of invoking the application service is extremely easy. If you choose to use a different data structure, then you need to map the event object data to the service data objects. The code to invoke the service can be implemented as a convenience method that obtains the EJB component, or you could have the action class code directly invoke the EJB service component. In the case of the business logic foundation, the `ServiceData` object has the name of the actual service to execute, so you can simply pass this object to a convenience method and have it do the work.

In some cases, you may also want to use a value object that holds data for a larger cross-section than a single business object. You could create object definitions in the metadata that don't have a corresponding business object in order to do this. However, in many cases, application services use value objects that map directly to business objects so that they can instantiate and populate them in order to execute business logic particular to the entity.

CORE RESPONSIBILITY FIVE The fifth core responsibility of the controller architecture is to invoke any applicable services from the Service-Based Architecture. This is the access point to the business logic, that is, the model in the MVC pattern. Any errors that occur should be handled and integrated into the presentation layer.

The service components throw a `BlfException` with a list of business errors if any errors have occurred. Thus, the action classes should always wrap a call to a service with a try-catch block. This logic is a part of the "manage user context" responsibility.

Managing the User Context

After the service is executed, the action must set the context for the next page and potentially future pages if the data will be needed again. There are a number of options within the Web tier for accomplishing this. The options will be discussed in detail later in this section under the state management design consideration.

CORE RESPONSIBILITY SIX The sixth core responsibility of the controller architecture is to manage the user context. This includes both communicating between Web components on a single page request as well as managing application state across the many user events (that is, HTTP requests) of a user's session within the application.

The action class forms a loop with the JSP and its resulting HTML through which HTTP requests travel. The JavaServer Pages typically expect a certain context that is set by the action. The JavaServer Pages create the HTML for the browser to display. The HTML is used to create the next request, which goes back through the controller architecture. This user event triggers an action that sets both the application data and error context for the next page to be displayed. This cycle will be illustrated in the many page examples discussed in the next chapter. In terms of page navigation, events can have action classes that prepare data for the JSP, or else the page itself can create the context. Figure 7.5 illustrates this loop between actions, JavaServer Pages, and the resulting HTML.

Web-Page Navigation

It was stated earlier that the user event was a key determinant of page navigation. This approach can be described as event-based navigation. In this approach, you map out all of the pages of an application and define the events that cause the user to travel from one page to another. In fact, this type of information can be captured in a UML model that could potentially be used to generate event navigation metadata. In some cases, a static model can define the default page flow, but it is usually not sufficient to

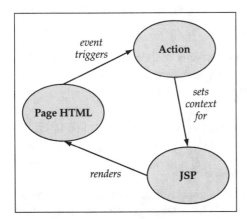

Figure 7.5   The User Interaction Loop.

capture all of the navigation possibilities. For this reason, the action class is given the flexibility to override the metadata and return the next page. Usually the action class uses the metadata to determine the next page, but there will be instances in which this is not the case. Thus, the general page navigation rule can be defined as:

```
Event + Action Result => Next Page
```

Navigation references in action class code should be to logical page names such as changeAddress or transferFunds. This is done purposely so that you do not have to hard-code URLs into the user interaction code. Page directory structures and physical URLs can always change, so it is a good idea to abstract pages out to the metadata.

BEST PRACTICE Abstract physical URLs out of the application into metadata in order to enable automation, avoid broken links, and have more maintainable pages.

Thus, the metadata maps logical page names to their physical URLs. As an example, the logical page changeAddress could be mapped to the physical URL/Change-Address.jsp.

CORE RESPONSIBILITY SEVEN The seventh core responsibility of the controller architecture is to determine what page (that is, view component) to display next. The majority of the page flow in an application can be captured in the event metadata. You can abstract the page flow of an application using an event-based navigation approach, in which the next page is determined by the user event and the success or failure of the resulting action. This predefined page flow can also be overridden by the action class for more dynamic scenarios in which navigation is determined at run time.

The last core responsibility is actually to dispatch the request once the next page has been determined. These two responsibilities are separated, because the navigation is ultimately the decision of the action class, while the controller is used actually to dispatch the request to the corresponding JSP.

CORE RESPONSIBILITY EIGHT The last core responsibility of the controller architecture is actually to perform the page forward to the appropriate view component (that is, JSP).

The previous discussion begs the question of what components are used to implement all of the core responsibilities. This is discussed in the next design consideration.

Automation and the Partitioning of Responsibility

If you look at the core responsibilities listed within the controller architecture, there are a number of things that can be automated through foundation components configured by metadata. Thus, it is worthwhile to look at the partitioning of responsibilities between the common controller component and the action classes written specifically for each application. Many of these responsibilities are common across all application requests, so perhaps you do not need to write them each time in every action class. For example, many user actions trigger a service to be invoked. The logic to obtain a service component, invoke it, and handle any error conditions can be generalized and implemented in the foundation logic. The metadata could also potentially define which service is invoked based on the user event that has taken place. The service component invocation logic includes catching any application exceptions and putting the error list in the request scope so that the next JSP can display the errors. Should this logic be in every action class, or should it be implemented as part of a configurable controller component? Well, for many simple forms such as the change address form, a standard implementation of this works fine. However, for more complicated scenarios, you may also want to store part of the output data from the service in the session for use in a future page. There may also be other presentation logic you need to execute in order to display the next page. If you limit the entire action to a standard implementation, you lose the extensibility and flexibility needed to handle the many different cases that arise out of the single controller servlet. This will likely be the case for a large number of the action classes. Thus, rather than automate the entire process, you can encapsulate repeated functions in utility classes that take the same arguments (that is, `HttpServletRequest`, `HttpServletResponse`) so that you can easily reuse the object from within either a configurable controller servlet or a specific action class.

Another option to provide more reusability in terms of action class functionality is to create an action base class that provides a template for handling requests. The hooks that would probably be necessary are a preservice invocation method and a postservice invocation method. The template could follow the basic pattern:

```
try {
    // Validation of event already invoked by controller

    // Convert event object to service data if necessary.
    ServiceData data = createServiceData(formBean);

    // hook method implemented by subclass
    // before service invocation
    preService(data, request, response);

    // Invoke service.
    data = executeService(data);

    // Hook method implemented by subclass
    // before service invocation
    postService(data, request, response);

} catch (BlfException be) {
    // Set error context.
}
```

Another option is to continue to have action classes own their responsibilities but to provide some set of foundation action classes that process the standard vanilla forms covered by a large majority of pages. These standard actions would be parameterized and could be configured by application metadata.

State Management

Core responsibility number six was to manage the user's context within an application across multiple HTTP page requests. The JSP and servlet specifications provide a number of choices for storing and accessing attributes, or objects, within a Web application. The different scope levels available are:

- Page: A single request in a single JSP
- Request: A single request for any Web component that is forwarded the request
- Session: All requests within a particular user's session
- Application: All requests for all users of a Web application

These scope levels provide places within the application server to store context for an application. A fifth option that is outside of the J2EE specification, client-side HTTP parameters, can be added to this list. You can use parameters in either a URL link or as hidden input form fields to manage state across multiple HTTP requests. The JSP can generate these parameters, which are then sent back to the browser when the user either submits the form or clicks the link. This is an effective option with little overhead if you don't mind exposing the data to the user. Any parameters within the HTML are visible to the end user either directly in the URL or through the view source function of the browser.

As far as the server-side options specified by J2EE, the page scope is the equivalent of instantiating an object in a scriptlet code within a JSP and then using it later in the same page. Thus, the page scope is largely used in custom tags within a JSP. The request scope, however, is a widely used aspect of the servlet API because it provides a means to communicate data between Web components within a single request. The request scope should be used wherever possible instead of the session or application scope because it has almost no overhead, comparatively speaking. It exists only for a single request and can be used to communicate between the controller servlet and the JavaServer Pages used to render the page. For example, application data retrieved through a service as well as error information can be set as attributes of the request so that the JSP can easily access it and display it on the page.

BEST PRACTICE Keep the session size fairly small, especially for applications that need to scale to large numbers of users.

As was discussed earlier, it is extremely important to keep the session size small. This can be tough to do in practice, but a large session size can quickly degrade the performance and scalability of a Web application. Sessions can quickly eat up memory as concurrent users are added, and if failover is a requirement, the overhead becomes more significant. If one application server in a cluster goes down, the session must be recoverable from either a replicated session in memory within the cluster or from a persistent session in the database. This adds additional overhead to each request. Thus, you should not store large amounts of data in the session. Before you decide to use the session to store context, analyze how often the data will be used throughout the application. If the answer is infrequently, store the minimum context used to perform a database query to get the rest, if possible. For accessing and paging through large data sets, it may be better to use the application database rather than the session object to manage the result set. The application database is usually well-tuned for its access patterns and may perform better than using the session, which consumes large amounts of memory and potentially adds database access. The performance results seen by different application servers can vary based on the failover mechanism used for sessions, so it is probably best to prototype and do some performance testing early on in your development cycle if you have this type of situation in your application. Be sure to note how the application scales as concurrent users are added toward your target levels, because this is where a significant difference can be seen. The other danger of using the session is that the data may change underneath you within another user's session. This makes the data you have stored in the user session outdated. This is discussed in more detail in the next section on MVC and state management. One last thing to note about using the session scope is that objects can also be taken out of scope. If you are done with a particular item in an application, for example, if the user closes out of a particular section of an application, be sure to remove any applicable objects from the session scope.

The application scope is seen by every Web component across all user sessions, so it is not a good option for managing state for a particular user. Thus, the primary options for managing state are client-side HTTP parameters, the request scope, and the session scope. Table 7.1 summarizes these primary options for state management with typical data scenarios in an application.

MVC and State Management

In thick-client MVC architectures, the view has direct access to the model objects. For example, a `JTable` GUI control is directly connected to the model object that holds its data. If the model is updated, the `JTable` receives a notification and refreshes its view so the up-to-date data is shown to the user. This connection between the view and the model continues across user requests on the screen. In thin-client Web applications, you do not have this long-lasting connection because the JSP implementation, which has access to the model's data, generates the page content and then goes on to process another user's request for that page. This occurs because the container converts JavaServer Pages to servlets, multithreaded server components used to process multiple users' requests for that page. There is the option of using the session scope to store model objects in order to emulate that connection; however, there are issues with this approach. In addition to the overhead, there is also the issue of what to do if the data stored in the session is updated in the database by another user of the application. If the same user updates the object, you can use the same notification approach and refresh the data in the session. However, if a different user performs the update, there is no way to automatically notify all of the user session objects that may contain that data. A JMS publish/subscribe mechanism is one of the only ways this could be accomplished. This is another reason to consider using the session to store only the minimal data needed to recreate the state from the database. The session can be used to

Table 7.1   Primary State Management Options

TYPE OF DATA	EXAMPLE	CLIENT-SIDE HTTP PARAMETERS	REQUEST SCOPE	SESSION SCOPE
Data used for current page request	Account data retrieved from service component to be displayed on next page	Not applicable	Use the request scope to communicate between Web components in a given request	Do not use the session for this purpose
Data used for next page; can be visible to user	Presentation control parameters	Use either hidden form fields or parameters in URL	Not applicable	Can be used, but avoid if possible so session does not become overloaded
Data used for next page; should not be visible to user	Internal account identifier on change address form	Do not use HTTP parameters for this purpose; they are visible to the user through browser view source function	Not applicable	Use session (see also server-side parameters section later in this chapter)
Data used across many page requests	User object	Not practical	Not applicable	Use session, keeping overall session size in mind

store data either if you do not care about concurrent updates or if only the current user can modify the data. However, this is rarely the case in business applications. Usually multiple users are allowed to update entities, although there are cases in which only single users have update access to a particular set of objects. If a pessimistic locking approach is used, only a single user would be able to update an object, and it would be safe to store that data in that user's session. Nonetheless, these exception cases provide limited usefulness in terms of state management.

HTTP Parameters versus Server-Side Parameters

Of the state management options, HTTP parameters provide a nice, efficient way to manage state from one page request to another. It should also be noted that HTTP parameters stored in the HTML are unique across multiple frames or browser instances that are spawned from a Web application. This is not the case when you use the session scope on the server side. With these advantages, however, comes one major disadvantage. Any HTML parameters can be seen by the end user. While this may not seem that bad at first, consider also that this is a parameter that is sent from the client to the server. Thus, it can be modified and resubmitted by a technically savvy user. The application controls the value of data that is stored on the server; however, a client-side parameter is sent to the server each time from the browser. Although the initial value for this parameter is created and sent in the HTML content, it is still a named parameter expected by an HTTP request sent over a network such as the Internet. As an example, say that you place the account ID in the URL of a list of links to view the account detail. A hacker can then modify the value of that parameter in the URL in an attempt to view another customer's account information. You then rely on the security of the server to catch these types of conditions. Normally, you can handle all of these conditions. In this example, the action class or JSP processing the request should first check to see that the account identifier belongs to that particular customer identified by a user object stored in the session. This would prevent any other user from successfully viewing another user's account data by modifying the HTML parameter. The risk level for your particular application should be assessed if you are considering using client-side parameters.

For the cases in which you do not want to expose these parameters to the end user, you should have a mechanism to easily link a set of server-side parameters to a particular user event. This is not always as straightforward as just putting a value in the session. On the view accounts page, there are a number of links for each page, and you need to identify the particular account for each link. If you want to hide the internal or external account ID from the URL, you need to use a server-side parameter that is associated with each link. You can use the session to store the server-side parameters, although you need an identifier to connect the link to the parameters in the session. This identifier can be a random identifier; in fact, it is best if it is meaningless so that the likelihood of faking a value is very low. The URL links would contain the random identifier that is then used to extract the proper set of server-side parameters for the user event. This provides a secure mechanism for managing state for different page and event instances within a user session. The downside of this approach is that it can quickly fill up the session object. It becomes necessary to remove parameters over time to manage the size of the session, thus creating the possibility that older pages can expire because no server-side context exists for them anymore. Thus, this approach should be used only when it is deemed necessary to secure an application.

View Components: JavaServer Pages

The view components, typically JavaServer Pages in the J2EE architecture, are responsible for taking the user context and application data in order to create the content for the particular Web page requested. As stated earlier, JavaServer Pages are document-based, HTML-centric servlets. Although you have the ability to put Java code directly in JavaServer Pages in the form of scriptlets, you should try and minimize this as much as possible so that you have readable, maintainable view components. Thus, the user interaction chapters of this book look at moving the presentation logic more to action components, additional JavaBeans components used in the pages, and custom JSP tags. An action class that does some setup work can make a JSP much simpler to implement. JSP tag libraries were also a magnificent addition to the JSP specification. They allow developers to encapsulate presentation logic in a form that is native to the content, that is, HTML tags. They can also be easily used by Web developers with HTML/XML skillsets as opposed to Java programming. Simply put, they are an extremely powerful mechanism for quickly building robust application pages with great quality and maintainability. Another technique that should be used to create modular, maintainable pages is the concept of a JSP template mechanism. A template pulls in reusable page fragments that make up the common look and feel of an application.

Minimize Java Code in a JSP

When JSP technology first became available, Java developers were given a powerful HTML-centric way to create page content that allowed them to embed any Java code directly into the presentation. This was a very tempting approach to use for all kinds of presentation logic, and it was not unusual to see JavaServer Pages that went on for pages and pages. If you compare this to good object-oriented programming practices, such as the general rule that no method should be longer than a single page, you can easily see that the JavaServer Pages were becoming too big to manage. On top of this, the code is interspersed with HTML, which makes it significantly more difficult to read and follow the logic of what is being done.

BEST PRACTICE Minimize the amount of actual Java code in a JSP. Large amounts of Java code interspersed with HTML in a JSP can quickly become unreadable and unmanageable. Instead, use custom tags wherever possible to encapsulate presentation logic and integrate with the controller architecture. You can also move logic out to action classes that perform setup work for the page or JavaBeans that are referenced by the page. If you do have scriptlets within the JSP, try to use a few large scriptlets as opposed to interspersing Java code throughout the entire HTML content.

You should minimize the amount of scriptlet code in a JSP. If possible, you should primarily put presentation logic in either JavaBeans or JSP custom tags. This limits the Java code to either expressions or small scriptlets that primarily invoke bean methods. In the case of custom tags, no Java code is required. You can simply embed the tag in the rest of the content. Introduced in the JSP 1.1 specification, this is a very powerful mechanism that you should take advantage of. It is a great way to encapsulate presentation logic and integrate it into the presentation. You will see numerous examples of how this mechanism can be used in the next chapter on building the User Interaction Architecture.

Use a JSP Template Mechanism

Web pages within an application normally share a common look and feel. This can include standard headers and footers as well as navigation bars that appear on the left of the page. The main content of the screen usually falls in the middle of the page. For example, this would be the actual table of account data in a view accounts page or the actual form with drop-down lists to choose accounts and enter a dollar amount in a transfer funds page. In order to make the view components more manageable, a template JSP can be created that pulls all of these common pieces together to create the overall page. Doing this prevents you from repeating common code in every JSP and makes it easier to change or configure the look and feel of all the screens in an application.

BEST PRACTICE Use a JSP template mechanism to apply a common look and feel to your application Web pages. This approach makes it easy to globally change common aspects of pages and reduces the amount of duplicated code.

For the sample bank application, a simple template that is used by most of the pages was structured. The template contains a header and footer as well as a navigation bar on the left-hand side. The main content of the screen, which is described by the next page in the navigation approach described earlier, fills the majority of the space on the page. Figure 7.6 shows the structure of the template.

Abstracting the Template

You will notice quickly that this template is fairly simplistic. Each section of the template is parameterized and specified by a given page. The standard sections, such as the header and footer, can be given default values for convenience, and the specific page instances can override them if necessary. For example, the bank application has a standard navigation bar that is used once a customer has logged on to the bank's Web site. However, when a user is going through the wizard to sign up as a new customer, this navigation bar does not make sense because the user does not yet have an account with the bank. Thus, the new customer pages would override the default navigation bar to show one that has links between the different pages of the multipage form.

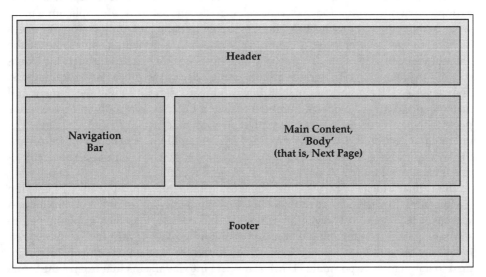

Figure 7.6 A Simple Page Template Structure.

The fact that the sections are parameterized provides a high level of maintainability, but all of the pages use the same template structure of header, footer, and navigation bar. For the sample application, this suffices just fine. However, for many complex applications, you have different types of templates for different pages. You can remedy this quite easily by abstracting the template. For example, perhaps some templates have an informational bar going down the right side as well. One of the definitions for each page can be what actual template to use. You could create <Template> tags in the metadata to define the sections of each template. In this book, however, the template as shown is used for simplicity, but you can easily see how to make this concept much more flexible to suit your application's needs.

An Overview of Jakarta Struts

Jakarta Struts is an open-source project launched by Craig Mclanahan to provide an MVC-based Web application framework for use with Java servlets, JSP, and JavaBeans components. This project embodies many of the best practices and design principles discussed in this chapter. The foundation of Struts is a generic implementation of the Model 2 architecture pattern applied to J2EE. This section looks at the elements of the Struts framework. The next chapter walks through how you can implement pages from the bank example using Struts.

The primary elements of Struts are:

- A controller `ActionServlet` that delegates specific request handling to `Action` classes

- An extensive JSP custom tag library

- A library of utility classes to support Web application development

If you look at the core responsibilities defined earlier for the controller architecture, the basic controller component and the action paradigm can be fairly straightforward to implement once you understand the relevant design patterns. A simple implementation of the controller architecture could probably be done with only a couple of pages of code. Struts does provide a controller servlet implementation, but some of the greatest value provided by a framework like Struts actually comes through the extensive JSP tag library that integrates into the remainder of the presentation framework. The power of JSP tag libraries is that they can greatly simplify JSP development and maintenance. Struts provides a number of custom JSP tags to rapidly integrate forms processing, error handling, and internationalization functionality into Web pages. The internationalization functionality provided by the tag libraries is based on features of the Java language such as `Locale` and `ResourceBundle`. The basic Struts architecture is shown in Figure 7.7.

The primary focus of Struts is functionality contained within the User Interaction Architecture. In particular, it provides a robust implementation of the controller and view aspects of the MVC design pattern. The business logic is then implemented in separate model components that can be either regular JavaBeans or Enterprise JavaBeans. As will be discussed later in detail, the `ActionServlet` can be configured to automatically populate HTML form data into JavaBeans that extend the Struts

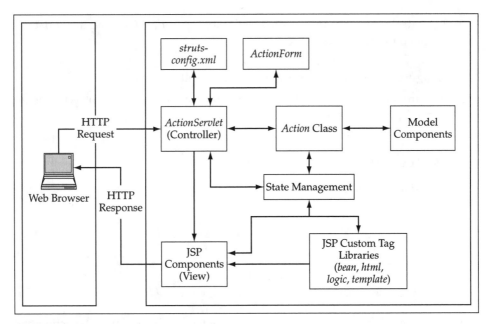

Figure 7.7   Basic Struts Architecture.

class `ActionForm`. These classes are closely tied to the servlet architecture and the controller's configuration data. Thus, they really are comparable to event objects that represent the data of a particular user event. If these were also used as the business object components, they would be limited in scope to the JSP container. This is sufficient for smaller applications; however, you can also use Struts as the user interaction layer of an enterprise architecture that implements the model components using Enterprise JavaBeans. The entry point into the model from Struts can be provided by the Service-Based Architecture, which is then built on top of the business object components.

At the core of the Struts framework is `ActionServlet`, a controller servlet that is the hub of the MVC implementation. It is a flexible metadata-driven component that dispatches specific request handling to subclasses of the Struts `Action` class. The application configuration of `ActionServlet` is controlled through an XML file called `struts-config.xml` that defines how user events map to actions and how those actions are processed. The controller is primarily used to process form submissions. For the most part, links go directly to a JSP view component. Thus, the basic logic of the controller is focused on forms processing. Each form maps to a particular `Action` in the configuration file `struts-config.xml`. In this file, the action can be defined to have an associated form bean (`ActionForm`). The controller logic can be summarized as follows:

1. Check for the existence of a form bean in the configured page scope (request, session, and so on).

2. Retrieve the existing form bean or instantiate one automatically if one is not found.

3. Populate the form bean based on direct mapping from HTML parameter names to bean property names.

4. Invoke the appropriate action class with the following arguments: the action configuration, form bean, and servlet request and response objects.

5. Forward the request to the JSP defined by the `ActionForward` object returned from the `Action` class.

Struts Actions

The standard action method overridden by subclasses and invoked by `Action-Servlet` is:

```
public ActionForward perform(ActionMapping mapping,
                             ActionForm form,
                             HttpServletRequest request,
                             HttpServletResponse response)
     throws IOException, ServletException;
```

The `ActionMapping` class holds all of the metadata for the particular action that is being invoked. It also defines how a user event maps to this action.

> **NOTE** The classes described here as a part of the Struts controller architecture can be found in the `org.apache.struts.action` package.

Mapping User Events to Actions

The Struts framework does not explicitly define user events. Rather, it uses URLs to indicate the particular user event that occurred. The URLs are referred to as action paths in the configuration. This is just one example of the great flexibility that exists in terms of implementing these concepts within J2EE technology. Rather than map a single URL to the controller servlet, the sample Struts configuration and examples map a URL pattern (http://<host:port>/*.do) to `ActionServlet`. Thus, any URL within the Web server domain that has the extension .do will be processed by the controller servlet. The actual servlet path can then be used to identify the event. For instance, consider the following HTML <form> elements. Each one will be processed by `ActionServlet` but with different servlet paths that identify the event. The `changeAddress` event has the following form definition:

```
<form name="changeAddressForm" method="POST"
     action="/bank/struts/changeAddress.do">
```

> **NOTE** Note that /bank is the root directory of the Web server. You place most of the JSP files in the /bank/struts directory. Thus, the context-relative servlet path (as given by the method `HttpServletRequest.getServletPath`) in this example is /struts/changeAddress.do.

Struts always strips off the extension for the purposes of mapping actions; thus, the event can be thought of as the path /struts/changeAddress in this example. Likewise, a transfer funds form defined by the following <form> tag will also be processed by `ActionServlet`.

```
<form name="transferFundsForm" method="POST"
      action="/bank/struts/transferFunds.do">
```

In this case, the event, as described by the servlet path, is /struts/transferFunds. The Struts examples in this book happen to be placed into a `struts` subdirectory, but you can easily see how the remaining path almost directly corresponds to the event names. Struts uses the context-relative path names to map HTTP requests to actions. Each action mapping in `struts-config.xml` defines a path that causes a request to be processed by this action. For example, look at the action mapping for the change address event:

```
<action    path="/struts/changeAddress"
           type="bank.struts.ChangeAddressAction"
           name="addressForm"
           scope="request"
           input="/struts/changeAddress.jsp">
</action>
```

Thus, the first of the preceding HTML <form> examples would be processed by this action because the servlet path /struts/changeAddress is defined as the `path`.

Action Mappings

The action configurations defined in the metadata are referred to as action mappings and are represented by `ActionMapping` objects. The <action> elements in `struts-config.xml` are actually located inside of an <action-mappings> element. Attributes of each <action> include:

`path`:   The servlet path that maps to this action. This is referenced from the custom tag <html:form action="`path`">.

`type`:   The class name of the `Action` subclass to handle the request.

`name`:   The name of the form bean to use. This is referenced in the <form-beans> section of the XML where the actual class name is defined. This is an optional attribute.

`scope`:   The JSP/servlet page scope (that is, request, session, and so on) to store the form bean. If not specified, this defaults to session, so be sure to set it to request whenever possible to avoid unnecessary overhead in the session.

`validate`:   An indicator of whether the `validate` method of the form bean should be automatically invoked by `ActionServlet`. This defaults to true.

`input`:   The URL from which this action originated. This optional attribute can be used in the case of errors to forward the request back to the original input form so that the errors can be displayed and the form can be resubmitted.

`unknown`:   This attribute can be set to true if you want this to be the default action for requests if no other mapping can be found. This defaults to false.

Page Navigation

Navigation from one page to another is represented as a forward within Struts. As stated earlier, the `Action` subclasses return an instance of `ActionForward` which represents the particular page to go to next. Forwards exist on two levels, a global level and an action level. Both are defined within the configuration XML so that the actual physical URLs are abstracted from the application code.

Global Forwards

Global forwards can be referenced from any action class or JSP and are defined in `struts-config.xml` under a <global-forwards> element. They are equivalent to a pure navigation event from the earlier design discussion. Some of the global forwards for the bank sample are defined as follows:

```
<global-forwards>
    <forward name="logon" path="/struts/login.jsp"/>
    <forward name="main"  path="/struts/main.jsp"/>
    <forward name="viewAccounts"
            path="/struts/viewAccounts.jsp"/>
    <forward name="changeAddress"
            path="/struts/changeAddress.jsp"/>
</global-forwards>
```

Action-Level Forwards

Action-level forwards can be used or seen only by the particular action in which they are defined. They are defined as <forward> subelements of the <action> tag. A common use of this mechanism is an implementation of the event-based navigation concept, which determines the next page based on the event and the success of the action. For example, take the transfer funds example, which goes to different places based on the result of the transaction. Its action mapping can be defined as follows:

```
<action     path="/struts/transferFunds"
            type="bank.struts.TransferFundsAction"
            name="transferFundsForm"
            scope="request"
    <forward name="success"
            path="/struts/viewAccounts.jsp" />
    <forward name="failure"
            path="/struts/transferFunds.jsp" />
</action>
```

These named forwards are then referenced by the `Action` class to communicate the navigation information back to the controller servlet. There is also a special action-level forward that is predefined by the framework, the `input` attribute of the <action> tag. This is an optional attribute that can be used to define the page that triggered this action. Notice that the actual URL of the page is different from the servlet path that maps to `ActionServlet`, so this is a nice convenience if you want to use it within an

`Action` implementation to return control back to the input form as is typically the case when errors occur.

Form Beans

All form beans extend the Struts class `ActionForm`. Form beans are really event objects that store the data from HTML form input fields. These classes are implemented like value objects and have explicit getter and setter methods for each form property so that they may be manipulated using Java introspection. This is a critical aspect of the framework that is used throughout the controller architecture as well as the custom tag library that integrates well with these form beans. In addition to property management methods, form bean classes typically also implement a few template methods, in particular one method for data validation.

Form beans are defined in `struts-config.xml` within a <form-beans> element. For the two samples thus far, the form beans are defined as follows:

```
<form-beans>

  <form-bean     name="transferFundsForm"
                 type="bank.struts.TransferFundsForm"/>

  <form-bean     name="addressForm"
                 type="bank.struts.AddressForm"/>

</form-beans>
```

These form beans were referenced by the `name` attribute of the previous action mappings. Additionally, the `name` attribute of each form bean is used as the attribute name in the defined page scope for the action (that is, request, session, and so on). The `type` attribute defines the actual class name of the form bean.

Populating Form Beans

The controller servlet populates form beans automatically. In order for this to happen, the beans' property names must equal the HTML parameter names. As you will see later, there is a complete tag library for creating the HTML input controls that map to the form beans' properties. Thus, you are really linking the parameters of the HTML tag library to the form bean names. This is a primary linkage point between the custom tag libraries and the controller architecture, and it provides a powerful basis for developing presentation functionality.

There are two reasons why you may want to use form beans as pure event objects. One is the fact that form beans are tied to the servlet API. The other reason is the one that you just encountered, the fact that the form beans' property names must equal the HTML parameter names. So that you do not have to tie the business object property names to the front end, it is sometimes a good idea to use the event object and service object abstractions. You can use the form bean data to create separate service data objects that are then actually serialized and sent to remote EJB method invocations within

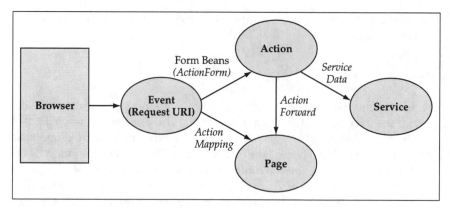

Figure 7.8   User Interaction Abstractions Using Struts.

the Service-Based Architecture. Thus, the abstractions in the front end can be mapped as shown in Figure 7.8 with Struts.

Form Beans as a Template

Form beans have two template methods that can be overridden for each subclass. The first is a `validate` method that can be used for basic data validation. In this sense, form beans are the equivalent of value objects or lightweight business objects. They have some additional functionality beyond just being data structures. Unless configured otherwise (see the `validate` attribute of the action mapping), the `validate` method is automatically invoked after the servlet populates the form bean but before the action is invoked. If `validate` returns a list of errors through `ActionErrors`, they are stored in the request scope, and control is forwarded to the `input` form for that action mapping. Error handling and `ActionErrors` are described in the next section. The interface for `validate` is defined as follows:

```
public ActionErrors validate(ActionMapping mapping,
                             HttpServletRequest request);
```

The second template method is `reset`, which is invoked before the servlet populates a form bean. It can be used to initialize property values of the bean, but be aware that it is also invoked when the bean is repopulated; consequently, you can overwrite the existing values if the bean was being stored in the session. The interface is defined as follows:

```
public void reset(ActionMapping mapping,
                  HttpServletRequest request);
```

Aggregated Form Beans

You may have noticed that the action configuration lets you define only a single form bean. If Struts stopped here, you would be limited to a single list of properties, analogous to your `ArgumentList`. But this is not the case because you can aggregate, or have nested form beans, within the form bean defined in the action mapping. In fact, you can go many levels deep as well. Form beans and their related `html` and `bean` tag libraries can also use a nested object syntax that separates each property with a dot notation. As an example, assume the `AddressForm` class described earlier was aggregated inside of a `CustomerForm` class. Standard getter methods for the aggregated object need to be defined on the customer such as the following example:

```
public class CustomerForm extends ActionForm {

    // AddressForm member
    private AddressForm address = new AddressForm();

    // Rest of properties declared here

    // Aggregated AddressForm
    public AddressForm getAddress() {
        return address;
    }

    // Rest of methods to follow
}
```

Assuming the `AddressForm` follows the normal JavaBeans naming standards, you can then use the nested syntax to access address fields from the `CustomerForm` object. The following examples show how the simple and nested syntax maps to method invocations on the customer form bean:

```
firstName       =>  getFirstName();
lastName        =>  getLastName();
address.city    =>  getAddress().getCity();
address.state   =>  getAddress().getState();
```

For multipage forms such as wizards, you can define a single parent form bean that can have many child form beans if you want to segregate the input data. This is actually the easiest way to implement pages within a wizard interface. Using nested form beans also allows for pages in a wizard to change without greatly affecting the remainder of the presentation logic.

Figure 7.9 represents the form beans within the controller architecture as a UML class diagram.

Error Handling

Earlier you saw that the `validate` method on the form beans returned a class called `ActionErrors`. This class implements the concept of an error bucket. Each individual error in the bucket is an instance of `ActionError`. Each `ActionError` is constructed with an error key and possibly some substitution arguments. This part is analogous to your `ErrorList` construct; however, the error messages are internationalized through property resource bundles. The actual error messages are stored in

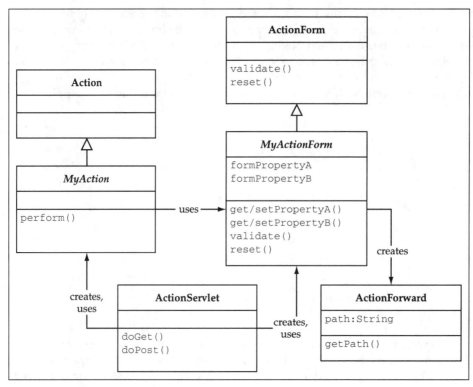

Figure 7.9   UML Representation of Struts Controller Architecture.

an application properties file that is configured by the application initialization parameter to `ActionServlet`. Thus, you have an `ApplicationResources.properties` file that defines all of the error messages, as well as other messages or labels that can go on the page. This allows you to define what text to use based on the `Locale` of the user. Some of the sample error messages are defined as follows in the properties file:

```
INVALID_ZIP=<li>The zip code {0} must be 5 digits.</li>.
CHECKING_MIN_BALANCE=<li>Minimum balance of $100 is not met for
                    the checking account.</li>
```

The messages themselves use `java.text.MessageFormat` to process substitution values. You notice that there is also HTML code surrounding the messages. This text is placed directly into the HTML page content, so you can add some standard formatting here if you wish. The primary method that is used on `ActionErrors` is the `add` method that puts errors in the bucket. This method is defined as follows:

```
public void add(String property, ActionError error);
```

Each error is linked to a form bean property that is indicated by the first argument. Optionally, this can also be defined as a global error that is not directly tied to an individual field. The constant `ActionErrors.GLOBAL_ERROR` is used in this case. For example, if you wanted to issue the invalid zip code error and tie it to the zip property, you would use the following code:

```
ActionErrors errors = new ActionErrors();

// Edit the zip code property
if (zip.length() != 5) {
    errors.add("zip", new ActionError("INVALID_ZIP",zip));
}
```

If you wanted to add the minimum balance as a global error, you could use the following code:

```
errors.add(ActionErrors.GLOBAL_ERROR,
           new ActionError("CHECKING_MIN_BALANCE"));
```

You can also ask the `ActionErrors` class if it is `empty()`, get the `size()`, or access the errors in their entirety or by specific properties.

View Components

The powerful JSP tag libraries make up the second major portion of the Struts framework. First, this section looks at the `html` tag library, which is focused on HTML forms but also adds support for things such as creating links and rendering images. Struts has created tags that also encapsulate the interaction with the form beans for each aspect of the HTML form.

HTML Tag Library

The <html:form> tag is used to wrap the entire form. Its `action` attribute specifies the context-relative path that is mapped to the appropriate action class as discussed earlier. Within an <html:form>, you can use any of the HTML tags that represent the various input controls, such as text fields, checkboxes, cancel buttons, and submit buttons, just to name a few.

HTML Form Tags

The primary input control is the text field. The <html:text> tag has the following basic format:

```
<html:text property="propertyName" />
```

This tag creates a text input field using the property name as the HTML name. It also defaults the value to the bean property of the same name. Notice it does this automatically to enforce the requirement that the HTML names and form bean property names be the same. You can also override the initial value of the text field with the `value` attribute. Similarly, <html:text> accepts most of the normal HTML <input> attributes, such as `size` and `maxlength`. Also note that the `property` can be either a simple reference or a nested syntax reference. Thus, if you had customer and address data on the same form using an earlier example, you could have the following content in your JSP:

```
<%@ taglib uri="/WEB-INF/struts-html.tld" prefix="html" %>
<html:html>
<head><title>Update Customer Page</title></head>
<body>

<html:form action="/struts/updateCustomer" focus="firstName">

    First Name: <html:text property="firstName" /> <br/>
    Last Name:  <html:text property="lastName" /> <br/>
    Address:    <html:text property="address.line1" /> <br/>
    City:       <html:text property="address.city" /> <br/>
    State:      <html:text property="address.state" /> <br/>
    Zip Code:   <html:text property="address.zip" /> <br/>

    <html:submit property="submit" value="Update Customer"/>
    <html:cancel />

</html:form>

</body>
</html:html>
```

There are a couple of things to note about this code snippet. This form is processed by the action mapping that defines the `path /struts/updateCustomer`. On the first submission of this form, the defined form bean is instantiated and stored in the scope configured by the action mapping. Initially, the form bean might be empty and no values would be shown in the text fields. After the form is submitted, the form bean is populated by the servlet and stored again in the proper page context. Thus, if this page is redisplayed with errors, the HTML tags automatically take care of retrieving the property values from the form bean.

In this example, you also see for the first time the `<html:submit>` tag, which creates a submit button with the given value. You also see an `<html:cancel>` tag with no additional attributes. This tag uses the value Cancel by default and uses a standard parameter name that is recognized by the `Action` class. The `Action` subclasses can actually ask `isCancelled()` to check for this user event. In addition to the HTML tags you have seen already, there are others that work similarly to the `<html:text>` tag for almost all input field types including checkboxes, hidden fields, password fields, radio buttons, reset buttons, select lists, and text areas. You will see some of these used in the upcoming examples. Finally, the `<html:html>` tag is used to wrap the entire page.

If you wanted to display any errors that may have occurred on the form submission, you could add the `<html:errors>` tag to display any `ActionErrors` that were stored in the request scope.

The HTML Link Tag

The `<html:link>` tag can be used to create URL links within a JSP. It takes care of encoding to ensure that URL rewriting will work if cookies are turned off. It also plugs into the navigation metadata defined in `struts-config.xml`. You must specify one of the following attributes to define the link:

`forward:` Refers to a global forward defined in <global-forwards>.

`href:` Defines the URL for the link.

`page:` The context-relative path that can map to an action class.

`linkName:` An intrapage link.

Thus, if you wanted to create a link to the bank's logon page, you could do so and reference the global forward shown earlier named logon:

```
<html:link forward="logon">Go to the Bank's Home Page
                          and Logon</html:link>
```

This creates an anchor tag <A> without any additional query parameters. If you want to add parameters to the URL, you can do so with additional tag attributes specifying either a single bean property or multiple parameters contained in a Java collection stored somewhere in the page context.

Bean Tag Library

The `bean` tag library provides access to beans and their properties as well as creates internationalized messages for inclusion into JSP content. The `<bean:write>` tag is used to retrieve the value of a specific bean property. Its format is similar to the core format of `<html:text>`. As an example, this code puts the value of the address line1 field into the page content:

```
<bean:write name="customerForm" property="address.line1" />
```

Another often used tag in this library is the `<bean:message>` tag. This tag pulls in content from an internationalized set of messages stored in property bundles. Internationalization uses the `Locale` object stored in the session. This can be set up automatically by using the `Locale` attribute of the `<html:html>` tag. Thus, you can modify the earlier JSP code snippet to internationalize the labels of each text field in the following manner by using the `<bean:message>` tag.

```
<html:html locale="true">

<!-- BEGINNING OF PAGE CONTENT -->

<bean:message key="prompt.state" /> :
    <html:text property="address.state" /> <br/>

<bean:message key="prompt.zip" /> :
    <html:text property="address.zip" /> <br/>

<!-- REST OF PAGE CONTENT TO FOLLOW -->

</html:html>
```

In your `ApplicationResources.properties` file for English, you would then have the following messages defined:

```
prompt.state=State
prompt.zip=Zip Code
```

In order to generate your Web pages in another language, you would create additional versions of the properties file named `ApplicationResources_xx.properties` where xx is equal to the ISO language code. This would then get picked up and used by Struts based on the request's `Accept-Language` header, if any is specified.

Template Tag Library

The Struts framework provides a `template` tag library to abstract the JSP template concept discussed earlier in the design considerations section. It lets you create template JavaServer Pages that have placeholders for content. The placeholders are defined with the `<template:get>` tag. This tag takes a `name` attribute to identify

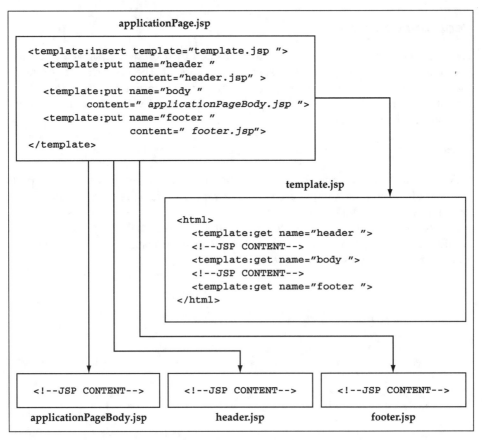

Figure 7.10 Struts Template Tag Design.

the page fragment. The JSP that invokes the template uses the `<template:insert>` tag to pull in a template. Within the `<template:insert>` tag, you can place `<template:put>` tags to define where the placeholders get their content. This design is depicted in Figure 7.10.

The JSP template can be defined as follows using the Struts `template` tag library to implement the basic design discussed earlier in this chapter. This design includes a header at the top of the page, a navigation bar on the left, and a footer at the bottom, all surrounding the main content in the middle.

```
<%@page import="blf.*"%>
<%@ taglib uri="/WEB-INF/struts-html.tld" prefix="html" %>
<%@ taglib uri='/WEB-INF/struts-template.tld'
          prefix='template' %>

<html:html>
<head><title><template:get name='title' /></title></head>
<body>
<template:get name='<%=PageConstants.TEMPLATE_HEADER%>' />
<table width="100%">
<tr>
<td width="20%" align="right" valign="top">
<template:get name='<%=PageConstants.TEMPLATE_NAVBAR%>' />
</td>
<td width="60%" >
<template:get name='<%=PageConstants.TEMPLATE_BODY%>' />
</td>
<td width="20%" align="right">
</td>
</tr>
</table>
<template:get name='<%=PageConstants.TEMPLATE_FOOTER%>' />
</body>
</html:html>
```

NOTE The `PageConstants` class is used to define string constants used throughout the User Interaction Architecture. In this case, it is used to define the parameters of the JSP template.

The actual JavaServer Pages then use this template using the `<template:insert>` tag. For example, the bank's main page uses the template and just displays a welcome message. The main JSP looks like this:

```
<%@ taglib uri='/WEB-INF/struts-template.tld'
          prefix='template' %>

<template:insert template='/struts/template.jsp'>
  <template:put name='title' content='Bank Main Page'
                direct='true'/>
```

```
    <template:put name='header' content='/struts/header.jsp' />
    <template:put name='navbar' content='/struts/navBar.jsp' />
    <template:put name='body' content='/struts/mainContent.jsp'/>
    <template:put name='footer' content='/struts/footer.jsp' />
</template:insert>
```

The `name` attribute identifies the page section, and the `content` attribute specifies the URL to use for the section. In the case of the page title, the `direct` attribute, which tells the template tags to put the text value directly in the page, is added. The example pages follow the pattern shown in Figure 7.10. The overall page that contains this reference to the template uses what you might consider the normal page name (that is, `main.jsp`). The main body of the page then is put in a JSP with a body prefix (that is, `mainBody.jsp`). Thus, the majority of the presentation logic is in the body JavaServer Pages. In this case, `mainBody.jsp` simply has the welcome message:

```
<table width=100%>
<tr><td witdh=100%>Welcome to the Main Bank Page</td></tr>
</table>
```

The `template` tag library provides a nice way to standardize the look and feel of the pages in your application. It also greatly increases the maintainability of your JSP code. You could also take the abstraction a step further and create a generic JSP to invoke the templates. The specific `content` attributes could be defined in page metadata so that you do not need to create a high-level JSP for each page. The bank examples pages continue to have a `pageName.jsp` and a `pageNameBody.jsp` for each logical page.

Logic Tag Library

The `logic` library provides tags to manage conditional flow in a page as well as iteration over a collection of objects. This includes tags, such as `<logic:equals>`, `<logic:notEquals>`, `<logic:lessThan>`, and `<logic:greaterThan>`, which evaluate bean properties and, based on the tag's meaning, evaluate the body of the tag only if the conditional test was satisfied. These tags are typically used for content that is data-driven or based on control parameters sent into the page. A particularly helpful tag is `<logic:iterate>`, which is used to iterate over a collection of objects. This tag can simplify some pages that would otherwise use JSP scriptlets to manage this. You will see an example of this tag being used in the upcoming Struts version of the view accounts page.

Best Practices for Designing the User Interaction Architecture

A summary of the best practices for designing the User Interaction Architecture is given in this section.

Use a Generic MVC Implementation

A generic MVC, or Model 2, implementation such as Jakarta Struts provides an excellent foundation on which to build the User Interaction Architecture. This approach automates much of the front-end processing while providing a flexible and extensible foundation to meet all types of application requirements. This practice adheres to a key design principle, which is to make the normal case as simple as possible through automation and configuration but to give the application the ability to override automated, configurable elements when necessary for complex cases. The true value that comes with a package like Struts is the tight integration between the controller architecture and the tag library used to rapidly create JSP components. This automates much of the forms processing, keeps the JSP code relatively clean, and allows the control logic to be isolated in action classes.

Abstract the Key Elements of User Interaction

The core responsibilities of the User Interaction Architecture revolve around four key abstractions: the user event, action, service, and Web page. The HTTP request should be abstracted as a user event in order to isolate the HTTP protocol from the business logic. The user event can then be configured through metadata and the controller architecture to drive the rest of the processing. The event determines the action class that handles the request and influences the service used to invoke the business logic. The event and the result of the action or service are then used to determine the next page to display to the user. By abstracting these key elements of user interaction, a good portion of the front-end processing can be automated and defined through metadata.

Don't Hard-Code Physical URLs into the Application

Abstract physical URLs out of the application into metadata in order to enable automation, avoid broken links, and have more maintainable pages. The controller architecture can use the metadata to resolve logical page names and forward control to the corresponding physical URL, typically implemented by a JSP.

Keep the Session Size to a Minimum

Keep the session size fairly small, especially for applications that need to scale to large numbers of users. Use the request scope wherever possible to pass data from the controller architecture to JSP components.

Minimize the Amount of Java Code in a JSP

Large amounts of Java code interspersed with HTML in a JSP can quickly become unreadable and unmanageable. Use custom tags wherever possible to encapsulate presentation logic and integrate with the controller architecture. You can also move logic out to action classes that perform setup work for the page or JavaBeans that are referenced by the page. If you do have scriptlets within the JSP, try to use a few large scriptlets as opposed to interspersing Java code throughout the entire HTML content.

Use a JSP Template Mechanism

A JSP template mechanism is an excellent way to apply a common look and feel to your application Web pages. This approach makes it easy to make global changes to common aspects of pages and it also reduces the amount of duplicated code. Jakarta Struts includes a tag library that can be used to implement this mechanism.

Summary

The cornerstone of the User Interaction Architecture is a generic implementation of the MVC architecture applied to J2EE. Jakarta Struts provides an excellent implementation that is readily available for developers to use. It provides a powerful tag library that integrates well with the Struts controller architecture to rapidly build transactional Web pages. The typical functionality provided by the controller architecture can be broken down into eight core responsibilities that revolve around four key abstractions: the user event, action, service, and Web page. The responsibilities center on the user-event abstraction that can be configured through metadata to drive the rest of the processing. The last step the controller servlet takes on each request is to forward to the next page, typically implemented as a JSP component. JSP components use should tag libraries as much as possible to encapsulate presentation logic and avoid large amounts of Java code interspersed with HTML. A JSP template mechanism provides a powerful way to apply a common look and feel to your application's Web pages.

With the design considerations and best practices from this chapter in mind, the next chapter walks through the implementation of the User Interaction Architecture. Web pages from the bank application are implemented that build on the service component and business object functionality implemented in previous chapters. User interaction functionality is implemented on top of Jakarta Struts, which is the first best practice that is discussed in this chapter.

Building the User Interaction Architecture

This chapter looks at how you can build pages from the bank application using the Struts framework. The existing business logic components created in earlier chapters are used for the implementation of the model in this MVC architecture. The Struts action classes invoke the service components as an entry point to the back-end business logic. The overall JSP content is constructed using the Struts template tag mechanism as was discussed in the last chapter.

The Change Address Page

This section shows how to build a Web page that contains a simple update form. The change address example is used to illustrate the implementation of the core responsibilities of the controller architecture using Struts. The change address page allows bank customers to change their address. It updates only one object, the Address object, which must already exist in the database. In order to construct the page, the current address information needs to be retrieved from the database and displayed on the page. Once the user edits the information and submits the form, the data should be validated and updated back to the database. In order to simplify the JSP, it is built to assume that the page context has already been set up prior to the JSP being executed. Thus, the

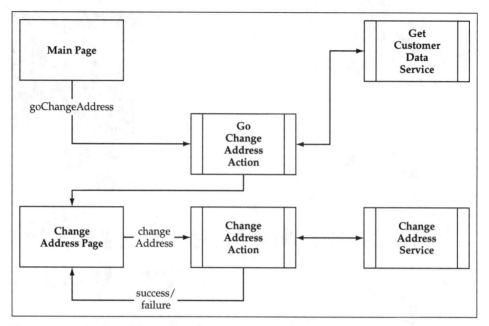

Figure 8.1   Change Address Page Flow.

navigation event that takes the user to the change address page invokes an action to do the setup work. This user event, which is defined as goChangeAddress, will be processed by a GoChangeAddressAction class that retrieves the user's address and makes the data available through a request attribute to the JSP for display. The actual form submission event is named changeAddress, which can then be processed by a ChangeAddressAction class. The flow through this page-generation loop is defined in Figure 8.1.

Each action class invokes an appropriate service component to access the data and business logic. The GetCustomerData service returns the customer and address value objects. The ChangeAddress service takes an address value object and uses the corresponding business object to update the database.

The relevant configuration for the change address page is shown here from struts-config.xml:

```
<struts-config>
    <form-beans>
        <form-bean  name="addressForm"
                    type="bank.struts.AddressForm"/>
    </form-beans>
    <global-forwards>
        <forward   name="changeAddress"
                   path="/struts/changeAddress.jsp" />
    </global-forwards>
    <action-mappings>
        <action   path="/struts/goChangeAddress"
                   type="bank.struts.GoChangeAddressAction" />
```

```
<action    path="/struts/changeAddress"
           type="bank.struts.ChangeAddressAction"
           name="addressForm"
           scope="request"
           input="/struts/changeAddress.jsp" />
       </action>
     </action-mappings>
</struts-config>
```

NOTE The `<action>` path attribute defines the user events discussed earlier. In the example, the customer pages are placed in the **/struts** directory, thus the last portion of the action path, for all intents and purposes, defines the named event. The path **/struts/goChangeAddress** defines the `goChangeAddress` event. This is the metadata used to support the controller's determination of the event that occurred and the action class to invoke (core responsibility one).

As described earlier, the `GoChangeAddressAction` retrieves the initial data for display on the form. From this point, the `changeAddress.jsp` form is processed by the `ChangeAddressAction` that invokes the change address service, which results in the update to the database. The page is then redisplayed with either a confirmation message or a list of errors.

Displayed using the template, the change address page looks like Figure 8.2.

The Go Change Address Event and Action

The change address process is initiated by the `goChangeAddress` navigation event (core responsibility 1). There is no event object to create (core responsibility 2) or application validations to perform (core responsibility 4) because this was a page navigation event. There is, however, an action class to invoke (core responsibility 3). The `GoChangeAddressAction` is implemented as shown later. It invokes an application service to retrieve the address data (core responsibility 5), manages the context for the change address page (core responsibility 6), and defines that page as the next page to display (core responsibility 7). After the action class has been executed, the controller servlet forwards the request to the next page (core responsibility 8). Even though `goChangeAddress` is just a navigation event, the page flow is made much cleaner by implementing the setup logic for the change address page in the `GoChangeAddress-Action` class. This reduces the amount of code in the change address JSP and isolates the call to the data retrieval service.

BEST PRACTICE One technique that you can use to minimize the amount of Java code in a JSP is to move page setup logic out to an action class. This isolates the service invocation from the page and also simplifies the page implementation in many cases by allowing the JSP to assume that a form bean is passed in as context.

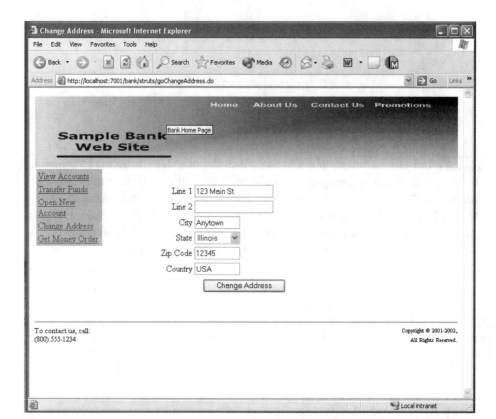

Figure 8.2   The Change Address Page.

This implementation of GoChangeAddressAction uses a Struts form bean as the event object and the AddressData value object as part of the service data.

```java
package bank.struts;

import java.io.IOException;
import java.util.*;
import javax.servlet.*;
import javax.servlet.http.*;
import org.apache.struts.action.*;
import org.apache.struts.util.MessageResources;
import blf.*;
import bank.AddressData;


/**
 * Action class that implements the go change address action
 */
public class GoChangeAddressAction extends Action {
```

```java
/**
 * The Struts action interface
 */
public ActionForward perform(ActionMapping mapping,
                             ActionForm form,
                             HttpServletRequest request,
                             HttpServletResponse response)
 throws IOException, ServletException {

    // Get hold of the session.
    HttpSession session = request.getSession(true);

    // Validate the request parameters.
    ActionErrors errors = new ActionErrors();

    try {
        // You need to run a data retrieval service
        // to initially get the address data.
        // This service takes an argument list
        // of just the customer identifier.
        ServiceData sdata =
            new ServiceData("GetCustomerData");
        ArgumentList argList = new ArgumentList();

        // Get the customer out of the session.
        // This was set by the logon action.
        argList.setProperty("customerId",
                  (String)session.getValue("customerId"));
        sdata.setArgumentList(argList);

        // Invoke the application service.
        BlfService service =
            ServiceObjectFactory.getBlfService();
        sdata = service.executeService(sdata);
        service.remove();

        // Service output has two value objects:
        // 0 - Customer, 1 - Address;
        // You just want the address.
        AddressData addrData =
            (AddressData) sdata.getOutputData(1);
        // Store the address ID as a server-side parameter.
        session.setAttribute("addressId",
            addrData.getProperty("id"));
        // Set the context for the next page.
        AddressForm formBean = new AddressForm();
        BlfStrutsConverter.convertValueObjToFormBean(
                                        addrData,formBean);
        request.setAttribute("addressForm",formBean);
```

```
                // Return the input page to redisplay the form.
                return (mapping.findForward("changeAddress"));

        } catch (BlfException be) {

                // Map BLF errors to action errors.
                BlfStrutsConverter.convertErrorList(
                                        be.getErrorList(),errors);
                // Set the errors so the next page can see them.
                saveErrors(request, errors);
                // Return the input page to redisplay the form.
                return (mapping.findForward("changeAddress"));

        } catch (Exception e) {

                // Create a general action error for the exception.
                errors.add(ActionErrors.GLOBAL_ERROR,
                        new ActionError("GENERAL_SERVICE_ERROR"));
                // Set the errors so the next page can see them.
                saveErrors(request, errors);
                // Return the input page to redisplay the form.
                return (mapping.findForward("changeAddress"));
        }
    }
}
```

There are a few interesting things to note about this action implementation using Struts. The first is the use of `ActionErrors` as the error bucket. No actual edits are done explicitly in this action class, but errors can be received back from the service invocation. However, the service returns the `ErrorList` business errors, not the action errors that are particular to the front end of the architecture. Thus, the business errors need to be converted to action errors. Because there is also a need to convert between value objects and form beans, a utility class can be created to do these conversions. The utility used for this purpose is a class named `BlfStrutsConverter`. The action class invokes the `convertErrorList` method to create a set of `Action-Errors` from the list of business errors. Also notice that when the context is set for the next page in the case of an error, the `saveErrors` method on the `Action` base class is used to store the errors in the request scope. The `BlfStrutsConverter` class was also used to convert the address value object returned from the service to its corresponding form bean used by the Struts controller architecture. This conversion class will be discussed in detail later in this section when the `ChangeAddressAction` class is discussed.

The other interesting aspect of this action class is the portion that sets the context for the change address JSP. The address identifier is set as a session attribute so that the change address action is able to determine later on what address instance is being updated. Alternatively, the identifier could have been placed as a hidden HTML form field and then sent back to the server with the rest of the object's properties. However, you might not want to expose the internal identifier of the address entity in the HTML based on security or other considerations. The strategy to mitigate this concern is to use server-side parameters that feed to the service. In the bank application, the customer id is also already stored in the session from the login page. The login process and security in general will be discussed in detail in the next chapter. However, for the time being, assume that the customer id is available in the session from any page in order to identify the user. Because the bank object model has only a single address for each customer, you could easily identify the address instance with an extra database lookup on the customer table. This functionality would go in the ChangeAddress service rather than the action. In the current example, the action adds the customer id from the session as another property in the AddressData input value object. These kinds of decisions are related to trade-offs that are made for highly scalable, secure applications. Each case will likely have different considerations. In this example, another string (the address id) adds very little to the session, so it makes sense to store it as a server-side parameter in the session.

The other step to manage user context in the GoChangeAddressAction class is related to the immediate rendering of the change address page. This is accomplished by adding an address form bean to the request scope. Remember that the change address action was defined as having the form bean named addressForm in the request scope. This action creates the form bean from the data retrieval service and puts it in the request scope so that it is automatically picked up by the Struts servlet and JSP architecture. Lastly, the ActionMapping.findForward method is used to return a reference to the changeAddress forward defined in the global forwards section of the struts-config.xml.

The Change Address JSP

The GoChangeAddressAction class returns the next logical page, change-Address. This logical page maps to the /struts/changeAddress.jsp URL in the Struts metadata. The Struts controller forwards the request to this JSP, which is the manifestation of the generic template for the change address page. The template includes the URL, /struts/changeAddressBody.jsp, as the main content. Now the actual JSP is executed and it has the address bean to use to display the existing values in the form. The user can modify the values and then click the submit button. The form is posted and processed by the controller servlet. It is determined that the event is changeAddress from the form's action. This is defined in the JSP by the action parameter of the <html:form> custom tag.

The changeAddress.jsp, which uses the Struts template tag library, is shown here:

```
<%@ taglib uri='/WEB-INF/struts-template.tld'
           prefix='template' %>

<template:insert template='/struts/template.jsp'>
  <template:put name='title' content='Change Address'
                direct='true'/>
  <template:put name='header' content='/struts/header.jsp' />
  <template:put name='navbar' content='/struts/navBar.jsp' />
```

```
        <template:put name='body'
                        content='/struts/changeAddressBody.jsp'/>
        <template:put name='footer' content='/struts/footer.jsp' />
    </template:insert>
```

BEST PRACTICE Use the Struts template tag library or an analogous mechanism to simplify the development and maintenance of the common aspects of application Web pages. A standard naming scheme can be used to distinguish between JSP components that implement template instances and page content.

The main content is then found in `changeAddressBody.jsp`.

```
<%@page import="bank.struts.AddressForm"%>
<%@ taglib uri="/WEB-INF/struts-html.tld" prefix="html" %>
<%@ taglib uri="/WEB-INF/struts-bean.tld" prefix="bean" %>
<%@ taglib uri="/WEB-INF/blf.tld"          prefix="blf" %>

<table width="100%">
<tr align="center"><td><ul><html:errors/></td></tr>
</table>


<%
    // You need to get the state value so you can pass it
    // to your custom drop-down tag.
    AddressForm formBean =
        (AddressForm) request.getAttribute("addressForm");
    String currentState = formBean.getState();
%>


<html:form action="/struts/changeAddress" focus="line1">
<table width="100%">
<tr>
<td align=right><bean:message key="prompt.line1" /></td>
<td><html:text property="line1" size="20" maxlength="30"/></td>
</tr>
<tr>
<td align=right><bean:message key="prompt.line2" /></td>
<td><html:text property="line2" size="20" maxlength="30"/></td>
</tr>
<tr>
<td align=right><bean:message key="prompt.city" /></td>
<td><html:text property="city" size="10" maxlength="20"/></td>
</tr>
<tr>
<td align=right><bean:message key="prompt.state" /></td>
<td><blf:dropDown htmlName="state" cache="States"
                    selectedOption='<%=currentState%>' /> </td>
</tr>
<tr>
<td align=right><bean:message key="prompt.zip" /></td>
```

```
<td><html:text property="zip" size="10" maxlength="20"/></td>
</tr>
<tr>
<td align=right><bean:message key="prompt.country" /></td>
<td><html:text property="country" size="10"
                maxlength="20"/></td>
</tr>
</table>
<table width=100%>
<tr>
<td align="center"><html:submit property="submit"
                            value="Change Address"/></td>
</tr>
</table>

</html:form>
```

Note that the <HTML> and associated tags are not needed because this page is being included inside of the master JSP template. The page itself is actually fairly straightforward. The <html:errors> tag is used to display any errors that occur on submissions. All of the form controls except the select list are created using <html:text> tags that directly reference the AddressForm bean defined for this action. The only scriptlet here is used to ascertain the current value of the state field for the drop-down tag. A Business Logic Foundation drop-down tag is used so that it can integrate directly into the CacheList mechanism developed in the Business Object Architecture chapters. If you wanted to use the Struts <html:select> tag to create this drop-down, you could store the cached data as JavaBeans with getter methods for the values and labels. It is important to note that the power of Struts is based on introspection and the JavaBeans convention for properties. Consequently, if components in the reference architecture use a different interface, you need to map these objects to JavaBeans in order to take advantage of all of the functionality. Thus, in the case of value objects, you may want to implement both the standard property interface and JavaBeans getters and setters. Examples of this concept were shown in the business object chapters. In this example, the BlfStrutsConverter class is used to convert between generic value objects and JavaBeans in order to plug them into the Struts framework. A version of this example using a combined value object and event object is discussed later. You may still want to have some type of abstraction between the form beans and the value objects because of the Web-centric nature of the form beans. As is the case here, you would need an extra conversion to take full advantage of Struts.

NOTE The <blf:dropdown> tag used in changeAddressBody.jsp illustrates the great power of custom JSP tag libraries. This tag seamlessly integrates the cached data stored within the CacheList mechanism into a form field in the page. It takes care of creating the HTML for the form field by accessing the state cache and mapping the state code from the form bean to its corresponding display value. This example also shows how you can create your own tag libraries and easily integrate them into JavaServer Pages that have been created using Struts as a foundation. The code for the drop-down tag is shown at the end of the example.

The Address Form Bean

The address form bean is implemented as follows. It is primarily a JavaBean used as a data structure, but it also implements the two `ActionForm` template methods, `validate` and `reset`. The `validate` method checks that required fields were populated on the form and that the zip code is the proper length. In this example, 5 digits were arbitrarily assumed to be the correct length of the zip code in order to demonstrate a simple application-specific validation:

```java
package bank.struts;

import javax.servlet.http.HttpServletRequest;
import org.apache.struts.action.ActionError;
import org.apache.struts.action.ActionErrors;
import org.apache.struts.action.ActionForm;
import org.apache.struts.action.ActionMapping;

/**
 * Form bean for the address entity
 */
public final class AddressForm extends ActionForm {

    private String line1 = null;
    private String line2 = null;
    private String city  = null;
    private String state = null;
    private String zip   = null;
    private String country  = null;

    public String getLine1() {
     return line1;
    }

    public void setLine1(String value) {
        line1 = value;
    }

    public String getLine2() {
     return line2;
    }

    public void setLine2(String value) {
        line2 = value;
    }

    public String getCity() {
     return city;
    }

    public void setCity(String value) {
        city = value;
    }
```

```java
public String getState() {
 return state;
}

public void setState(String value) {
    state = value;
}

public String getZip() {
 return zip;
}

public void setZip(String value) {
    zip = value;
}

public String getCountry() {
 return country;
}

public void setCountry(String value) {
    country = value;
}

/**
 * Reset all properties to their default values.
 */
public void reset(ActionMapping mapping,
                  HttpServletRequest request) {

    this.line1 = null;
    this.line2 = null;
    this.city = null;
    this.state = null;
    this.zip = null;
    this.country = null;
}


/**
 * Validate the properties that have been set from this
 * HTTP request and return any errors.
 */
public ActionErrors validate(ActionMapping mapping,
                             HttpServletRequest request) {

    ActionErrors errors = new ActionErrors();
    if ((line1 == null) || (line1.length() < 1))
        errors.add("line1",
          new ActionError("REQ_FIELD","line1"));
```

```
            if ((city == null) || (city.length() < 1))
                errors.add("city",
                    new ActionError("REQ_FIELD","city"));
            if ((state == null) || (state.length() < 1))
                errors.add("state",
                    new ActionError("REQ_FIELD","state"));
            if ((zip == null) || (zip.length() < 1)) {
                errors.add("zip",
                    new ActionError("REQ_FIELD","zip"));
            } else if (zip.length() != 5) {
                errors.add("zip",
                        new ActionError("INVALID_ZIP",zip));
            }
            if ((country == null) || (country.length() < 1))
                errors.add("country",
                    new ActionError("REQ_FIELD",
                                    "country"));


            return errors;
        }
    }
```

The ChangeAddressAction in this example is triggered when the user submits
the change address form. In this case, the controller implements the first four core
responsibilities. It determines that the changeAddress event occurred and that the
request should be delegated to the ChangeAddressAction. It populates the
AddressForm bean shown earlier from the input data and invokes its validate
method to perform the validations required for the page. It is now the responsibility of
the ChangeAddressAction class to invoke the ChangeAddress service, manage
the user context, handle any errors that occur, and define the next page. In this case, the
change address form is always shown next with either confirmation or error messages.
The ChangeAddressAction class is implemented as follows:

```
package bank.struts;

import java.io.IOException;
import java.util.*;
import javax.servlet.*;
import javax.servlet.http.*;
import org.apache.struts.action.*;
import org.apache.struts.util.MessageResources;
import blf.*;
import bank.AddressData;


/**
 * Action class that implements the go change address action
 */
public class ChangeAddressAction extends Action {
```

```java
/**
 * The Struts action interface
 */
public ActionForward perform(ActionMapping mapping,
                             ActionForm form,
                             HttpServletRequest request,
                             HttpServletResponse response)
    throws IOException, ServletException {

    // Get hold of the session.
    HttpSession session = request.getSession(true);

    // Get the request parameters.
    ActionErrors errors = new ActionErrors();
    String line1 = ((AddressForm) form).getLine1();
    String line2 = ((AddressForm) form).getLine2();
    String city  = ((AddressForm) form).getCity();
    String state = ((AddressForm) form).getState();
    String zip   = ((AddressForm) form).getZip();
    String country = ((AddressForm) form).getCountry();

    try {
        // Create a service data object for this service.
        ServiceData sdata =
            new ServiceData("ChangeAddress");
        AddressData addrData = new AddressData();
        addrData.setProperty("line1",line1);
        addrData.setProperty("line2",line2);
        addrData.setProperty("city",city);
        addrData.setProperty("state",state);
        addrData.setProperty("zip",zip);
        addrData.setProperty("country",country);
        addrData.setProperty("id",
                        session.getAttribute("addressId"));
        sdata.addInputData(addrData);

        // Invoke the application service.
        BlfService service =
            ServiceObjectFactory.getBlfService();
        sdata = service.executeService(sdata);
        service.remove();

        // Add a confirmation message to inform the user
        // that the update was successful.
        errors.add(ActionErrors.GLOBAL_ERROR,
                   new ActionError("ADDR_CONFIRMATION"));
        // Set the context so the next page can see them.
        saveErrors(request, errors);

        // Return the input page to redisplay the form.
        return (new ActionForward(mapping.getInput()));
```

```
        } catch (BlfException be) {

            // Map BLF errors to action errors.
            BlfStrutsConverter.convertErrorList(
                                be.getErrorList(),errors);
            // Set the errors so the next page can see them.
            saveErrors(request, errors);
            // Return the input page to redisplay the form.
            return (new ActionForward(mapping.getInput()));

        } catch (Exception e) {

            // Create a general action error for the exception.
            errors.add(ActionErrors.GLOBAL_ERROR,
                    new ActionError("GENERAL_SERVICE_ERROR"));
            // Set the errors so the next page can see them.
            saveErrors(request, errors);
            // Return the input page to redisplay the form.
            return (new ActionForward(mapping.getInput()));
        }
    }
}
```

The `validate` method of the `AddressForm` bean was automatically invoked by the controller servlet prior to this class being executed; thus, if any required fields are missing or basic data validations fail, you automatically get the input form redisplayed with the error messages. The change address JSP, which is the input form in this case, is shown if the update is a success or a failure. After the call to the service, the `ADDR_CONFIRMATION` message is added to the error bucket to provide the confirmation message. Note that this is only an informational message, but because this is the action class and it is used after the call to the Session Bean, it could not have affected the transaction anyway.

Using a Conversion Utility with Separate Event and Value Objects

In the preceding `ChangeAddressAction` code, the service data was explicitly populated from the form bean so that you could see the process. However, you can also automate this process and encapsulate the logic in the `BlfStrutsConverter` class that was introduced earlier. The relevant portion of the code could be rewritten to create the service data using `BlfStrutsConverter`.

```
// Create a service data object for this service.
ServiceData sdata =
    new ServiceData("ChangeAddress");
AddressData addrData = new AddressData();
BlfStrutsConverter.convertFormBeanToValueObj(
                                form,addrData);
sdata.addInputData(addrData);
```

The code for the conversion method in `BlfStrutsConverter` uses the `PropertyUtils` class and the list of attributes from the reference architecture metadata to populate the value object. The code for this method is shown here:

```
public static void convertFormBeanToValueObj(
    ActionForm formBean, ValueObject valueObject)
    throws BlfException {

    try {
        Set propNames =
            valueObject.getAttributeMetadata().keySet();
        Iterator iter = propNames.iterator();
        while (iter.hasNext()) {
            String propName = (String) iter.next();
            try {
                Object value =
                    PropertyUtils.getProperty(formBean,
                                              propName);
                valueObject.setProperty(propName,value);
                // If the property does not exist
                // on the form bean, it can be
                // ignored. Sometimes, not all
                // of the fields of an object
                // are on a given form.
            } catch (NoSuchMethodException ignore) {}
        }
    } catch (Exception e) {
        throw new BlfException(e.getMessage());
    }
}
```

Validation

As mentioned earlier, the `validate` method of the form bean is automatically invoked to perform required field checking and data validation. As an example, say that the user did not enter the `line1` and `city` fields in the change address form. These are required fields that should be caught by the value object's `validate` method. One such validation is shown here:

```
if ((line1 == null) || (line1.length() < 1))
    errors.add("line1",
       new ActionError("REQ_FIELD","line1"));
```

The REQ_FIELD error message is defined in the `ApplicationResources.` `properties` file that Struts uses for action errors. This string is added to the message list at run time to provide a helpful note to the user:

```
REQ_FIELD=<li>The field {0} is required.</li>
```

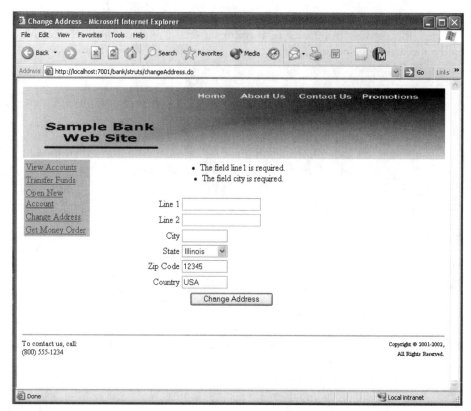

Figure 8.3 Change Address Page with Required Field Errors.

Any errors that are either returned from the `validate` method or saved using the `saveErrors` method in the action class are displayed using the <html:errors> tag. In this validation example, in which the user fails to enter a value for `line1` or `city`, the form bean adds two REQ_FIELD errors to the list, which then get displayed on the page as shown in Figure 8.3.

Using the Validation Template in the Form Bean

Although this example works fine as is shown earlier, there is a slight design problem with the validation logic in that it is duplicated both in the form bean `validate` method and the `validate` template of the value object. In earlier chapters, a validate template was created that used the application metadata to perform required field edits and data type validations. This template also called a `blfValidate` method that was optionally implemented by the application developer to implement application-specific edits. It would not make sense to have to implement this validation logic all over again in each form bean. The same set of logic used in the base value object and business object implementations can also be used within the Struts form bean structure. The same inheritance structure can be used to provide this functionality.

BEST PRACTICE Use the same Template Method pattern within form beans to implement a validate template. This mechanism can reuse much of the property validation and handling logic implemented for use with the business objects. This prevents a duplication of code and effort.

A base class called `BaseFormBean` can act just like the base business object class. The relevant code from the business object base class can be used almost exactly as is because all of the property manipulation is based on introspection and the generic property methods found in the `ValueObject` interface. In fact, it makes sense to have `BaseFormBean` implement the `ValueObject` interface.

NOTE There is one minor difficulty with having `BaseFormBean` extend Strut's `ActionForm` class and implement the `ValueObject` interface. An earlier version of Struts used a `validate` method with no arguments that returned an array of strings. Thus, the `validate` method as it was defined in `ValueObject` conflicts with the existing method signature. To resolve this issue, the `validate` method needs to be moved up to the business object interface so that it does not override the return type of the `validate` method. A `StrutsValueObject` interface that extends `ValueObject` can be used to provide a `validate-FormBean` method for this purpose that does not conflict with any other methods. Only Web-tier components ever need to refer to the form beans by this interface. If the form bean is used as both the event object and value object, the service implementations still need to refer to them only by the `ValueObject` interface.

The class diagram for form beans as value objects is shown in Figure 8.4.
The `StrutsValueObject` interface simply contains the `validateFormBean` method.

```
package blf.struts;

import blf.ValueObject;
import blf.BlfException;
import org.apache.struts.action.ActionErrors;

/**
 * This interface is needed because the original
 * value object interface overrode the return
 * value of a deprecated validate method in
 * the StrutsFormBean.
 */
public interface StrutsValueObject extends ValueObject {

    /**
     * Validate method.
     */
    public ActionErrors validateFormBean() throws BlfException;

}
```

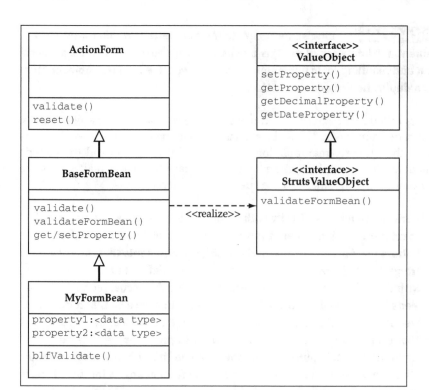

Figure 8.4   Class Diagram for Struts Form Beans as Value Objects.

The implementation of BaseFormBean calls the validateFormBean method, which now becomes the validate Template Method for form beans used as value objects. One interesting thing to note is that the generic validation methods such as validateRequiredFields and validatePropertyValues should check only those properties that have been modified. This is not true for business objects that are required to check all properties specified in the object metadata. However, an event object or value object does not necessarily populate all of the object's properties. This is true for two primary reasons:

- Some properties are supplied through context management rather than the input form. For example, the id property of the address is not specified on the form because it is set in the action class from a value stored in the session. Thus, you would not want to issue an error in this case.

- Some pages allow a user to update only a subset of an object's properties; thus, you would not want to validate what has not been specified.

Optionally, you could define metadata specifically for event objects, in which case you could always validate all of the properties of the bean. However, it is often much easier to reuse object metadata, as is the case with the change address example. The change address form contains all of the address fields; thus, you can point to the same Address definition in the metadata to avoid duplication.

How can you tell if a property was modified? It turns out that the form bean needs to be refactored to capture this data. A collection of property names is maintained for those properties that were modified. The generic `setProperty` method adds the name to this list for each property if it has not already been modified. Because Struts uses the regular setter methods through introspection, another mechanism is also needed to track this. Thus, the `setModified` method, which will need to be called in the subclass implementation of the setter methods, was added. The address form bean later in this section will illustrate this concept.

The relevant code from `BaseFormBean` is shown here:

```
public class BaseFormBean extends ActionForm
    implements StrutsValueObject, java.io.Serializable {

    protected HashMap attributeMetadata;
    protected String  objectName;
    // Collection of property names that were modified
    protected ArrayList modifiedProperties;
    // Error list to hold validation errors
    protected ActionErrors errorList;


    private BaseFormBean() {
    }

    public BaseFormBean(String objectName) {
        try
        {
            BusinessObjectMetadata bom =
                MetadataManager.getBusinessObject(objectName);
            attributeMetadata = bom.getPropertyMap();
            this.objectName = objectName;
            modifiedProperties = new ArrayList();
        }
        catch (Exception e)
        {
            e.printStackTrace();
        }
    }

    protected ActionErrors getErrorList() {
        if (errorList == null) {
            errorList = new ActionErrors();
        }
        return errorList;
    }

    /**
     * Validate the properties that have been set from this
     * HTTP request and return any errors.
     */
```

```java
public ActionErrors validate(ActionMapping mapping,
                             HttpServletRequest request) {

    try {
        // Run the standard validate template.
        validateFormBean();

        // Run a validation template that takes
        // the request object and action
        // mapping.
        blfValidate(mapping,request);

    } catch (BlfException be) {
        errorList.add(ActionErrors.GLOBAL_ERROR,
            new ActionError("GENERAL_SERVICE_ERROR",
                            be.getMessage())));
    }

    return errorList;

}


/**
 * Validation template method particular to form beans,
 * which takes request object and action mapping
 */
public void blfValidate(ActionMapping mapping,
                        HttpServletRequest request) {
    // Base class implementation does nothing.
}


/**
 * Set that a property was modified.
 */
protected void setModified(String propertyName) {
    if (!modifiedProperties.contains(propertyName)) {
        modifiedProperties.add(propertyName);
    }
}


/**
 * Validate the value object's data.
 */
public ActionErrors validateFormBean()
    throws BlfException {

    // Initialize the error list.
    errorList = new ActionErrors();

    // Validate all required fields.
    validateRequiredFields();
```

```
        // Validate data types.
        validatePropertyValues();
        // Invoke the Template Method for the application.
        // Specific validation
        blfValidate();

        return errorList;
}


/**
 * Template Method for application-specific validation;
 * base class implementation is empty.
 */
public void blfValidate() throws BlfException {
}


/**
 * For each modified property, check that a value exists
 * if it is defined as required in the metadata.
 */
public void validateRequiredFields() throws BlfException {

    // Validate only those that have been populated.
    Iterator iter = modifiedProperties.iterator();
    while (iter.hasNext()) {
        // Get the properties metadata.
        String propName = (String) iter.next();
        PropertyMetadata prop =
            getPropertyMetadata(propName);

        if (prop.isRequired()) {
            //
            // Field is required, so check that it
            // has a value.
            //
            String value = null;
            try {
              value = getProperty(prop.getName());
            } catch (PropertyException ignore) {}

            // Add an error to the bucket if no value.
            if ((value == null) || (value.equals(""))) {
                errorList.add( prop.getName(),
                    new ActionError("REQ_FIELD",
                                    prop.getName())));
            }
        }
    }
}
```

```java
/**
 * Use the property validator mechanism to validate
 * data types for populated properties.
 */
public void validatePropertyValues() throws BlfException {

    // Validate only those that have been populated.
    Iterator iter = modifiedProperties.iterator();
    while (iter.hasNext()) {
        // Get the properties metadata.
        String propName = (String) iter.next();
        PropertyMetadata pmd =
            getPropertyMetadata(propName);
        String propValue = getProperty(pmd.getName());

        // Invoke helper method to invoke
        // appropriate property validator.
        try {
            validatePropertyDataType(pmd.getType(),
                                     propValue);
        } catch (BlfException be) {
            // Add to the error bucket if an error
            // was detected.
            getErrorList().add( propName,
                new ActionError("INVALID_VALUE",propValue));
        }
    }
}


/**
 * Property management methods
 */
public void setProperty(String propertyName, Object value)
    throws PropertyException {

    // Mark that this property is modified.
    // Only modified properties are validated,
    // unlike business objects, due to incomplete
    // data that can come from the front end.
    setModified(propertyName);

    // Validate the data type first because you
    // are going to set the actual member variable.
    PropertyMetadata prop =
        getPropertyMetadata(propertyName);
    String propType = prop.getType();

    try {
        // Use the utility class to invoke the set method.
        PropertyUtils.setProperty(this,propertyName,
            convertToObjectFormat(propType,value));
```

```
        } catch (BlfException ex) {
            throw new PropertyException(ex.getMessage(),
                                        ex.getErrorList());
        } catch (Exception ex) {
            throw new PropertyException(ex.getMessage());
        }
    }

public String getProperty(String propertyName)
    throws PropertyException {

    Object value = null;

    try {
        // Get the member variable value as an object.
        Object obj =
            PropertyUtils.getProperty(this,propertyName);

        // Convert the object to a string using the
        // property-handler mechanism.
        PropertyMetadata prop =
            getPropertyMetadata(propertyName);
        String type = prop.getType();
        value = convertToStringFormat(type,obj);

    } catch (NoSuchMethodException ex) {
        // This happens when a property specified
        // in the metadata does not exist. Ignore it
        // so that you can use the same metadata with
        // Java business objects, Entity Beans,
        // and form beans.
        // Log a note just in case this is
        // actually the cause of an error.
        System.out.println("BaseFormBean missing getter "
            + propertyName);
        return null;
    } catch (Exception ex) {
        throw new PropertyException(ex.getMessage());
    }

    if (value == null) return null;
    return value.toString();
}

public BigDecimal getDecimalProperty(String propertyName)
    throws PropertyException {

    Object value = null;
    try {
        value =
            PropertyUtils.getProperty(this,propertyName);
```

```
        } catch (Exception e) {
            throw new PropertyException(e.getMessage());
        }
        return (BigDecimal) value;
    }


    // Rest of property management methods to follow ...


}
```

The new AddressFormBean does not have to implement required field checking in a validate method. Rather, it only has to implement the specific edits for the event object in the blfValidate Template Method. The validate method is defined with no arguments as was the case with business objects and regular value objects. It is also defined to match the signature of the Struts form bean validate method that takes the request object and the action mapping as arguments. The validate template in BaseFormBean invokes both, so you can place your logic in either one.

With regards to properties, the setModified method is invoked in each setter method because there is no other way to know if a given property was modified. This is a small inconvenience that can be easily resolved if you are using code-generation tools to create your form beans. Otherwise, be sure to add this method to each setter method, or else the validate template as it was implemented earlier will not validate the properties. The blfValidate Template Method is now automatically invoked through the form bean's validate template, which in turn was invoked by the Struts controller servlet. The validate method in BaseFormBean runs the standard validation template first shown in the business object chapters. The code for Address-FormBean is shown here. Again, note that the setModified method is used in setter methods to track which properties are modified for validation purposes.

```java
public class AddressFormBean extends BaseFormBean {

    private String id = null;
    private String line1 = null;
    private String line2 = null;
    private String city  = null;
    private String state = null;
    private String zip   = null;
    private String country  = null;

    /**
     * Default constructor
     */
    public AddressFormBean() {
        super("Address");
    }

    public String getId() {
     return id;
    }
```

```java
public void setId(String value) {
    setModified("id");
    id = value;
}

public String getLine1() {
 return line1;
}

public void setLine1(String value) {
    setModified("line1");
    line1 = value;
}

// Rest of property accessors to follow...

/**
 * Template Method for application-specific validation;
 * base class implementation is empty.
 */
public void blfValidate() throws BlfException {

    // Validate only fields that have
    // been populated in value objects.
    if (modifiedProperties.contains("zip")) {
        String zip = getProperty("zip");
        if (zip.length() != 5) {
            getErrorList().add("zip",
                new ActionError("INVALID_ZIP",zip));
        }
    }
}
}
```

Using the Form Bean as Both the Event Object and Value Object

The version of the address form bean that implements the ValueObject interface can be used as both the event object and the service data object. This eliminates the data conversion between the two separate structures. However, the form bean does have methods that would not be applicable as a pure value object. For example, the validate method that takes the HttpServletRequest object would not be relevant on the EJB tier. The ActionForm base class, in fact, has a reference to the servlet as a member. However, it is marked as transient, so it is not serialized and sent to a remote EJB, as is the case with the Session Bean service components. If your service components are local Session Beans, the servlet reference would be available to the service component but should not be used. Thus, the only reasons you may want to keep the event and value objects separate is if you want the additional flexibility or if the Web-centric nature of the form bean bothers you enough to forgo the option. Clearly, if the form bean is used as a value object that is sent back and forth from the EJB tier, there is a small amount of training or documentation needed to educate your development staff on its proper use.

To implement this option in the change address example, you should make sure that the `ChangeAddress` service refers only to the `ValueObject` interface, in which case it does not matter what the actual implementation of the value object is. The relevant lines of the `ChangeAddressServiceImpl` are shown here to illustrate the insignificance of the value object implementation.

```
ValueObject addressData =
    (ValueObject) serviceData.getInputData(0);
String addressId = addressData.getProperty("id");

Address addr = (Address)
    BusinessFactoryImpl.findByPrimaryKey("Address",
                                         addressId);
addr.setProperties(addressData);
addr.save();
```

The address metadata needs to be modified to define a version of the form bean named `AddressFormBean` as the value object class. The action classes are not required to use the `BlfStrutsConverter` class in this case. They can directly reference the value object that is sent back from the `GetCustomerData` service. The `GoChangeAddressAction` implementation now references only the `ValueObject` interface as shown here in the portion of the code that invokes the service and sets the page context:

```
// Invoke the application service.
BlfService service =
    ServiceObjectFactory.getBlfService();
sdata = service.executeService(sdata);
service.remove();

// Service output has two value objects:
// 0 - Customer, 1 - Address;
// You just want the address.
ValueObject addrData =
    (ValueObject) sdata.getOutputData(1);
// Store the address ID as a server-side parameter.
session.setAttribute("addressId",
                     addrData.getProperty("id"));
// Set the context for the next page.
request.setAttribute("addressForm",addrData);
```

The `ChangeAddressAction` applies the same type of changes. It references the form bean as a `ValueObject` and uses it to invoke the service. The relevant code from `ChangeAddressAction` is shown below.

```
// Create a service data object for this service.
ServiceData sdata =
    new ServiceData("ChangeAddress");
```

```
ValueObject formBean = (ValueObject) form;
formBean.setProperty("id",
            session.getAttribute("addressId"));
sdata.addInputData(formBean);

// Invoke the application service.
BlfService service =
    ServiceObjectFactory.getBlfService();
sdata = service.executeService(sdata);
service.remove();
```

The Drop-Down Tag

In the `changeAddress.jsp`, it was noted earlier that a custom tag was used to create the drop-down list of states for the user to choose from on the form. This is a common recurrence in business applications, so it makes sense for the logic to be encapsulated in a custom tag. It is also common for the values in the list to come from one of the cache lists. Drop-down data commonly takes the form of relatively static data, such as the fifty United States. Thus, you can integrate the tag with the `CacheList` mechanism. The HTML to invoke the tag is the following:

```
<td><blf:dropDown htmlName="state" cache="States"
                selectedOption='<%=currentState%>' /> </td>
```

The drop-down tag takes the HTML name of the input control, the name of the cache to get the code/values from, and an optional preselected option. It uses the cache keys as the values of the list with the cached objects being the labels. In this case, the cache is usually implemented as a `LookupCache` that deals with all strings, although it is not required to be a `LookupCache`. The cached objects can implement the `toString()` method to represent their values in the list. The code for `DropDownTag` is shown here. It is a bit more complex than the current illustration because it can also support the creation of lists from any collection of value objects that is stored in the page context. In this case, the property names to be used for the labels and values of the list must be specified.

```
package blf;

import java.io.IOException;
import javax.servlet.http.HttpServletRequest;
import javax.servlet.http.HttpSession;
import javax.servlet.jsp.JspException;
import javax.servlet.jsp.JspWriter;
import javax.servlet.jsp.PageContext;
import javax.servlet.jsp.tagext.TagSupport;
import java.util.*;

/**
 * Drop-down tag
 */
public class DropDownTag extends TagSupport {
```

```java
// Name to make the HTML control.
private String htmlName = null;
// A name of a collection of value objects;
// either this or a cache name must be
// specified.
private String collection = null;
// For collections, the property name
// that is the label on the list
private String labelProperty = null;
// For collections, the property name
// that is the value on the list
private String valueProperty = null;
// The cache name to use for this
// drop-down
private String cache = null;
// For any configuration, the option
// that should be preselected
private String selectedOption = null;

public String getHtmlName() {
    return htmlName;
}

public void setHtmlName(String value) {
    htmlName = value;
}

public String getCollection() {
    return collection;
}

public void setCollection(String value) {
    collection = value;
}

public String getLabelProperty() {
    return labelProperty;
}

public void setLabelProperty(String value) {
    labelProperty = value;
}

public String getValueProperty() {
    return valueProperty;
}

public void setValueProperty(String value) {
    valueProperty = value;
}
public String getSelectedOption() {
    return selectedOption;
}
```

```java
public void setSelectedOption(String value) {
    selectedOption = value;
}
public String getCache() {
    return cache;
}

public void setCache(String value) {
    cache = value;
}


/**
 * Process the start of this tag.
 */
public int doStartTag() throws JspException {

    StringBuffer buffer = new StringBuffer();
    buffer.append ("<select name=\"" + htmlName +
                   "\" size=\"1\">\n");

    // Determine if you use a single collection
    // of objects from a cache
    // or two separate collections of labels and values.
    if (collection != null) {
        //
        // Using a collection of value objects
        //
        Collection coll = (Collection)
            pageContext.findAttribute(collection);
        Iterator iter = coll.iterator();
        while (iter.hasNext ()) {
            ValueObject collObject =
                (ValueObject) iter.next();
            String label = null;
            String value = null;
            try {
                label = (String)
                    collObject.getProperty(labelProperty);
                value = (String)
                    collObject.getProperty(valueProperty);
            } catch (PropertyException pe) {
                throw new JspException(pe.getMessage());
            }

            if (selectedOption == null) {
                writeOption(buffer,label,value,false);
            } else {
                if (value.equals (selectedOption)) {
                    writeOption(buffer,label,value,true);
                } else  {
                    writeOption(buffer,label,value,false);
                }
```

```java
            }
        }
    } else {
        //
        // Using a cache
        //
        ObjectCache objCache = null;
        try {
            objCache =
                CacheList.getInstance().getCache(cache);
        } catch (BlfException be) {
            throw new JspException(be.getMessage());
        }
        Iterator labelIter = objCache.valuesIterator();
        Iterator valueIter = objCache.keysIterator();
        while (labelIter.hasNext ()) {
            String label = (String) labelIter.next();
            String value = (String) valueIter.next();

            if (selectedOption == null) {
                writeOption(buffer,label,value,false);
            } else {
                if (value.equals (selectedOption)) {
                    writeOption(buffer,label,value,true);
                } else  {
                    writeOption(buffer,label,value,false);
                }
            }
        }
    }

    // Close the HTML tag.
    buffer.append ("</select>\n");

    // Write out the HTML to the page.
    JspWriter writer = pageContext.getOut();
    try {
        writer.print(buffer.toString());
    } catch (IOException e) {
        throw new JspException(e.getMessage());
    }

    // Evaluate the included content of this tag.
    return (EVAL_BODY_INCLUDE);
}


/**
 * Process the end of this tag.
 */
public int doEndTag() throws JspException {
```

```
          // Evaluate the remainder of this page.
          return (EVAL_PAGE);
      }


      /**
       * Release any acquired resources.
       */
      public void release() {
      }


      /**
       * Helper method to write HTML
       * for an individual option
       */
      public void writeOption(StringBuffer buffer, String label,
          String value, boolean isSelected) {

          if (isSelected) {
              buffer.append ("<option selected value=\"");
          } else {
              buffer.append ("<option value=\"");
          }
          buffer.append(value);
          buffer.append("\">");
          buffer.append(label);
          buffer.append("</option>\n");
      }
  }
}
```

The tag library descriptor referred to in the JavaService Pages is defined for this tag as follows. The `collection`, `labelProperty`, and `valueProperty` tag attributes were not used in the change address example. They are used for the creation of drop-down lists from any collection of value objects stored in the page context. Any subsequent Business Logic Foundation tags are added to this descriptor.

```
<?xml version="1.0" encoding="UTF-8"?>

<!DOCTYPE taglib PUBLIC
    "-//Sun Microsystems, Inc.//DTD JSP Tag Library 1.1//EN"
    "http://java.sun.com/j2ee/dtds/web-jsptaglibrary_1_1.dtd">
<taglib>
  <tlibversion>1.0</tlibversion>
  <jspversion>1.1</jspversion>
  <shortname>blf</shortname>
  <tag>
    <name>dropDown</name>
    <tagclass>blf.DropDownTag</tagclass>
    <bodycontent>empty</bodycontent>
    <attribute>
      <name>htmlName</name>
```

```
                <required>true</required>
                <rtexprvalue>false</rtexprvalue>
            </attribute>
            <attribute>
                <name>selectedOption</name>
                <required>false</required>
                <rtexprvalue>true</rtexprvalue>
            </attribute>
            <attribute>
                <name>cache</name>
                <required>false</required>
                <rtexprvalue>true</rtexprvalue>
            </attribute>
            <attribute>
                <name>collection</name>
                <required>false</required>
                <rtexprvalue>false</rtexprvalue>
            </attribute>
            <attribute>
                <name>labelProperty</name>
                <required>false</required>
                <rtexprvalue>false</rtexprvalue>
            </attribute>
            <attribute>
                <name>valueProperty</name>
                <required>false</required>
                <rtexprvalue>false</rtexprvalue>
            </attribute>
        </tag>
    </taglib>
```

The drop-down tag illustrates a powerful concept used by Jakarta Struts and the reference architecture. The custom tag integrates directly into the caching component of the Business Logic Foundation. This adds reusable functionality to the page in a straightforward manner that simplifies the JSP code and maintainability of the overall application.

BEST PRACTICE Use JSP custom tags to encapsulate presentation logic and provide tight integration with the reference architecture. This simplifies the JSP code through standards-based, reusable page components.

The View Accounts Page

The view accounts page invokes a data retrieval service to get the list of accounts for the customer. It displays the list of accounts and their current balances in a table as shown in Figure 8.5.

The viewAccounts event triggers the ViewAccountsAction, which prepares for the JSP by retrieving the collection of account value objects for that customer. It

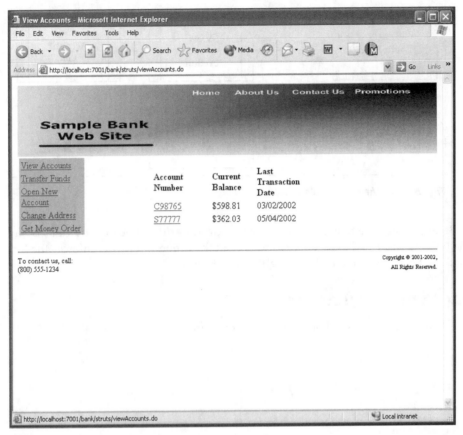

Figure 8.5 The View Accounts Page.

invokes the `GetAccountList` service to access the database that takes an argument list with the customer `id` as a parameter. All it has to do then is set the output data from the service, which is a collection of account value objects, in the request scope. The page flow for view accounts is shown in Figure 8.6.

The Struts configuration data for this page is shown here. Notice that there is no form bean or other associated information. This is analogous to a navigation event being processed by an action class. In fact, the HTML link in the navigation bar to get to this page is as follows:

```
<a href="/bank/struts/viewAccounts.do">View Accounts</a>
```

The action mapping is defined like this:

```
<action     path="/struts/viewAccounts"
            type="bank.struts.ViewAccountsAction">
    <forward   name="viewAccounts"
               path="/struts/viewAccounts.jsp"/>
</action>
```

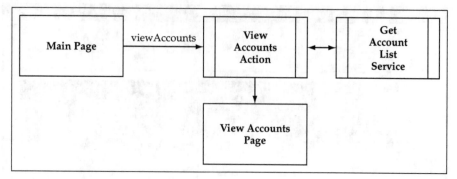

Figure 8.6 View Accounts Page Flow.

Because you have to execute the ViewAccountsAction before you can display the JSP, you need to define the forward only at the action level. This enforces the fact that you have to get to the JSP through the action class.

The View Accounts Action

The ViewAccountsAction is implemented as follows:

```
package bank.struts;

import java.io.IOException;
import java.util.*;
import javax.servlet.*;
import javax.servlet.http.*;
import org.apache.struts.action.*;
import org.apache.struts.util.MessageResources;
import blf.*;
import bank.CustomerData;

/**
 * Action class that implements the view accounts action
 */
public class ViewAccountsAction extends Action {

    /**
     * The Struts action interface
     */
    public ActionForward perform(ActionMapping mapping,
                                 ActionForm form,
                                 HttpServletRequest request,
                                 HttpServletResponse response)
        throws IOException, ServletException {

        // Get hold of the session.
        HttpSession session = request.getSession(true);
        // Create an empty list of errors.
        ActionErrors errors = new ActionErrors();
```

```
try {
    // Run a data retrieval service
    // to initially get the address data.
    // This service takes an argument list
    // of just the customer identifier.
    ServiceData sdata =
        new ServiceData("GetAccountList");
    ArgumentList argList = new ArgumentList();
    argList.setProperty("customerId",
                (String)session.getValue("customerId"));
    sdata.setArgumentList(argList);

    // Invoke the application service.
    BlfService service =
        ServiceObjectFactory.getBlfService();
    sdata = service.executeService(sdata);
    service.remove();

    //
    // Set context for the next page.
    //
    request.setAttribute(PageConstants.DATA,
                        sdata.getOutputData());

    // Set next page to main page.
    return (mapping.findForward("viewAccounts"));

} catch (BlfException be) {

    // On an error, set an empty list in the context.
    request.setAttribute(PageConstants.DATA,
                        new ArrayList());

    // Map BLF errors to action errors
    // and set so the next page can see them.
    BlfStrutsConverter.convertErrorList(
                        be.getErrorList(),errors);
    saveErrors(request, errors);

    // Go to the view accounts page and display
    // the errors.
    return (mapping.findForward("viewAccounts"));

} catch (Exception e) {

    // On an error, set an empty list in the context.
    request.setAttribute(PageConstants.DATA,
                        new ArrayList());

    // Create a general action error for the exception
    // and set so the next page can see them.
    errors.add(ActionErrors.GLOBAL_ERROR,
```

```
                    new ActionError("GENERAL_SERVICE_ERROR",
                                    e.getMessage())));
            saveErrors(request, errors);

            // Go to the view accounts page and display
            // the errors.
            return (mapping.findForward("viewAccounts"));
        }
    }
}
```

The account value object in this case is implemented as an extension of Base-ValueObject, but explicit getters and setters are added so that the Struts tags can be used within the JSP. A portion of AccountData is shown here to illustrate this. Note that this is just one option; you could also use a Struts AccountFormBean that implements the ValueObject interface, similar to the alternative shown for the change address page.

```
public class AccountData extends BaseValueObject
    implements java.io.Serializable {

    /**
     * Default constructor
     */
    public AccountData() {
        super("Account");
    }

    //
    // JavaBean property methods
    //
    public String getId() throws PropertyException {
        return getProperty("id");
    }
    public void setId(String value) throws PropertyException {
        setProperty("id",value);
    }

    public String getNumber() throws PropertyException {
        return getProperty("number");
    }
    public void setNumber(String value)
        throws PropertyException {
        setProperty("number",value);
    }

    //
    // Rest of accessors to follow...
    //
}
```

The `PageConstants.DATA` key was used to designate the account data to the JSP. The `PageConstants` class is shown here:

```
package blf;

/**
 * This class defines constants to be used by actions and JavaServer Pages
 * for dealing with attribute names of the request
 * and session scope, and so on.
 */
public class PageConstants {

    /**
     * The application data from the service invocation
     */
    public static final String DATA = "blfData";

    //
    // The sections of the JSP template
    //

    public static final String TEMPLATE_HEADER = "header";
    public static final String TEMPLATE_FOOTER = "footer";
    public static final String TEMPLATE_NAVBAR = "navbar";
    public static final String TEMPLATE_BODY   = "body";

}
```

The View Accounts JSP

The `viewAccounts.jsp` uses the standard JSP template. The interesting part is in `viewAccountBody.jsp`. An implementation of this page using the Struts `<bean:write>` tag to access properties is shown here:

```
<%@page import="blf.*"%>
<%@ taglib uri="/WEB-INF/struts-logic.tld" prefix="logic" %>
<%@ taglib uri="/WEB-INF/struts-bean.tld" prefix="bean" %>
<%@ taglib uri="/WEB-INF/blf.tld" prefix="blf" %>


<html:errors/>

<table width=60% align=center>
<tr><td width=40%><B>Account Number</B></td>
    <td width=30%><B>Current Balance</B></td>
    <td width=30%><B>Last Transaction Date</B></td></tr>

<logic:iterate name="<%=PageConstants.DATA%>"
               id="acctValueObject" scope="request"
               type="bank.AccountData"  >
```

```
<tr><td><a href="/bank/struts/accountDetail.do?id=
          <bean:write name="acctValueObject" property="id" />">
   <bean:write name="acctValueObject" property="number" />
       </a></td>
     <td><bean:write name="acctValueObject"
                   property="currentBalance" /></td>
     <td><bean:write name="acctValueObject"
                   property="lastModifiedDate" /></td></tr>

</logic:iterate>

</table>
```

The Struts `<logic:iterate>` tag is used to go through the output data of the service and create the HTML for each account. The logic tag has a `name` attribute and a `scope`, which points to the `PageConstants.DATA` stored in the request from `ViewAccountsAction`. The data in this case is a collection of account value objects. The `id` attribute of the `<logic:iterate>` tag is the name of a page scope attribute that makes each iterated object available to the JSP body of the tag. Finally, the `type` is the casting done to each object in the collection. This example actually casts each value object to its implementation class and uses the `<bean:write>` tag to get the values.

View Accounts Using Custom Tags

There is actually one slight problem with the previous implementation of the `changeAddressBody.jsp`. The `<bean:write>` tag uses the standard getter method to get the values from the beans. Thus, the `getCurrentBalance` method on `AccountData` that is invoked returns values such as 123.45 rather than values that are formatted for display such as $123.45. The property-handling mechanism created earlier in the business object chapters included a `getDisplayProperty` method exactly for this purpose. A custom tag `<blf:getProperty>` can be created that uses the `getDisplayProperty` method on the standard `ValueObject` interface rather than the standard getter method as defined by introspection. The implementation of `changeAddress.jsp` that uses this tag is shown here. Note that the value objects are cast to the `ValueObject` interface rather than their specific implementation class.

```
<%@page import="blf.*"%>
<%@ taglib uri="/WEB-INF/struts-html.tld" prefix="html" %>
<%@ taglib uri="/WEB-INF/struts-logic.tld" prefix="logic" %>
<%@ taglib uri="/WEB-INF/blf.tld" prefix="blf" %>

<html:errors/>

<table width=60% align=center>
<tr><td width=40%><B>Account Number</B></td>
    <td width=30%><B>Current Balance</B></td>
    <td width=30%><B>Last Transaction Date</B></td></tr>
```

```
<logic:iterate name="<%=PageConstants.DATA%>"
               id="acctValueObject"
               scope="request"
               type="blf.ValueObject" >
<tr><td>
<a href="/bank/struts/accountDetail.do?id=
  <blf:getProperty bean="acctValueObject" property="id" />">
    <blf:getProperty bean="acctValueObject"
                 property="number" /></a></td>
    <td><blf:getProperty bean="acctValueObject"
                         property="currentBalance" /></td>
    <td><blf:getProperty bean="acctValueObject"
                         property="lastModifiedDate" />
</td></tr>
</logic:iterate>

</table>
```

The code for the `<blf:getProperty>` tag is quite simple and is as follows:

```
public class GetPropertyTag extends TagSupport {

    /**
     * The bean from which to get a property
     */
    private String bean = null;

    public String getBean() {
        return bean;
    }

    public void setBean(String value) {
        bean = value;
    }

    /**
     * The property to get
     */
    private String property = null;

    public String getProperty() {
        return property;
    }

    public void setProperty(String value) {
        property = value;
    }

    /**
     * Process the start of this tag.
     */
```

```java
public int doStartTag() throws JspException {

    try {
        // First, get hold of the bean.
        // This method searches request, session, ...
        ValueObject obj =
            (ValueObject) pageContext.findAttribute(bean);

        // Get the value. If null, return
        // empty string.
        String value = obj.getDisplayProperty(property);
        if (value == null) {
            value = "";
        }

        // Write out the value.
        JspWriter writer = pageContext.getOut();
        writer.print(value);

    } catch (Exception be) {
        throw new JspException(be.getMessage());
    }

    // Skip the included content of this tag.
    return (SKIP_BODY);

}


/**
 * Process the end of this tag.
 */
public int doEndTag() throws JspException {

    // Evaluate the remainder of this page.
    return (EVAL_PAGE);

}


/**
 * Release any acquired resources.
 */
public void release() {
}

}
```

The `getDisplayProperty` method of the value object uses the `convertTo-DisplayFormat` method of the property handler. In this case, the `current-Balance` property is defined as a Currency property. The property-handler class is a standard place to do value formatting. The `CurrencyHandler` class, which formats it using a dollar sign and decimal places, is shown here:

```java
package blf;

import java.math.BigDecimal;
import java.text.NumberFormat;

/**
 * Currency handler is used to display currency properties.
 */
public class CurrencyHandler extends DecimalHandler
    implements PropertyValidator, PropertyHandler {

    public String convertToDisplayFormat(Object value)
        throws PropertyException {

        // Get the currency in the BigDecimal format.
        BigDecimal amount = null;
        if (value instanceof String) {
            amount = (BigDecimal)
                this.convertToObjectFormat(value);
        } else if (value instanceof BigDecimal) {
            amount = (BigDecimal) value;
        } else {
            throw new PropertyException(
                "Invalid object type for currency property.");
        }

        // Use the currency formatter to display
        // for presentation.
        NumberFormat formatter =
            NumberFormat.getCurrencyInstance();
        return formatter.format(amount.doubleValue());
    }

}
```

BEST PRACTICE Integrate the property formatting mechanism originally implemented for business objects into the User Interaction Architecture. This avoids a duplication of effort and simplifies the JSP code.

Variations on the Account Detail Link

The previous example used a fairly straightforward approach to creating the detail link for each account. The JSP explicitly created the `<a>` tag and added an `id` parameter to identify the account. The first alternative is to use the `<html:link>` tag provided by Struts. In this case, the link includes a dynamic query parameter, so you need to tell it to reference a property somewhere in the page scope. The relevant portion of a JSP that uses the <html:link> tag is shown here:

```
<logic:iterate name="<%=PageConstants.DATA%>"
               id="acctValueObject" scope="request"
               type="bank.AccountData" >
<tr><td>
  <html:link href="/bank/struts/accountDetail.do" paramId="id"
             paramName="acctValueObject" paramProperty="id"
             paramScope="page">
    <bean:write name="acctValueObject"
                property="number" />
  </html:link></td>
    <td><bean:write name="acctValueObject"
                    property="currentBalance" /></td>
    <td><bean:write name="acctValueObject"
                    property="lastModifiedDate" /></td></tr>
</logic:iterate>
```

Another option is to use a server-side parameter if you do not want to expose the internal account identifier in the URL. You could create a custom tag that creates a link identifier as a session key to store the actual account ID. The account detail page then uses this link identifier to get the account ID out of the session for processing.

The New Customer Wizard

The new customer wizard is a multipage form that visitors of the bank Web site link to from the logon page. It has three screens that collect customer data to be aggregated together in the session until the final confirmation is made and the NewCustomer service is invoked. At this point, the event data should have the customer, address, and account information. Preliminary validations are performed after each intermediate page, and then the service does complete business validations at the end once again to ensure data integrity. Figure 8.7 shows the new customer pages and the flow between them.

The Page Flow through the Wizard

The implementation flow for these pages is shown in Figure 8.8.

The Struts configuration metadata for these pages is defined as follows. Only global forwards are defined for the first two pages because you can link directly to these pages from the new customer navigation bar. The last two pages of the wizard can be reached only by successfully completing the previous pages that are processed by the NewCustomerAction class.

```
<global-forwards>
    <forward   name="newCustomer1"
               path="/struts/newCustomer1.jsp"/>
```

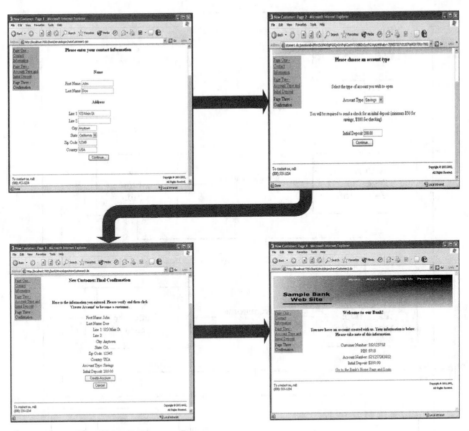

Figure 8.7 The New Customer Pages.

```
        <forward    name="newCustomer2"
                    path="/struts/newCustomer2.jsp"/>
    </global-forwards>

    <form-beans>
        <form-bean name="customerForm"
                   type="bank.struts.CustomerForm"/>
    </form-beans>

    <action-mappings>
        <action    path="/strutslogon/newCustomer1"
                   type="bank.struts.NewCustomerAction"
                   name="customerForm"
                   scope="session"
                   validate="false" >
          <forward name="success"
                   path="/strutslogon/newCustomer2.jsp" />
          <forward name="failure"
                   path="/strutslogon/newCustomer1.jsp" />
        </action>
```

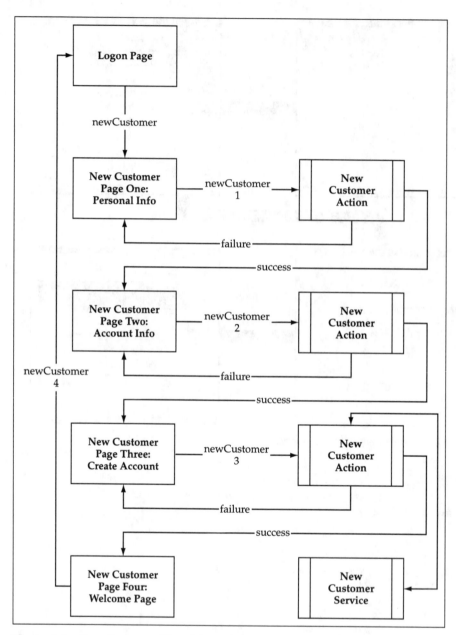

Figure 8.8 New Customer Wizard Page Flow.

```
<action    path="/strutslogon/newCustomer2"
           type="bank.struts.NewCustomerAction"
           name="customerForm"
           scope="session"
           validate="false" >
```

```
        <forward name="success"
                path="/strutslogon/newCustomer3.jsp" />
        <forward name="failure"
                path="/strutslogon/newCustomer2.jsp" />
    </action>

    <action   path="/strutslogon/newCustomer3"
              type="bank.struts.NewCustomerAction"
              name="customerForm"
              scope="session"
              validate="false" >
        <forward name="success"
                path="/strutslogon/newCustomer4.jsp" />
        <forward name="failure"
                path="/strutslogon/newCustomer3.jsp" />
    </action>
</action-mappings>
```

The page flow for this multipage form is as follows:

- Page one collects the customer name and address information. The new-Customer1 event is used to capture this data and store it in the Customer-Form and AddressForm event objects. AddressForm is aggregated inside of the CustomerForm object that is stored in the session and will be accessed as a starting point for the remainder of the pages in the wizard. Basic data validation is done on the submission, and any errors are displayed so the user can correct the data.

- Page two allows users to select the account type they want to open from a drop-down list. They are also required to enter an amount for initial deposit to meet the minimum balance requirements. The newCustomer2 event captures the account type and amount in the AccountForm event object that is also aggregated by CustomerForm. The deposit amount is validated against the minimum balance requirement for the type of account selected, and the page is redrawn with any error messages if necessary.

- Page three is a confirmation page that displays the user-entered data and allows users to click either the Create New Account or Cancel button. This submission generates the newCustomer3 event. A positive confirmation here causes the NewCustomer service to be invoked with ServiceData containing the event data from the customer, address, and account beans.

- Page four is a new customer information page. It displays a message that the transaction was successful and provides the new customer number, account number, and generated PIN number. It provides a link to the logon page so the customer can immediately begin to bank online at the Web site.

- A different navigation bar, which allows the user to go back and forth between pages in the wizard, is used for the new customer pages. These links are pure navigation events that use the global forwards newCustomer1 and newCustomer2, respectively, for the first two pages. Pages three and four can be reached only by successfully completing their predecessors.

The Address and Account as Aggregated Form Beans

The new customer multipage form exercises two aspects of Struts that have not been utilized much thus far, action-level forwards and nested form beans. This section looks at the use of nested form beans within the new customer pages. The `CustomerForm` bean aggregates both the address and account form beans. The code for the `CustomerForm` bean is shown here:

```java
package bank.struts;

import javax.servlet.http.HttpServletRequest;
import org.apache.struts.action.ActionError;
import org.apache.struts.action.ActionErrors;
import org.apache.struts.action.ActionForm;
import org.apache.struts.action.ActionMapping;

public class CustomerForm extends ActionForm {

    // Properties
    private String firstName = null;
    private String lastName = null;

    // Relationships
    private AddressForm address = null;
    private AccountForm account = null;

    /**
     * Default constructor
     */
    public CustomerForm() {
        // Create aggregated objects
        address = new AddressForm();
        account = new AccountForm();
    }

    public String getFirstName() {
     return firstName;
    }


    public void setFirstName(String value) {
        firstName = value;
    }


    public String getLastName() {
     return lastName;
    }
```

```java
public void setLastName(String value) {
    lastName = value;
}

public AddressForm getAddress() {
 return address;
}

public void setAddress(AddressForm value) {
    address = value;
}

public AccountForm getAccount() {
 return account;
}

public void setAccount(AccountForm value) {
    account = value;
}


/**
 * Validate the properties that have been set from
 * the HTTP request.
 *
 * @param mapping The mapping used to select this instance
 * @param request The servlet request you are processing
 */
public ActionErrors validate(ActionMapping mapping,
                             HttpServletRequest request) {

    ActionErrors errors = new ActionErrors();
    if ((lastName == null) || (lastName.length() < 1)) {
        errors.add("lastName",
            new ActionError("REQ_FIELD",
                            "lastName"));
    }
    return errors;

}
}
```

NOTE This implementation of `CustomerForm` validates only the customer fields. The topic of validation, particularly the validation of nested form beans within this example, will be revisited later in this section.

This implementation initializes all of the aggregated objects in the constructor, but you could easily have used lazy instantiation as well in the getter methods. The Struts nested syntax is used in the JSP to access the aggregated form beans.

Page One: The Customer and Account Information

The first page, which has customer and address data, shows the use of nested form beans in the HTML tags:

```
<%@page import="java.util.*,blf.*,bank.struts.*"%>
<%@ taglib uri="/WEB-INF/struts-html.tld" prefix="html" %>
<%@ taglib uri="/WEB-INF/struts-bean.tld" prefix="bean" %>
<%@ taglib uri="/WEB-INF/blf.tld" prefix="blf" %>
<table width=100%>
<tr><td align=center>
    <H3> Please enter your contact information </H3>
</td></tr>
</table>

<table width="100%">
<tr align="center"><td><ul><html:errors/></td></tr>
</table>

<%
    // You need to get the state value so you can pass it
    // to your custom drop-down tag.
    String currentState = "";
    CustomerForm formBean =
        (CustomerForm) session.getAttribute("customerForm");
    if (formBean != null) {
        currentState = formBean.getAddress().getState();
    }
%>

<html:form action="/strutslogon/newCustomer1"
     focus="firstName">
<br/><center><b>Name</b></center><br/>
<table width=100%>
<tr>
<td align=right>First Name</td>
<td><html:text property="firstName" size="20"
             maxlength="30"/></td>
</tr>
<tr>
<td align=right>Last Name</td>
<td><html:text property="lastName" size="20"
             maxlength="30"/></td>
</tr>
</table>
<br/><center><b>Address</b></center><br/>
<table width="100%">
<tr>
<td align=right>Line 1</td>
```

```
<td><html:text property="address.line1" size="20"
                maxlength="30"/></td>
</tr>
<tr>
<td align=right>Line 2</td>
<td><html:text property="address.line2" size="20"
                maxlength="30"/></td>
</tr>
<tr>
<td align=right>City</td>
<td><html:text property="address.city" size="10"
                maxlength="20"/></td>
</tr>
<tr>
<td align=right>State</td>
<td><blf:dropDown htmlName="address.state" cache="States"
                selectedOption='<%=currentState%>' /></td>
</tr>
<tr>
<td align=right>Zip Code</td>
<td><html:text property="address.zip" size="10"
                maxlength="20"/></td>
</tr>
<tr>
<td align=right>Country</td>
<td><html:text property="address.country" size="10"
                maxlength="20"/></td>
</tr>
</table>
<table width=100%>
<tr>
<td align=center><html:submit property="submit"
                            value="Continue..."/></td>
</tr>
</table>

</html:form>
```

The New Customer Action

Because the wizard's events and actions are related, the controller delegates the handling of all these requests to the same action class. The action mappings shown earlier configured all of the new customer pages to be processed by the NewCustomer-Action. This is done to simplify things for someone reading the code and trying to understand it. This action class is responsible for handling the form submissions of all four pages. This example shows how the different URLs used by each of the forms signify the different events that are occurring. If you look at the action code, there is a helper method that is used to derive the event name from the servlet path. This code mirrors that of the code used by ActionServlet; however, it is modified to take only the text after the last slash (/) character. Thus, the request path /struts/newCustomer1 maps to the event newCustomer1. The action code for NewCustomerAction is shown here:

```
package bank.struts;

import java.io.IOException;
import java.util.*;
import javax.servlet.*;
import javax.servlet.http.*;
import org.apache.struts.action.*;
import org.apache.struts.util.MessageResources;
import blf.*;
import bank.AccountValidator;
import java.math.BigDecimal;
import bank.CustomerData;
import bank.AddressData;
import bank.AccountData;


/**
 * Action class that implements the new customer wizard
 */
public class NewCustomerAction extends Action {


    /**
     * The Struts action interface
     */
    public ActionForward perform(ActionMapping mapping,
                                 ActionForm form,
                                 HttpServletRequest request,
                                 HttpServletResponse response)
        throws IOException, ServletException {

        // Get hold of the session.
        HttpSession session = request.getSession(true);

        // Create error bucket.
        ActionErrors errors = new ActionErrors();

        // Get the event.
        String event = determineEvent(request);

        if (event.equals("newCustomer1")) {
            //
            // Page One - Customer and Address Info
            //

            // Get the form beans out of the defined scope.
```

```
CustomerForm custForm = (CustomerForm)
    session.getAttribute("customerForm");
AddressForm addrForm = custForm.getAddress();

// Validate the input data.
errors = custForm.validate(mapping,request);
ActionErrors addrErrors =
    addrForm.validate(mapping,request);
// If there were address errors, add
// them to the overall list.
if (!addrErrors.empty()) {
    Iterator iter = addrErrors.get();
    while (iter.hasNext()) {
        ActionError error =
            (ActionError) iter.next();
        errors.add(ActionErrors.GLOBAL_ERROR,
                                error);
    }
}

// If there were any errors, set error data in
// request scope and go back to first page.
if (errors.empty()) {
    // Go to the next page.
    return (mapping.findForward("success"));

} else {
    saveErrors(request, errors);
    // Return to the input page to redisplay
    // the form.
    return (mapping.findForward("failure"));
}
} else if (event.equals("newCustomer2")) {
    //
    // Page Two - Account Type and Initial Deposit
    //

    // Get the form bean out of the defined scope.
    CustomerForm custForm = (CustomerForm)
        session.getAttribute("customerForm");

    // Validate input data.
    AccountForm acctForm = custForm.getAccount();
    errors = acctForm.validate(mapping,request);
    if (!errors.empty()) {
        saveErrors(request, errors);
        return (mapping.findForward("failure"));
    }
    // Use the account validator class to verify the
    // minimum balance.
```

```java
                    try {
                        BigDecimal balance =
                            new BigDecimal(acctForm.getAmount());
                        AccountValidator.validateMinimumBalance(
                                        acctForm.getType(), balance);
                    } catch (BlfException be) {
                        // Map BLF errors to action errors.
                        BlfStrutsConverter.convertErrorList(
                                        be.getErrorList(),errors);
                        saveErrors(request, errors);
                        return (mapping.findForward("failure"));
                    }
                    // Go to the next page.
                    return (mapping.findForward("success"));


            } else if (event.equals("newCustomer3")) {
                //
                // Page Three - Confirmation
                //
                if (isCancelled(request)) {
                    // In case the user clicked the cancel
                    // button, go back to the logon page.
                    session.removeAttribute("customerForm");
                    return (mapping.findForward("logon"));
                }

                try {
                    // Get the form bean out of the defined scope.
                    CustomerForm custForm = (CustomerForm)
                        session.getAttribute("customerForm");

                    // Create the service data.
                    ServiceData sdata =
                        new ServiceData("NewCustomer");

                    // Populate the service data by
                    // converting form beans to value objects.
                    CustomerData custData = new CustomerData();
                    AccountData acctData = new AccountData();
                    ArgumentList argList = new ArgumentList();
                    argList.setProperty("amount",
                            custForm.getAccount().getAmount());
                    BlfStrutsConverter.convertFormBeanToValueObj(
                            custForm,custData);
                    BlfStrutsConverter.convertFormBeanToValueObj(
                            custForm.getAddress(),
                            custData.getAddress());
                    BlfStrutsConverter.convertFormBeanToValueObj(
                            custForm.getAccount(),acctData);
```

```
                custData.getAccounts().add(acctData);
                sdata.addInputData(custData);
                sdata.setArgumentList(argList);

                // Invoke the application service.
                BlfService service =
                    ServiceObjectFactory.getBlfService();
                sdata = service.executeService(sdata);
                service.remove();

                // Store the data so the final page can see it.
                request.setAttribute(PageConstants.DATA,
                                     sdata);
                return (mapping.findForward("success"));

            } catch (BlfException be) {

                // Map BLF errors to action errors.
                BlfStrutsConverter.convertErrorList(
                                 be.getErrorList(),errors);
                // Set the errors so the next page can see them.
                saveErrors(request, errors);
                return (mapping.findForward("failure"));

            } catch (Exception e) {

                // Create a general action error
                // for the exception.
                errors.add(ActionErrors.GLOBAL_ERROR,
                    new ActionError("GENERAL_SERVICE_ERROR",
                                    e.getMessage())));
                // Set the errors so the next page can see them.
                saveErrors(request, errors);
                return (mapping.findForward("failure"));
            }
        }

        // You should never get here.
        return null;
    }


/**
 * Helper method to determine the event name
 * from the servlet request path
 */
private String determineEvent(HttpServletRequest request) {

    // Remove the extension and get the
    // path after the last slash.
    // This is the name of your event.
```

```
        // For example, /struts/newCustomer1.do
        // becomes newCustomer1.
        String path = request.getServletPath();
        int slash = path.lastIndexOf("/");
        int period = path.lastIndexOf(".");
        if ((period >= 0) && (period > slash)) {
            path = path.substring(slash + 1, period);
        }
        return (path);
    }
}
```

The first thing the action does is use the helper method to determine what event occurred, that is, which page had a form submitted. When processing the first page's form, there isn't much to do. The `ActionServlet` automatically populates the form beans. The automatic validation by the servlet is turned off in the configuration. The `validate` methods on the form beans are called explicitly because the `CustomerForm` bean could have been triggered by a number of different action mappings. Thus, there may be incomplete data in the aggregated form beans, or you may want only errors from the data just entered. If there are any errors from the form, they are saved in the request using `saveErrors`, and control is forwarded to the failure page. Otherwise, the action forwards to the success page that is the second page in the wizard. Remember that in the metadata, success and failure are defined as action-level forwards for each step in the process.

An interesting thing to note about this action class is that it actually overrides the navigation metadata when processing page three. At the point the user submits that form, there are three possible outcomes:

- User clicks Create New Account and no errors are detected (success).
- User clicks Create New Account and errors are detected (failure).
- User clicks Cancel.

The third possible outcome, cancel, really does not map to anything in the navigation scenarios. Thus, the action class overrides the metadata in this situation and returns the logon page, which takes users back to the point where they originally started. Note that this could also have been designed other ways. The situations of a form with multiple submit buttons tends to recur periodically in business applications. An alternative way to design this type of situation would have been to equate different submit buttons on the page to different events. You would need to change the event helper method to additionally check for an HTTP parameter representing the submit button. In the JSP, the name of the submit buttons could be "event," and the different values could represent the different event names. The HTML for this would be similar to the following:

```
<table width=100%>
<tr>
<td align=center><input type="submit" name="event"
                    value="Create" /></td>
```

```
</tr>
<tr>
<td align=center><input type="submit" name="event"
                        value="Cancel"/></td>
</tr>
</table>
```

The validation logic for page two is application specific and goes beyond straight data type or required field edits. This validation logic checks to see that the initial deposit meets the required minimum balance for the account type chosen. This is done as a preliminary edit at this point, but it is also logic that is shared by the business object. For these types of situations, it is sometimes helpful to move the validation logic out to a separate validation class that can be used both by the action class and the business object. In this case, an `AccountValidator` class was created with a static method that checks the minimum balance and throws a `ValidationException` with business errors if any were detected.

The third page, which confirms all of the information and invokes the service, shows how you can use the `BlfStrutsConverter` utility to create value objects from each of the aggregated form beans to create an overall instance of `ServiceData`. The output data of the service is saved in the request scope so that the welcome page can display the new account numbers and PIN.

Page Two: The Account Information

The second page is only slightly different than the previous example. The implementation of `newCustomer2Body.jsp` is shown here:

```
<%@page import="java.util.*,blf.*,bank.struts.*"%>
<%@ taglib uri="/WEB-INF/struts-html.tld" prefix="html" %>
<%@ taglib uri="/WEB-INF/struts-bean.tld" prefix="bean" %>
<%@ taglib uri="/WEB-INF/blf.tld" prefix="blf" %>

<table width=100%>
<tr>
<td align=center><H3> Please choose an account type </H3></td>
</tr>
</table>


<table width="100%">
<tr align="center"><td><ul><html:errors/></td></tr>
</table>


<%
    // You need to get the type value so you can pass it
    // to your custom drop-down tag.
    String currentType = "";
    CustomerForm formBean =
        (CustomerForm) session.getAttribute("customerForm");
```

```
        if (formBean != null) {
            currentType = formBean.getAccount().getType();
        }
%>

<html:form action="/strutslogon/newCustomer2"
            focus="account.type">
<br/><center>Select the type of account you wish to
            open</center><br/>

<table width=100%>
<tr>
<td align=right>Account Type</td>
<td><blf:dropDown htmlName="account.type" cache="AccountTypes"
            selectedOption='<%=currentType%>' /></td>
</tr>
</table>
<br/><center>You will be required to send a check for an
    initial deposit (minimum $50 for savings, $100 for
    checking)</center><br/>
<table width="100%">
<tr>
<td align=right>Initial Deposit</td>
<td><html:text property="account.amount" size="10"
            maxlength="20"/></td>
</tr>
</table>
<table width=100%>
<tr>
<td align=center><html:submit property="submit"
                            value="Continue..."/></td>
</tr>
</table>

</html:form>
```

Page Three: The Confirmation Page

The next JSP, newCustomer3Body.jsp, uses the <bean:write> tag simply to display the values stored within the form beans. Two interesting things to note about this page are:

■ The use of the Struts <html:cancel> tag. It creates a cancel button that is checked by the isCancelled(request) method of the action class.

■ A new <blf:lookupValue> custom tag that takes a code value, in this case the account type, and returns the full description from the specified cache. Thus, the codes S and C would appear as Savings and Checking, respectively, on the page.

The third page, `newCustomer3Body.jsp`, is implemented as follows:

```
<%@page import="java.util.*,blf.*,bank.struts.*"%>
<%@ taglib uri="/WEB-INF/struts-html.tld" prefix="html" %>
<%@ taglib uri="/WEB-INF/struts-bean.tld" prefix="bean" %>
<%@ taglib uri="/WEB-INF/blf.tld" prefix="blf" %>


<table width=100%>
<tr>
<td align=center><H3> New Customer: Final Confirmation
                                             </H3></td>
</tr>
</table>



<table width="100%">
<tr align="center"><td><ul><html:errors/></td></tr>
</table>
<%
    // You need to get the type value so you can pass it
    // to your custom drop-down tag.
    String currentType = "";
    CustomerForm formBean =
        (CustomerForm) session.getAttribute("customerForm");
    if (formBean != null) {
        currentType = formBean.getAccount().getType();
    }
%>


<html:form action="/strutslogon/newCustomer3">
<br/><center><b>Here is the information you entered.  Please
    verify and then click 'Create Account' to become a
    customer.</b></center><br/>
<table width="100%">
<tr><td align=right>First Name:</td>
  <td><bean:write name="customerForm"
                  property="firstName" /></td></tr>
<tr><td align=right>Last Name:</td>
  <td><bean:write name="customerForm"
                  property="lastName" /></td></tr>
<tr><td align=right>Line 1:</td>
  <td><bean:write name="customerForm"
                  property="address.line1" /></td></tr>
<tr><td align=right>Line 2:</td>
  <td><bean:write name="customerForm"
                  property="address.line2" /></td></tr>
<tr><td align=right>City:</td>
  <td><bean:write name="customerForm"
                  property="address.city" /></td></tr>
```

```
<tr><td align=right>State:</td>
  <td><bean:write name="customerForm"
                  property="address.state" /></td></tr>
<tr><td align=right>Zip Code:</td>
  <td><bean:write name="customerForm"
                  property="address.zip" /></td></tr>
<tr><td align=right>Country:</td>
  <td><bean:write name="customerForm"
                  property="address.country" /></td></tr>
<tr><td align=right>Account Type:</td>
  <td><blf:lookupValue cache="AccountTypes"
                       value='<%=currentType%>' /></td></tr>
<tr><td align=right>Initial Deposit:</td>
  <td><bean:write name="customerForm"
                  property="account.amount" /></td></tr>
</table>
<table width=100%>
<tr>
<td align=center><html:submit property="submit"
                              value="Create Account"/></td>
</tr>
<tr>
<td align=center><html:cancel /></td>
</tr>
</table>

</html:form>
```

The Lookup Value Custom Tag

The code for the custom lookup tag is fairly straightforward. It obtains the cache by name and gets the lookup value. The code for `LookupValueTag` is shown here:

```
public class LookupValueTag extends TagSupport {

    // The name of the cache to get the lookup data
    private String value = null;

    public String getValue() {
        return value;
    }
    public void setValue(String value) {
        this.value = value;
    }

    // The name of the cache to get the lookup data
    private String cache = null;

    public String getCache() {
        return cache;
```

```
    }
    public void setCache(String value) {
        cache = value;
    }

    /**
     * Process the start of this tag.
     */
    public int doStartTag() throws JspException {

        String outputValue = null;

        ObjectCache objCache = null;
        try {
            objCache = CacheList.getInstance().getCache(cache);
            if (!(objCache instanceof LookupCache)) {
                throw new JspException("Cache " + cache
                            + " is not a lookup cache.");
            }
            outputValue = (String) objCache.get(value);
        } catch (BlfException be) {
            throw new JspException(be.getMessage());
        }

        // Write out the error HTML.
        JspWriter writer = pageContext.getOut();
        try {
            writer.print(outputValue);
        } catch (IOException e) {
            throw new JspException(e.getMessage());
        }

        // Evaluate the included content of this tag.
        return (EVAL_BODY_INCLUDE);
    }

    /**
     * Process the end of this tag.
     */
    public int doEndTag() throws JspException {

        // Evaluate the remainder of this page.
        return (EVAL_PAGE);
    }

    /**
     * Release any acquired resources.
     */
    public void release() {
    }
}
```

Page Four: The New Customer Information Page

The fourth page, `newCustomer4Body.jsp`, retrieves the updated output data of the service so that it can display the newly generated account numbers and PIN. The entire `ServiceData` object is placed in the request so the page can access it:

```
<%@page import="java.util.*,blf.*,bank.*"%>
<%@ taglib uri="/WEB-INF/struts-html.tld" prefix="html" %>
<%@ taglib uri="/WEB-INF/struts-bean.tld" prefix="bean" %>
<%@ taglib uri="/WEB-INF/blf.tld" prefix="blf" %>


<table width=100%>
<tr>
<td align=center><H3> Welcome to our Bank! </H3></td>
</tr>
</table>


<table width="100%">
<tr align="center"><td><ul><html:errors/></td></tr>
</table>
<%
    // Get hold of the output data
    // from the session.
    ServiceData sdata = (ServiceData)
        request.getAttribute(PageConstants.DATA);
    CustomerData custData =
        (CustomerData) sdata.getOutputData(0);
    // There will only be one account returned.
    AccountData acctData = (AccountData)
        custData.getAccounts().iterator().next();
    // Set the value objects in the page context
    // so the <blf:getProperty> tag can see them.
    pageContext.setAttribute("custData",custData);
    pageContext.setAttribute("acctData",acctData);
%>


<br/><center><b>You now have an account created with us.
    Your information is below.
    Please take note of this information.</b></center><br/>
<table width="100%">
<tr><td align=right>Customer Number:</td>
    <td><blf:getProperty bean="custData"
                        property="customerNumber" /></td></tr>
<tr><td align=right>PIN:</td>
    <td><blf:getProperty bean="custData"
                        property="pin" /></td></tr>
<tr><td align=right>Account Number:</td>
```

```
    <td><blf:getProperty bean="acctData"
                      property="number" /></td></tr>
<tr><td align=right>Initial Deposit:</td>
    <td><blf:getProperty bean="acctData"
                      property="currentBalance" /></td></tr>
</table>

<table width=100%>
<tr><td align=center><html:link href="/bank/struts/logon.do">
    Go to the Bank's Home Page and Login</html:link></td></tr>
</table>
```

Using JSP Templates

One thing that you haven't seen yet are the JavaService Pages that invoke the templates. They have one major difference from the earlier examples in that they pull in a different navigation bar for the wizard. For example, look at newCustomer1.jsp:

```
<%@ taglib uri='/WEB-INF/struts-template.tld'
            prefix='template' %>

<template:insert template="/struts/template.jsp'>
  <template:put name='title'
                content='New Customer: Page 1' direct='true'/>
  <template:put name='header' content='/struts/header.jsp' />
  <template:put name='navbar'
                content='/struts/navBarNewCustomer.jsp' />
  <template:put name='body'
                content='/struts/newCustomer1Body.jsp'/>
  <template:put name='footer' content='/struts/footer.jsp' />
</template:insert>
```

The navigation bar for this wizard uses the <html:link> tag and references the two global forwards defined for the first two pages. In these cases, the request is forwarded directly to the JSP without going through the controller servlet:

```
<%@ taglib uri="/WEB-INF/struts-html.tld" prefix="html" %>

<table align="left" bgcolor="#c0c0c0" width="80%">
<tr><td>
<html:link forward="newCustomer1">
    Page One - Contact Information</html:link>
</td></tr>
<tr><td>
<html:link forward="newCustomer2">
    Page Two - Account Type and Initial Deposit</html:link>
</td></tr>
<tr><td>Page Three - Confirmation</td></tr>
</table>
```

Refactoring to Use Form Beans as Value Objects

The new customer example can also easily be implemented using the form beans as value objects, similar to the alternative discussed for the change address page. Just like `AddressFormBean`, the `CustomerForm` and `AccountForm` classes can be converted to implement the `ValueObject` interface by extending `BaseFormBean`. Neither the customer nor the account contains any application-specific edits. The normal validation template uses the application metadata to drive the data validations, such as checking that a valid numeric was given for the initial deposit amount.

Validation of Aggregated Event Objects

In the business object chapter, a mechanism was created to automatically validate any aggregated objects. If the helper methods such as `getOneToOneRelationship` are added to `ValueObject` to access aggregated objects, the same code from the base business object class can be used within the value object or form bean structure. If this approach is taken, then the `NewCustomerAction` needs only to call `validate` on the customer form bean, and it will also validate the address and account data. Optionally, the metadata configuration could be set back to `validate='true'`, which is the default. You would need to implement lazy instantiation on the form beans and validate aggregated objects only if they are already instantiated in order for this to work. This step is necessary due to the first execution of the first page. In this particular case, only the customer and address data are on the form, thus you should not issue required field errors for account data that isn't even on the page.

A Template for the Action Class

Many of the action implementations share a similar pattern, especially for simple update and data retrieval scenarios. A foundation component can be created that implements this basic logic as a template pattern. This base class would have hooks before the service is invoked as well as afterwards for both success and failure conditions. If you look at the basic responsibilities of the action class, the most complicated responsibility to implement in a general fashion is probably "manage user context." Without creating a wildly intricate mechanism for dealing with this, action metadata could be defined that determines the servlet/JSP scope in which either the input or output data should be stored. Typically this is either the request or session scope. As you have seen, some services such as `ViewAccountsAction` store the whole collection of value objects, whereas others such as `ChangeAddressAction` need only a single object. Thus, the metadata can also define whether the collection of output data should be used or just an individual value object. This concept can be called the "data container" for lack of a better term. The metadata also needs to define the service to be invoked.

The base class can be called `BasicAction`. The action metadata for a version of the change address that extends `BasicAction` would be defined as follows:

```
<Action name="changeAddress"
        class="bank.BasicChangeAddressAction"
        service="ChangeAddress" />
```

For an implementation of the view accounts action using this template, the metadata would be specified as follows:

```
<Action name="viewAccounts"
        service="GetAccountList"
        dataScope="R"
        dataContainer="C" />
```

The name of the action corresponds to the event that triggers the action. The data scope values are R for Request, S for Session, and A for application. The data container values are C for collection and I for Individual. The code for `BasicAction` is shown here:

```java
package blf.struts;

import javax.servlet.*;
import javax.servlet.http.*;
import java.util.*;
import java.rmi.RemoteException;
import javax.ejb.RemoveException;
import java.io.IOException;
import org.apache.struts.action.*;
import bank.struts.BlfStrutsConverter;
import blf.*;

public class BasicAction extends Action {

    public static final String REQUEST_SCOPE = "R";
    public static final String SESSION_SCOPE = "S";
    public static final String APPLICATION_SCOPE = "A";

    public static final String COLLECTION_DATA = "C";
    public static final String INDIVIDUAL_DATA = "I";

    /**
     * The Struts action interface
     */
    public ActionForward perform(ActionMapping mapping,
                            ActionForm form,
                            HttpServletRequest request,
                            HttpServletResponse response)
        throws IOException, ServletException {
```

```
// Get hold of the session.
HttpSession session = request.getSession(true);
// The error bucket
ActionErrors errors = new ActionErrors();
// The service data
ServiceData sdata = null;
// The next page
ActionForward nextPage = null;
// The action metadata
ActionMetadata am = null;

try {
    String event = determineEvent(request);
    am = MetadataManager.getAction(event);
    if (am == null) {
        throw new BlfException(
            "No action defined in metadata for event: "
            + event);
    }

    // Process the form input and
    // create the service data structure.
    ValueObject formBean = (ValueObject) form;
    sdata = new ServiceData(am.getService());
    sdata.addInputData(formBean);

    // Template Method
    preService(sdata,errors,form,
                mapping,request,response);

    // Invoke the application service.
    sdata = executeService(sdata);

    // Template Method
    // This method returns the next page.
    nextPage = postService(sdata,errors,
                            mapping,request,response);

    // Set the errors so the next page can see them.
    saveErrors(request, errors);

    // Manage state based on action metadata.
    manageState(am, sdata, request);

    // Use the next page returned from the subclass.
    // Otherwise, return to the input form.
    if (nextPage != null) return nextPage;
    return (new ActionForward(mapping.getInput()));

} catch (BlfException be) {
```

```
            // Template Method for service failure
            nextPage = serviceFailed(be,sdata,
                                request,response);


            // Map BLF errors to action errors.
            BlfStrutsConverter.convertErrorList(
                                be.getErrorList(),errors);
            // Set the errors so the next page can see them.
            saveErrors(request, errors);


            // Manage application state based on metadata.
            manageState(am, sdata, request);


            // Use the next page returned from the subclass.
            // Otherwise, return to the input form.
            if (nextPage != null) return nextPage;
            return (new ActionForward(mapping.getInput()));


        } catch (Exception e) {


            // Template Method for service failure
            nextPage = serviceFailed(e,sdata,request,response);


                // Create a general action error for the exception.
            errors.add(ActionErrors.GLOBAL_ERROR,
                new ActionError("GENERAL_SERVICE_ERROR",
                            e.getMessage())));
            // Set the errors so the next page can see them.
            saveErrors(request, errors);


            // Manage state based on action metadata.
            manageState(am, sdata, request);


            // Use the next page returned from the subclass.
            // Otherwise, return to the input form.
            if (nextPage != null) return nextPage;
            return (new ActionForward(mapping.getInput()));
        }
    }


    /**
     * Template Method executed before service is invoked
     */
    public void preService(ServiceData sdata,
        ActionErrors errors, ActionForm form,
        ActionMapping mapping, HttpServletRequest request,
        HttpServletResponse response)
        throws BlfException {
    }
```

```java
/**
 * Template Method executed after service is invoked;
 * return null to use standard
 * navigation metadata.
 */
public ActionForward postService(ServiceData sdata,
    ActionErrors errors, ActionMapping mapping,
    HttpServletRequest request,
    HttpServletResponse response)
    throws BlfException {

    return null;
}


/**
 * Template Method executed if exception is caught
 * out of action; return null to use standard
 * navigation metadata.
 */
public ActionForward serviceFailed(Exception executeAction,
    ServiceData sdata, HttpServletRequest request,
    HttpServletResponse response) {

    return null;
}


/**
 * Helper method to invoke application service
 */
protected ServiceData executeService(ServiceData sdata)
    throws BlfException, RemoteException, RemoveException {
    BlfService service =
        ServiceObjectFactory.getBlfService();
    sdata = service.executeService(sdata);
    service.remove();
    return sdata;
}


/**
 * Helper method to store service data in scope
 * based on metadata
 */
protected void manageState(ActionMetadata am,
    ServiceData sdata, HttpServletRequest request) {

    try {
        String dataScope      = am.getDataScope();
        String dataContainer  = am.getDataContainer();
        if (dataScope != null) {
            if (dataScope.equals(REQUEST_SCOPE)) {
                if (dataContainer.equals(COLLECTION_DATA)) {
```

```
                        request.setAttribute(
                            PageConstants.DATA,
                            sdata.getOutputData());
                    } else {
                        request.setAttribute(
                            PageConstants.DATA,
                            sdata.getOutputData(0));

                    }
                } else if (dataScope.equals(SESSION_SCOPE)) {
                    if (dataContainer.equals(COLLECTION_DATA)) {
                        request.getSession(true).setAttribute(
                            PageConstants.DATA,
                            sdata.getOutputData());
                    } else {
                        request.getSession(true).setAttribute(
                            PageConstants.DATA,
                            sdata.getOutputData(0));

                    }
                }
            }
        } catch (BlfException ignore) {}
}


/**
 * Helper method to determine the event name
 * from the servlet request path
 */
private String determineEvent(HttpServletRequest request) {

    // Remove the extension and get the
    // path after the last slash.
    // This is the name of your event.
    // For example, /struts/newCustomer1.do
    // becomes newCustomer1.
    String path = request.getServletPath();
    int slash = path.lastIndexOf("/");
    int period = path.lastIndexOf(".");
    if ((period >= 0) && (period > slash)) {
        path = path.substring(slash + 1, period);
    }
    return (path);
}

}
```

Template Implementation of Change Address Action

The BasicChangeAddressAction subclass has two responsibilities. The first is to add the address identifier from the session to the service data. The second is to add a confirmation message on a successful update. Because the change address page is shown on success or failure, no navigation logic needs to be implemented because BasicAction defaults the next page to the input form. The code for Basic-ChangeAddressAction is shown here:

```
public class BasicChangeAddressAction extends BasicAction {

    /**
     * Template Method executed before service is invoked
     */
    public void preService(ServiceData sdata,
        ActionErrors errors, ActionForm form,
        ActionMapping mapping, HttpServletRequest request,
        HttpServletResponse response)
        throws BlfException {

        // Set the identifier that is stored in the session.
        ValueObject formBean = (ValueObject) form;
        formBean.setProperty("id",
            request.getSession(true).getAttribute("addressId"));
    }

    /**
     * Template Method executed after service is invoked;
     * return null to use standard
     * navigation metadata.
     */
    public ActionForward postService(ServiceData sdata,
        ActionErrors errors, ActionMapping mapping,
        HttpServletRequest request,
        HttpServletResponse response)
        throws BlfException {

        // Add a confirmation message to inform the user
        // that the update was successful.
        errors.add(ActionErrors.GLOBAL_ERROR,
                new ActionError("ADDR_CONFIRMATION"));

        // Use the default next page, which is the input form.
        return null;
    }
}
```

Template Implementation of View Accounts Action

The subclass implementation of BasicViewAccountsAction is fairly straightforward. It uses the action metadata to store the results of the service in the request scope so that it is available to the change address JSP. Its only responsibilities are to set the input argument for the data retrieval service and return the next page. The code for

`BasicViewAccountsAction` is shown here:

```
public class BasicViewAccountsAction extends BasicAction {

    /**
     * Template Method executed before service is invoked
     */
    public void preService(ServiceData sdata,
        ActionErrors errors, ActionForm form,
        ActionMapping mapping, HttpServletRequest request,
        HttpServletResponse response)
        throws BlfException {

        // Prepare the input data for the service.
        ArgumentList argList = new ArgumentList();
        argList.setProperty("customerId", (String)
            request.getSession(true).getValue("customerId"));
        sdata.setArgumentList(argList);
    }

    /**
     * Template Method executed after service is invoked;
     * return null to use standard
     * navigation metadata.
     */
    public ActionForward postService(ServiceData sdata,
        ActionErrors errors, ActionMapping mapping,
        HttpServletRequest request,
        HttpServletResponse response)
        throws BlfException {

        // Set next page to view accounts page.
        return (mapping.findForward("viewAccounts"));
    }
}
```

If you have a lot of basic update and retrieval screens, this design pattern can be used quite effectively. However, many business applications are more dynamic than this and require additional presentation logic. The `BasicAction` concept can add some value to repetitive applications, but clearly many action implementations will be required to add logic to the hook methods. If nothing else, this pattern does add consistency to the action implementations. Use it as you see fit, or consider creating other base actions that implement repeatable patterns in your application to provide greater quality and consistency in your code.

Web Services

The user interaction element of Web services is usually fairly simple. Most Web service frameworks, particularly those that implement the SOAP protocol, provide an easy way to map HTTP requests directly to method invocations on objects. These packages

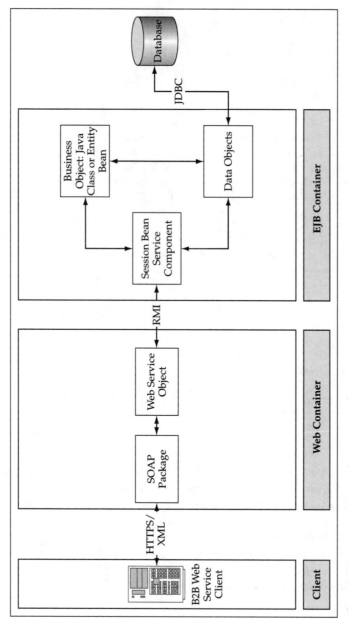

Figure 8.9 Basic SOAP Web Service Architecture.

wrap the HTTP protocol and allow developers to concentrate on the actual data handling and application service invocations. The actual additional work of the Web service is done in a proxy object that resides on the Web tier. Figure 8.9 shows how this object exposes your application services as Web services.

Best Practices for Implementing the User Interaction Architecture

A summary of the best practices for implementing the User Interaction Architecture is given in this section.

Consider Minimizing Page Logic through Action Classes

One technique that you can use to minimize the amount of Java code in a JSP is to move page setup logic out to an action class. This isolates the service invocation from the page and also simplifies the page implementation in many cases by allowing the JSP to assume that a form bean is passed in as context. If you are going to include Java code in a JSP, try to group logic into a few large scriplets rather than having it interspersed throughout the HTML content. This makes the JSP code much easier to read and maintain.

Use the Struts Template Tag Library

Use the Struts template tag library or an analogous mechanism to simplify the development and maintenance of the common aspects of application web pages. A standard naming scheme can be used to distinguish between JSP components that implement template instances and page content. In the examples shown in this chapter, the naming scheme used was `<logicalPageName>.jsp` for the template instance and `<logicalPageName>Body.jsp` for the page content. Standard headers and footers were used for most of the pages, although a different navigation bar was used for the new customer wizard. You can also consider abstracting the JSP template itself and using metadata to define the page fragments used for a given Web page.

Automate Data Validation in Form Beans

The same Template Method pattern used by the business objects can also be used within form beans to implement a validate template. This should reuse the same property-handling and validation mechanism used by business objects to prevent duplication of code and effort. There should not be anything specific to the Web tier or EJB tier about the property-handling mechanism that would cause a problem with this approach. A base class for form beans that is similar in form and function to the business object base classes can be implemented for this purpose.

Encapsulate and Reuse Presentation Logic through JSP Custom Tags

JSP custom tags can be used to encapsulate presentation logic and provide tight integration with the reference architecture. This technique simplifies JSP code through standards-based, reusable page components. The JSP tags provided by J2EE are a very powerful mechanism that developers should take advantage of. This does not mean that you should necessarily implement all the features of a programming language with custom tags, but you should look for opportunities to encapsulate presentation logic with custom tags, particularly if they are reusable across pages in your application.

Integrate a Property Formatting Mechanism into JSP Components

Integrate reusable property definitions and formatting routines into the user interaction architecture. This mechanism should be tied in to custom tags used by the pages. This approach avoids duplication of effort and simplifies the JSP code. Another option is to encapsulate property-formatting logic in the data retrieval services. This approach allows the JSP to put the property values directly into the HTML content.

Summary

Struts provide a robust implementation of the Model 2 architecture for JavaServer Pages, servlets, and JavaBeans components. If you integrate a strong Business Logic Foundation with Struts, you have an excellent architecture for developing quality Web-based applications. The overall unified architecture diagram is shown in Figure 8.10.

The basic flow of the user interaction architecture is to determine the user event and invoke the appropriate action class. Most action class implementations follow a similar pattern that includes invoking an application service and managing page context for the next JSP. Struts implementations are configured to map HTTP request data automatically into form beans that are then passed to the action class through the standard interface. The data from the form beans can be moved into value objects as service input data, or the form beans themselves can be modified to implement the value object interface. A small conversion utility can be used to convert between Web-centric objects in Struts and reference architecture artifacts if necessary. For example, a conversion utility is used in the examples to convert business errors from the application service to action errors that are displayed on the page. The JSP template tags in Struts provide a nice mechanism that can be used to structure your pages and standardize the application's look and feel. Java code should be minimized in your JSP components through the use of action classes, custom tags, and JavaBeans where appropriate.

This chapter covered the implementation of basic update and data retrieval pages using Jakarta Struts. Some of the main pages in the bank application were implemented as examples. The next chapter will expand on these concepts and apply security to the banking Web applications. Some of the more advanced design concepts that come up frequently in Web applications will also be discussed.

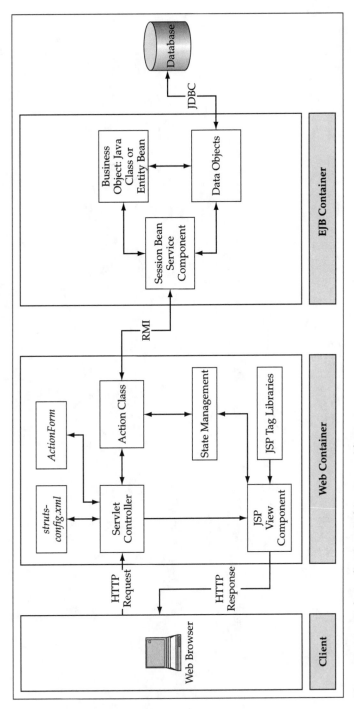

Figure 8.10 Web Application Architecture with Struts.

Strengthening the Bank Application: Adding Security and Advanced Functionality

You have already seen many of the core functions of the sample bank application. This chapter looks at some of the more interesting design and implementation aspects of this application. First, the topic of J2EE security is discussed and then applied to the bank application. Following this, some of the remaining pages and back-end functionality are discussed to illustrate some of the more complex design aspects of Web applications.

Up to this point, you have seen two different sets of pages within the application. The first set includes all of the customers' pages when they log onto the bank's Web site. This includes pages such as view accounts and change address. The second set of pages is part of the new customer wizard that takes a new user through the process of becoming a customer. There is also a third set of pages within the sample application for an administrative user. There are a few functions implemented here that help a system administrator manage the Web site and the bank's operations. The overall page hierarchy is shown in Figure 9.1.

Application Security

There are a number of declarative and programmatic tools for security built into the J2EE application environment throughout all of the tiers. This section first takes a look at the application's Web pages. This is a critical aspect of application security because

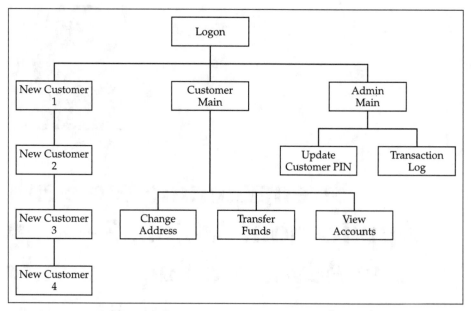

Figure 9.1 Overall Page Hierarchy.

the Web pages are the interface into all of the system functionality. In fact, some implementations can base their entire security model solely on this aspect of security. There are three categories of access on the bank Web site:

- **Bank logon page and new customer wizard pages:** Anyone is allowed to view these pages to either log on or open an account with the bank.

- **Bank's customer pages:** Only bank customers can access their account pages.

- **Bank's administrative pages:** Only administrators of the bank's Web application can access these pages, which have functions to update transaction logs and reset PINs for customers.

The basic security model is primarily based on the following concepts:

Authentication.   Verifying that users are who they claim to be. This is usually done with a username and password logon, although certificates or other mechanisms can also be used. In J2EE, a user is roughly analogous to a principal. Once authenticated, the principal's profile consists of a set of roles that the user participates in.

Authorization.   Verifying that the user is allowed to perform a given function. The authorization to invoke a particular function is usually based on the user's participation in a given role.

Confidentiality.   Data is available only to authorized users and is protected during transit over any networks.

Thus, there is a need for at least three roles within the bank's security model. The first of these is actually the absence of a role, an unauthenticated user. A new user is not required to authenticate himself or herself with a username and password in order to visit the new customer pages because new users do not have credentials with the bank yet. Once they complete the new customer application, they will be given a customer number and PIN, and at that point they can go to the logon page and authenticate themselves. This second role is the `Customer` role, which allows users to access all pages dealing with their bank accounts. When new customers create an account with the bank, they automatically become a `Customer`. The third category is for Web site administrators that have either the role of `AdminUser` or `SuperUser`. The administrator gets a completely different set of Web pages than the regular customers do. An `AdminUser` is allowed to change a customer's PIN while a `SuperUser` can also update the transaction logs for an account.

Web Application Security

When looking at Web application security, the first choice is between using container-managed security services or implementing them yourself within the application. Security management services are available for almost every component type within the J2EE architecture in most containers. For example, components that can be secured include JSP, servlets, EJB, and JNDI lookups, and the list goes on. Do you need secure controls on every single one of these components? Well, each one is like another layer of an onion that someone has to peel in order to break into your system. Adding security on each of these components can marginally increase the level of security provided by the first line of defense.

This first layer, the Web tier, is of course critical to the overall security model, but at some point underneath that in the architecture, the concept of the trusted server usually enters into the picture. For example, not every user of the bank application is assigned a database username and password. When a new customer number and PIN is created, the application does not also create a new logon for the database. The application server uses a pool of database connections to perform all database activity. Thus, the database server trusts the application server to have authenticated and authorized users for the particular activity they are about to perform. This concept can bubble up as far as you want in a multi-tier Web architecture. For example, if users authenticate at the Web tier, you may not feel it is necessary to either reauthenticate them or apply EJB security at the service component level if you trust the JSP tier to have addressed these issues. The controller architecture has already enforced access control on the URL, and the action class may have already ensured that this user is authorized to invoke a given service. Typically, you would have the option to forgo authentication at the EJB tier because of the network and hardware architecture. An EJB tier typically would be behind a number of Internet firewalls that would prevent direct access from all locations except the Web container.

For many applications, this type of security approach can work well; however, it depends on the security risk of the application as well as its design. If there are a large number of fine-grained services with different authorization requirements, it would not make sense to program this logic into the application when you can have the container manage this for you. As long as the security model is based on roles, you can use declarative J2EE security measures to handle this. If other security requirements are based on application data or additional business logic, you can still use the J2EE authentication mechanisms to get the user's profile (that is, what roles the user belongs to), and then programmatically use the servlet or EJB APIs to access this information in conjunction with the appropriate business logic.

Thus, at the Web tier, you can either implement the security yourself or use the container's security. The alternative of implementing the security in the application is discussed first.

NOTE Examples are shown in this book of both application-managed security and container-managed security. In either case, the user's credentials are specified by the `Customer` object, and hence the `customer` database table. The customer number is the username and the PIN is the user's password. The database also has a table `cust_roles` that links customer numbers to security roles. The entity is managed by a `UserRole` business object that maps to the table.

A typical scenario for a Web application that manages its own security is to use a logon form to validate the user's ID and password and then store a token in the session to identify the user. All secure pages then first check the session for that token before rendering the page. If that token is not present, then the application redirects the user to the logon page. This logic is usually implemented at the beginning of the controller servlet logic as well as in every JSP either as scriptlet code at the top of the page or more preferably, as a reusable custom tag. The token within the session can also contain role or user group information to implement authorization for application services. In the bank application, the `LogonAction` stores a `customerId` attribute in the session that is used throughout the application to identify the user and provide input data for some of the service invocations. In this case, the session token provides both security benefits and state management across page requests.

Application-Managed Web Security

This section looks at authentication in an application-managed scenario. A bank login page is used as an example to illustrate this. The Struts configuration for the login event is defined as follows:

```
<action     path="/struts/login"
            type="bank.struts.LogonAction"
            name="logonForm"
            scope="request"
            input="/struts/login.jsp">
</action>
```

The `logon.jsp` is a simple HTML form with the two input fields previously defined, `custNumber` and `pin`. The `LogonAction` code, which simply invokes the logon service, is shown here:

```java
public class LogonAction extends Action {

    /**
     * The Struts action interface
     */
    public ActionForward perform(ActionMapping mapping,
                                 ActionForm form,
                                 HttpServletRequest request,
                                 HttpServletResponse response)
        throws IOException, ServletException {

    // Validate the request parameters specified by the user.
    ActionErrors errors = new ActionErrors();
    String custNumber = ((LogonForm) form).getCustNumber();
    String pin = ((LogonForm) form).getPin();

        try {
            // Create a service data object for this service.
            ArgumentList argList = new ArgumentList();
            argList.setProperty("custNumber",custNumber);
            argList.setProperty("pin",pin);
            ServiceData sdata = new ServiceData("Logon");
            sdata.setArgumentList(argList);

            // Invoke the application service.
            BlfService service =
                ServiceObjectFactory.getBlfService();
            sdata = service.executeService(sdata);
            service.remove();

            // Store the customer ID as a session token.
            CustomerData custData =
                (CustomerData) sdata.getOutputData(0);
            HttpSession session = request.getSession(true);
            session.putValue("customerId",
                             custData.getProperty("id"));

            // Set next page to main page.
            return (mapping.findForward("main"));

        } catch (BlfException be) {

            // Map blf errors to action errors.
            BlfStrutsConverter.convertErrorList(
                             be.getErrorList(),errors);

            // Set the errors so the next page can see them.
            saveErrors(request, errors);
            // Return the input page to redisplay the form.
            return (new ActionForward(mapping.getInput()));

        } catch (Exception e) {

            // Create a general action error for the exception.
```

```
            errors.add(ActionErrors.GLOBAL_ERROR,
                    new ActionError("GENERAL_SERVICE_ERROR"));
            // Set the errors so the next page can see them.
            saveErrors(request, errors);
            // Return the input page to redisplay the form.
            return (new ActionForward(mapping.getInput()));
        }
    }
}
```

The logon service is implemented as follows:

```
public class LogonServiceImpl implements BlfServiceObject {
    public void doService(ServiceData serviceData)
        throws BlfException, RemoteException {

        // Get hold of the input data.
        ValueObject argumentList =
            serviceData.getArgumentList();
        String custNumber =
            argumentList.getProperty("custNumber");
        String pin = argumentList.getProperty("pin");

        // Use ObjectList to locate the customer.
        ObjectList customerListObj =
            new ObjectList("Customer");
        ArrayList args = new ArrayList(1);
        args.add(custNumber);
        ArrayList custList =
            customerListObj.getValueObjects("byNumber",args);

        // Put results in output data if any.
        int size = custList.size();
        if (size != 1) {
            // If more than one or no customers are found,
            // the customer number is invalid.
            serviceData.getErrorList().addError(
                                "INVALID_CUST_NUMBER");
        } else {
            // If the customer number is valid,
            // ensure that the PIN is valid.
            CustomerData custData =
                (CustomerData) custList.get(0);
            if (!(custData.getProperty("pin").equals(pin))) {
                serviceData.getErrorList().addError(
                                "INVALID_LOGON");
            } else {
                serviceData.addOutputData(custData);
            }
        }
    }
}
```

If you also wanted to address authorization within this process, you would need to store some type of customer bean in the session that also included role information for that particular user. The logon action would need to differentiate between administrative users and customers. Rather than going ahead and implementing this logic, the container-managed model for accomplishing this action is discussed in the following section.

Container-Managed Web Security

If you look back at the code for the application-managed user logon, the logic is fairly straightforward. However that is only one part of the overall security scheme. Each servlet and Web page must check the session token and possibly any role information stored within it in order to safely protect the Web resources of the application. Any programming mistake in this logic within any of the components can introduce a security leak. Thus, this is one good reason to rely on the container's security mechanism, which has already been thoroughly tested and used in multiple production environments.

The other compelling reason not to implement this portion of the security in the application code is portability across applications and across the enterprise. If you use the container's authentication mechanism, your application is easily portable across J2EE deployment environments and enterprise security architectures. A typical single sign-on scenario involves storing user credentials in an LDAP (lightweight directory access protocol) repository that can then be accessed by authentication mechanisms on multiple platforms and applications throughout the enterprise. Authentication information that is stored in text files, databases, or other custom security modules can be accessed by most J2EE application server products. This type of approach provides a robust, reusable Web security model that is recommended over coding this portion of the security directly into the application, unless there is an otherwise compelling reason to do so.

BEST PRACTICE Use J2EE security whenever possible to safely protect application resources. Container-managed security is portable across J2EE environments and integrates well with enterprise security architectures. Protecting Web-tier resources is critical because they are the entry point to the application. Consider the network security model and the trusted server concept when determining how many EJB tier resources you want explicitly secured using container-managed security. For application-specific requirements, both the servlet and EJB APIs offer programmatic access to information about user credentials.

If you look at the sample application, there are not a lot of fine-grained security requirements. For the most part, once customers are authenticated, they are allowed to access any page within their account and invoke any of the services behind those pages. The examples still use a `customerId` session token as a shortcut to avoid an extra database lookup on many of the page requests. You can, in fact, get the user `Principal` on each request from the `HttpServletRequest.getUserPrincipal()` API;

Figure 9.2 Web Directory Structure.

however, this is the external customer number that was used as the username. The internal customer id is what is used in the relational database to link to other entities; thus, the id is saved as a shortcut for input to some of the services. You may feel that using the session token and the security roles overlaps the same function, in which case you could easily omit the session token and pass the principal information to each service. The services that require the customer id would then perform the additional database select or table join when it is required.

Much of the Web security model is based on controlling access to pages within defined URL patterns. Earlier, three groups of users were identified for the bank application: unauthenticated users, customers, and administrative users. Consequently, the page URLs were structured according to Figure 9.2 so that they could correspond to the user roles.

Table 9.1 describes the contents of each directory.

The web.xml file in the WEB-INF directory contains the J2EE configuration for Web-tier components. In addition to defining servlets and tag libraries, it includes the definition of container-managed security constraints. These constraints can force URL patterns to require user authentication as well as define what roles are authorized to view the pages. Thus, for the customer pages, security constraints that require authentication and allow access to all of the customer roles and the admin user roles are

Table 9.1 Contents of Web Directories

DIRECTORY	CONTENTS
/bank	The root directory of the Web application.
/bank/struts	Contains all the customer JavaServer Pages for the bank application.
/bank/struts/admin	Contains all the administration JavaServer Pages for the bank application.
/bank/strutslogon	Contains all pages for unauthenticated users including the logon page and the new customer wizard pages.
/bank/WEB-INF	This directory contains all of the Web application configurations files such as web.xml and struts-config.xml, and all of the tag library descriptor files such as blf.tld, struts-html.tld, and so on.

defined in the web.xml file. Note that /bank/ is defined as the root directory, so URLs in this file start from that directory:

```
<security-constraint>
  <web-resource-collection>
    <web-resource-name>BankApp</web-resource-name>
    <url-pattern>/struts/*</url-pattern>
    <http-method>GET</http-method>
    <http-method>POST</http-method>
  </web-resource-collection>
  <auth-constraint>
    <role-name>Customer</role-name>
    <role-name>AdminUser</role-name>
    <role-name>SuperUser</role-name>
  </auth-constraint>
  <user-data-constraint>
    <transport-guarantee>NONE</transport-guarantee>
  </user-data-constraint>
</security-constraint>
```

This constraint was defined to cover the collection of Web resources under the /struts/* directory. This includes both HTTP GET and POST requests. The <auth-constraint> tag lists the roles that have access to these resources, in this case both the customer and admin roles. Finally, the <user-data-constraint> is specified as NONE here because the example wasn't run using SSL (Secure Socket Layer), so this value would be set to CONFIDENTIAL in production. This will be discussed further in a moment.

You can define a separate security constraint for the administrative pages and allow only the AdminUser or SuperUser role to access them:

```
<security-constraint>
  <web-resource-collection>
  <web-resource-name>BankApp</web-resource-name>
    <url-pattern>/struts/admin/*</url-pattern>
    <http-method>GET</http-method>
    <http-method>POST</http-method>
  </web-resource-collection>
  <auth-constraint>
    <role-name>AdminUser</role-name>
    <role-name>SuperUser</role-name>
  </auth-constraint>
  <user-data-constraint>
    <transport-guarantee>NONE</transport-guarantee>
  </user-data-constraint>
</security-constraint>
```

What has not been specified yet is the method of authentication to use. This is defined in the <login-config> section of web.xml. There are a couple of options available. The first and most primitive is basic authentication, although it is also quite effective. Basic authentication causes the Web server to return a 401 Authentication

Required HTTP response. This response is recognized by the browser and opens a pop-up window to prompt the user for his or her username and password. If the user is authenticated based on the credentials that are supplied, the original request for the secured page is processed. This authentication actually happens on every page request because HTTP is a stateless protocol, but the browser remembers the user's credentials and passes them along with each request. Once a user closes the browser, he or she needs to retype the username and password, although some browsers offer the option of remembering the credentials for future visits to the Web site. To use basic authentication, the `web.xml` file would include the following section:

```
<login-config>
  <auth-method>BASIC</auth-method>
  <realm-name>Sample Bank App</realm-name>
</login-config>
```

The pop-up window displays the name of the security realm, but that is about it in terms of customizing the look and feel. An example is shown in Figure 9.3.

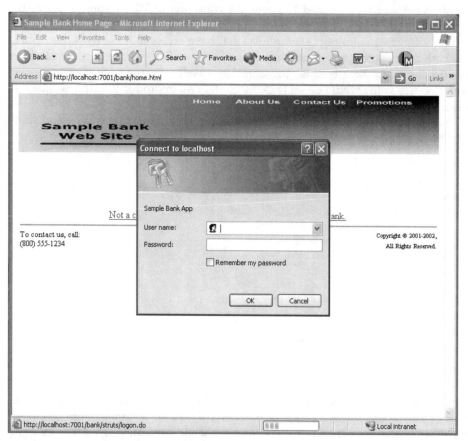

Figure 9.3 Example of Basic Authentication Logon.

The basic authentication mechanism does not address the confidentiality aspect of security. In fact, the username and password are sent over the network by way of a simple base64 encoding. Thus, you typically combine this with a secure transport layer such as SSL through HTTP(S) or a secure network solution such as a VPN. There is another authentication mechanism called digest authentication that works the same as basic authentication except that it uses a stronger encryption scheme for sending the username and password. This encryption, however, is still not as strong as SSL, and thus it is not a required aspect of the servlet specification. In order to ensure that SSL is being used in combination with these authentication mechanisms, configure your Web server appropriately and specify the <user-data-constraint> as follows:

```
<user-data-constraint>
  <transport-guarantee>CONFIDENTIAL</transport-guarantee>
</user-data-constraint>
```

As was mentioned earlier, you cannot customize the pop-up window used with basic authentication. However, you can use your own HTML logon page when you use form-based authentication. The HTML logon form that you use does require a certain action string and predefined input fields for the username and password, but other than that, the page is completely up to you. In the <login-config> section of web.xml, you can simply define form-based authentication and supply the URL of the logon page and an error page to use if the logon is incorrect. Thus, the configuration can be changed to the following:

```
<login-config>
  <auth-method>FORM</auth-method>
  <realm-name>Sample Bank App</realm-name>
  <form-login-config>
    <form-login-page>/strutslogon/formlogon.jsp
                              </form-login-page>
    <form-error-page>/strutslogon/formlogonerror.jsp
                              </form-error-page>
  </form-login-config>
</login-config>
```

Note that the logon pages are placed with the rest of the unauthenticated content. Making these pages secure can cause an infinite loop because the user can never authenticate to get to the logon page. The form-based logon page is shown in Figure 9.4.

The form action of the logon page must be the string "j_security_check". The username and password input fields must be named "j_username" and "j_password", respectively. The formlogon.jsp page is shown here:

```
<form action="j_security_check" method="POST">
<table width=100%>
<tr>
<td width=40% align=right>Customer Number:</td>
<td width=60%><input type="text" name="j_username" size="10"
                maxlength="20"/></td>
</tr>
```

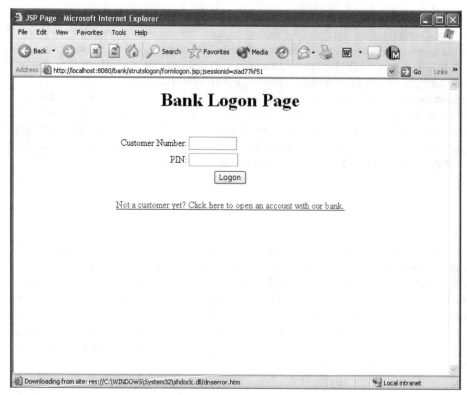

Figure 9.4   Sample Form-Based Logon Page.

```
<tr>
<td align=right>PIN:</td>
<td><input type="password" name="j_password" size="10"
          maxlength="20" /></td>
</tr>
</table>
<table width=100%>
<tr>
<td align=center><input type="submit" name="submit"
                        value="Logon"/></td>
</tr>
</table>
<P/>
<table width=100%>
<tr>
<td align=center><html:link forward="newCustomer1">
   Not a customer yet?  Click here to open an account with our
   bank.</html:link></td>
</tr>
</table>

</form>
```

> **NOTE** In many Web architectures, there is a separate Web server in front of the J2EE application server that handles authentication and confidentiality. For example, Apache can be used to handle authentication as well as the encryption and decryption of a secure transport mechanism such as SSL. In these cases, it may not be necessary to secure the transport internally within the architecture; the Web server may choose to forward clear text to the JSP container.

The last authentication option is client authentication that requires a public key certificate.

User Authentication Data

There are a number of options for storing and accessing the user and role information. As mentioned earlier, many organizations use an LDAP repository to store the information, although most products also support authentication data in properties files, database tables, or custom security modules. For simplicity, the examples will use the database to store the user information. There is already a `customer` table with the customer number and PIN, so the only missing piece is a table to store the customer roles. Thus, a `cust_roles` table was created with two columns, `cust_number` and `role_name`. The `cust_number` column links to the `customer` table and the `role_name` column specifies a role that the user participates in. This information is broken out into a separate table so that a customer may belong to more than one role. The same customer table will actually be used to store the administrative users as well. In an enterprise environment, you would likely break out the user information to a separate table and generalize the column names so that they apply to all types of users. However, for the sample application, certain customer numbers will simply be picked for the administrative users.

Access to different authentication data sources in products is commonly referred to as a particular realm. For example, using the database is referred to as the JDBC realm, whereas using a directory service would be called an LDAP realm. In either case, the particular database or directory structures are defined in the configuration. For example, this is what allows you to use the existing `customer` table as the source of the username and password fields.

Bank Implementation of Container Security

The bank application has a home page located in the root directory so that unauthorized users can access it. This page has the following Enter link that goes to a protected Web resource that will be processed by a `ContainerLogonAction`.

```
<a href="/bank/struts/logon.do" >Click here to enter</a>
```

The user first goes to the home page and then clicks on the link. Because the URL is under the `/struts/*` URL pattern, the form-based authentication mechanism is triggered and `formlogon.jsp` is shown. The user enters his or her username and password, and the container processes the form. Authentication is completed against the `customer` and `cust_roles` database tables that are shown in the example. If the credentials are invalid, the `formlogonerror.jsp` is shown. Otherwise, if the credentials are valid, the initial request to /bank/struts/logon.do is processed. This path is mapped by the following action configuration:

```
<!— Process a user logon —>
<action    path="/struts/logon"
           type="bank.struts.ContainerLogonAction">
</action>
```

The `ContainerLogonAction` uses the `isUserInRole` method to determine if this was an administrative user logging in to the application. In this case, the user is forwarded to the main administrative page. In all other cases, the action looks up the customer entity and stores the customer `id` in the session as a time-saver. Remember that this is not necessary because you could alternatively use the `getUserPrincipal` method in each action to get the customer number and perform a database join on subsequent transactions. For authenticated users in a customer role, the action then forwards to the main customer page. The `ContainerLogonAction` code is as follows:

```
public class ContainerLogonAction extends Action {

    /**
     * The Struts action interface
     */
    public ActionForward perform(ActionMapping mapping,
                                 ActionForm form,
                                 HttpServletRequest request,
                                 HttpServletResponse response)
        throws IOException, ServletException {

        // Create an error bucket.
        ActionErrors errors = new ActionErrors();

        // The customer number is the user
        // principal, that is, the username
        // from the authentication (basic or form).
        Principal principal = request.getUserPrincipal();
        String custNumber = principal.getName();

        // If this is an admin user,
        // go to the administrator's main page.
        if (request.isUserInRole("AdminUser") ||
            request.isUserInRole("SuperUser")) {
            return (mapping.findForward("adminMain"));
        }

        try {
            // Create the service data to invoke
            // the logon service.
            ArgumentList argList = new ArgumentList();
            argList.setProperty("custNumber",custNumber);
```

```
        ServiceData sdata =
            new ServiceData("GetCustomerByNumber");
        sdata.setArgumentList(argList);

        // Invoke the application service.
        BlfService service =
            ServiceObjectFactory.getBlfService();
        sdata = service.executeService(sdata);
        service.remove();

        // Store the customer ID in the session.
        CustomerData custData =
            (CustomerData) sdata.getOutputData(0);
        HttpSession session = request.getSession(true);
        session.putValue("customerId",
                            custData.getProperty("id"));

        // Set next page to main page.
        return (mapping.findForward("main"));

    } catch (BlfException be) {

        // Map BLF errors to action errors.
        BlfStrutsConverter.convertErrorList(
                            be.getErrorList(),errors);

        // Set the errors so the next page can see them.
        saveErrors(request, errors);
        // Return the input page to redisplay the form.
        return (mapping.findForward("main"));

    } catch (Exception e) {

        // Create a general action error for the exception.
        errors.add(ActionErrors.GLOBAL_ERROR,
            new ActionError("GENERAL_SERVICE_ERROR"));
        // Set the errors so the next page can see them.
        saveErrors(request, errors);
        // Return the input page to redisplay the form.
        return (mapping.findForward("main"));
    }
  }
}
```

Use of Roles to Customize Content

In this last section, you saw the user roles used as a trigger to change the content of the application. In this case, if the user was in an administrative role, he or she was sent to an entirely different page. However, you can also use roles within a given JSP to provide dynamic content based on the type of user. One such example of this concept in practice is provided by the Struts JSP template mechanism. You can specify that a page fragment be included only if the user is in a certain role. For example, there are two types of administrative roles, AdminUser and SuperUser. As you will see in the next section, the administrative functions are triggered from the navigation bar. You can use the admin template.jsp to pull in a different navigation bar based on the user role. The changes to do this are shown in bold here:

```
<html:html>
<head><title><template:get name='title' /></title></head>
<body>
<template:get name='<%=PageConstants.TEMPLATE_HEADER%>' />
<table width="100%">
<tr>
<td width="20%" align="right" valign="top">
<template:get name='<%=PageConstants.TEMPLATE_NAVBAR%>'
               role='AdminUser' />
<template:get name='supernavbar' role='SuperUser' />
</td>
<td width="60%" >
<template:get name='<%=PageConstants.TEMPLATE_BODY%>' />
</td>
<td width="20%" align="right">
</td>
</tr>
</table>
<template:get name='<%=PageConstants.TEMPLATE_FOOTER%>' />
</body>
</html:html>
```

Any admin page that uses this template can then add the following lines in bold to show either navBar.jsp for someone in the AdminUser role or superNavBar.jsp for someone in the SuperUser role. As an example, the template instance for the administrative main page is shown here:

```
<%@ taglib uri='/WEB-INF/struts-template.tld'
           prefix='template' %>

<template:insert template='/struts/admin/template.jsp'>
  <template:put name='title' content='Administrative Main Page'
                direct='true'/>
  <template:put name='header' content='/struts/header.jsp' />
  <template:put name='navbar'
                content='/struts/admin/navBar.jsp' />
  <template:put name='supernavbar'
                content='/struts/admin/superNavBar.jsp' />
  <template:put name='body'
                content='/struts/admin/mainBody.jsp'/>
  <template:put name='footer' content='/struts/footer.jsp' />
</template:insert>
```

The different pages for the two users are shown in Figure 9.5.

AdminUser **Main Page**   *SuperUser* **Main Page**

 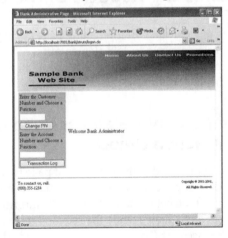

Figure 9.5 Customized Administrative Pages.

NOTE The example was structured such that a user is either an `AdminUser` or a `SuperUser`. If the security roles were modeled such that a `SuperUser` was also an `AdminUser`, the current implementation would give you two navigation bars on the page because both conditions would be satisfied. In this case, you would want to move the template and role-based content down to the navigation bar JSP level. Within a navigation bar template, you could pull in the additional content for the `SuperUser` role.

EJB Security

The bank Web application will use the container-managed security model described earlier. There is also the option of adding security to the EJB tier. As was discussed earlier, you can use the EJB tier as a trusted server, using the Web tier to enforce the security constraints. You are not required to authenticate in order to use an EJB, although you can do that as well. The Web tier can pass the user credentials (username and password) to the remote EJB method invocation. You also have the option of mapping principals in the Web tier to different principals on the EJB tier if your two application areas have modeled the security differently. EJB containers have the same kind of authentication mechanisms available to them as discussed earlier on the Web tier. On some integrated JSP and EJB containers, it may not be necessary to explicitly pass the user credentials as this may happen automatically. Method-level permissions can be placed on EJB components to allow access only to certain roles. In the bank application, a standard Session Bean service component is used, so access would have to be granted to the `Customer`, `AdminUser`, and `SuperUser` roles. This would ensure that the client was authenticated, but it would not add any additional authorization functionality. The bank application also does not make heavy use of Entity Beans, so the decision was made simply to implement the security model using the Web tier and make the EJB tier a trusted server.

Interesting Aspects of the Bank Application

There are a number of interesting pages in the bank application that illustrate interesting design aspects and implementation concepts not seen in the earlier examples. The first of these is the account detail page that shows a data retrieval example including the display of multiple object types in the same page.

The Account Detail Page and the Transaction Object

Earlier you saw that the account list page had links for each account to a details screen. The details page is interesting because it has both parent and child data on it. The Account object contains the header information such as the account number, type, and current balance while the remainder of the page is a list of Transaction objects for that account. The account detail page is shown in Figure 9.6.

The implementation of the account detail page that is shown in this chapter uses Entity Bean business objects and ObjectList to deal with the collection of Transaction objects. The transaction object is defined in the metadata as follows.

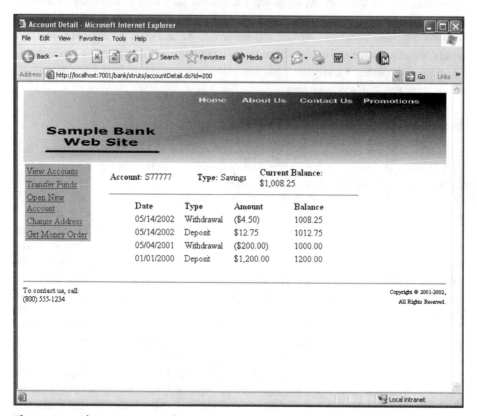

Figure 9.6 The Account Detail Page.

Note that the database information is defined in the metadata so that the JDBC utility underneath `ObjectList` can access the database:

```
<BusinessObject name="Transaction"
                valueObjClass="bank.TransactionData"
            ejbHomeClass="bank.entity.TransactionLocalHome"
                table="transaction">
<Property name="id" dbname="id" type="String"
          required="true" key="true" autogen="true" />
<Property name="type" dbname="type" type="String"
          required="true" />
<Property name="transactionDate" dbname="transaction_date"
          type="Date" />
<Property name="amount" dbname="amount" type="Currency"
          required="true" />
<Property name="description" dbname="description"
          type="String" />
<Collection name="byAccount"
query="where account_id = ? order by transaction_date desc" />
  </BusinessObject>
```

The page is also interesting because it calculates a running total as it displays the transactions so that the current balance can be shown after each transaction. Alternatively, you could have created a `balance` property on the `Transaction` object that captured the balance at the time of the transaction. However, this example does the calculation for illustrative purposes.

The request for the account details page sends an `id` parameter in the URL to indicate what account information to display. The `AccountDetailAction` that processes this request is fairly straightforward. It uses the `id` to retrieve the account information. The relevant portion of `AccountDetailAction` is shown here:

```
// You need to run a data retrieval service
// to get the transaction history.
// This service takes an argument list
// of just the account identifier
// that was passed in as a request
// parameter.
ServiceData sdata =
    new ServiceData("GetAccountDetail");
ArgumentList argList = new ArgumentList();
argList.setProperty("accountId",
                    request.getParameter("id"));
sdata.setArgumentList(argList);

// Invoke the application service.
BlfService service =
    ServiceObjectFactory.getBlfService();
sdata = service.executeService(sdata);
service.remove();
```

```
//
// Set context for the next page.
//
request.setAttribute(PageConstants.DATA,
                     sdata.getOutputData());
return (mapping.findForward("accountDetail"));
```

In order to get the data for the account detail page, a new service was created called `GetAccountDetail`. This service needs to return the account object and its transaction objects. Because the service data structure returns a collection of value objects, the output data of the service will have the 0th element be the `AccountData` object while any additional objects are `TransactionData` objects. As input data, the service takes either an account identifier or an account number, because as you will see, it ends up being used in both the customer and administrative pages that have different contexts. The code for this service is as follows. It uses the business object factory to select the individual account object and `ObjectList` to retrieve the list of transaction objects. This service also shows an example of directly using the EJB Home interface to invoke a finder method. Optionally, a general `find` method that uses reflection to generically invoke finder methods could be implemented on `EJBFactory`. In this example however, it is done explicitly. The `FinderException` is mapped to the `ObjectNotFoundException`, a subclass of `BlfException` that communicates the corresponding business error. This is an incarnation of a best practice described earlier, which states that system-level exceptions should be mapped to application-level exceptions with corresponding user-friendly error messages.

BEST PRACTICE Map EJB-level exceptions to application exceptions with defined business errors for user-friendly error messages. This approach also simplifies the client code because there is only one high-level application exception that needs to be handled. The application exception always contains the list of errors in case any have occurred.

```
public class GetAccountDetailServiceImpl
    implements BlfServiceObject {

    public void doService(ServiceData serviceData)
        throws BlfException, RemoteException {

        // Get hold of the input data.
        ValueObject argumentList =
            serviceData.getArgumentList();
        String accountId =
            argumentList.getProperty("accountId");
        String accountNumber =
            argumentList.getProperty("accountNumber");

        //
        // Depending on the input, use the appropriate
        // database mechanism to get the account.
        //
```

```
        if (accountId != null) {
            // Use the findByPrimaryKey.
            AccountLocal account = (AccountLocal)
                EJBFactoryImpl.findByPrimaryKey("Account",
                                                accountId);
            serviceData.addOutputData(
                account.getValueObject());
        } else if (accountNumber != null) {
            // Use the EJB finder method.
            AccountLocalHome accountHome = (AccountLocalHome)
                EJBFactoryImpl.getHomeInterface("Account",
                    MetadataManager.getBusinessObject(
                                                "Account"));
            try {
                AccountLocal account = (AccountLocal)
                    accountHome.findByNumber(accountNumber);
                ValueObject accountData =
                    account.getValueObject();
                serviceData.addOutputData(accountData);
                accountId = accountData.getProperty("id");
            } catch (FinderException fe) {
                throw new ObjectNotFoundException("Account",
                                                accountNumber);
            }
        } else {
            throw new BlfException("Account id or number " +
                " required for GetAccountDetail service.");
        }

        // Use ObjectList to get the collection of accounts.
        ObjectList accountsListObj =
            new ObjectList("Transaction");
        ArrayList args = new ArrayList(1);
        args.add(accountId);
        Collection accountList =
            accountsListObj.getValueObjects("byAccount",args);

        // Put the results in the output data.
        Iterator iter = accountList.iterator();
        while (iter.hasNext()) {
            serviceData.addOutputData(
                (ValueObject)iter.next());
        }
    }
}
```

The actual `accountDetailBody.jsp` uses a number of Struts custom tags to iterate over the collection of output objects. There is a set of logic tags that evaluate the body of the tag only if the test condition is met. As the page iterates over the collection of output value objects from the service, the `<logic:equal>` and `<logic: notEqual>` tags are used to determine what index is being processed. If it is the

0th index, this is the account value object and the header is displayed. If the index is not equal to zero, then the page is processing one of the transaction value objects, and a new row is created within an HTML table containing the transaction data. From the account object, a `BigDecimal` variable is initialized with the current balance that will be used to keep track of the running account balance total after each transaction. Note that the collection of transactions is defined in the metadata to be in descending date order, so the transaction amount is subtracted each time from the running total. The code for `accountDetailBody.jsp` is shown here:

```
<%@page import="java.util.*,blf.*,bank.TransactionData"%>
<%@page import="bank.AccountData,java.math.BigDecimal"%>
<%@ taglib uri="/WEB-INF/struts-html.tld" prefix="html" %>
<%@ taglib uri="/WEB-INF/struts-logic.tld" prefix="logic" %>
<%@ taglib uri="/WEB-INF/struts-bean.tld" prefix="bean" %>
<%@ taglib uri="/WEB-INF/blf.tld" prefix="blf" %>

<%
    //
    // The service data has the following objects:
    // 0        Account value object
    // 1 - n    Transaction value objects
    //

    // You are going to keep
    // a running total of
    // the current balance
    // after each transaction.
    BigDecimal tempBalance = null;
%>
<logic:iterate name="<%=PageConstants.DATA%>" id="data"
    indexId="indexVar" scope="request" type="blf.ValueObject" >
<logic:equal name="indexVar" scope="page" value="0" >
<%
    // The first item in the collection
    // is the account object, so
    // get the starting balance for
    // your running total and display
    // the header information.
    tempBalance = data.getDecimalProperty("currentBalance");
    tempBalance = tempBalance.setScale(2);
%>
<table width=100% align=center>
<tr><td width=35%><B>Account: </B>
    <blf:getProperty bean="data" property="number" /></td>
    <td width=25%><B>Type: </B>
      <blf:lookupValue cache="AccountTypes"
              value='<%=data.getProperty("type")%>' /></td>
    <td width=40%><B>Current Balance: </B>
      <blf:getProperty bean="data" property="currentBalance" />
</td></tr>
</table>
```

```
<hr noshade>

<table width=80% align=center>
<tr><td width=25%><B>Date</B></td>
    <td width=25%><B>Type</B></td>
    <td width=30%><B>Amount</B></td>
    <td width=20%><B>Balance</B></td></tr>
</logic:equal>
<logic:notEqual name="indexVar" scope="page" value="0" >

<tr><td><blf:getProperty bean="data"
                         property="transactionDate" /></td>
    <td><blf:lookupValue cache="TransactionTypes"
                value='<%=data.getProperty("type")%>' /></td>
    <td><blf:getProperty bean="data" property="amount" /></td>
    <td><%=tempBalance%></td></tr>
<%
    // Calculate the resulting balance after this transaction.
    // Note that you are going in descending date order, so
    // substract to get the correct balance.
    tempBalance =
        tempBalance.subtract(data.getDecimalProperty("amount"));
%>
</logic:notEqual>
</logic:iterate>
</table>
```

The Transfer Funds Page

The transfer funds function has been mentioned many times throughout the earlier chapters. This section takes a look at how this page is implemented. The transfer funds form has two drop-down lists, each containing the customer's accounts, as well as an amount field as shown in Figure 9.7.

The page flow for the transfer funds function is shown in Figure 9.8. The next page after a successful transfer is the view accounts page, while the form is redrawn if any errors occurred.

The form data is captured using Struts into a `TransferFundsForm` bean that has three corresponding properties. The only field-level data validations are on the amount field because the user is forced to select valid accounts using the drop-down lists. Thus, the form bean class is fairly simple except for the `validate` method, which checks first that an amount was specified and second that it was a valid decimal value. Because there is already a set of `PropertyHandler` classes that manipulate string values for all data types, the decimal property validator can be used to ensure that it has a valid value. The code for `TransferFundsForm` is shown here:

```
public class TransferFundsForm extends ActionForm {

    private String fromAcct = null;
    private String toAcct = null;
    private String amount = null;
```

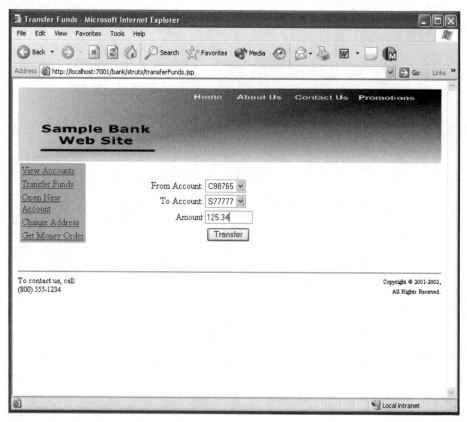

Figure 9.7 Transfer Funds Page.

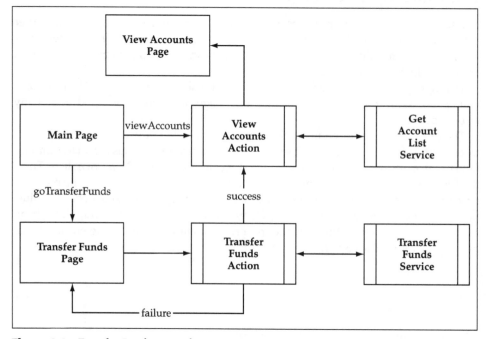

Figure 9.8 Transfer Funds Page Flow.

```java
public String getFromAcct() {
  return fromAcct;
}
public void setFromAcct(String value) {
    fromAcct = value;
}

public String getToAcct() {
  return toAcct;
}
public void setToAcct(String value) {
    toAcct = value;
}

public String getAmount() {
  return amount;
}
public void setAmount(String value) {
    amount = value;
}

/**
 * Reset all properties to their default values.
 */
public void reset(ActionMapping mapping,
                  HttpServletRequest request) {
}


/**
 * Validate the properties that have been set from this
 * form submission.
 */
public ActionErrors validate(ActionMapping mapping,
                             HttpServletRequest request) {

    ActionErrors errors = new ActionErrors();
    // Check that an amount was specified.
    if ((amount == null) || (amount.length() < 1)) {
        errors.add("amount",
                   new ActionError("TRANSFER_AMT_REQ"));
    } else {
        // Check that there is a valid decimal amount
        // using your standard property validator.
        try {
            PropertyValidator validator =
                (PropertyValidator)
                    CacheList.getInstance().getObject(
                        "PropertyTypeCache","Decimal");
            validator.validateProperty(amount);
```

```
            } catch (BlfException be) {
               errors.add("amount",
                            new ActionError("INVALID_AMOUNT"));
            }
        }
        return errors;
    }
}
```

Rather than use the converter for the errors, this form bean simply catches `Blf-Exception` and adds an `ActionError` for the user message. The error messages for this page are defined as follows:

```
TRANSFER_AMT_REQ=<li>You must specify an amount to transfer.</li>
INVALID_AMOUNT=<li>The amount is invalid.</li>
INVALID_TRANSFER=<li>You must choose another account to transfer
                     funds.</li>
INSUFFICIENT_FUNDS=<li>There are insufficient funds for the withdrawal.
                     The current balance is {0}.</li>
```

You will see how the last two error messages are used later in this section.

For smaller development projects, this approach to form validation works just fine. However, for larger projects, it may seem a bit tedious to have to code standard validation logic like this, such as required field and data type checking, in every form bean. In the case of forms that correspond directly to objects, the form beans can implement the `ValueObject` interface and use the standard validation template discussed earlier. This was done for the address form bean in the change address example. However, the transfer funds form data does not correspond directly to an object. If you still wanted to use the automated validation provided by the reference architecture, you could define an object in the metadata that corresponds to the transfer funds form. It would have three properties, all of which are required, and their data type information would be specified. You would not specify a business object class name, only a value object class name. You could then handle all of the form's basic data validation simply by having the form bean extend `BaseFormBean`. In some situations, you may also end up using a combination of explicit and metadata-driven techniques.

The other validation that needs to be performed is to check that the user did not select the same account for both the from and the to accounts. This type of validation could also easily go into the form bean `validate` method, but the decision was made to move this edit to the action class and limit the form bean to straight data validation. This is purely a design decision, and the consistency of the approach or guidelines used throughout your application is probably more important than the individual choice here. Form beans like this are usually particular to a page as compared to value objects that easily can be reused across pages. This simply continues the value object paradigm of performing field-level validation in these objects, although it was certainly not necessary. Consequently, the `TransferFundsAction` performs this edit and then creates an argument list to invoke the `TransferFunds` service. An interesting aspect of this action class is page navigation. If an error occurs, the action class returns back to the input form. However, on a successful transfer, the user is shown the new account balances on the view accounts page. The account list page requires some setup work done in the ViewAccountsAction class. Thus, the concept of action chaining is used and the request is forwarded on to that action class, similar to service chaining discussed in the Service-Based Architecture chapter. The ActionForward class has previously been constructed using the logical forwards defined in struts-config.xml; however, it can be constructed using a servlet path that maps to the action class. Thus, an ActionForward is returned that goes to /struts/viewAccounts.do, which gets mapped to the next action class in the chain. The entire code for TransferFunds-Action is shown here:

```java
public class TransferFundsAction extends Action {

    /**
     * The Struts action interface
     */
    public ActionForward perform(ActionMapping mapping,
                                 ActionForm form,
                                 HttpServletRequest request,
                                 HttpServletResponse response)
        throws IOException, ServletException {

        // Validate the request parameters.
        ActionErrors errors = new ActionErrors();

        try {
            String fromAcct =
                ((TransferFundsForm) form).getFromAcct();
            String toAcct =
                ((TransferFundsForm) form).getToAcct();
            String amount =
                ((TransferFundsForm) form).getAmount();

            // Verify that the transfer is between
            // different accounts.
            if (fromAcct.equals(toAcct)) {
                errors.add(ActionErrors.GLOBAL_ERROR,
                        new ActionError("INVALID_TRANSFER"));
            } else {

                // Process the form input and
                // create the service data structure.
                ServiceData sdata =
                    new ServiceData("TransferFunds");
                ArgumentList argList = new ArgumentList();
                argList.setProperty("fromAccount",fromAcct);
                argList.setProperty("toAccount",toAcct);
                argList.setProperty("amount",amount);
                sdata.setArgumentList(argList);
```

```
                // Invoke the application service.
                BlfService service =
                    ServiceObjectFactory.getBlfService();
                sdata = service.executeService(sdata);
                service.remove();

                // Chain actions together to get to the
                // view accounts page.
                return (
                  new ActionForward("/struts/viewAccounts.do"));
            }

        } catch (BlfException be) {
            // Map blf errors to action errors.
            BlfStrutsConverter.convertErrorList(
                                    be.getErrorList(),errors);

        } catch (Exception e) {
            // Create a general action error for the exception.
            errors.add(ActionErrors.GLOBAL_ERROR,
                    new ActionError("GENERAL_SERVICE_ERROR"));
        }

        // If you get here, an error occurred.
        // Set the errors so the next page can see them.
        saveErrors(request, errors);
        // Return the input page to redisplay the form.
        return (new ActionForward(mapping.getInput()));
    }
}
```

In the case of the view accounts page, the setup logic was moved out to an action class to simplify the JSP. Otherwise, this class could have forwarded directly to the page itself. This separation of logic was done in order to minimize the amount of code in the JSP for readability and maintainability. Should the design always have this type of separation? Well, in some applications, the clean separation and modular design might not seem worth it, or else you may have a very small amount of preparation work to do that seems wasteful to create another action class. If this is the case, the recommendation is still to minimize the actual Java code in the JSP, but you can also use a common technique and put a single scriptlet at the top of the page that performs this logic. It usually defines any page variables that are referenced later in the JSP. Although this introduces measurable amounts of Java code in the JSP, at least it is isolated to a separate section at the top. This avoids the biggest danger of having large amounts of HTML and Java code intertwined. The transferFundsBody.jsp uses this technique. The drop-down lists are created at run time from the customer's account list. A call is made to the GetAccountList service to get this data and store it in the page context for the <blf:dropDown> custom tag. It also gets the form bean out of the request in case this page is being redisplayed after an error. This needs to be done in order to get the selected values for the drop-down list tags. This type of logic is automatically handled for text fields by the <html:text> tag. The only context this page expects is the `customerId` in the session that is used to call the service. The `transferFundsBody.jsp` code is shown here:

```
<%@page import="java.util.*,blf.*"%>
<%@page import="bank.struts.TransferFundsForm"%>
<%@ taglib uri="/WEB-INF/blf.tld" prefix="blf" %>
<%@ taglib uri="/WEB-INF/struts-html.tld" prefix="html" %>

<%
    // Get hold of existing values for drop-down lists.
    String toAcct = null;
    String fromAcct = null;
    TransferFundsForm formBean = (TransferFundsForm)
        request.getAttribute("transferFundsForm");
    if (formBean != null) {
        toAcct = formBean.getToAcct();
        fromAcct = formBean.getFromAcct();
    }

    // Get the list of accounts for the drop-down.
    ArrayList accountList = null;
    try {
        // Call the GetAccountList service.
        ServiceData sdata = new ServiceData("GetAccountList");
        ArgumentList argList = new ArgumentList();
        argList.setProperty("customerId",
                        (String)session.getValue("customerId"));
        sdata.setArgumentList(argList);
        BlfService service =
            ServiceObjectFactory.getBlfService();
        sdata = service.executeService(sdata);
        accountList = sdata.getOutputData();
        // Set this so your drop-down tag can see it.
        pageContext.setAttribute("accounts",accountList);
        service.remove();

    } catch (BlfException be) {
        be.printStackTrace();
        accountList = new ArrayList(0);
    }


%>

<table width="100%">
<tr align="center"><td><ul><html:errors/></td></tr>
</table>

<html:form action="/struts/transferFunds" focus="fromAcct">
<table width=100%>
<tr>
```

```
<td width=40% align=right>From Account:</td>
<td width=60%>
<blf:dropDown htmlName="fromAcct" collection="accounts"
    labelProperty="number" valueProperty="id"
    selectedOption='<%=fromAcct%>' />
</td>
</tr>
<tr>
<td align=right>To Account:</td>
<td>
<blf:dropDown htmlName="toAcct" collection="accounts"
    labelProperty="number" valueProperty="id"
    selectedOption='<%=toAcct%>' />
</td>
</tr>
<tr>
<td align=right>Amount</td>
<td><html:text property="amount" size="10"
              maxlength="20"/></td>
</tr>
</table>
<table width=100%>
<tr>
<td align=center>
    <html:submit property="submit" value="Transfer"/></td>
</tr>
</table>
</html:form>
```

Finally, the `TransferFunds` service implementation performs the business logic. It uses the Entity Bean implementation of the `Account` and `Transaction` business objects. The service object itself uses the `EJBFactory` to locate both of these account components. It then invokes the `deposit` method on the to account and the `withdraw` method on the from account. The logic to create the transaction records of the transfer is encapsulated within the account object. If an error occurs within either component, such as insufficient funds on the withdrawal, a `BlfException` is thrown back out to the service component. The service base class handles this automatically. This foundation class catches these exceptions, votes to roll back the transaction, and then rethrows the exception to communicate the errors back to the action class. The `TransferFundsServiceImpl` class is shown here:

```
package bank.entity;

import blf.*;
import java.math.BigDecimal;
import java.rmi.RemoteException;

public class TransferFundsServiceImpl
    implements BlfServiceObject {
```

```
public void doService(ServiceData data)
     throws BlfException, RemoteException {

    // Get the input data from the argument list.
    ValueObject args = data.getArgumentList();
    String fromAccountId = args.getProperty("fromAccount");
    String toAccountId   = args.getProperty("toAccount");
    BigDecimal amount = args.getDecimalProperty("amount");

    // Use EJBFactory to locate components.
    Account fromAcct = (Account)
        EJBFactoryImpl.findByPrimaryKey("Account",
                                            fromAccountId);
    Account toAcct = (Account)
        EJBFactoryImpl.findByPrimaryKey("Account",
                                            toAccountId);

    // Perform the transfer by depositing the amount
    // into the to account and withdrawing from
    // the from account.
    toAcct.deposit(amount);
    fromAcct.withdraw(amount);
   }
 }
```

The relevant portions of the `AccountBean` implementation of the Entity Bean are shown here. The `Transaction` Entity bean that is used here does not contain any additional business logic; it is primarily used for persistence to the database:

```
public void blfPreSave() throws BlfException {

    // Initialize any fields.
    setProperty("lastModifiedDate",
        new java.sql.Date(System.currentTimeMillis()));
}

public void deposit(BigDecimal value) throws BlfException {
    deposit(value,null);
}

public void deposit(BigDecimal value,
                    String transactionDescription)
    throws BlfException {

// Add the amount to the balance.
setProperty("currentBalance",
    getDecimalProperty("currentBalance").add(value));

// Create a record of the transaction.
TransactionData transData = new TransactionData();
transData.setProperty("type","D");
```

```java
        transData.setProperty("amount",value);
        if (transactionDescription == null) {
            transData.setProperty("description",
                                  "Normal Deposit");
        } else {
            transData.setProperty("description",
                                  transactionDescription);
        }
        TransactionLocal transaction = (TransactionLocal)
            EJBFactoryImpl.create("Transaction",transData);
        Collection coll = getTransactions();
        coll.add(transaction);


        // Invoke the save template.
        save();
    }

public void withdraw(BigDecimal value)
    throws BlfException {
    withdraw(value,null);
}

public void withdraw(BigDecimal value,
    String transactionDescription) throws BlfException {

    // Ensure that this account will not be
    // overwithdrawn.
    BigDecimal currBalance =
        getDecimalProperty("currentBalance");
    if (currBalance.compareTo(value) < 0) {
        throw new ValidationException("Insufficient Funds",
            ErrorList.createSingleErrorList(
                            "INSUFFICIENT_FUNDS",
                            currBalance.toString())));
    }

    // Remove the amount from the balance.
    setProperty("currentBalance",
                currBalance.subtract(value));

    // Create a record of the transaction.
    TransactionData transData = new TransactionData();
    transData.setProperty("type","W");
    transData.setProperty("amount",value.negate());
    if (transactionDescription == null) {
        transData.setProperty("description",
                              "Normal Withdraw");
    } else {
        transData.setProperty("description",
                              transactionDescription);
    }
```

```
        TransactionLocal transaction = (TransactionLocal)
            EJBFactoryImpl.create("Transaction",transData);
        Collection coll = getTransactions();
        coll.add(transaction);

        // Invoke the save template.
        save();
    }

    public void blfValidate() throws ValidationException {

        // Clear out the error list for the business object.
        getErrorList().clear();

        try {
            // Get hold of the current balance.
            BigDecimal balance =
                getDecimalProperty("currentBalance");

            // Validations for a checking account
            if (getProperty("type").equals("C")) {
                // Validate that the balance is above
                // the minimum allowed.
                if ((balance.compareTo(
                        new BigDecimal("100.00"))) == -1) {
                    errorList.addError("CHECKING_MIN_BALANCE",
                                        balance.toString());
                }
            }

            // Validations for a savings account
            if (getProperty("type").equals("S")) {

                // Validate that the balance is above
                // the minimum allowed.
                if ((balance.compareTo(new
                        BigDecimal("50.00"))) == -1) {
                    errorList.addError("SAVINGS_MIN_BALANCE",
                                        balance.toString());
                }
            }
        } catch (PropertyException pe) {
            errorList.addError("GEN_PROPERTY_ERROR",
                            pe.getMessage());
        }

        // Use the error list utility to automatically throw
        // an exception with the business errors if any
        // occurred.
        errorList.throwExceptionIfErrors();
    }
```

The Administration Pages

If an administrator logs on to the bank Web site, he or she sees a different screen and navigation bar than customers do. The administrator's home page was shown earlier in the role-based customization example. Administrators can enter either a customer number or an account number to access the administrative function for these entities. Thus, the admin navigation bar is implemented as a form to capture this input data. The admin functions available in the sample application are:

- Change a customer's PIN
- Update an account transaction log

All of the administrative pages are configured to be processed by a single action, AdminUserAction, as well as a single form bean, AdminForm. This was done for simplicity to isolate the administrative functions as well as to illustrate the flexibility in terms of designing the user interaction components.

Multiple Submit Buttons on a Form

The admin navigation bar actually is one HTML form with multiple submit buttons. So how does it distinguish between the different events? The submit buttons are given different names and then the existence of their parameter values is checked in the action class. Only one submit button can be clicked, so if one of the parameters has a value, you know that was the user event. The navigation bar JSP is shown here. The input fields both map to properties of the AdminForm bean:

```
<%@ taglib uri="/WEB-INF/struts-html.tld" prefix="html" %>


<table align="left" bgcolor="#c0c0c0" width="80%">
<html:form action="/struts/adminUser" >
<tr><td>Enter the Customer Number and Choose a
        Function</td></tr>
<tr><td>
<html:text property="customerNumber" size="10" maxlength="20"/>
</td></tr>
<tr><td>
<html:submit property="updatePINSubmit" value="Change PIN" />
</td></tr>
<tr><td>Enter the Account Number and Choose a
        Function</td></tr>
<tr><td>
<html:text property="accountNumber" size="10" maxlength="20"/>
</td></tr>
<tr><td>
<html:submit property="updateTransactionSubmit"
             value="Transaction Log" />
</td></tr>
</html:form>
</table>
```

The `AdminUserAction` is structured so that it determines the actual event and then uses a helper method to process the request.

BEST PRACTICE If multiple events are processed by the same action, as is the case with multiple submit buttons on a form, first determine the event that occurred using either the request URL or the submit button parameters. This type of logic should be isolated from the code that handles each event. The processing of each event can be broken out into a helper method.

`AdminUserAction` processes both the navigation events to get to the admin pages as well as the actual update form submissions. The control logic to distinguish between navigation events and update events is shown here. If neither submit button was clicked, that means this is an update form submission and the `determineEvent` helper method is used to get the event name from the last string token in the servlet context path. This is the same helper method that is used in the `NewCustomer-Action` class, which also processed multiple events based on the request URL:

```
/**
 * The Struts action interface
 */
public ActionForward perform(ActionMapping mapping,
                             ActionForm form,
                             HttpServletRequest request,
                             HttpServletResponse response)
    throws IOException, ServletException {

    // Create error bucket.
    ActionErrors errors = new ActionErrors();

    try {
        //
        // Check to see if this was a navigation bar event.
        //
        if (request.getParameter("updatePINSubmit")
                                        != null) {
            return processPINNavigation(mapping,form,
                                  request,response,errors);
        }
        if (request.getParameter("updateTransactionSubmit")
                                        != null) {
            return
                processTransactionNavigation(mapping,
                          form,request,response,errors);
        }

        //
        // Otherwise, this was an admin form submission.
        // Determine the event by the URL.
        //
        String event = determineEvent(request);
```

```
        // Process the event accordingly.
        if (event.equals("updatePIN")) {
            return (processUpdatePIN(mapping,form,
                            request,response,errors));
        }
        if (event.equals("updateTransactions")) {
            return (processUpdateTransactions(mapping,form,
                            request,response,errors));
        }
    } catch (BlfException be) {
        BlfStrutsConverter.convertErrorList(
                        be.getErrorList(),errors);
        saveErrors(request, errors);
        return (mapping.findForward("adminMain"));
    } catch (Exception e) {
        errors.add(ActionErrors.GLOBAL_ERROR,
                new ActionError("GENERAL_SERVICE_ERROR"));
        saveErrors(request, errors);
        return (mapping.findForward("adminMain"));
    }

    // If all else fails...
    return (mapping.findForward("adminMain"));
}
```

Update Form with Multiple Object Instances

The account transaction log page is particularly interesting because it is the first update form in the bank application that has multiple instances of the same object. In this case, a single form can have zero to many transaction objects. The administrator can update the transaction amount and description in order to make manual adjustments and correct mistakes. Remember that during the discussion of the User Interaction Architecture, the logic behind mapping HTML form parameters to multiple instances of the same object was discussed. Struts handles this situation by using indexed nested form beans. If you take the AccountForm bean, a collection member variable could be added and exposed as an indexed property. An indexed property has the following methods:

```
getProperty(int index);
setProperty(int index, Object value);
```

If you named the indexed property transaction, you would use the following nested syntax to refer to the description property of the first and second instance:

```
transaction[0].description
transaction[1].description
```

If you don't know the number of items ahead of time, as is the case with the transactions log, you need to dynamically generate the indices for each input tag within the

JSP. In the implementation of the transaction log page, the `AccountForm` bean is aggregated inside of `AdminForm`, the form bean used by the entire set of administrative pages. Thus, the nested syntax to refer to the description of the first transaction is as follows:

```
account.transaction[0].description
```

The relevant code from `AccountForm` is shown here:

```java
public class AccountForm extends ActionForm {
    private ArrayList transactions = new ArrayList();

    public TransactionForm getTransaction(int index) {
        return (TransactionForm) transactions.get(index);
    }

    public void setTransaction(int index,
                               TransactionForm transaction) {
        transactions.set(index,transaction);
    }

    public ArrayList getTransactions() {
        return transactions;
    }

    public void setTransactions(ArrayList list) {
        transactions = list;
    }
}
```

BEST PRACTICE Use aggregated, indexed form beans to manage forms with Struts that update multiple instances of the same object. Struts takes care of mapping request data to the corresponding form bean instance. The list of form beans can then easily be converted to value objects, or the form beans can be used as value objects themselves as input data for an update service.

The function used by the `AdminUserAction` to prepare for the page is as follows. It gets the account number from the form bean that the user entered and uses it to invoke the account detail service. Note that this is the same service used by the customer account detail page. The output data of this service is the account object followed by zero to many transaction objects. This collection of objects is converted to the aggregated form bean hierarchy and set in the session context so it is available to the `updateTransactions.jsp`:

```java
private ActionForward processTransactionNavigation(
        ActionMapping mapping,
        ActionForm form,
        HttpServletRequest request,
```

```
                    HttpServletResponse response,
                    ActionErrors errors)
        throws BlfException,RemoteException,RemoveException {

        // Get the transaction list.
        AdminForm adminForm = (AdminForm) form;
        String accountNumber = adminForm.getAccountNumber();
        ArgumentList argList = new ArgumentList();
        argList.setProperty("accountNumber",accountNumber);
        ServiceData sdata =
            new ServiceData("GetAccountDetail");
        sdata.setArgumentList(argList);

        // Invoke the application service.
        BlfService service =
            ServiceObjectFactory.getBlfService();
        sdata = service.executeService(sdata);
        service.remove();

        // Set context for the next page.
        // Map value objects to form beans.
        // 0 - account, 1-n transaction
        ArrayList transactionList = sdata.getOutputData();
        BlfStrutsConverter.convertValueObjToFormBean(
                    (ValueObject)transactionList.get(0),
                    adminForm.getAccount());
        transactionList.remove(0);
        Collection transactionFormBeanList =
            BlfStrutsConverter.convertValueObjsToFormBeans(
                    transactionList,new TransactionForm());
        adminForm.getAccount().setTransactions(
            (ArrayList)transactionFormBeanList);
        request.getSession(true).setAttribute("adminForm",
                                        adminForm);

        // Go to transaction log page.
        return (mapping.findForward(
                        "adminUpdateTransactions"));
    }
```

The updateTransactionsBody.jsp that uses the output data of the account
detail service is shown here. It uses Struts HTML tags to create input fields that correspond to each instance of the TransactionForm bean. The logic iteration tag is used
to drive the processing of each transaction. Nested property strings are created on each
loop to refer to the indexed transaction's properties. On the form submission, Struts
then takes care of mapping the input data to the AdminForm bean hierarchy containing the account and transaction objects:

```
<%@page import="bank.struts.AdminForm"%>
<%@ taglib uri="/WEB-INF/struts-html.tld"  prefix="html" %>
<%@ taglib uri="/WEB-INF/struts-bean.tld"  prefix="bean" %>
```

```
<%@ taglib uri="/WEB-INF/struts-logic.tld" prefix="logic" %>
<%@ taglib uri="/WEB-INF/blf.tld"           prefix="blf" %>


<table width="100%">
<tr align="center"><td><ul><html:errors/></td></tr>
</table>

<html:form action="/struts/adminUser/updateTransactions">

<table width=100% align=center>
<tr><td width=35%><B>Account: </B>
     <bean:write name="adminForm"
                 property="account.number" /></td>
   <td width=25%><B>Type: </B>
       <blf:lookupValue cache="AccountTypes"
                     value='<%=((AdminForm)
session.getAttribute("adminForm")).getAccount().getType()%>' />
   </td>
   <td width=40%><B>Current Balance: </B>
       <bean:write name="adminForm"
                   property="account.currentBalance" />
   </td>
</tr>
</table>

<hr noshade>

<table width=80% align=center>
<tr><td width=25%><B>Date</B></td>
   <td width=25%><B>Type</B></td>
   <td width=30%><B>Amount</B></td>
   <td width=20%><B>Description</B></td></tr>

<logic:iterate name="adminForm" property="account.transactions"
     id="data" indexId="indexVar" scope="session"
     type="bank.struts.TransactionForm" >
<%
   // Define nested property strings to be
   // used as attribute values of HTML tags.
   String amtStr =
     "account.transaction[" + indexVar + "].amount";
   String descStr =
     "account.transaction[" + indexVar + "].description";
   String idStr = "account.transaction[" + indexVar + "].id";
%>
<tr><td><%=data.getTransactionDate()%></td>
   <td><blf:lookupValue cache="TransactionTypes"
                     value='<%=data.getType()%>' /></td>
   <td><html:text property='<%=amtStr%>' /></td>
   <td><html:text property='<%=descStr%>' /></td></tr>
```

```
            <html:hidden property='<%=idStr%>' />
</logic:iterate>
</table>
<table width=100%>
<tr>
<td align="center"><html:submit property="submit"
                        value="Update Transaction Log"/></td>
</tr>
</table>

</html:form>
```

This page ends up looking something like Figure 9.9.

The code in `AdminUserAction` uses a new method on `BlfStrutsConverter` to convert the collection of `TransactionForm` beans to their corresponding `TransactionData` value objects. Note that this example can also be implemented easily by using `TransactionForm` as a value object as well. You can complete the implementation by extending `BaseFormBean`. However, this implementation shows a more complex mapping example between event objects and value objects. It still turns out to be fairly simple due to the `BlfStrutsConverter` utility. The slightly

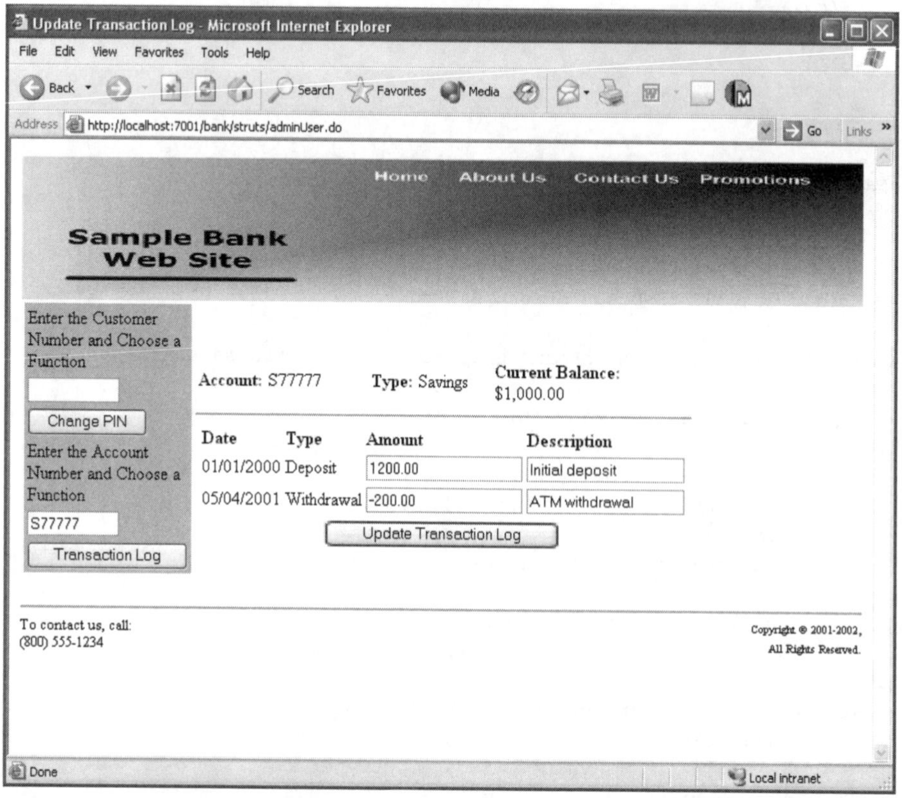

Figure 9.9 Update Transactions Log Page.

more complicated aspect is mapping the collection of value objects back into the form bean hierarchy due to the fact that the first element in the collection is the account value object. Another option would have been to implement the transaction value objects as aggregated within the account value object. This option could also possibly lead to a more automated conversion. Consequently, there are a number of options for how this could be implemented. In any case, once the form beans are converted to a collection of `TransactionData` objects, they are passed as input to an `Update-Transactions` service. If the service is successful, a confirmation message is added to the error list, and control is forwarded back to the transactions log page:

```
private ActionForward processUpdateTransactions(
        ActionMapping mapping,
        ActionForm form,
        HttpServletRequest request,
        HttpServletResponse response,
        ActionErrors errors)
    throws BlfException,RemoteException,RemoveException {

    // Create service data from the multiple
    // transaction objects on the form.
    ServiceData sdata =
        new ServiceData("UpdateTransactions");
    AdminForm adminForm = (AdminForm)form;
    ArrayList transactions =
        adminForm.getAccount().getTransactions();
    Iterator iter = transactions.iterator();
    sdata.setInputData(
        BlfStrutsConverter.convertFormBeansToValueObjs(
            transactions, new TransactionData()));

    // Invoke the application service.
    BlfService service =
        ServiceObjectFactory.getBlfService();
    sdata = service.executeService(sdata);
    service.remove();

    // Set context for the next page.
    // Map value objects to form bean:
    // 0 - account, 1-n transaction.
    ArrayList transactionList = sdata.getOutputData();
    BlfStrutsConverter.convertValueObjToFormBean(
                (ValueObject)transactionList.get(0),
                adminForm.getAccount());
    transactionList.remove(0);
    Collection transactionFormBeanList =
        BlfStrutsConverter.convertValueObjsToFormBeans(
                transactionList,new TransactionForm());
    adminForm.getAccount().setTransactions(
        (ArrayList)transactionFormBeanList);
    request.getSession(true).setAttribute("adminForm",
                                adminForm);
```

```
            // Add a confirmation message to inform the user
            // that the update was successful.
            errors.add(ActionErrors.GLOBAL_ERROR,
                new ActionError("TRANSACTION_LOG_CONFIRMATION"));
            saveErrors(request, errors);
            // Go to transaction log page.
            return (mapping.findForward(
                            "adminUpdateTransactions"));
    }
```

The UpdateTransactions service iterates through this collection and updates each entity with the new data. As it processes each transaction, it checks whether the amount was changed from the original amount. Any amount adjustments made on the update form are tallied in a running total that is used at the end of the service to update the current balance of the Account object itself. This service implementation uses the Entity Bean implementation of the business objects to make the updates:

```
public class UpdateTransactionsServiceImpl
    implements BlfServiceObject {

    public void doService(ServiceData serviceData)
        throws BlfException, RemoteException {

        // Keep track of any balance adjustments made
        // through this update.
        BigDecimal currentBalanceAdjustment =
            new BigDecimal(0);

        // Keep hold of the output data separately.
        ArrayList outputData = new ArrayList();

        // Remember the account ID.
        String accountId = null;

        // Get hold of the input value objects.
        Iterator iter = serviceData.getInputData().iterator();
        while (iter.hasNext()) {
            ValueObject data = (ValueObject) iter.next();

            // Use EJB BusinessObjectFactory to
            // locate component.
            TransactionLocal transaction = (TransactionLocal)
                EJBFactoryImpl.findByPrimaryKey("Transaction",
                                    data.getProperty("id"));

            // Calculate current adjustment value.
            BigDecimal oldAmount =
                transaction.getDecimalProperty("amount");
            BigDecimal newAmount =
                data.getDecimalProperty("amount");
```

```
        if (oldAmount.compareTo(newAmount) != 0) {
            currentBalanceAdjustment =
                currentBalanceAdjustment.add(
                        newAmount.subtract(oldAmount));
        }

        // Make the update.
        transaction.setProperty("amount",
                            data.getProperty("amount"));
        transaction.setProperty("description",
                        data.getProperty("description"));
        transaction.save();

        // Add each transaction to the output data.
        outputData.add(transaction.getValueObject());
        AccountLocal account = transaction.getAccount();
        accountId = account.getProperty("id");

    }

    // Adjust the current balance on the account.
    AccountLocal account = (AccountLocal)
      EJBFactoryImpl.findByPrimaryKey("Account",accountId);
    BigDecimal currentBalance =
        account.getDecimalProperty("currentBalance");
    currentBalance =
        currentBalance.add(currentBalanceAdjustment);
    account.setProperty("currentBalance",currentBalance);
    account.save();

    // Set the order of the output to be:
    // 0       Account
    // 1 - n   Transaction
    outputData.add(0,account.getValueObject());
    serviceData.setOutputData(outputData);
  }
}
```

Best Practices for Advanced Web Application Development

A summary of the best practices discussed in this chapter is given in this section.

Using Container-Managed Security Whenever Possible

Use J2EE security whenever possible to safely protect application resources. Container-managed security is portable across J2EE environments and integrates well with enterprise security architectures. Protecting Web-tier resources is critical because they are the entry point to the application. Consider the network security model and the trusted server concept when determining how many EJB tier resources you want explicitly secured using container-managed security. For application-specific requirements, both the servlet and EJB APIs offer programmatic access to user credentials.

Mapping EJB-Level Exceptions to Application-Defined Errors

Map EJB-level exceptions to application exceptions with defined business errors for user-friendly error messages. This approach also simplifies the client code because there is only one high-level application exception that needs to be handled. The application exception then always contains the list of errors. This is a variation on a best practice discussed earlier, which states that all system-level exceptions should be mapped to user-friendly messages. As is the case with `ObjectNotFoundException`, you can predefine certain application exception subclasses to map to defined business errors.

Implementing Actions with Multiple Events

If multiple events are processed by the same action, as is the case with multiple submit buttons on a form, first determine the event that occurred using either the request URL or the submit button parameters. This type of logic should be isolated from the code that handles each event. The actual processing of each event can be broken out into helper methods. This approach is a result of a best practice described earlier in the user interaction chapters, which states that user events should be abstracted and used to drive front-end processing.

Implementing Forms with Multiple Object Instances

Use aggregated, indexed form beans to manage forms with Struts that update multiple instances of the same object. Struts automatically maps request data to the corresponding form bean instance. The list of form beans can then easily be converted to value objects, or else the form beans can be used as value objects themselves as input data for an update service. To implement this in a JSP, you need to create the appropriate nested syntax string to refer to each property instance. This can be done within a loop structured using the Struts custom tag `<logic:iterate>`, which iterates over a collection of objects.

Summary

Application security is largely based on three concepts: authentication, authorization, and confidentiality. J2EE container-managed security has a number of benefits that should be considered. It provides a well-tested solution, portability across J2EE environments, and fairly easy integration with most enterprise security solutions.

Applications can also manage security directly, or they can use the servlet and EJB APIs to extend the basic security model provided by the container. One example of a combined approach is a scenario in which the container is used to integrate with authentication data and application-specific code is used to perform authorization. If possible, however, use J2EE security to enforce authorization against component resources, in particular Web-tier resources that are the entry point into the application. At some point in the architecture, network security models, firewalls, and the trusted server concept come into play; therefore, not all EJB-tier resources need to be explicitly secured using container-managed security.

This chapter covered concepts that can be used to strengthen your Web applications. Application security was covered using J2EE and a number of interesting design scenarios were discussed. These include Web pages with multiple events and object instances being triggered by the same HTML form. The examples in this chapter expanded on the architecture concepts and best practices that were discussed in earlier chapters. The next chapter looks at strengthening your applications from the perspective of performance.

CHAPTER 10

Performance

There is simply no way around the fact that the performance of any real-time Web application is critical to the success or failure of the product. Most user communities today are very unforgiving of applications with substantial page response times. Time is a valuable commodity in today's fast-paced Internet world, so performance is an essential aspect of user acceptance for any software product. Thus, it is critical that performance be considered from the beginning of the software development process. Now, there is a lot of common wisdom on this topic, particularly about the dangers of spending too much time up front on optimization. As in many things, the best answer is to take things in moderation and find a middle ground. Performance should be considered first at the architecture level and then at increasingly lower levels of detail as the iterative software development process continues. To begin, this chapter looks at the overall software development process and how performance engineering fits into the picture.

Overall Performance Approach

A basic development lifecycle with performance engineering integrated into the process is shown in Figure 10.1. Note that this process itself is often performed in an iterative manner that includes both prototypes and multiple production releases.

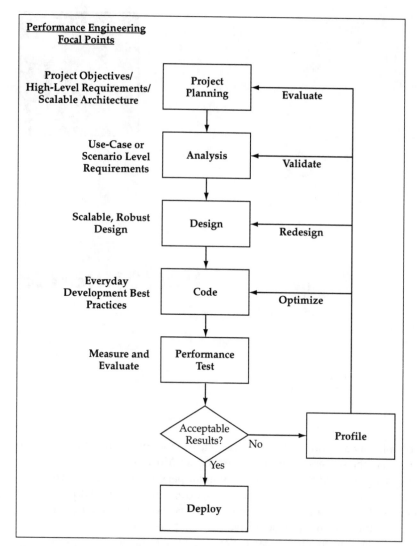

Figure 10.1 A Development Process with Performance Engineering.

It is no surprise to see that the corrective measures after an unacceptable performance test get increasingly more expensive and detrimental as you are required to go farther back in the process. Thus, it is very important to spend some initial time considering performance during the establishment of the overall software architecture. It is much easier to refactor portions of the application code than it is to change the underlying software architecture. As was alluded to earlier, there should still be a balance in terms of how much time and effort is spent on this topic, but the following guidelines usually hold true:

- A scalable, efficient architecture is a must for high-performance applications.
- Lower-level optimizations can always be done later.

As this chapter looks at performance both in the overall software development process and in J2EE technology, more clarity will be brought to these two important points. The next section takes a look at each of the development steps in a bit more detail from the perspective of performance.

Performance Engineering in the Development Process

At the beginning of a software development effort, one of the first steps is to determine the high-level objectives and requirements of the project. In addition to identifying the key functionality provided by the system, the project objectives can include such things as the flexibility of the system or the overall performance requirements. During this time, the overall system architecture is also being developed. For performance-intensive applications and projects with demanding requirements, a scalable architecture is an absolute must. Early architecture reviews cannot ignore the performance aspect of the system.

BEST PRACTICE A scalable, efficient architecture is essential for high-performance applications. Initial architecture reviews during the early stages of a project can be used to help benchmark and validate high-level performance requirements.

At this point, you are talking about the high-level software architecture including such things as component interaction, partitioning of functionality, and the use of frameworks and common design patterns. At this point you do not need to spend large amounts of effort or consideration on detailed optimizations such as the use of `StringBuffer` versus `String` or data caching down to the entity level. You are, however, still looking at high-level strategies such as the component implementation model, data caching strategies, and possibilities for asynchronous processing.

The creation of the basic software architecture at this point usually includes some kind of narrow but deep prototype, or proof-of-concept, which executes the communication through all of the layers and primary components of the architecture. This could include a user interface that retrieves data from the database and then sends an update all the way back through the architecture. Some basic load testing can occur at this point to obtain a ballpark estimate of transactions per second, page response time, or some other meaningful unit of measure that can help to frame the discussion on performance. This kind of data can be very helpful in terms of determining the validity of any high-level performance requirements that are being agreed upon during the project's early stages.

Once the individual use cases or scenarios of the system move into the analysis step, specific performance requirements often emerge for different functions and business processes. The analysis step allows you to apply the high-level project objectives against the specific functional requirements in order to derive these lower-level performance requirements for particular functions or pages.

Using the combination of the project objectives, functional requirements, and any case-specific performance requirements, the process moves into the design phase. It is important that performance be considered at this phase because in many cases, there are trade-offs that must be made between competing objectives on both the business and technical sides of the project. Planning for performance can sometimes require a give and take between business requirements, such as the overall flexibility of the system and technical constraints, such as adherence to pure object-oriented design techniques. Thus, you cannot ignore performance as a consideration during the design phase, yet at the same time, you should not let it drive every decision.

In the coding phase, the everyday coding best practices become a focal point that lead directly into the resulting quality of the product. At this point, common design patterns have been prototyped, optimized to the extent that they can be in limited-use situations, and are being applied to the application functionality. It is the responsibility of the development team to then follow any guidelines set forth, such as the aforementioned use of `StringBuffer` when a large amount of string concatenation is being done to avoid the creation of many small, temporary objects. These are the more minor things that, if done simply out of habit, can all add up to a robust set of application code and the best possible performance results. These types of things can also be caught during code reviews and used as a way to validate and communicate best practices to a development team.

In iterative software development, performance tests are typically run after significant intermediate iterations have been completed or before releases go into production. Testing tools are often used to generate a target number of simulated clients, and the results are measured, again resulting in a set of metrics such as average page response time and transactions per second. If the results are not satisfactory and the root causes are not immediately apparent, profiling tools can be used to determine where the trouble spots are in the code.

NOTE If your project or organization is on a small budget, there is a nice load-testing tool called OpenSTA available under a GPL (GNU General Public License) license that can be found at http://www.opensta.org. This tool is fairly easy to set up and use to run simulated load tests on Web applications. It may lack all of the features available within some commercial packaged solutions, but it provides almost all of the basic capabilities and reporting functions.

Even at the end of a development cycle, there are still many lower-level code optimizations that can be done, for example, additional data caching or the use of more efficient Java collections classes. However, major changes to the code involving the component implementation and interaction models are difficult to make unless a modular architecture has already been put in place. Likewise, if the architecture itself is not scalable or efficient for its purposes, you have an entire codebase that may be affected by changes sitting on top of it. If a commonly used pattern in the application is redesigned at this point, it likely has many incarnations across the codebase that need to be changed. Alternatively, if you are talking about something like moving components from Entity Beans to regular Java classes, the migration is much more difficult if you do not have a service layer isolating the business logic from the presentation layer. These types of changes can be costly at this point in the game. Similarly, changes to the application design can have a significant effect. For example, you may have made much of the business logic of the application configurable through database tables in order to meet a project objective of flexibility. A potential resulting effect of this, in terms of performance, is that the application becomes terribly slow due to the extensive database I/O throughout each transaction. A change to this aspect of the design, such as moving more of the logic back into the application code, could very easily affect the overall flexibility. Now, the role of architecture in this project is not only to provide an efficient foundation to implement these designs but also to allow for a mitigation plan. If you have wrapped access to the configuration data and isolated it to a set of objects, you may be able to cache the data in memory and easily speed up the performance of the application. You may also need to build in a refresh mechanism based on the requirements. In terms of implementing this type of change, it is much less painful to go back and recode a wrapper class than it is to update every business component that used the configuration data. In fact, the foundation logic for the business objects followed this same pattern through the use of the `MetadataManager` and `CacheList` components.

As a last resort, there may be a need to go back and review the specific performance requirements and possibly even validate that the project objectives are in line with what can realistically be done to provide the most value to the user community. To avoid having to go through this, the time and effort spent on performance can be spread a bit more evenly throughout the life of the project in order to mitigate, measure, and meet the performance requirements spelled out for your application.

Measuring Performance

Fully evaluating the performance capabilities and capacity of an application often requires the use of different metrics and different perspectives. Initially, it is usually best to put the focus at the transaction level and measure the individual transaction time or page response time. As the development process continues, the focus expands to include measurements of the transaction throughput, the ability to support concurrent users, and the overall scalability of the application. One of the main challenges in terms of performance in application development is to try to balance these vantage points.

Individual Transaction Response Time

During the early prototyping stages, the first question to ask is, "How fast can I push a single transaction through the system?" This is easy to test, requiring only a simple client program with a timer, yet it provides the basic unit of measure upon which the vast majority of performance metrics will be based. The result of a load test or sizing exercise is usually a multiple of the processing speed of each individual unit of work. Thus, the first area of focus is the basic patterns and architecture components exercised by some basic transactions. If you create efficient patterns going through the core of the user interface and business component models, these basic transactions can be optimized and used as a foundation for the application. Keep in mind, however, that your work does not end here because the next perspective may impact some of the strategies chosen during this first exercise.

Transaction Throughput and Scalability

The second aspect of performance that you want to measure takes the area of focus up a level to the behavior of the application operating under a heavy user load. Scalability is one of the main concerns here that can potentially impact some of the optimizations you want to perform at the individual transaction level. The J2EE component architecture provides a foundation for highly scalable and available applications on which to base your approach. However, there are a couple of things to keep in mind, primarily the memory consumption of the application and the size of the user HttpSession object. As an example, you may have a blazing fast page response time for a single user, but that may have been enabled by storing an entire result set from the database in the HttpSession. Subsequent page requests can then page through the data without having to go back to the database. If you are in this situation with a large data set, however, you may be able to get only a handful of concurrent users on an individual box because of the memory footprint involved with the application components.

As you look at the transaction throughput with various concurrent user levels, you also want to ask the question, "Does the system performance degrade as I add concurrent users and transactions?" You hope not, as you would like to see a linear response time as you add concurrent users to an application. Once you have hit the maximum number of users by pushing the current hardware to its limit, you would then like to see a linear response time as you add additional hardware. This type of scalability is made possible through the clustering and load balancing of the application components on the Web and EJB tiers. It enables you to add additional hardware and create redundant instances of the application server to meet the demands of your application. The value of the EJB component model is that it provides a standard method of building components to plug into a container and automatically take advantage of these infrastructure services.

Object Instantiation, Garbage Collection, and Scalability

In the Java language, there is also another aspect of code running in a JVM that affects the ideal of linear response time. There are actually two performance hits incurred by the JVM, both associated with instantiating an object in Java:

1. The initial cost of allocating memory to create the object
2. The secondary cost of tracking the object and later running it through the garbage collection (GC) process, potentially multiple times, until it is eventually destroyed and the memory is freed up for other use

Every object that is created in your code must later be checked by the JVM to see if it is being used by another object. This must be done before it can be freed and the memory reallocated for other use. The more objects that are created, the longer this garbage collection process takes, and the less free memory that is available, which then leads to the garbage collection process running more often. You can easily see how this can create a downward spiral that quickly degrades both the transaction throughput and the individual response times.

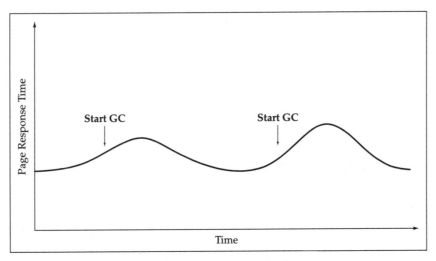

Figure 10.2   Theoretical Response Time with a Single JVM.

NOTE To quickly see the effects of garbage collection, use the `-verbose:gc` JVM flag. This causes the JVM to write information to the output log showing the time spent in GC, memory used, and memory freed each time GC is run.

The problem of the downward spiral is magnified if only one JVM is being used because transactions can continue to become backlogged until they eventually start to time out or reach completely unacceptable levels. Figure 10.2 shows a graph to represent the effects of garbage collection on response time for a single JVM under a heavy transaction load.

The secondary cost of object instantiation also prevents you from simply applying the tempting cure of adding more memory to the heap. With a larger heap size, the garbage collection process can become even more cumbersome to manage and then takes away valuable computing cycles that could be used for processing user transactions. Thus, adding more memory works to an extent, but at some point, it may have a marginally negative effect. Once again, the clustering and load-balancing capabilities of the J2EE application server come to the rescue to provide the scalability you need to help maintain a relatively even response time. Because requests are distributed across a cluster of application server instances, you can typically avoid having to use the JVMs that are garbage collecting to process the current transaction. The load-balancing algorithm, of course, is usually not tied directly into the GC status of the JVM, but it does use the law of averages and probabilities to work in your favor. What the clustering also allows you to do is to use a moderately sized memory heap for each JVM instance so that you can find the optimal setting for your application. Tuning this JVM parameter can often have a meaningful affect on the overall performance of an application. Usually it takes a number of trial and error load tests in order to determine the optimal settings for the heap size, although a few general guidelines include setting the minimum size to be half of the maximum size, which usually does not exceed 512 MB. The

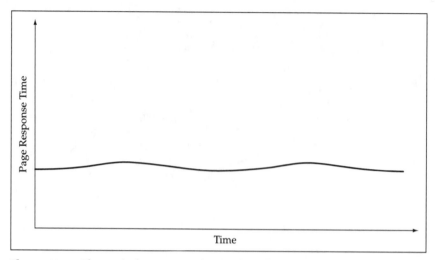

Figure 10.3   Theoretical Response Time with Multiple JVMs.

net result of all of this is a much more even response time and consistent transaction throughput as concurrent user levels increase. Figure 10.3 shows what an improved response time might be for an application clustered across multiple JVMs. Barring other extraneous factors, some minor blips in the curve still appear due to the occasional time periods when a number of the JVMs happen to be collecting garbage at the same time. This is largely unavoidable, but it has a much smaller effect on the overall response curve than in the scenario with a single JVM.

ECperf—An EJB Performance Benchmark

Another performance metric you can use is the ECperf benchmark created through the Java Community Process that is now a part of the J2EE suite of technologies. Its goal is to provide a standard benchmark for the scalability and performance of J2EE application servers and, in particular, the Enterprise JavaBean aspect that serves as the foundation for middle-tier business logic. The focus of the ECperf specification is not the presentation layer or database performance; these aspects are covered by other measures such as the series of TPC benchmarks. The focus of the ECperf tests is to test all aspects of the EJB component architecture including:

- Distributed components and transactions
- High availability and scalability
- Object persistence
- Security and role-based authentication
- Messaging, asynchronous processing, and legacy application integration

The software used for the test is intended to be a nontrivial, real-world example that executes both internal and external business processes, yet it has an understandable workflow that can be consistently executed in a reasonable amount of time. Four business domains are modeled in the ECperf 1.1 specification as part of a worldwide business case for the tests:

- Manufacturing
- Supplier
- Customer
- Corporate

A number of transactions are defined for each of the domains, each of which is given a method signature to be used by an EJB component in the test. These transactions include such things as `ScheduleWorkOrder` and `CreateLargeOrder` in the manufacturing domain, as well as `NewOrder` and `GetOrderStatus` in the customer domain. Subsequently, two applications are built using these domains. The first is an `OrderEntry Application` that acts on behalf of customers who enter orders, makes changes to them, and can check on their status. The second is a `Manufacturing Application` that manages work orders and production output. The throughput benchmarks are then determined by the activity of these two applications on the system being tested. Reference beans are given for the test, and Entity Beans can be run using either BMP or CMP. The only code changes allowed are for porting BMP code according to regulations set forth in the specification. Deployment descriptors for all of the beans must be used as they are given in order to standardize the transactional behavior as well as the rest of the deployment settings. The reference implementation of these transactions uses stateless and stateful Session Beans as a front to Entity Beans, although the ratio of components is fairly heavily weighted toward Entity Beans.

The primary metric used to capture the result is defined using the term BBops/min, which is the standard for benchmark business operations per minute. This definition includes the number of customer domain transactions plus the number of workorders completed in the manufacturing domain over the given time intervals. This metric must be expressed within either a standard or distributed deployment. In the standard, or centralized deployment, the same application server deployment can be used for all of the domains and can talk to a single database instance containing all of the tables. The distributed version requires separate deployments and different database instances. These two measurements are thus reported as `BBops/min@std` or `BBops/min@Dist`, respectively. For either of these measurements, there is a very helpful aspect built into the specification for technology decision makers, the measure of performance against price, that is, `$ per BBops/min@std`, also commonly referred to as Price/BBops.

The ECperf 1.1 specification also announced that it will be repackaged as SPECjAppServer2001 and reported by the Standard Performance Evaluation Corporation (http://www.spec.org). SPECjAppServer2001 will cover J2EE 1.2 application servers while SPECjAppServer2002 will cover J2EE 1.3 application servers. A good "apples-to-apples" comparison of application servers like this has been a long time coming. The Sun Web site currently refers you to http://ecperf.theserverside.com/ecperf/ for published results. To give you a ballpark idea, there are currently a couple posted results over 16,000 `BBops/min@std` for under $20/BBops.

Performance in J2EE Applications

This section takes a look at various techniques you can use to optimize the architecture, design, and code within your J2EE applications. As a first step, there are key aspects within all Java programs that need to be addressed for their potential impact on application performance. Additionally, there are various performance characteristics associated with J2EE components and technologies that are worth noting. Many solutions involve using enterprise Java services whenever they provide the most benefit, but not as a standard across the board. Using the enterprise components across the board from front to back in the software architecture is a common tendency in building J2EE architectures. A key example of this is the use of Entity Beans. Relatively speaking, Entity Beans are fairly heavyweight components, and thus should not be used to model every business object in an application, particularly if each Entity Bean maps to a row in the database. Doing this can quickly degrade the scalability, and thus the usability, of an application. This goes back to one of the main points, that a scalable architecture is a must for almost any system, and design guidelines must be applied when deciding on the foundation for software components as well as in building the individual components themselves.

Core Aspects of Java Application Performance

Two significant performance aspects to consider for almost all applications are:

- Object instantiation and garbage collection
- Disk and database I/O

Object Instantiation

A key point to take away from the earlier discussion regarding object instantiation and garbage collection is that, to some degree, objects should be instantiated wisely. Each new version of the JVM has seen significant gains in the efficiency of the garbage collection process, but if you can reasonably limit or delay the creation of objects, you can help yourself greatly in terms of performance. This is especially true for larger components that usually encompass the instantiation of many objects. Of course, this does not mean you should go back to doing pure procedural software development and put all of your logic in a single `main` method. This is where performance as a design consideration comes into play. You don't want to sacrifice the potential for reusability and flexibility through solid object-oriented design; thus, you don't let performance drive all of your decisions. Nonetheless, keep it in the back of your mind. And if you aren't quite sure of a potential impact, you can use an abstraction or design pattern to mitigate the concern by providing an escape route to take later. This means that if you have isolated an architecture layer or encapsulated a certain function, it can be changed in one place without great cost or side effects to the remainder of the application.

To maximize the efficiency of time spent considering performance in the design process, consider the following approach. Rather than look at every object in the entire object model, perhaps spend some time concentrating on the two extremes in your implementation: the extremely large objects and components and the extremely small objects. For obvious reasons, large objects and components rapidly increase the memory footprint and can affect the scalability of an application. In the case of larger components, they often spawn the creation of many smaller objects as well. Consider now the case of the very small object, such as the intermediate strings created by the following line of code:

```
String result = value1 + value2 + value3 + value4;
```

This is a commonly referenced example in which, because `String` objects are immutable, you find out that `value1` and `value2` are concatenated to form an intermediate `String` object, which is then concatenated to `value3`, and so on until the final `String` result is created. Even if these strings are only a few characters in size, consider now that each of these small `String` objects has a relatively equal impact on your secondary cost consideration, the object tracking and garbage collection process. An object is still an object, no matter what the size, and the JVM needs to track all of the other objects that reference this one before it can be freed and taken off of the garbage collection list. Thus, all of those little objects, although they do not significantly impact the memory footprint, have an equal effect on slowing down the garbage collection process as it runs periodically throughout the life of the application. For this reason, you want to look at places in the application where lots of small objects are created in order to see if there are other options that can be considered.

In the study of business object components, the concept of lazy instantiation, which delays the creation of an aggregated object until it is requested, was discussed. If strict encapsulation is used where even private methods used a standard `get<Object>` method, you can delay the instantiation of the object until it is truly necessary. This concept is particularly important for value objects or other objects used as data transport across a network. This practice minimizes the amount of RMI serialization overhead as well as reducing network traffic.

BEST PRACTICE Use lazy instantiation to delay object creation until necessary. Pay particular attention to objects that are serialized and sent over RMI.

Another common use of this concept can be put into practice when lists of objects are used. In many application transactions, a query is executed and a subset of the resulting objects is dealt with in a transactional manner. This concept is particularly important if the business object components are implemented as Entity Beans. For a collection of size n, as was discussed in the Business Object Architecture chapter, the potential exists for the (n + 1) Entity Bean finder problem, which results in additional database lookups that can be accomplished with a single JDBC query. However, you also want to consider the characteristics of Entity Beans and their effect on the container's performance. Although Entity Beans are fairly heavyweight components, the optimized transaction model is fairly efficient because Entity Bean instances are pooled and shared by the container for different client transactions. However, once an Entity Bean instance is pulled into a client transaction, it cannot be shared by another client until either the transaction ends or the container passivates the state of that instance for future use. This passivation comes at a cost and additional complexity because the container must activate the instance once again to complete the transaction later in a reliable, safe manner. Considering that the Entity Bean components have a relatively large fixed cost and that there may be many different types in a complex application, you want to size the component pools appropriately and find a balance between resource consumption and large amounts of activation and passivation that can slow down the application server. With all of this being said, if you can avoid using an Entity Bean for pure data retrieval, it is worth doing it. Perhaps not for that individual transaction, but it will aid the scalability and throughput of the overall application under a heavy user load. This comes back to the analysis of performance measurement that first starts at the individual transaction level, but then has to consider the effect on the overall application performance.

This concept is also in line with the idea of using business objects only for transactional updates as opposed to requiring that they be used for data retrieval as well. Thus, if your application deals with a collection of objects, it is perhaps best to first run the query using JDBC, similar to the `ObjectList` utility class. You can then iterate through the collection and instantiate or look up the Entity Bean equivalents when you want to perform a transaction update on a given instance. In the cases in which you do not update the entire collection, you can gain the greatest benefit from this technique. The database lookups for an n size collection are then somewhere between 1 and $(n + 1)$, depending on the particular circumstances of the transaction. You can also compare this to an aggressive-loading Entity Bean strategy that theoretically limits you to a single database query but then has the overall cost associated with using a significant portion of the free instance pool. In other words, you sacrifice the overall transaction throughput for the benefit of the individual transaction in a heavy user load setting. Note that if the transaction volume is quite sporadic for a given application, an aggressive-loading strategy for Entity Beans may be the better solution because the assumption of fewer concurrent transactions is made; thus the cross-user impact is limited.

Disk and Database I/O

Often, the first thing to look at when tuning an application is the amount of database and disk I/O because of its relative cost compared to regular computational cycles. Thus, look to minimize the amount of database calls and file read/writes in your application. The first strategy to do this is usually to analyze the access patterns and identify redundant or unnecessary database access. In many cases, a significant benefit can be derived from performing this step at the design review and code review stages of a project. Eventually, your application approaches the minimum level of access required, and then you need to look to other techniques to make further improvements, which is where data caching comes into play.

Data caching commonly refers to storing application data in the memory of the JVM, although in general terms, it could also involve storing the data somewhere closer to the client or in a less costly place than the original source. In a sense, you can refer to data stored in the `HttpSession` of a Web application as being cached if you are not required to go through an EJB component and to the application database to get it. In practice, the `HttpSession` could be implemented by the container through in-memory replication or persistent storage to a separate database, although, in both cases, the access time to get to the data is likely less than it would be to go to the definitive source. Now, of course, the definitive source is just that, and you need to be able to refresh the cache with the updated data if it changes and your application requirements dictate the need, which is often the case. In the Business Object Architecture chapter, a solution for this issue was looked at in the J2EE architecture using JMS as a notification mechanism for caches living within each of the distributed, redundant application server instances. Remember that even this approach has a minor lag time between the update of the definitive source and the notification message being processed by each of the caches. This may still not be acceptable for some mission-critical applications; however it does fit the needs of many application requirements.

The reference architecture uses an XML configuration file for application metadata, and many applications use a set of configuration values coming from a properties file. This type of data is a perfect candidate for caching because it does not change frequently and may not even require a refresh mechanism because changes to this data often require a redeployment of the application.

The use of Entity Beans to cache data should also be addressed here. Whereas Session Beans are used to deal with the state of a particular client at a time, Entity Beans represent an instance of a persistent object across all clients. So how much can you rely on Entity Beans to help with caching? Unfortunately, the benefit is not as great as one might think. Although an instance of an Entity Bean can be shared across clients, the same issue of updates to the definitive source applies here. If you deploy your EJB components to a single instance of an application server, then you can, in fact, take full advantage of this caching. However, most significant deployments wish to use the clustering and load-balancing features of the application servers, so multiple instances are deployed and the cached Entity Bean must consider the possibility of updates by another copy of that Entity Bean in another instance. Thus, in a clustered environment, the `ejbLoad` method must always be invoked at the beginning of a transaction to load the current state and ensure data integrity.

Object Caching

The concept of caching can also be applied to objects that are relatively expensive to instantiate. In a J2EE environment, this can include such objects as the JNDI Initial Context and the EJB Home interfaces. In your own application, you may also have complex components or objects that are expensive to instantiate. Some examples of this might be classes that make use of BeanShell scripts or other external resources that involve I/O, parsing, or other relatively expensive operations. You may want to cache instances of these objects rather than instantiate new ones every time if one of the following requirements can be met:

- Objects can be made thread-safe for access by multiple concurrent clients.
- Objects have an efficient way to clone themselves.

JNDI Objects

Relatively speaking, the JNDI operations can be somewhat expensive for an application. The creation of a `InitialContext` and the subsequent lookups for EJB Home interfaces should be looked at as a performance consideration. If your application does not use a large number of EJB, this may not be worth any further thought. For example, if your business logic is encompassed within Session Beans and you typically have only one EJB lookup in a transaction, it may not be worth the trouble to try and optimize this step. However, if you have a large number of Entity Beans used within a given transaction, it can make a noticeable difference if you can avoid the creation of an `InitialContext` and subsequent JNDI lookup for each component. Caching the JNDI objects should be used with caution, as there are a number of potential impacts to consider. The `InitialContext` object can be created once, such as on the Web tier in the controller servlet's `init` method, and then used for all client requests rather than a new one created for each individual request. In a set of tests with heavy user loads, a single shared `InitialContext` instance did not present any problems; however, you should thoroughly test in your target environment to become comfortable with the approach.

Before looking at the `EJBFactoryImpl` code for an implementation of this solution, you should also consider caching the EJB Home interface objects. This technique can also provide a performance boost in some cases but should be used only after careful consideration. Many application servers provide a Home interface that is aware of the available, redundant application server instances. However, ensure that this is the case for your environment before using this technique. If you are going to reuse an existing Home interface, you don't want one that pins you to a given instance, or you will lose all of your load-balancing and failover capabilities. The other aspect to consider of reusing the Home interface is that problems can result if one or more of the application server instances are brought up or down. A Home interface may become "stale" if the EJB server is restarted, and if instances are added or removed from the cluster, the existing home interface is likely not to be aware of this. In this sense, there also needs to be a refresh capability for the Home interface cache unless it is acceptable to restart the Web tier, or other such client tier, when a change is made to the EJB server configuration. This is likely to be a manual process unless a programmatic management capability can be introduced into the application.

Here are the relevant portions of `EJBFactoryImpl` that use a cached `Initial-Context` and cached collection of EJB Home interfaces keyed by the object name. In the examples in this book, this class is always used in the context of an EJB tier underneath a service component deployed as a Session Bean. Thus, note that the `InitialContext` is created without any properties in a static initialization block. In order to be used by remote clients, this class would need to be modified to pass in the provider URL and context factory, but you can see the basic idea from this example. Each time the `findByPrimaryKey` method is invoked, the helper method `getHomeInterface`, which first looks in a collection of Home interfaces to see if the interface was already created and cached, is called. If it is not there, then it is created and stored for future use. This implementation uses a lazy-instantiation approach in which the first time through is a bit slower and then subsequent requests benefit from the performance improvements. Alternatively, this initial cost could be incurred at server startup time:

```java
public class EJBFactoryImpl extends BusinessObjectFactory {

    // Cached initial context
    private static InitialContext jndiContext;

    // Cached set of home interfaces keyed by JNDI name
    private static HashMap homeInterfaces;

    static {
        try {
            // Initialize the context.
            jndiContext = new InitialContext();

            // Initialize the home interface cache.
            homeInterfaces = new HashMap();

        } catch (NamingException ne) {
            ne.printStackTrace();
        }
    }

    /**
     * Helper method to get the EJBHome interface
     */
    private static EJBHome getHomeInterface(String objectName,
                                    BusinessObjectMetadata bom)
        throws BlfException {

        EJBHome home = null;

        try {
            // Check to see if you have already cached this
            // Home interface.
            if (homeInterfaces.containsKey(objectName)) {
                return (EJBHome)
                    homeInterfaces.get(objectName);
            }

            // Get a reference to the bean.
            Object ref = jndiContext.lookup(objectName);

            // Get hold of the Home class.
            Class homeClass =
                Class.forName(bom.getEJBHomeClass());

            // Get a reference from this to the
            // Bean's Home interface.
```

```
        home = (EJBHome)
            PortableRemoteObject.narrow(ref, homeClass);

        // Cache this Home interface.
        homeInterfaces.put(objectName,home);

    } catch (Exception e) {
        throw new BlfException(e.getMessage());
    }

    return home;
}

/*
 * Discover an instance of a business object with the
 * given key object.
 */
public static Object findByPrimaryKey(String objectName,
                                        Object keyObject)
    throws BlfException {

    // Obtain the business object metadata.
    BusinessObjectMetadata bom =
        MetadataManager.getBusinessObject(objectName);

    // Get the Home interface.
    EJBHome home = getHomeInterface(objectName, bom);

    //
    // Use the Home interface to invoke the finder method...
    //
}
}
```

BEST PRACTICE For increased performance in applications that use a large number of Entity Beans, consider caching the JNDI `InitialContext` and EJB Home interfaces. This optimization should be encapsulated within the EJB business object factory so there is no effect on business object client code. Many application servers provide a Home interface that is aware of the available, redundant application server instances. However, ensure that this is the case for your environment before using this technique so you don't lose the load-balancing and failover capabilities of the application server.

Entity Beans

Many of the performance characteristics of Entity Beans have already been covered. Although they are fairly heavyweight components, the container pools instances of them, and the regular transaction model can be quite efficient. However, you can get into trouble when the container is forced to perform large amounts of activation and passivation that can occur under heavy, concurrent usage. There are a number of other things to keep in mind. For example, when using remote interfaces, you want to minimize the amount of remote method invocation and RMI overhead. Thus, you use value objects to communicate data to the Entity Bean. You also want to avoid iterating through collections of Entity Beans through finder methods unless you can mitigate the risks of the $(n + 1)$ database lookup problem.

If you are using a Session Bean layer as a front to Entity Beans, similar to the reference architecture and the services layer, you should use local interfaces to access your Entity Beans. This avoids the overhead of RMI and remote method invocations. This forces you to colocate all related Entity Beans in a transaction in a given application server deployment, although this usually does not cause much of a problem unless you have a truly distributed architecture. In many cases, all of the beans are running in a standard centralized deployment for performance reasons and you can do this with ease. At this point, the biggest overhead left for each Entity Bean is the JNDI lookup to access the local interface, and there are options to address this given the earlier discussion of JNDI and object caching.

In many cases, Container-Managed Persistence (CMP) provides the best option in terms of performance for Entity Bean persistence. Bean-Managed Persistence (BMP) does suffer from a serious performance flaw in that a single lookup of an Entity Bean can actually cause two database hits. This problem is similar to the $(n + 1)$ problem if considered for a collection of one. The container needs to look up the bean using the primary key after a Home interface method is invoked. Once the component is located and a business method is invoked from the remote or local interface, the `ejbLoad` method, which typically uses application JDBC code to select the remainder of the properties from the database, is called by the container. In the container-managed approach, the container can optimize these steps into one database call. This is a serious consideration for using BMP in your Entity Beans. There are also many other cases in which the container can optimize how persistence is implemented, such as checking for modified fields before executing `ejbStore`. Finally, a major benefit of using Entity Beans is the object persistence service, so carefully consider the benefits of using BMP before taking this approach.

Another factor that can affect the performance of Entity Beans is the transaction isolation setting. The safest option is `TRANSACTION_SERIALIZABLE`, but it is not surprisingly the most expensive. Use the lowest level of isolation that implements the safety required by the application requirements. In many cases, `TRANSACTION_READ_COMMITTED` provides a sufficient level of isolation in that only committed data is accessible by other beans. Transactions should also be kept to the smallest scope possible. However, this can sometimes be difficult to implement using container-managed transactions because you can give each method only a single transaction setting for the entire deployment. Often, methods are used across different contexts in an application, and you would like the setting to be different in various situations. For this, you need to use bean-managed transactions and control this aspect yourself. However, a nice benefit of the Session Bean to Entity Bean pattern is that Entity Beans are usually invoked within a transaction initiated by the Session Bean. In this case, a transaction setting of `TX_SUPPORTS` works in most cases because a transaction will have already been initiated if need be.

Session Beans

Stateless Session Beans are the most efficient type of Enterprise JavaBean. Because the beans are stateless, the container can use a single instance across multiple client threads; thus, there is a minimal cost to using a stateless Session Bean both for the individual transaction and the overall application scalability. Remember that this is not always the case with Entity Beans due to the potential for activation and passivation. The container implementation also has the option to pool instances of stateless Session Beans for maximum efficiency.

A stateful Session Bean is particular to the client that created it. Thus, there is a fixed cost for the individual transaction that uses a stateful Session Bean. Stateful Session Beans are sometimes used as an interface to a remote client that maintains some state about the application. In a Web application, this type of state can usually be stored in the HttpSession, although stateful Session Beans are particularly helpful for thick-client Swing front ends. Note that it is important that the client call the remove method on the stateful Session Bean when it is done; otherwise the container will passivate it for future use, and this adds to its overall overhead.

BEST PRACTICE Be sure to remove instances of stateful Session Beans to avoid unnecessary container overhead and processing.

One thing to note is that some J2EE containers, particularly earlier versions, do not support failover with stateful Session Beans, although the major containers are now doing this. Make sure this is the case in your environment if this is a factor for consideration in your application.

XML

If an application does a large amount of XML parsing, it is important to look at the parsing method being used to do it. Two of the basic parsing options are the Document Object Model (DOM) and the Simple API for XML (SAX). DOM parsers require much more overhead because they parse an entire XML document at once and create an in-memory object representation of the XML tree. This is helpful if the program requires either significant manipulation or the creation of XML documents. However, if your application simply needs to parse through a document once and deal with the data right away, the SAX parser is much more efficient. It reads through a document once and invokes hook methods to process each tag that it comes across in the document. A document handler is written specifically for the application. It is a little more complicated to write because the hook methods are called without much of the XML tag context, such as the name of the parent tag. Thus, it requires the developer to maintain some state in order to correctly process the document if it contains any nested tags. However, the difference in speed can be noticeable for large documents. The reasoning for this goes back to the initial discussion on object creation and garbage collection. A DOM parser creates a large number of objects underneath the covers. The actual number of objects created is a factor of the number of XML nodes because objects are created for each attribute and text node of each element.

Many applications that use XML as a messaging or communications framework will want to manipulate the data in a regular Java object format. There are binding frameworks such as the Java API for XML Binding (JAXB) that can be used to generate classes that can both extract their data from XML and write out their state as XML. These classes can be quite efficient because they know exactly where in the XML their properties belong and thus can avoid some of the overhead of a generic parsing API. These binding packages create a very powerful framework for exchanging data and dealing with it on both sides of a business service or process.

BEST PRACTICE If you use XML extensively throughout your application and performance is a concern, choose the most efficient parsing method available to you that meets your requirements. DOM parsers are usually the slowest due to the large number of objects instantiated underneath the covers and their generic nature. If your application simply needs to parse through a document once and deal with the data right away, the SAX parser is much more efficient. Binding frameworks such as JAXB will also be more efficient because they know exactly what they are looking for in the XML or what XML tags they need to create. These types of frameworks are also helpful because they use XML as a data transport but allow programs to access the data through objects.

Asynchronous Processing

Asynchronous processing is a strategy that can be used in certain circumstances to alleviate performance concerns. There are a limited number of situations for which this approach can be used; however, in the cases in which it is applicable, it can make a noticeable difference. Executing processes in parallel can be considered if any of the following conditions exist:

- Semi-real-time updates fit within the application requirements.
- There are a number of independent external applications to invoke.
- Application data and the relevant units-of-work can be partitioned.

Asynchronous processing can also be used to provide the benefit of perceived performance. For example, if a Web page is waiting on a response from a lengthy transaction, you may want to display the next page prior to the completion of the overall process to give the user the ability to continue work, thus increasing the perceived performance of the application. The next page might include a confirmation message, some intermediate or partial results, or else just a message informing users that they will be notified upon completion of the process, perhaps by email.

For a parallel processing approach to be effective, each asynchronous process needs to be significantly big enough to make the light overhead of a messaging framework, such as JMS, worth the benefit. One interesting thing to note about the J2EE environment is that JMS and Message-Driven EJBs are the only mechanisms provided to perform asynchronous processing. Strictly speaking, the EJB specification prohibits applications from managing their own threads. This makes sense when you think about the responsibilities of an application server. It is managing multiple threads for different types of components, and in order to effectively maximize performance and resource utilization, it requires control of the threads being run on a given machine. Thus, an application component cannot explicitly start a new thread in an object.

However, the Java Message Service provides a mechanism that goes through the container to invoke and start other threads. A message can be sent asynchronously from a client and a component that receives that message can process it in parallel with the execution of the original thread. This strategy is quite easy with the EJB 2.0 specification that provides a third type of Enterprise Bean, the Message-Driven Bean. This is an EJB component that is invoked when a particular type of JMS message is received. Thus, for asynchronous processing, a client can send a JMS message and a defined Message-Driven Bean can be used as a wrapper to invoke additional functionality in parallel.

BEST PRACTICE Consider the use of asynchronous processing to alleviate performance concerns in applications with semi-real-time updates, multiple external applications that can be invoked in parallel, or work that can be partitioned into segments. Use Message-Driven Beans and JMS to implement parallel processing in a J2EE container. Asynchronous processing can also be used to increase the perceived performance of an application.

The Web Tier

JavaServer Pages and servlets are extremely efficient in that they are multithreaded components with a very small amount of overhead. These components provide very useful APIs and functions without causing much of an impact to the performance of the application. Unlike EJBs, little or no thought is required in order to use either of these components with regard to performance. The exception to this rule is of course the use of `HttpSession`, something that was alluded to numerous times throughout this book. This state maintenance option can impact the scalability and throughput of an application, so careful attention does need to be paid to its use. Nonetheless, the front end of the J2EE platform provides a very efficient, robust architecture for implementing high-quality Web applications.

Best Practices for J2EE Performance Engineering

A summary of the performance best practices is given in this section.

Considering Performance throughout the Development Process

A scalable, efficient architecture is essential for high-performance applications. Initial architecture reviews during the early stages of a project can be used to help benchmark and validate high-level performance requirements. Lower-level optimizations can be done later in the process. In general, spread the time spent on performance engineering throughout the process rather than wait until the week prior to deployment to run a load test. Remember that performance problems uncovered later in the process become increasingly more expensive to resolve.

Minimizing Object Instantiation Whenever Possible

Use lazy instantiation to delay object creation until necessary. Pay particular attention to objects that are serialized and sent over RMI. If you are invoking a remote Session Bean, try to send only the object data that is required for the component method.

Caching EJB Home Interfaces

For increased performance in applications that use a large number of Entity Beans, consider caching the JNDI `InitialContext` and EJB Home interfaces. This optimization should be encapsulated within the EJB business object factory so that there is no effect on business object client code. Many application servers provide Home interfaces that are aware of the available, redundant application server instances. However, ensure that this is the case for your environment before using this technique so you don't lose the load-balancing and failover capabilities of the application server.

Removing Stateful Session Beans When Finished

Be sure to remove instances of stateful Session Beans when you are done with them to avoid unnecessary container overhead and processing.

Choosing an Efficient XML Parser Based on Your Requirements

The extensive use of XML in an application can have a noticeable effect on application performance. Choose the most efficient parsing method available to you that will meet your requirements. DOM parsers are usually the slowest due to the large number of objects instantiated underneath the covers and their generic nature. If your application simply needs to parse through a document once and deal with the data right away, the SAX parser is much more efficient. Binding frameworks such as JAXB will also be more efficient because they know exactly what they are looking for in the XML or what XML tags they need to create. These types of frameworks are also helpful because they use XML as a data transport, but you can program against the objects that receive the data.

Asynchronous Processing as an Alternative

Asynchronous processing is an option that can be used to alleviate performance concerns in applications with semi-real-time updates, multiple external applications that can be invoked in parallel, or work that can be partitioned into segments. Use Message-Driven Beans and JMS to implement parallel processing in a J2EE container. Asynchronous processing can also be used to increase the perceived performance of an application.

Summary

Performance should be considered throughout the development process. The initial focus is on developing a scalable architecture while lower-level optimizations can be saved until later. A typical approach involves a narrow but deep prototype, or proof-of-concept, which executes the communication through all of the layers and primary components of the architecture. Some basic load testing is done at this point to obtain basic performance metrics that help to validate both the high-level performance requirements and the proposed architecture. Performance should also be considered during the design phase because it often involves trade-offs against flexibility and other requirements. The application architecture and design should help to mitigate performance concerns by providing potential migration paths through the use of isolation and encapsulation. A key example of this concept is the use of a business object factory that provides a placeholder to optimize JNDI lookups without affecting the rest of the application code. Other key factors to consider when looking at J2EE performance include the use of Entity Beans and optimal pool sizes, choice of the right XML parser, and possibilities for asynchronous processing.

This chapter covered best practices for performance engineering in J2EE Web applications. The role of performance in the development process was considered and a number of techniques were discussed for the use of specific technologies such as Entity Beans, Message-Driven Beans, and XML. Whereas this chapter helped make your applications run faster, the next chapter addresses a number of best practices used to speed the development of your applications. These best practices focus on the topic of software reuse.

Moving toward Reuse in the Reference Architecture

The topic of reuse in the software industry is a very big and complicated issue. This chapter is not intended to tackle the entire problem. Instead, it takes a look at a few of the common roadblocks and discusses some corresponding best practices that can be used to help enable reuse. In particular, many of the practices discussed here are intended to be used in conjunction with a reference architecture that is similar to the one described in this book. Unfortunately, reuse has been difficult to achieve in many practical settings for a number of reasons, but a combination of the J2EE platform, the reference architecture, and the guiding principles discussed at the beginning of this book can go a long way toward making reuse an achievable goal. The J2EE platform provides a rich tool set and suite of standards to use in order to build highly reusable components and enterprise architectures. The application architecture approach that sits on top of the J2EE platform, which in this case is the reference architecture, can greatly help the direction that reuse takes. It shapes how components are plugged in to the application and how they fit in the strategic view of the architecture. Finally, the guiding principles of design patterns, automation, and metadata-driven components can be key enablers toward "reuse" architecture.

Common Roadblocks and Corresponding Best Practices

On paper, reusability looks like an easy way for many organizations to rapidly build new Web-based applications. However, there are difficult aspects that come into play from a number of different dimensions. Figure 11.1 shows a few of the common roadblocks from both the producer and consumer perspectives of a reusable asset. Best practices that can help address these issues are suggested for each hurdle. The rest of this chapter will discuss these practices in more detail.

The Social and Educational Dimensions

Generally speaking, most people want to meet their deadlines and be able to leave work at a decent hour. Additionally, given that consumers of technology are also in businesses that change very rapidly these days, the demands for new functionality are not slowing down, nor are they coming with relaxed development schedules. Consequently, the motivation to reuse would appear to be high, yet many organizations have been struggling to realize the benefits for quite some time.

In many cases, an existing software component is not reused because a potential consumer is either not aware of it, doesn't know how to use it, or doesn't like the way in which it was implemented. Yet, technologists are inextricably faced with the fact that today's demanding requirements and schedules simply do not allow them to build everything from scratch. Consequently, there needs to be a happy medium between reuse and new development.

Characteristics of Reuse

What are the characteristics of a successful reuse effort? In order to address the social and educational aspects of reuse, this is a helpful question to ask. There are many levels in the J2EE architecture where portions of code can be reused. The reference architecture, in fact, can be viewed as a number of layers that build on one another, reusing services and components from the lower levels. The J2EE platform itself is the lowest layer in the software architecture and provides many libraries and services for developers to use. Consequently, looking at J2EE for a moment, it seems quite easy to reuse services and components from this layer. Interestingly enough, it usually requires little motivation to do so on the part of the development staff. This is important to note, particularly because of the many roadblocks listed earlier.

For example, developers are inherently motivated to use the servlet API to get HTTP parameters out of a request. This is largely because the `HttpServletRequest.getParameter` method is easy to use, particularly when compared to the option of getting the servlet input stream and parsing the text to extract and access the named HTTP parameters. This illustrates one of the lowest levels of reuse in the layered view of the architecture, and it seems like a "no-brainer" decision. How can this be emulated in your own organization so that reuse bubbles up through the rest of the architecture

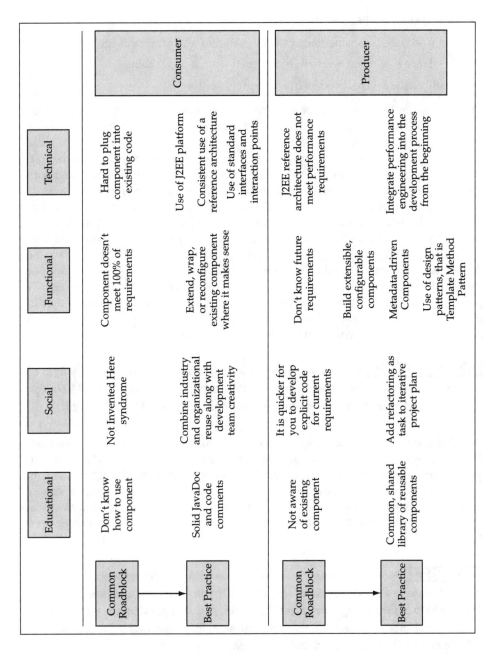

Figure 11.1 Dimensions of Reuse: Roadblocks and Best Practices.

layers and becomes a prevalent best practice among development teams? Well, the servlet API example exhibits a number of characteristics that can be applied to development projects. In particular, the `getParameter` method of the servlet API is:

- An easy to use API or method signature
- Published, well-documented, and has examples and sample usage
- Standards-based and a generally accepted way of doing things
- Readily available and comes from a trusted source

If you consider that the presence of these characteristics led to a "no-brainer" decision to use the servlet `getParameter` API rather than parsing the input stream, an assumption can be made that people are willing, and in fact have an incentive, to reuse software when it makes sense. To paraphrase the list of reuse characteristics, if the software component is easy to use and there seems to be a low level of risk associated with it, people will use it. How would someone determine the risk level of a component? Well, the fact that a component has a published API, uses standards-based technology, and is well documented leads to the impression that its use is a generally accepted practice. If you can apply even a subset of these same characteristics to your organization's software, you should be able to achieve better results and start to engrain the behavior of reuse within the development organization. How can this be done? For one, you should strive to achieve the same high levels of quality within internally developed software. As any technologist will tell you, there are never enough hours in the day to do all of this, but you can focus on a few key points in particular that will help the behavior and practice of reuse to grow.

BEST PRACTICE Make sure that your software components have easy to use APIs and are well documented. A little JavaDoc can go a long way toward helping someone understand an existing component and feel comfortable reusing it.

Making a software component easy to use is absolutely essential for it to be successfully reused by others. The API, or method signatures of an object, should have meaningful English names, and they should break up the work into chunks of functionality that are separable and meaningful on their own. If you are developing a service component, the API should be published to the user community and well documented. This means that it should be clearly stated what input data is expected and what output data will be returned.

THOUGHT People in general, but particularly software developers, get frustrated very easily if they try to use something on their own and need to go ask for help before being able to get it to work. At some point, many developers simply implement the functionality themselves before even making a simple phone call to ask a question about an existing component.

Consequently, for the most part, you want your reusable components to be consumable by developers without having to do much extra hand-holding. There are, of course, exceptions to this rule. Large, complex software components as well as comprehensive frameworks normally require additional training or consulting, but many reusable assets are fairly self-contained and, consequently, should be straightforward to use. Making components easy to use and well understood is accomplished both through making their APIs intuitive and having clear documentation for their use, particularly for the external interfaces. A common language for describing components is available through UML models that can very quickly communicate basic information about your components. In terms of documentation and UML models, if you have a limited amount of time to spend, use your time to document the external APIs and interfaces before writing anything else. This is what people see when they first look at a component. In terms of reuse, and even to some extent maintenance, the interface is the best place to start in order to understand how a component is used and accessed.

The aspect of standards-based software is a bit more difficult for most of the development community because in the majority of cases, the resulting components are not going to become part of the Java or J2EE specifications. But you can ensure that you are using standard design patterns and that you are building on top of existing specifications and technologies. For example, you would not likely build a service component as a pure RMI service anymore if you have an EJB infrastructure readily available. In terms of design patterns, if you are building a Web-tier architecture, your components are much more likely to be accepted if they are built using the Model-View-Controller design pattern as opposed to some other approach. Taking this even a step further, you are more likely to have reusable components if they are built upon generally accepted solutions for the Web tier, such as action classes or tag libraries built upon Jakarta Struts.

The last point on this example is awareness. You must ensure that components are available and accessible to those who might be able to use them. This may be through some kind of regular communications vehicle, searchable component library, or other mechanism. Quite simply, you can't reuse something that you don't know about or don't have access to.

Combining Reuse with Creativity

The "not-invented-here" syndrome has been a strong barrier to reuse for quite some time. It stems from the fact that many people are hesitant to put their faith in something new, unfamiliar, or put quite simply, done differently than they would have done it. In the author's opinion, it is, in fact, quite important that the eventual solution for strategically important projects involve some combination of subjunctive industry reuse, organizational reuse, and the creativity of the individuals involved. There are a number of observations that lead to this point. The first is that a large body of high-quality work, which represents years of proven designs and experience, already exists out in the industry, readily available for use. To ignore these as candidates for reuse would simply not be wise. Within an organization, there are a number of shared aspects that make reuse the right answer for productivity gains. In particular, organizations have domain expertise and component implementations in common that can usually be shared among development teams.

Going toward the other end of the spectrum, members of a development team should also have a sense of ownership and "pride of authorship" in the work that they do. Consequently it is also important that, to some degree, they are able to put their own signature on the technology solution that they implement. This should not be done just for the sake of doing so, but when it is required for the job. You could make a very simple case that this creativity is required more often than not. For example, try to find one application or project that looks exactly like another one you or your organization has done. Rarely, if ever, is this the case, because for some unknown reason, each software development project seems to take on a life of its own. Consequently, there will be the need for customized solutions that require the intelligent use of existing patterns, designs, and principles in order to find the best solution for the job. In this way, the development staff applies their own creativity to a solution and can feel good, knowing not only that they made their deadline and delivered a quality product, but that they were a part of something worthwhile that they created.

BEST PRACTICE For large, strategically important development projects, use a combination of industry and organizational reuse along with the creativity and innovation of the development team. Each of these sources brings unique value to the table. An approach that combines these aspects will help to alleviate the "not-invented-here" syndrome while at the same time providing a jumpstart to the development effort.

It is also important to note that creativity does not always strike on day one of a project. A robust, reusable design or component implementation may not come into focus until after the realization of the architecture starts to take shape. By nature, the more you learn about the project, technology, or requirements, the smarter you become. Consequently, it is recommended that you add refactoring as an explicit task to each iteration of a development plan. Even a small amount of time allotted for this purpose can yield great long-term benefits in terms of reusability and flexibility.

BEST PRACTICE Add refactoring as an explicit task in iterative software development. This helps not only to increase the overall quality of the software, but it often leads to more robust code that can be harvested into reusable assets.

The Technical and Functional Dimensions

Even if an existing component is well known and understood, two common reasons that it still may not be reused are that the component doesn't meet all of the functional requirements or else that it does not easily fit into the application architecture. These roadblocks can be addressed at two different levels:

- J2EE standards for component services and deployment
- A configurable, extensible, reference architecture built using proven design patterns

Figure 11.2 represents some of the primary aspects of J2EE and the reference architecture that enable reuse.

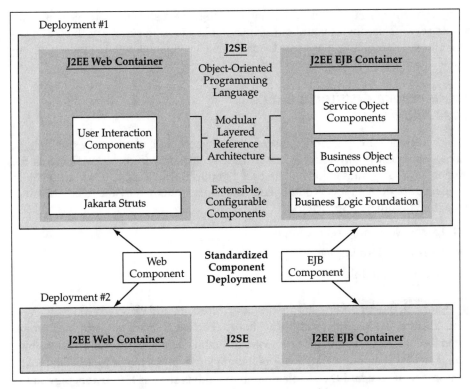

Figure 11.2 Reuse Aspects in J2EE and the Reference Architecture.

J2EE Component Standards

The standard component deployment model provided by J2EE provides a tremendous advantage in terms of building reusable assets for Web applications. If you first look at the Web tier, the JSP custom tag mechanism is a shining example of a powerful mechanism for building reusable pieces of presentation code that can easily be integrated into HTML-centric Web pages. There are already a number of prolific tag libraries from Struts, the Jakarta project, and the upcoming Java Standard Tag Library. Any of these libraries can be reused within your application to some degree, in many cases with even a small amount of effort. They provide common functions such as collection iteration, forms processing, and custom presentation logic. If you step back and look at the JSP and servlet specifications at a higher level, they actually have given the Java community almost a de facto standard for the implementation of MVC-based Web architectures. Servlets provide the component implementation for the controller while JSPs provide the view implementation.

The EJB specification provides a standard mechanism to distribute and manage component functionality. It makes it easier to pull an existing component off the shelf and drop it into your own environment because there are fewer worries about having to plug it into "infrastructure" type services. In fact, even if you are picking up a non-standard type component, you can usually wrap it with a Session EJB to integrate it into your environment and take advantage of the same distribution, transaction, and security services used with your homegrown applications. In summary, the J2EE platform removes a large hurdle to reuse by providing a consistent, interoperable environment for the interaction of components.

The Reference Architecture as a Reuse Architecture

A solid reference architecture is essential to a successful reuse effort. For one, it becomes the most highly reused code in the application because it implements the common aspects of transactional, Web-based applications. Second, it is a key enabler for the reuse of domain-level components. Concepts embodied by the reference architecture that promote reuse include:

- Extensible, configurable components
- Use of standard interfaces as interaction points
- A layered, modular architecture

BEST PRACTICE Choose a reference architecture and view it as a "reuse" architecture. Use it consistently throughout J2EE development projects. Incorporate standard interaction points for components with known interfaces. Use extensible, configurable components, such as the Jakarta Struts project, as a foundation. Take advantage of standard J2EE implementation models such as JSP custom tags and Session Bean EJB components.

Extensible, Configurable Components

Given that one cannot see into the future and accurately predict 100 percent of the upcoming requirements for a given application, most software components are developed to meet all of the current requirements and perhaps some percentage of potential future functionality. Likewise, when one looks to reuse assets, many existing components do not provide all of the functionality or else they do it a bit differently. Consequently, it is crucial that software components, particularly foundation components, be designed so that they can easily be extended or configured to behave differently.

THOUGHT One of most powerful forms of reuse is through inheritance and the use of the Template Method pattern that was used in the Business Logic Foundation layer. Almost all Web-application frameworks use this concept at length to create extensible foundation layers.

The Template Method pattern allows you to implement a standard process or set of logic with extensibility points that can be implemented by subclasses. Many foundation classes for business components use some aspect of this design pattern. In these cases, inheritance provides the extensibility needed to enable an existing asset to be specialized for your own needs, whether the object represents an entity, a process, or some other type of function.

The reference architecture uses metadata, similar to the J2EE specification, in order to configure and drive the behavior of components. The Struts controller architecture is a prime example of this concept. The configuration metadata determines how the controller servlet handles particular requests for a Web client. This allows it to be used as a foundation for almost any type of Web application. This same concept of declarative programming can be used to add flexibility and reusability to many types of software components.

Build to a Standard Interface

In Java, there is another very powerful mechanism at your disposal, the concept of an interface. The use of standard interfaces throughout the reference architecture is a best practice for both service and business object components. In terms of reuse in the reference architecture, this is a central concept. It addresses the technical roadblock of difficulty in plugging a new component into the architecture. If there are standard interaction points, developers can build new implementations of components and easily plug them into the architecture. Different implementations can also be configured using metadata and invoked dynamically.

Java interfaces also allow you to gain some of the shared interface benefits without the rigidity of inheritance and having to subclass an object. This is a powerful option to consider in designing your application. If an existing asset implements a common interface, it will be much easier for your application components to reuse it out of the box. This is a primary rationale for the use of common interfaces throughout the service components and business objects in the reference architecture.

The Layered, Modular Architecture

The fact that the reference architecture is structured into layers provides a great amount of flexibility. Applications can be structured such that each layer reuses components from lower levels in the architecture. Starting at the top layer, you can consider the actual "application" to be a particular view into the business component functionality. The form that the user's view takes is dependent on the user's role, security privileges, and the amount of personalization factored into the application. This concept is at the heart of a strategic view of the application architecture that will be discussed in further detail later in this chapter.

In terms of a modular architecture, each layer as a whole can be thought of as a building block upon which to build new functionality. Everything sits on top of J2EE with business objects being the core application component in the architecture. Continuing upward, service components form a layer on top of the business components, and then finally the user interaction layer exposes the component functionality to clients. In today's world, a key recipient of layered architecture benefits is the User Interaction Architecture because it can include a wide array of PCs and devices that wish to have access to the same services.

The Initial Investment of a Reference Architecture

Component frameworks are a core aspect of the reference architecture. The reference architecture is built upon the Jakarta Struts project and the Business Logic Foundation that was developed in the earlier chapters of this book. There are also many more options available in the form of both open-source projects and commercial products. Without a doubt, there is an initial investment required to take advantage of component frameworks, although the long-term benefits are clear and profound. Nonetheless, if your situation requires the rapid development of either fairly simple applications or "nonstrategic" software components, you may not be able to afford the additional learning curve of using such a product. In these cases, you might want to code directly on top of the J2EE specifications. No technology professional can escape the fact that time simply can become a bigger factor than either consistency or maintainability. Rarely, however, is quality not a concern. Component frameworks usually represent highly tested pieces of software that can provide reliable building blocks for your application logic. It is best to consider all of these aspects before making a decision one way or another for your next software development project.

Reuse in the Reference Architecture

This section looks at the reference architecture and considers the potential for reuse in each of the different layers.

Business Objects

Business objects tend to have a moderate level of reuse because they provide the transactional ability to update a particular business entity. In a shared portfolio of applications, you don't want to end up creating duplicate objects to represent the same entity, even though they are viewed somewhat differently. For example, in the bank application, consider the customer Web pages and the administrative Web pages as two different applications. From a strategic viewpoint, this is one way to look at things, in which each set of users has a different "view" into the same set of business functionality. The `Transaction` object is used in the customer pages to record withdrawals and deposits as well as in the administrative pages to display and update the history of transactions for a particular account. In these two different scenarios, the `Transaction` object is used differently, and it could have been implemented differently in both cases. For example, in the case of the administrative pages, only two properties of the `Transaction` object are updated, so one alternative would have been to write a stored procedure to update those two fields. This stored procedure could then be invoked from a corresponding service component. From a strategic long-term viewpoint, however, that may not be the best decision. By reusing the same `Transaction` business object, you ensure that all the updates pass through the same set of data validations. Additionally, if you change the structure of that object or the related database tables, there is only one place that you need to go to in order to make the changes. In this manner, reusability and ease of maintenance go hand-in-hand, as is often the case.

Similar to reuse with business objects, value objects and data objects will be reused if you are using these conventions in your architecture. This is particularly important if you are not using Container-Managed Persistence or if you are using JDBC outside of Entity Beans. In these cases, you want to have a shared set of objects so that all of your data access for each particular entity is encapsulated in a single place.

Service Objects

These components have a lower level of reuse because they implement specific business processes and transactions. In many cases, they are particular to the application in which they are built, although within a service, they do reuse existing business objects in order to do their work. One way in which services can be reused as building blocks is when smaller services are combined to form more coarse-grained services. Examples were discussed in the Service-Based Architecture chapter of workflow examples that used existing services to implement reusable steps within larger workflows.

If you look at services from the perspective of access through different types of clients, they can be considered to have a high level of reuse. In the bank application, there is a service that retrieves account transaction data that is reused across a couple of pages. In some cases, you may want to look at reusing services in this way, particularly for related data retrievals or updates of similar business entities. If a data retrieval service returns a few extra columns in order to satisfy a number of different screens, this can usually be done at a relatively low performance cost to get the benefit of easier maintenance through a reduced codebase. A different type of example for service reuse might be something like a "time" service that provides the system time across a distributed set of components. This service would be highly reusable across any component or application that needed the official time with regards to the application

User Interaction Objects

Web pages themselves are rarely reusable; however, the framework upon which they are built is highly reusable. In some cases, you may create domain-level tag libraries that could be reused across applications, but for the most part, each application provides its own view into the business functionality. Consequently, presentation layers can be highly customized and personalized for the particular user or user role.

Turning the Layers Upside Down

With regard to business objects and services, they may not always stack up in the layers shown in the earlier diagrams. Often, you may reuse a service from within a business object in addition to the examples thus far, which illustrated the services using business objects. You can create components that are implemented through a pyramid of building blocks made up of both service objects and business objects. Figure 11.3 represents such a component, typically implemented as an EJB component in order to provide distribution, transaction management, and all of the other common services provided by J2EE. Underneath the component interface are the building blocks of the architecture reused in order to provide the ultimate function.

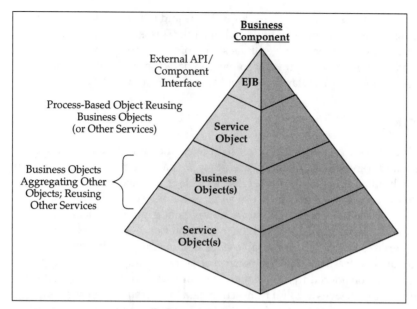

Figure 11.3 Service Component Implementation as Building Blocks.

At the bottom of this pyramid is usually a wide base of business objects that can be reused across services and applications. As you build up on top of lower layers, the pyramid gets narrower until it comes to a point. This represents the fact that domain-level reuse gets much more difficult to achieve as you build on top of business components and go higher and higher in this diagram. Eventually, you get to a point where you have customized services that are tailored to your specific application, although they may be built upon reusable building blocks by combining existing transactional components to create a specific process.

The Strategic View of the Architecture

A primary goal of having a strategic architecture vision is to plan for the future and be able to adapt quickly when the time comes. Consequently, reusability is a core aspect of any strategic architecture plan. The reference architecture, made up of extensible, configurable layers with defined interaction points, is another core aspect of the strategic view. This helps to enable the development of robust components that can easily be plugged into new components or extended to provide additional functionality. At its core, application architecture can be described as the definition of the application components and their interaction with each other. It is the interaction aspect of this definition that is crucial to the future viability of any existing software assets. Loosely coupled application components are simply more flexible than tightly coupled sets of components. The importance of the component interaction is exemplified by the sheer number of components that are included in a large-scale enterprise application. The definition of individual components may not make or break the architecture, but groups of related components that interact with other sets of components and define the structure of how this is done are vitally important if one wants to add new functionality or modify existing functionality. In the case of small modifications, the individual component definition, of course, becomes the key factor; but changes to the overall business vision or technology direction will cut right to the heart of the component interaction model. Consequently, it is important to look at what types of components exist in the application inventory and how they interact with one another.

From the context of a strategic viewpoint, the following types of components exist within the architecture layers:

Business object components. This is the core functionality of the application because it models the business. It contains the majority of the business logic and database interaction.

Service-based components. This layer represents the business processes. It also insulates the user interaction components from the specific business object implementation model and APIs. It is the exposure of the business transactions to the front end.

User interaction components. This layer provides the view into the application's functionality. It can vary widely based on the client device and business function being provided. Different views into the application can use the same set of services, retrieve the same data, and update the same entities, but they can potentially present the information and functions in very diverse ways.

Why is the separation of the business transactions into a conceptual service layer so important? One reason is that you want to be able to reuse the same business logic components to implement both browser-based applications as well as B2B Web services. Additionally, if your applications are deployed to wireless handheld devices, you want them to be able to reuse the same business logic and only have to change the presentation layer to cater to the language of the device. In some cases, this might be Wireless Markup Language (WML) instead of HTML. Or in other cases, you might want to plug existing functionality into another application that does not know anything about the existing business object model. Finally, in all of these cases, you want to be able to change the presentation layer and still access the same business functions. By having the service components in between the user interaction and the business entity components, development of the presentation layer can be simplified while at the same time the same business logic code can be reused.

In addition to Web services, two critical aspects of a strategic architecture include an Internet presence with personalized content and the integration of legacy applications to the architecture. If all these aspects together are put together in one picture, it starts to look like Figure 11.4.

For the most part, the major emphasis on integration thus far has been to integrate existing applications within your own enterprise. Already, however, the focus is expanding to include consuming Web services from third parties and other business partners external to the organization. A true services-based model may become a prevalent architecture direction as organizations look to integrate legacy functionality, newly developed components, and functionality available from business partners over the Internet.

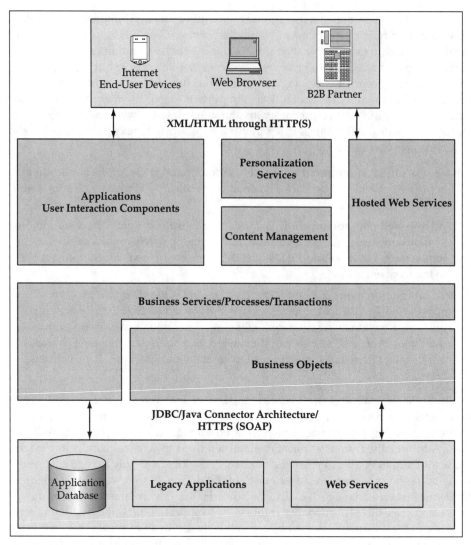

Figure 11.4 A Strategic Architecture.

Best Practices for Moving toward Reuse

A summary of the reuse best practices is given in this section.

Simplifying Life for the Consumer of Reusable Assets

As a producer of reusable assets, try to remove the potential barriers for a consumer. Emulate the characteristics of Java and J2EE APIs that are heavily used. Make sure that your software components have easy to use APIs and are well documented. A little JavaDoc can go a long way toward helping someone understand an existing component and feel comfortable reusing it. The use of proven design patterns and standard J2EE component models can help minimize any perceived risk of using an existing component.

Combining Reuse with Creativity

For large, strategically important development projects, use a combination of industry and organizational reuse along with the creativity and innovation of the development team. Each of these sources brings unique value to the table. An approach that combines these aspects helps to alleviate the "not-invented-here" syndrome while at the same time providing a jumpstart to the development effort.

Harvesting Reusable Assets through Iterative Development

Add refactoring as an explicit task in iterative software development. This helps not only to increase the overall quality of the software, but it often leads to more robust code that can be harvested into reusable assets. The most frequently used assets are usually not developed on day one. They are typically the result of iterative development processes and incremental investments that often provide a solid return.

Using a Reference Architecture as a Reuse Architecture

Choose a reference architecture and view it as a "reuse" architecture. Use it consistently throughout J2EE development projects. Incorporate standard component interaction points that use known interfaces. Use extensible, configurable components, such as the Jakarta Struts project, as a foundation. Take advantage of standard J2EE implementation models such as JSP custom tags and Session Bean EJB components.

Summary

Reuse is a very complex issue in the software industry. The potential benefits are immense, but the road to get there is not always so clear. Certainly, the entire problem cannot be addressed in a single chapter, but there are a number of common roadblocks that can be identified and remedied to some extent. These roadblocks span from the social and educational dimensions all the way to functional and technical issues. A number of best practices were identified to help alleviate these roadblocks. They primarily center on the consistent use of a reference architecture in conjunction with J2EE technology. J2EE has provided the standard development and deployment platform. The reference architecture is then used to build extensible, configurable components that have standard interaction points on top of J2EE. This allows the application to plug new components into the architecture in addition to using or extending existing components.

The strategic architecture built upon the J2EE platform uses all of the best practices that have been discussed in this book. Component interaction, which is so important to the overall flexibility of a solution, is largely based on proven design patterns. The rapid development of new functionality is largely based on the use of consistent, maintainable foundation layers that automate common functions through configurable, extensible components. Consider performance from the beginning of the development process because a scalable architecture is a prerequisite for any high-throughput application. You can always make lower-level optimizations later in the process, but you need to be within the ballpark to even get to that point. Finally, a good object design that represents the entities and processes of a business puts you in a position to achieve high levels of reuse and flexibility, allowing your organization to shift to new requirements and adapt to changes in the business.

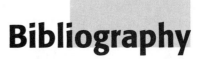

Bibliography

D. Alur, J. Crupi, D. Malks. 2001. *Core J2EE Patterns*. Upper Saddle River, NJ: Prentice Hall PTR.

E. Gamma, R. Helm, R. Johnson, J. Vlissides. 1995. *Design Patterns*. Boston, MA: Addison-Wesley.

I. Singh, B. Stearns, M. Johnson, Enterprise Team. 2002. *Designing Enterprise Applications with the J2EE Platform*. 2d ed. Boston, MA: Adddison-Wesley.

The Model/View pattern, *Journal of Object-Oriented Programming* 1(3):26–49, August/September 1988.

Index